VIZ GRAPHIC NOVEL

THE ALL-NEW TENCHI MUYŌ!

GIRLS GET BUSY

D0921059

STORY AND ART BY
HITOSHI OKUDA

The All-New Tenchi Muyô!
Vol. 4: Girls Get Busy
Action Edition

STORY AND ART BY HITOSHI OKUDA

English Adaptation/Fred Burke
Translation/Lillian Olsen
Touch-up & Lettering/Dan Nakrosis
Cover Design/Hidemi Sahara
Graphic Design/Hidemi Sahara
Editor/Eric Searleman

Managing Editor/Annette Roman
Editor-in-Chief/Alvin Lu
Production Manager/Noboru Watanabe
Sr. Dir. of Licensing & Acquisitions/Rika Inouye
Vp of Marketing/Liza Coppola
V.P. of Sales/Joe Morici
Sr. VP of Editorial/Hyoe Narita
Publisher/Seiji Horibuchi

© 2001 HITOSHI OKUDA © AIC/VAP • NTV Originally published in Japan in 2001 by KADOKAWA SHOTEN PUBLISHING CO., LTD., Tokyo. English translation rights arranged with KADOKAWA SHOTEN PUBLISHING CO., LTD., Tokyo.

Printed in Canada

Published by VIZ, LLC
P.O. Box 77010
San Francisco, CA 94107

Action Edition
10 9 8 7 6 5 4 3 2
First printing, April 2003
Second printing, August 2004
For advertising rates or media kit, e-mail advertising@viz.com

www.animerica-mag.com

www.viz.com   store.viz.com

CONTENTS

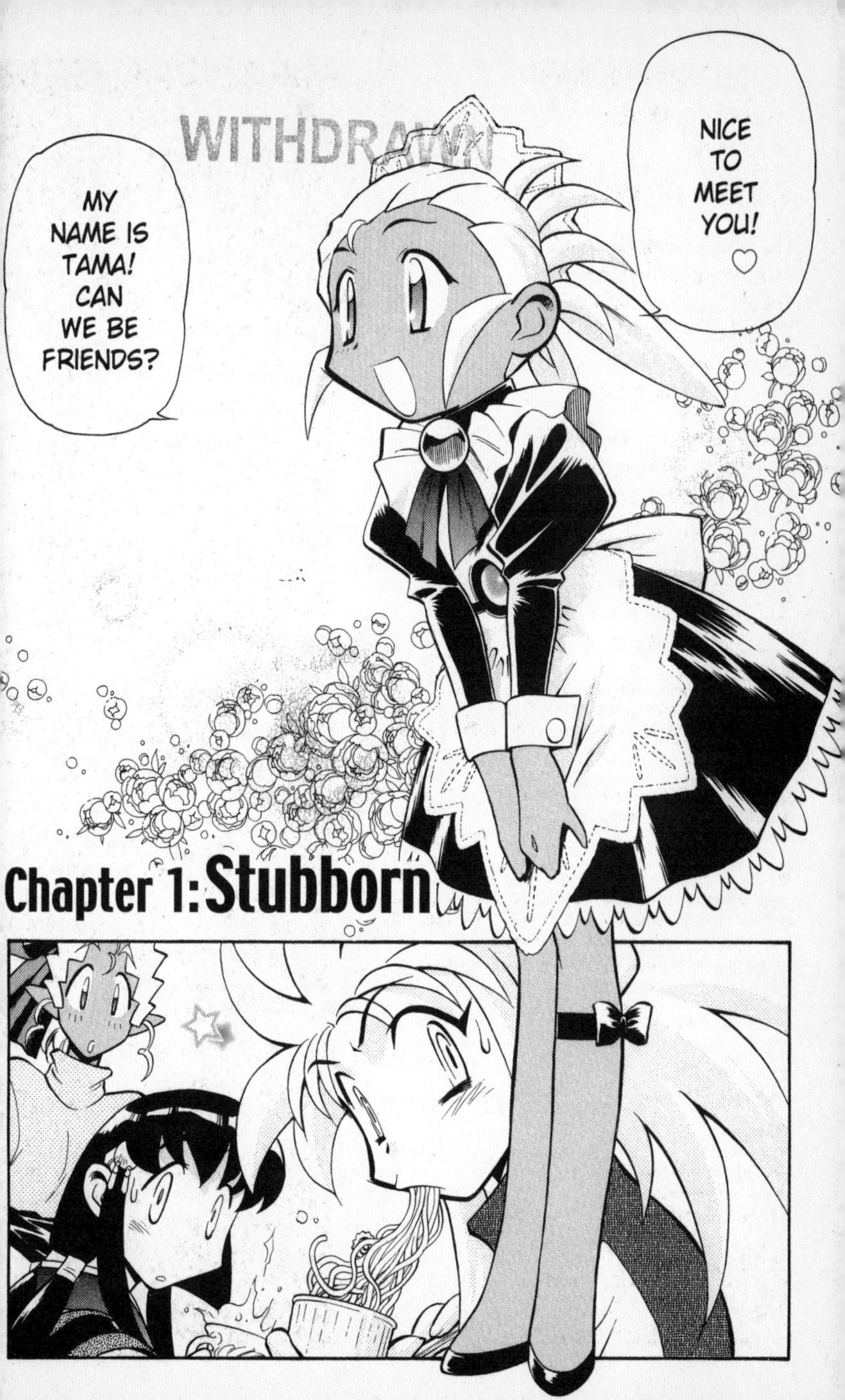
MY NAME IS TAMA! CAN WE BE FRIENDS?
NICE TO MEET YOU! ♡

Chapter 1: Stubborn

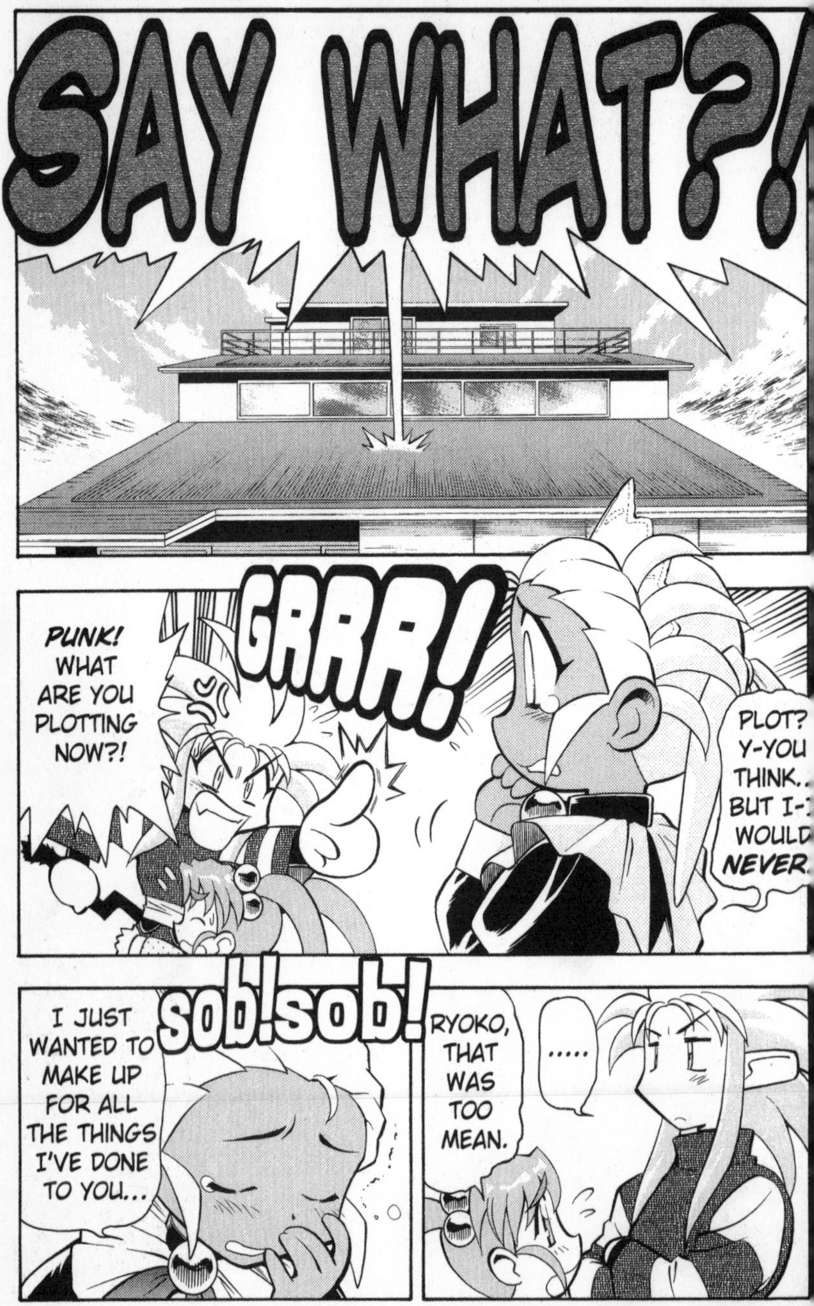
SAY WHAT?!
PUNK! WHAT ARE YOU PLOTTING NOW?!
GRRR!
PLOT? Y-YOU THINK... BUT I-I WOULD NEVER
I JUST WANTED TO MAKE UP FOR ALL THE THINGS I'VE DONE TO YOU...
sob!sob!
RYOKO, THAT WAS TOO MEAN.
.....

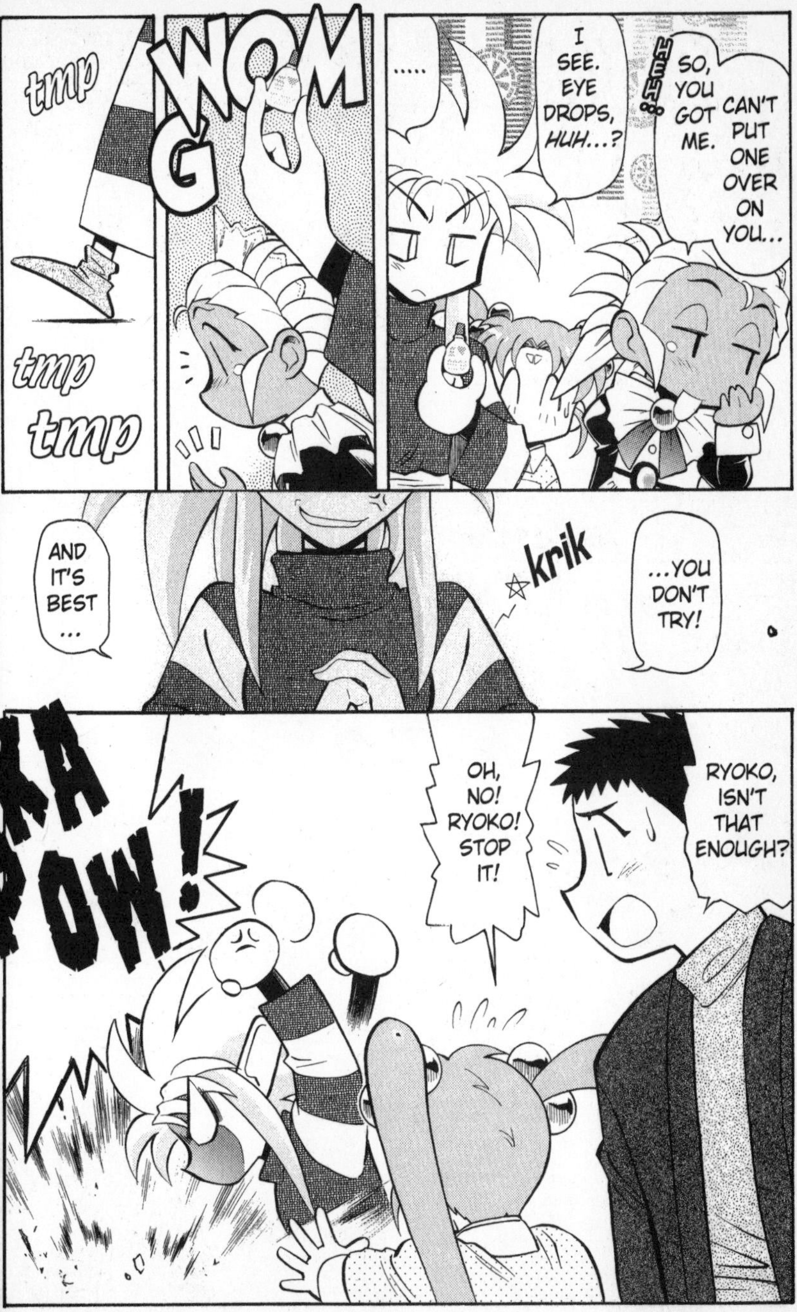
tmp
tmp
tmp
WOMG
.....
I SEE. EYE DROPS, HUH...?
HEH...
SO, YOU GOT ME. CAN'T PUT ONE OVER ON YOU...
AND IT'S BEST...
krik
...YOU DON'T TRY!
KA POW!
OH, NO! RYOKO! STOP IT!
RYOKO, ISN'T THAT ENOUGH?

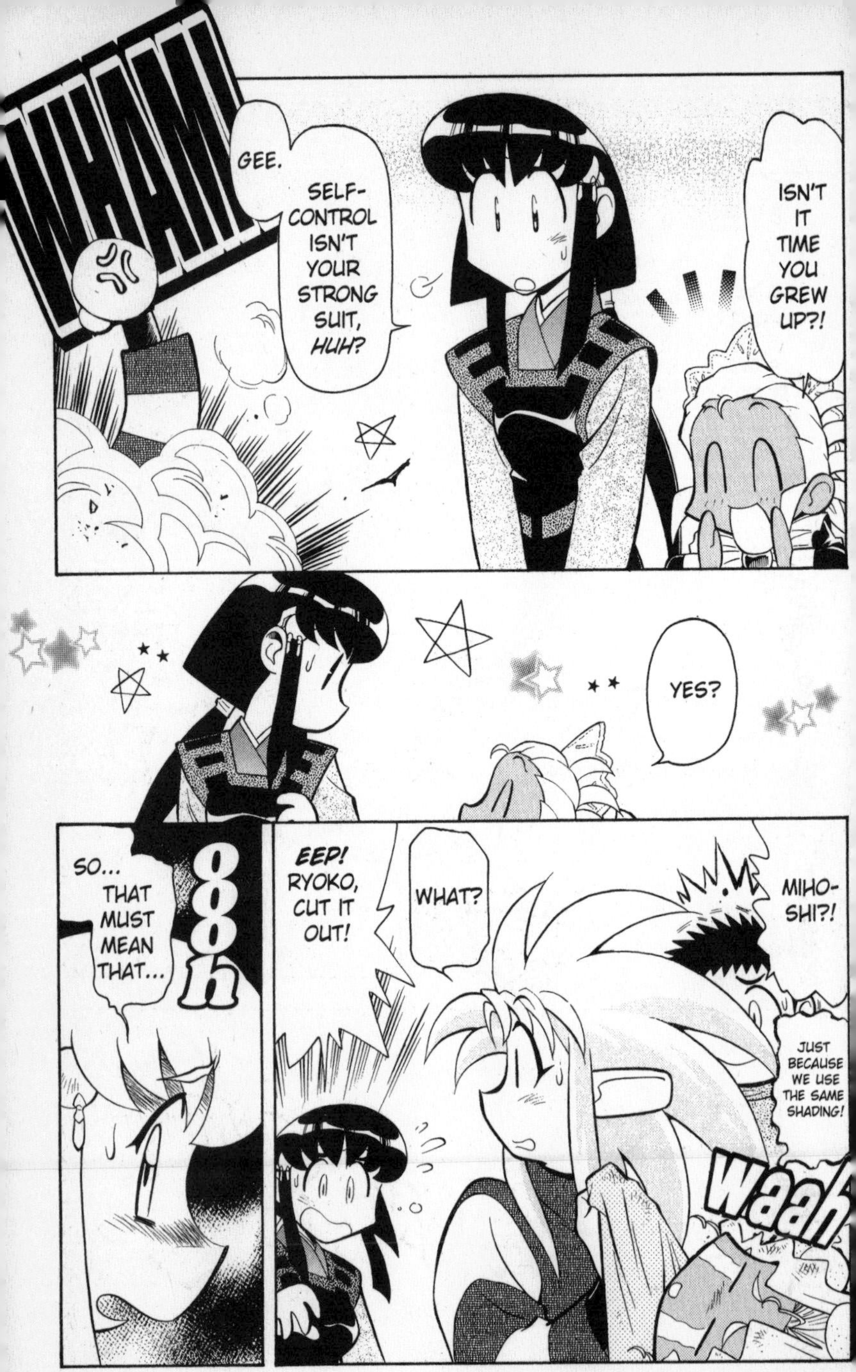

WHAM
GEE.
SELF-CONTROL ISN'T YOUR STRONG SUIT, *HUH?*
ISN'T IT TIME YOU GREW UP?!
YES?
SO... THAT MUST MEAN THAT...
oooh
EEP! RYOKO, CUT IT OUT!
WHAT?
MIHO-SHI?!
JUST BECAUSE WE USE THE SAME SHADING!
waah

ND SO A NEW MEMBER JOINED THE MASAKI HOUSEHOLD...
HOWEVER...

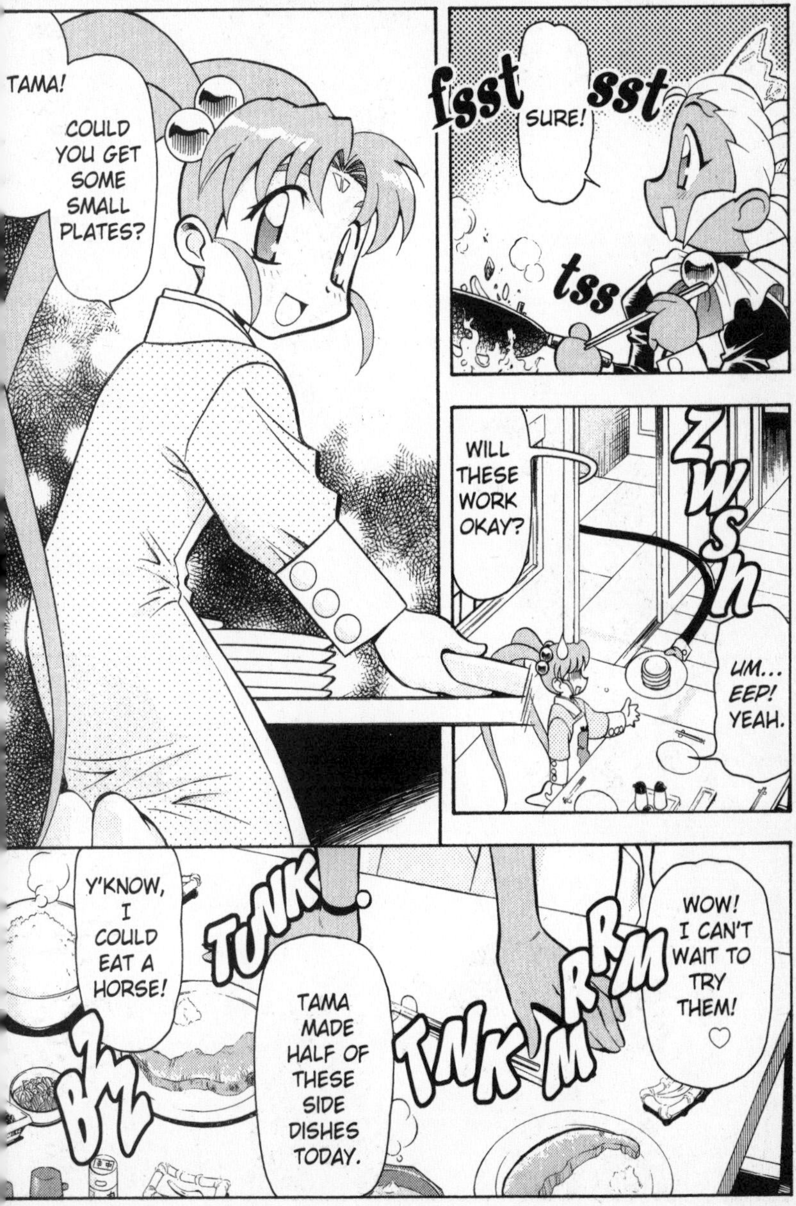
TAMA!
COULD YOU GET SOME SMALL PLATES?
fsst
SURE!
sst
tss
WILL THESE WORK OKAY?
ZWSH
UM... EEP! YEAH.
Y'KNOW, I COULD EAT A HORSE!
TUNK
BZZ
TAMA MADE HALF OF THESE SIDE DISHES TODAY.
TNK
MRRM
WOW! I CAN'T WAIT TO TRY THEM! ♡

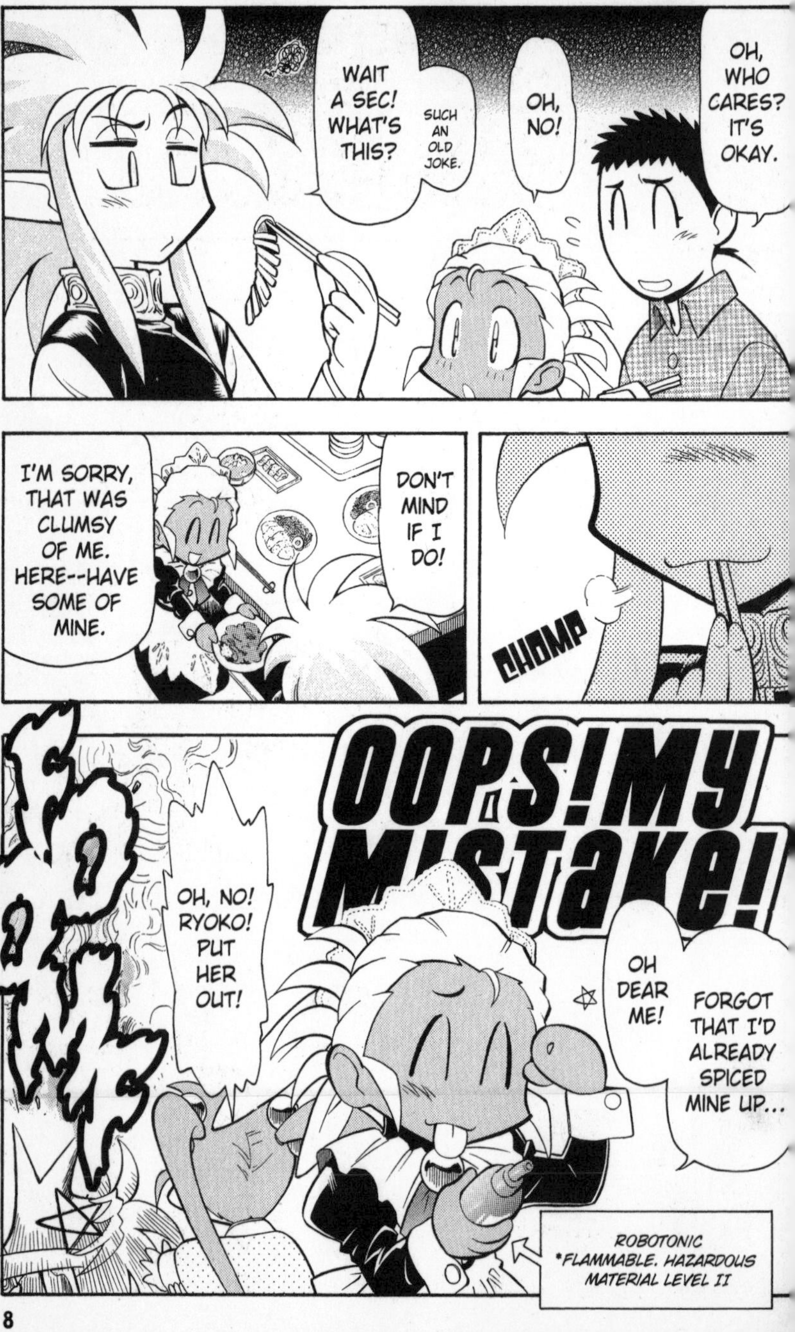
WAIT A SEC! WHAT'S THIS?
SUCH AN OLD JOKE.
OH, NO!
OH, WHO CARES? IT'S OKAY.
I'M SORRY, THAT WAS CLUMSY OF ME. HERE--HAVE SOME OF MINE.
DON'T MIND IF I DO!
CHOMP
OOPS! MY MISTAKE!
OH, NO! RYOKO! PUT HER OUT!
OH DEAR ME!
FORGOT THAT I'D ALREADY SPICED MINE UP...
ROBOTONIC
*FLAMMABLE. HAZARDOUS MATERIAL LEVEL II

A FEW DAYS LATER...

I CAN'T DEAL WITH THIS!

AYEKA, DIDN'T SHE DO HORRIBLE THINGS TO YOU, TOO?! HOW CAN YOU STAND...

...TO JUST LIVE WITH HER LIKE THIS?!

SLAM

HUH?!

FishCakes

hic

IT FELT WEIRD AT FIRST.

BUT...

NO ALCOHOL UNTIL YOU'RE 21!

...THAT EVIL DR. CLAY DID ALL THAT. IT WASN'T TAMA'S FAULT.

URK...

BESIDES, SHE'S TRYING SO HARD TO FIT IN-- WORKS AT IT EVERY DAY!

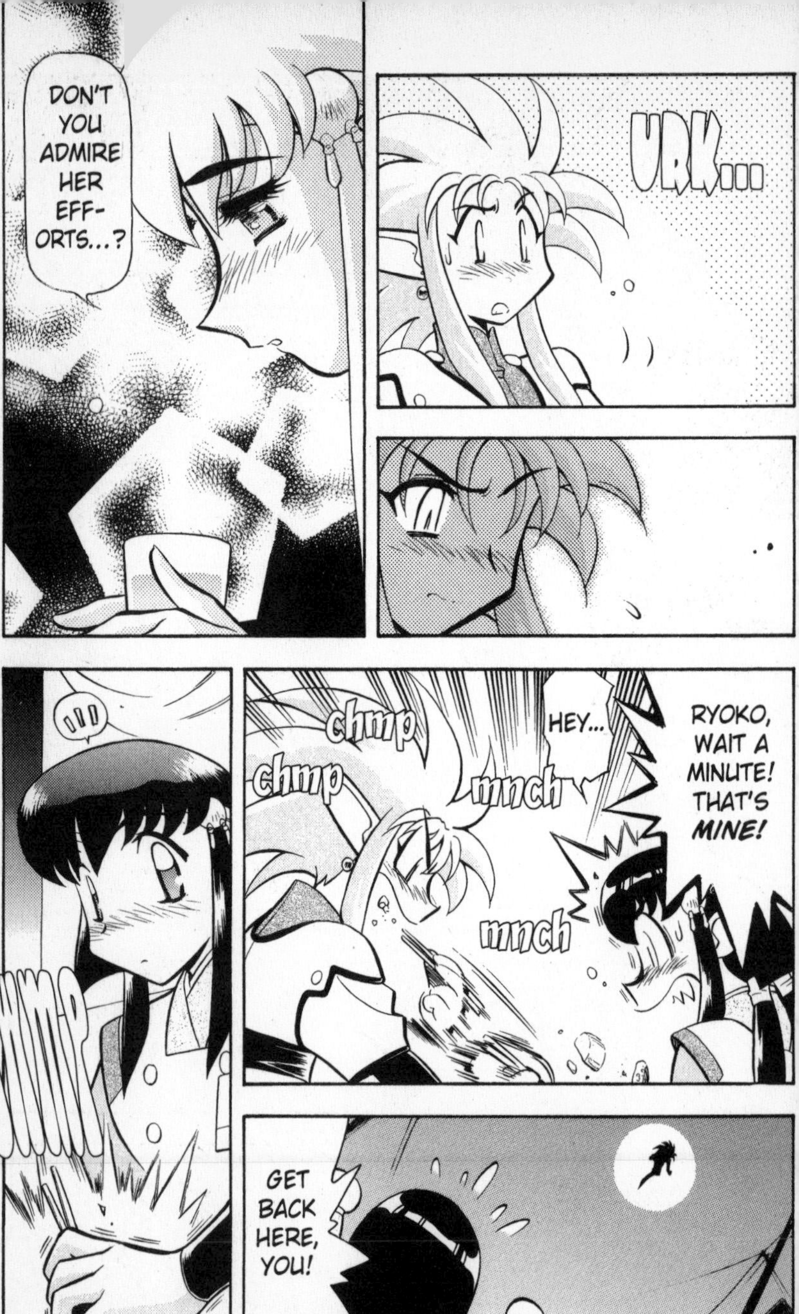

DON'T YOU ADMIRE HER EFF-ORTS...?
URK...
..
chmp
chmp
HEY...
mnch
mnch
RYOKO, WAIT A MINUTE! THAT'S *MINE!*
GET BACK HERE, YOU!

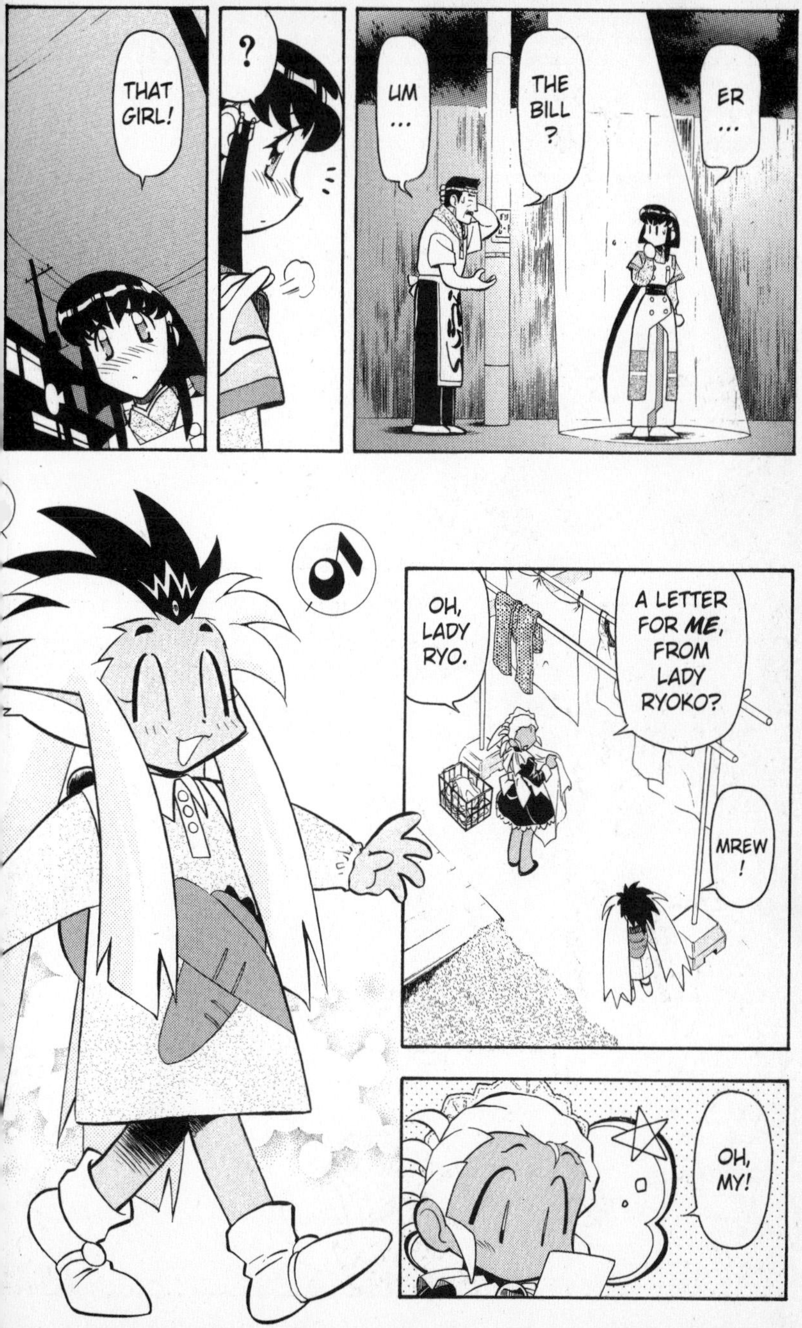
THAT GIRL!
?
UM ...
THE BILL ?
ER ...
OH, LADY RYO.
A LETTER FOR *ME*, FROM LADY RYOKO?
MREW !
OH, MY!

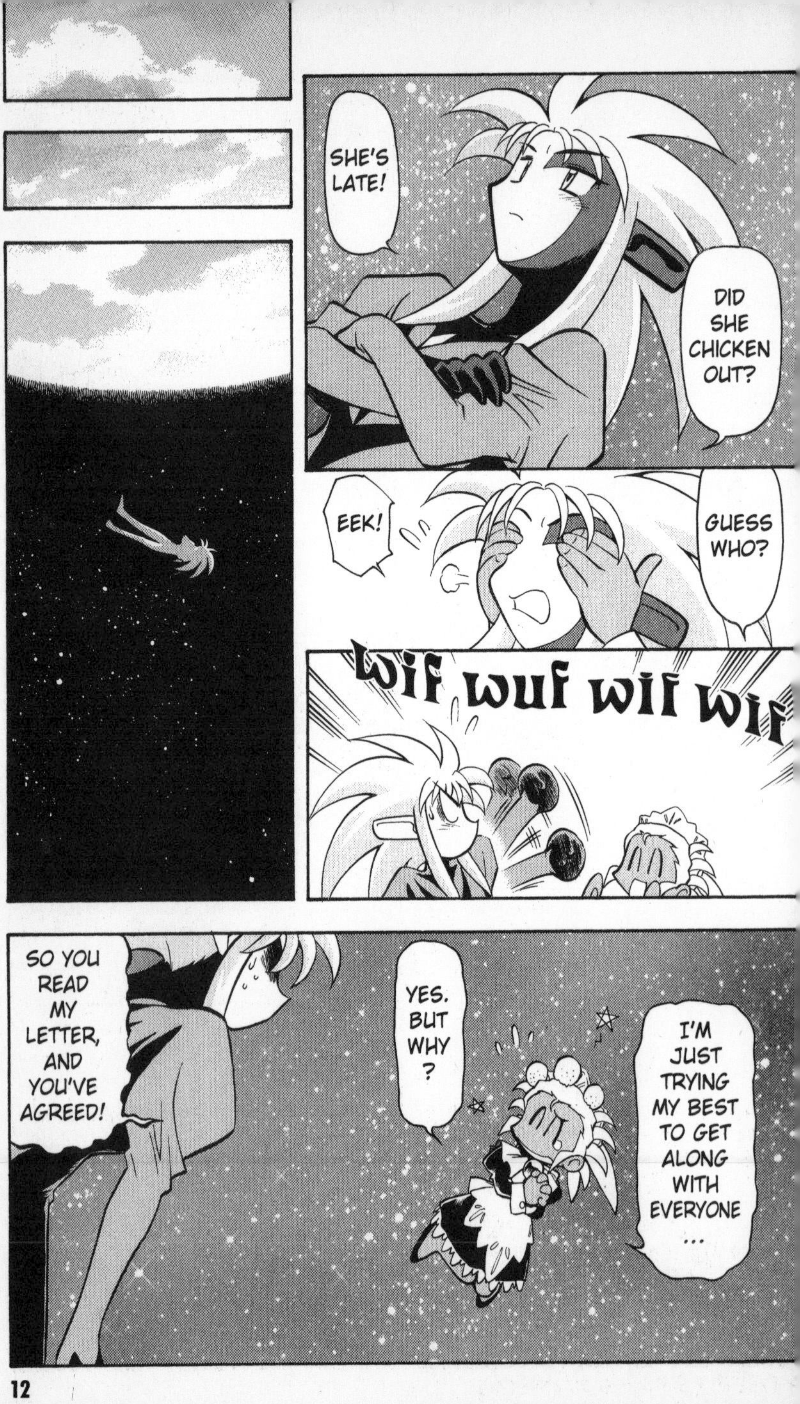
SHE'S LATE!
DID SHE CHICKEN OUT?
EEK!
GUESS WHO?
wif wuf wif wif
SO YOU READ MY LETTER, AND YOU'VE AGREED!
YES. BUT WHY?
I'M JUST TRYING MY BEST TO GET ALONG WITH EVERYONE...

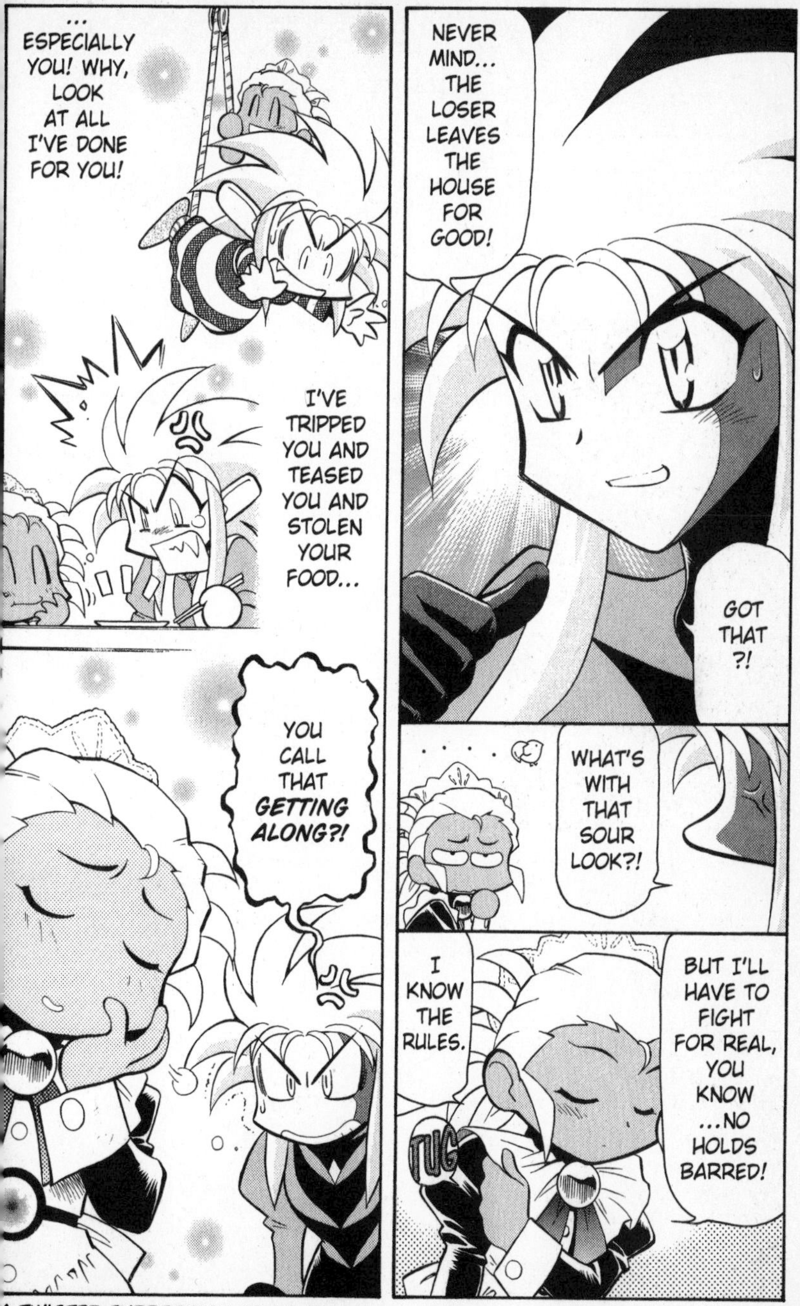

...ESPECIALLY YOU! WHY, LOOK AT ALL I'VE DONE FOR YOU!
I'VE TRIPPED YOU AND TEASED YOU AND STOLEN YOUR FOOD...
NEVER MIND... THE LOSER LEAVES THE HOUSE FOR GOOD!
GOT THAT?!
YOU CALL THAT *GETTING ALONG?!*
WHAT'S WITH THAT SOUR LOOK?!
I KNOW THE RULES.
BUT I'LL HAVE TO FIGHT FOR REAL, YOU KNOW ...NO HOLDS BARRED!
TUG

A TWISTED EXPRESSION OF LOVE

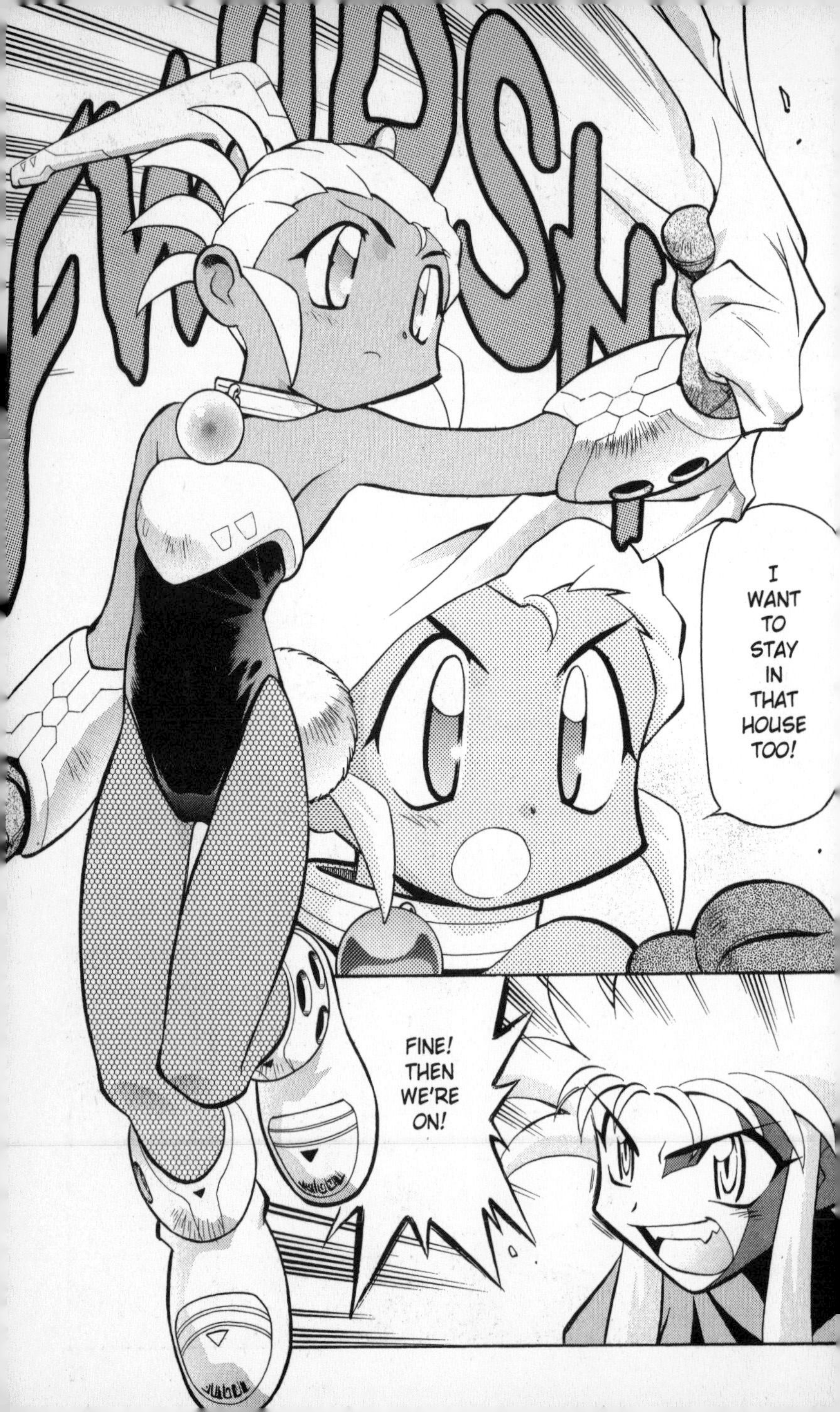
I WANT TO STAY IN THAT HOUSE TOO!
FINE! THEN WE'RE ON!

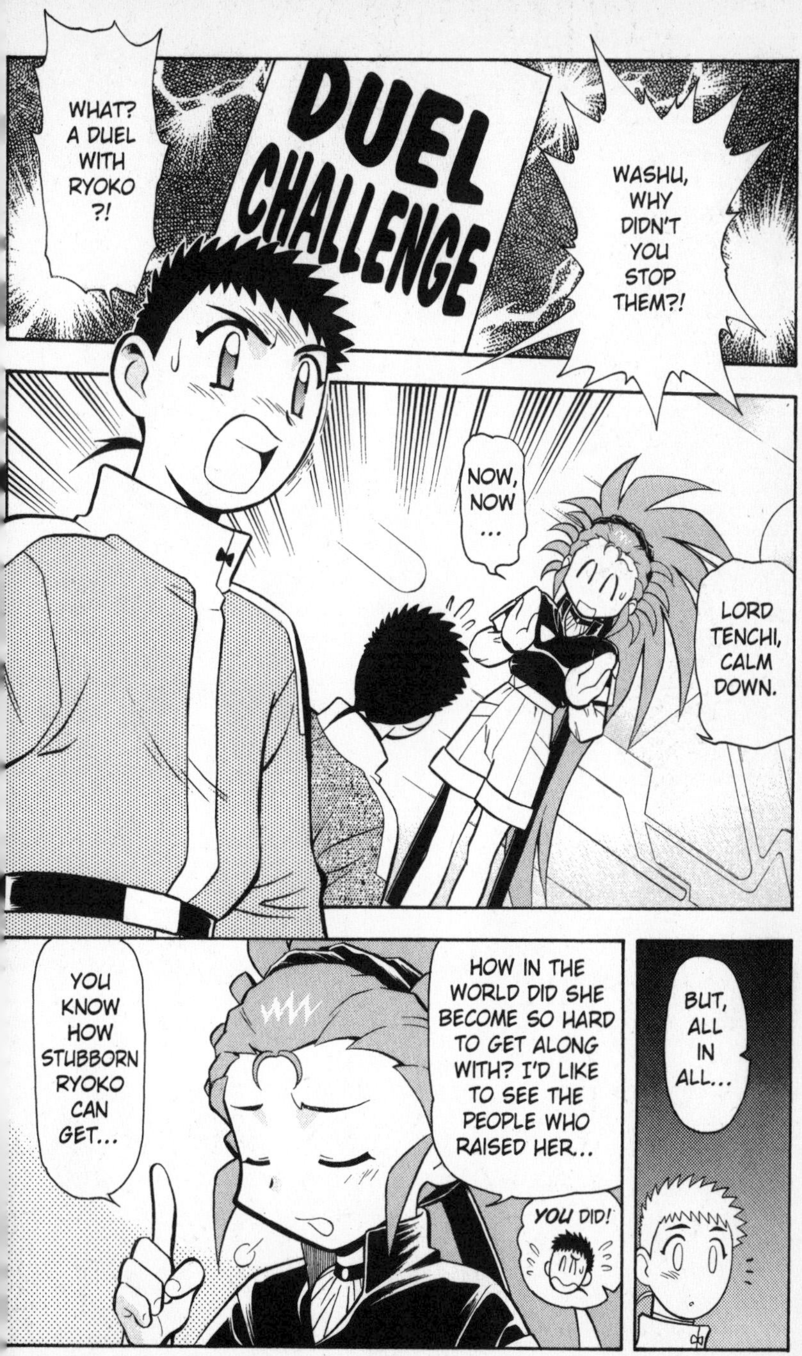
DUEL CHALLENGE
WHAT? A DUEL WITH RYOKO ?!
WASHU, WHY DIDN'T YOU STOP THEM?!
NOW, NOW ...
LORD TENCHI, CALM DOWN.
YOU KNOW HOW STUBBORN RYOKO CAN GET...
HOW IN THE WORLD DID SHE BECOME SO HARD TO GET ALONG WITH? I'D LIKE TO SEE THE PEOPLE WHO RAISED HER...
YOU DID!
BUT, ALL IN ALL...

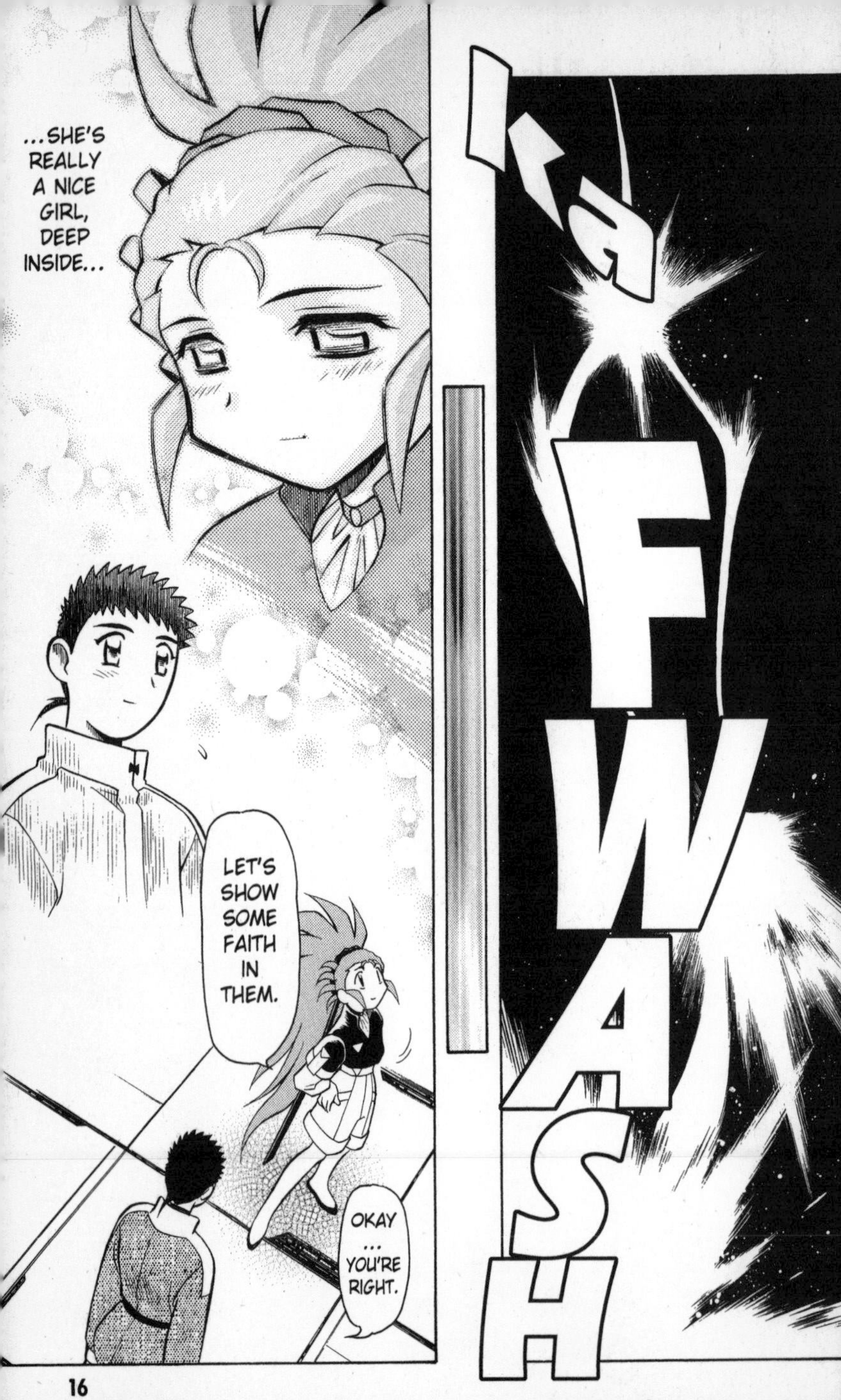
...SHE'S REALLY A NICE GIRL, DEEP INSIDE...
LET'S SHOW SOME FAITH IN THEM.
OKAY ... YOU'RE RIGHT.
ka
FWASH

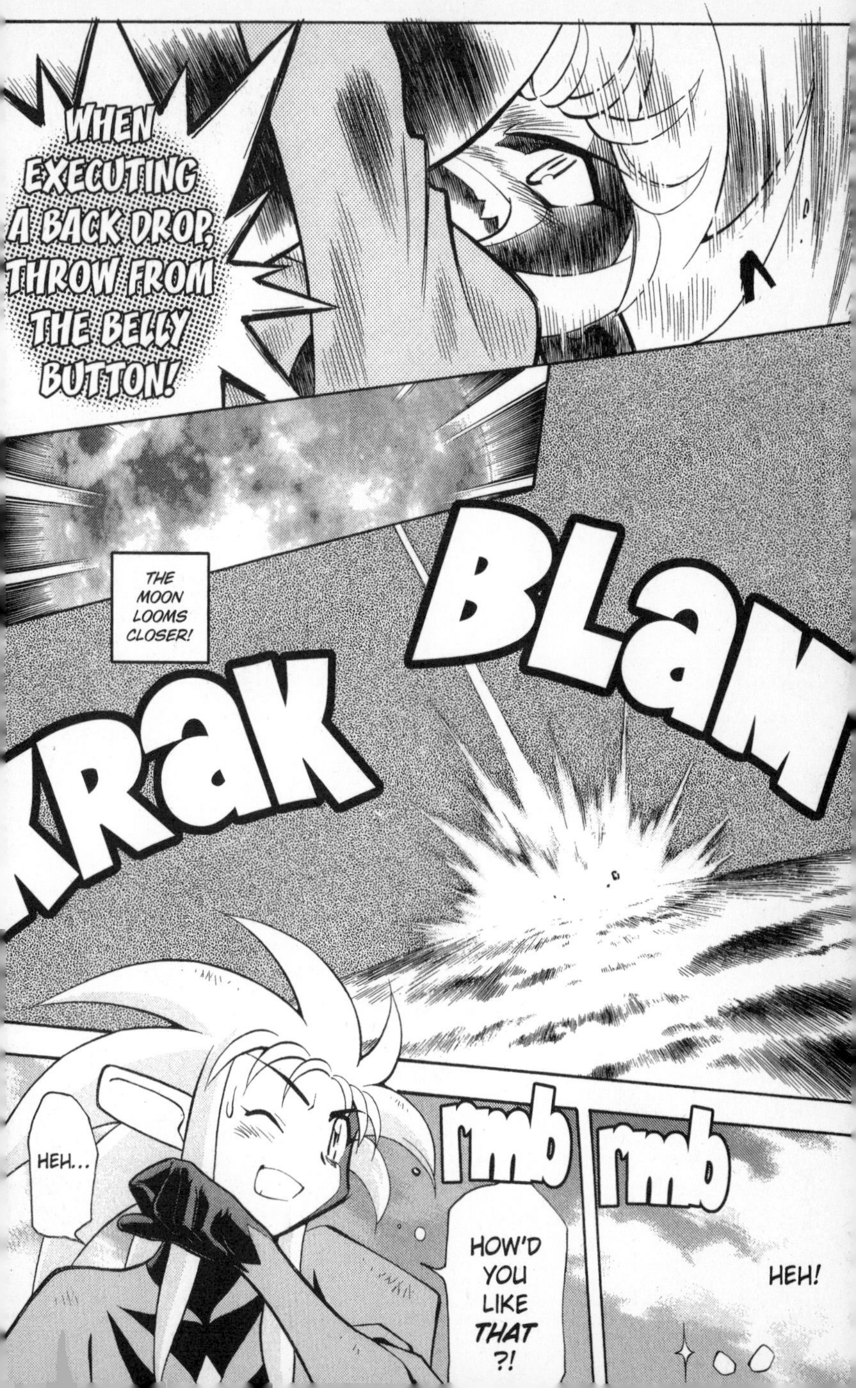
WHEN EXECUTING A BACK DROP, THROW FROM THE BELLY BUTTON!
THE MOON LOOMS CLOSER!
BLAM
KRAK
HEH...
rmb rmb
HOW'D YOU LIKE THAT ?!
HEH!

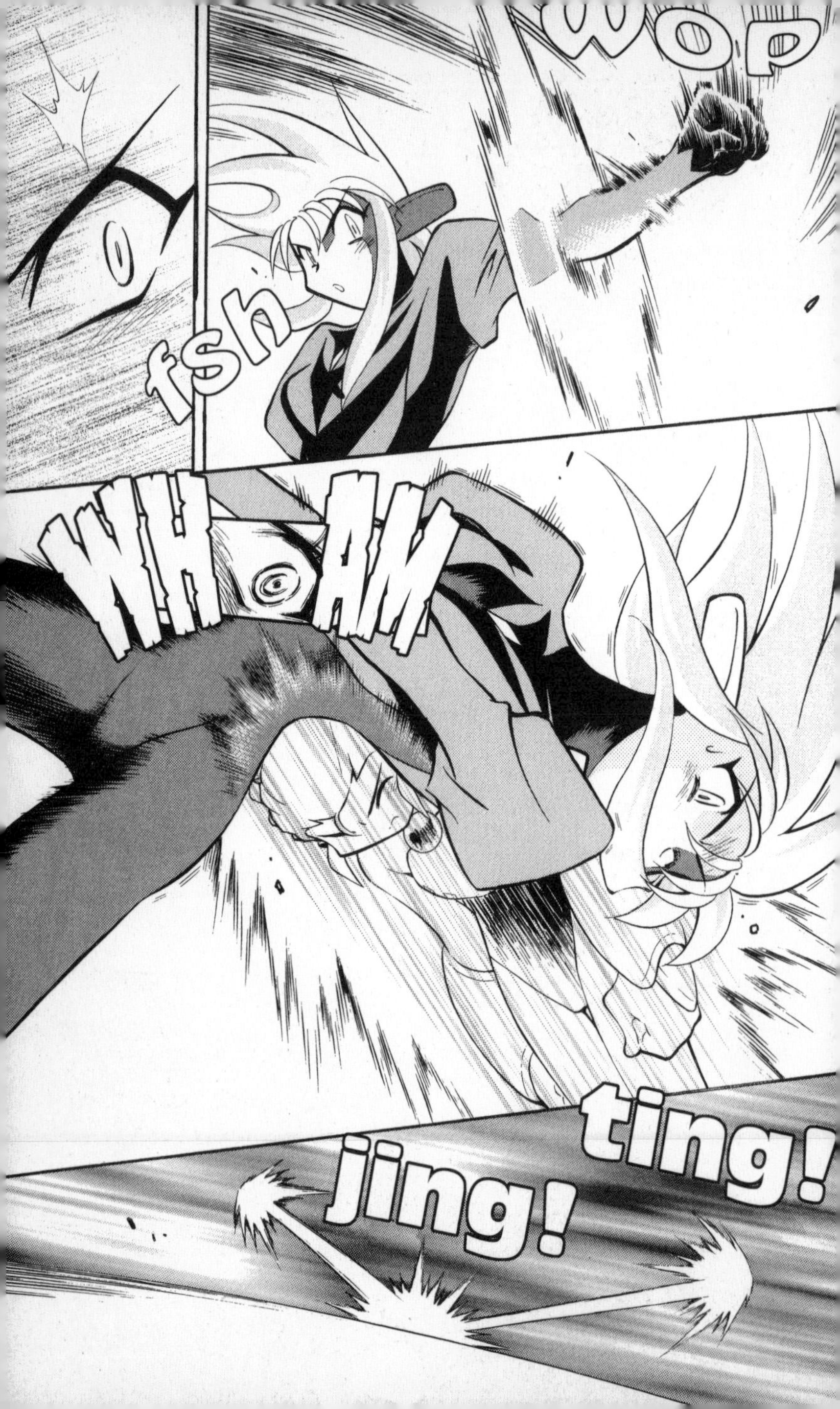
fsh
WOP
WHAM
ting!
jing!

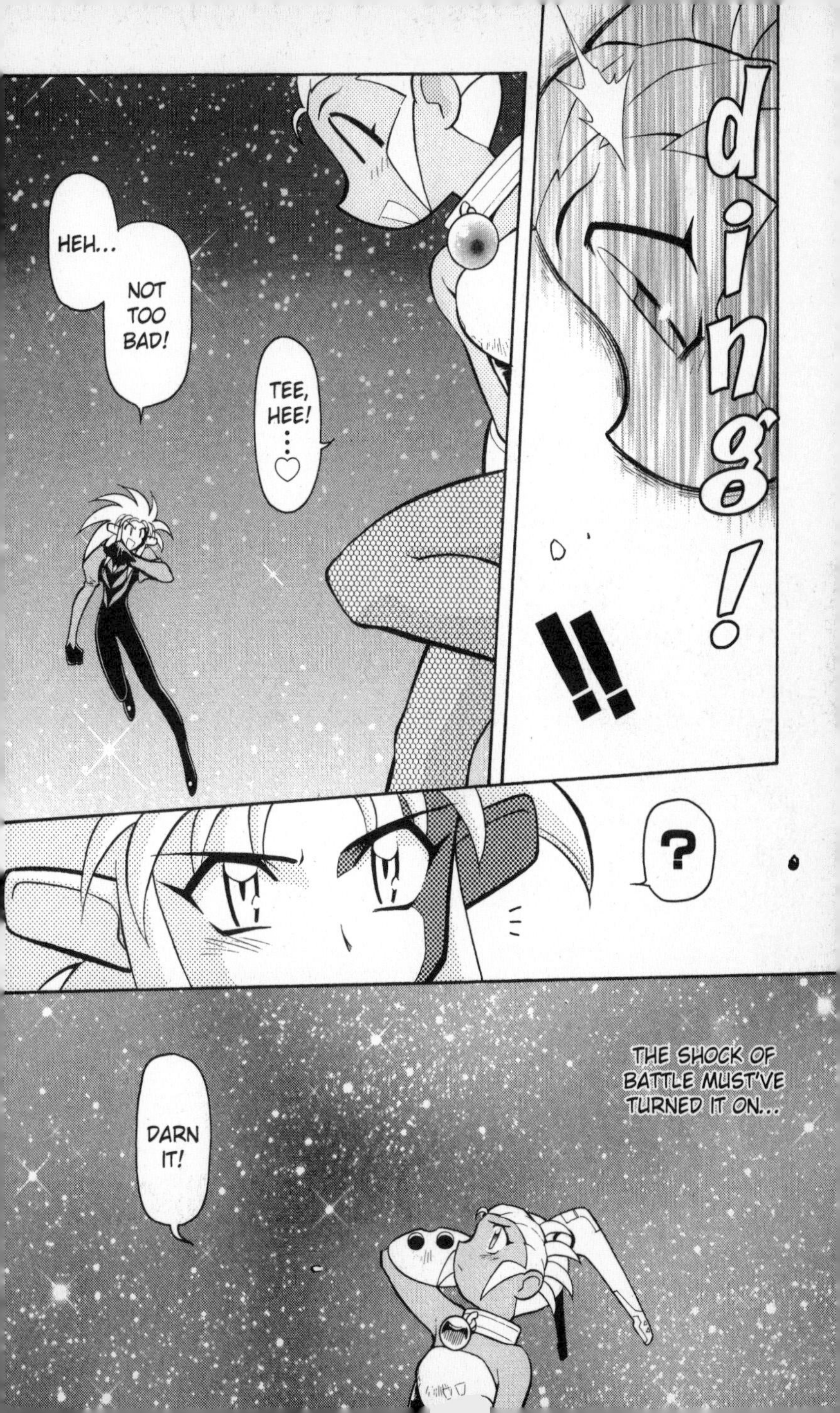
HEH...
NOT TOO BAD!
TEE, HEE! ...♡
ding!
!!
?
DARN IT!
THE SHOCK OF BATTLE MUST'VE TURNED IT ON...

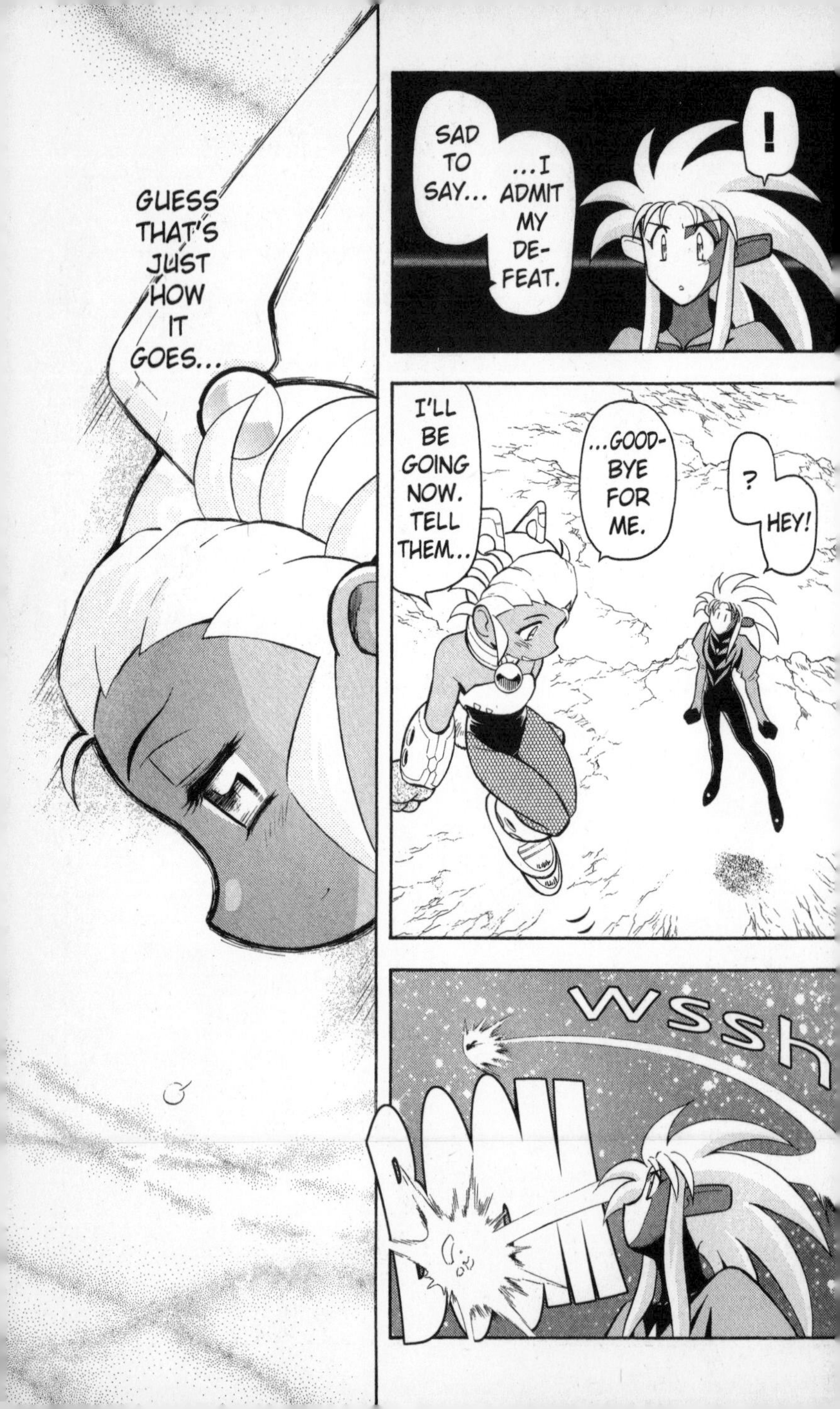
GUESS THAT'S JUST HOW IT GOES...
SAD TO SAY...
...I ADMIT MY DE-FEAT.
!
I'LL BE GOING NOW. TELL THEM...
...GOOD-BYE FOR ME.
?
HEY!
Wssh

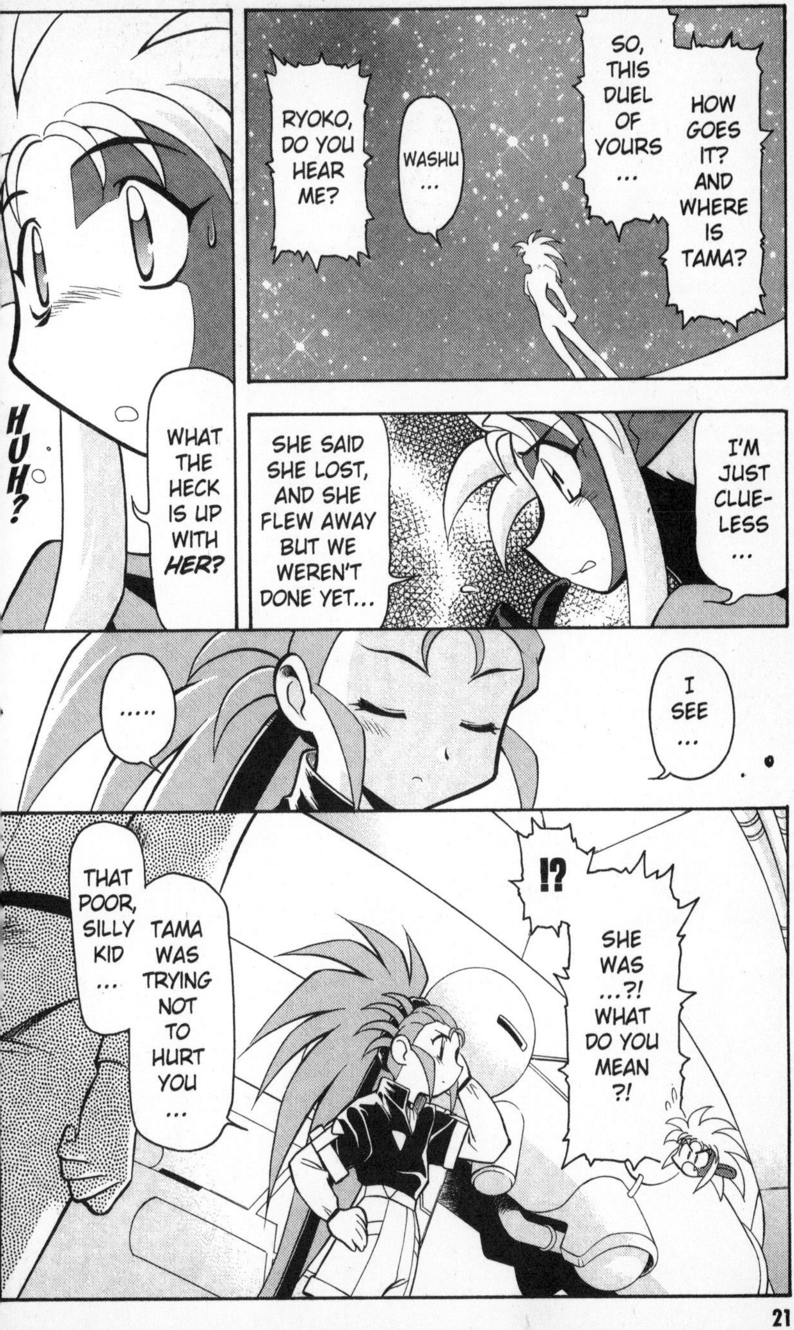
HUH?
WHAT THE HECK IS UP WITH *HER*?
RYOKO, DO YOU HEAR ME?
WASHU ...
SO, THIS DUEL OF YOURS ...
HOW GOES IT? AND WHERE IS TAMA?
SHE SAID SHE LOST, AND SHE FLEW AWAY BUT WE WEREN'T DONE YET...
I'M JUST CLUE-LESS ...
.....
I SEE ...
THAT POOR, SILLY KID ...
TAMA WAS TRYING NOT TO HURT YOU ...
!?
SHE WAS ...?! WHAT DO YOU MEAN ?!

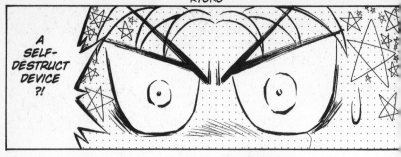

A SELF-DESTRUCT DEVICE?!

A-A BOMB?!

WHY'D YOU EQUIP HER WITH THAT?!

WELL... SHE ASKED ME TO WHEN I WAS RE-BUILDING HER.. AND IT SEEMED SO AMUS-ING...

SHE TRIES SO HARD...

NO FAIR! YOU TRICKED ME...

HUH? WHAT ARE YOU TALKING ABOUT?

THAT IDIOT ...

THAT SHOW-OFF!

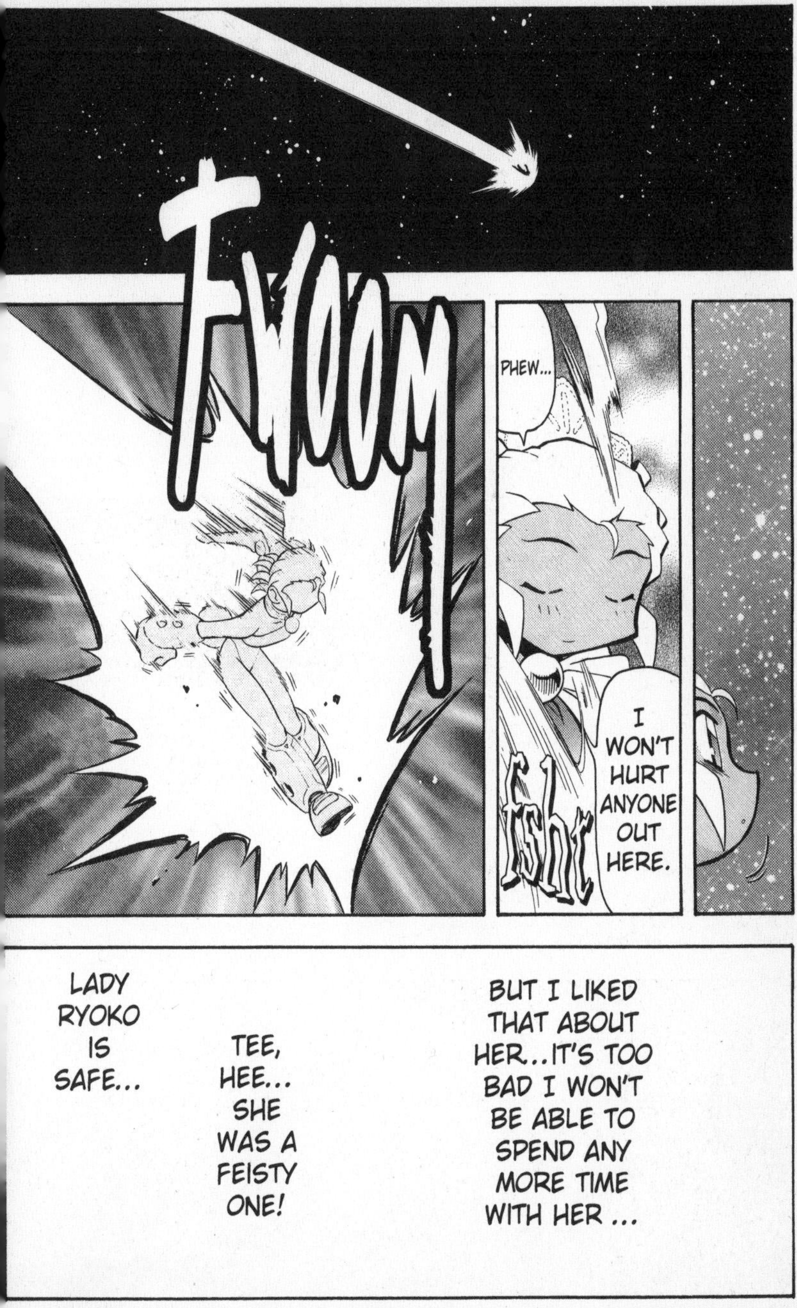
FWOOM
PHEW...
I WON'T HURT ANYONE OUT HERE.
fsht
LADY RYOKO IS SAFE...
TEE, HEE... SHE WAS A FEISTY ONE!
BUT I LIKED THAT ABOUT HER...IT'S TOO BAD I WON'T BE ABLE TO SPEND ANY MORE TIME WITH HER ...

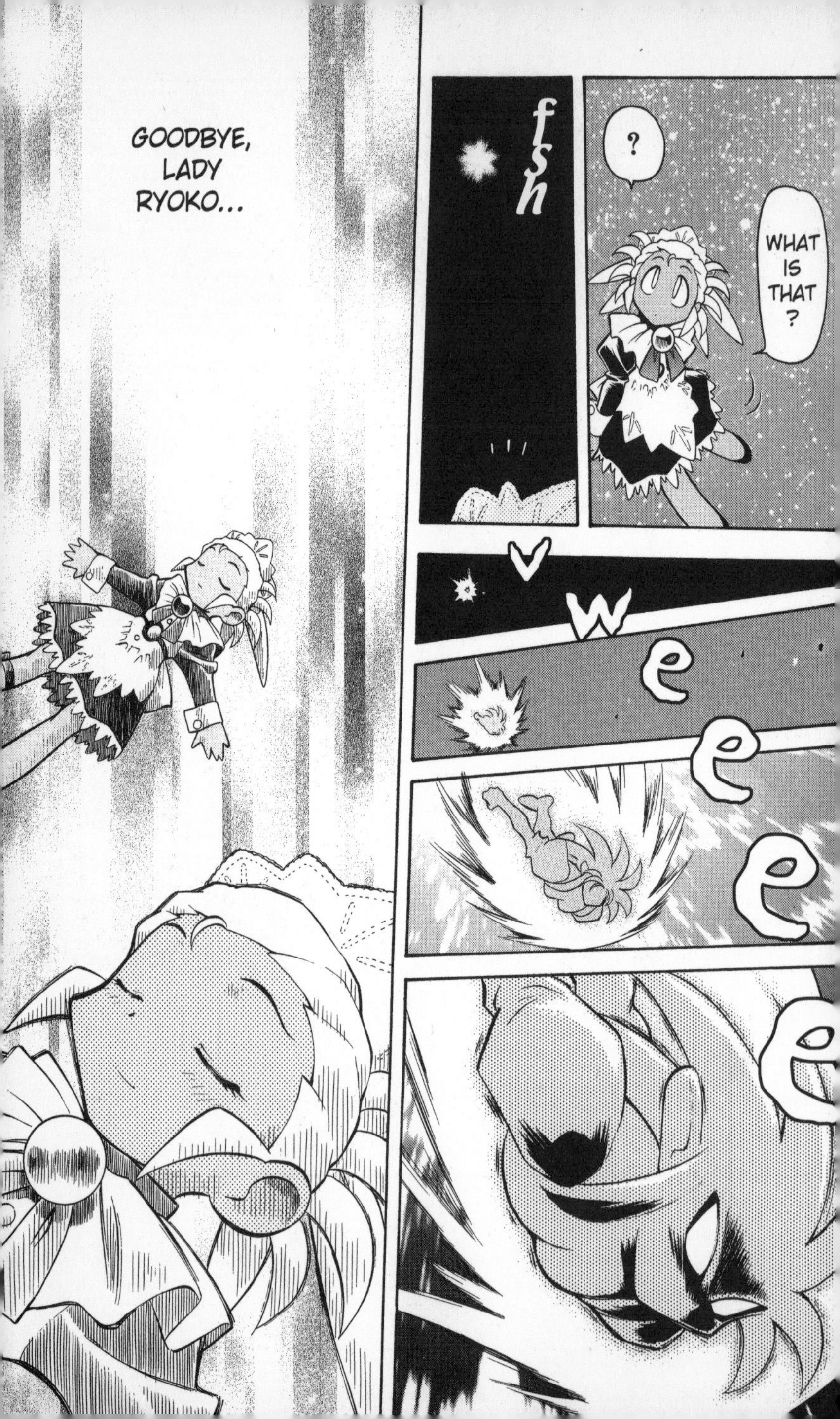
GOODBYE, LADY RYOKO...
fsh
?
WHAT IS THAT?
vweeee

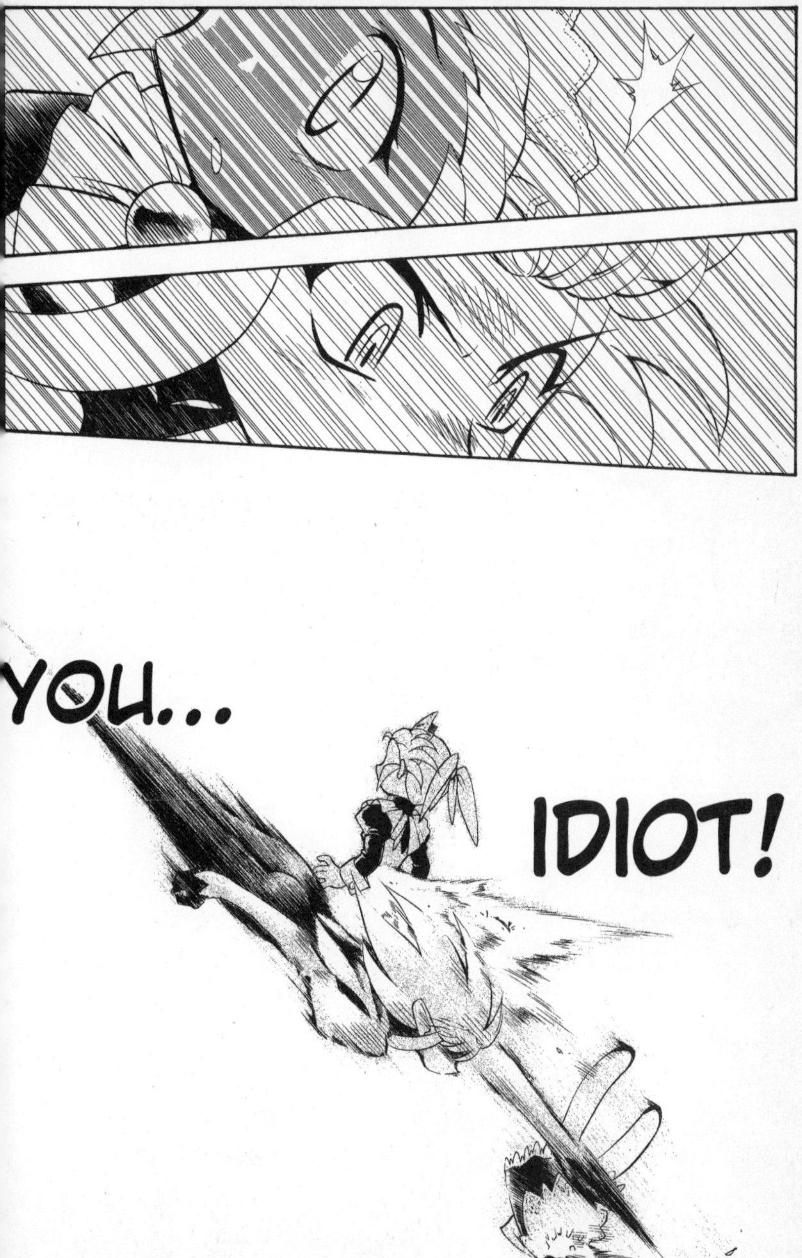
YOU...
IDIOT!

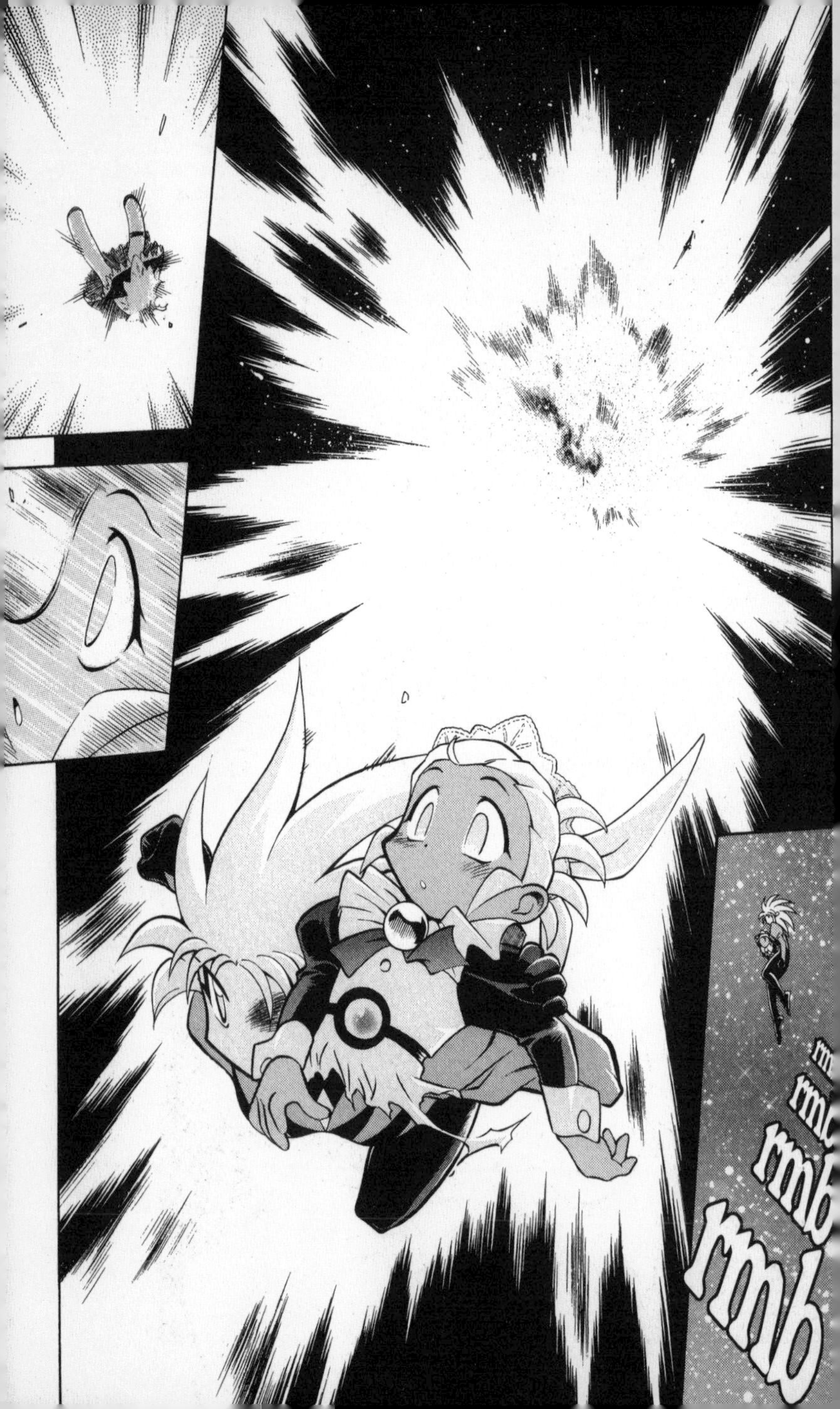
rm
rm
rmb
rmb

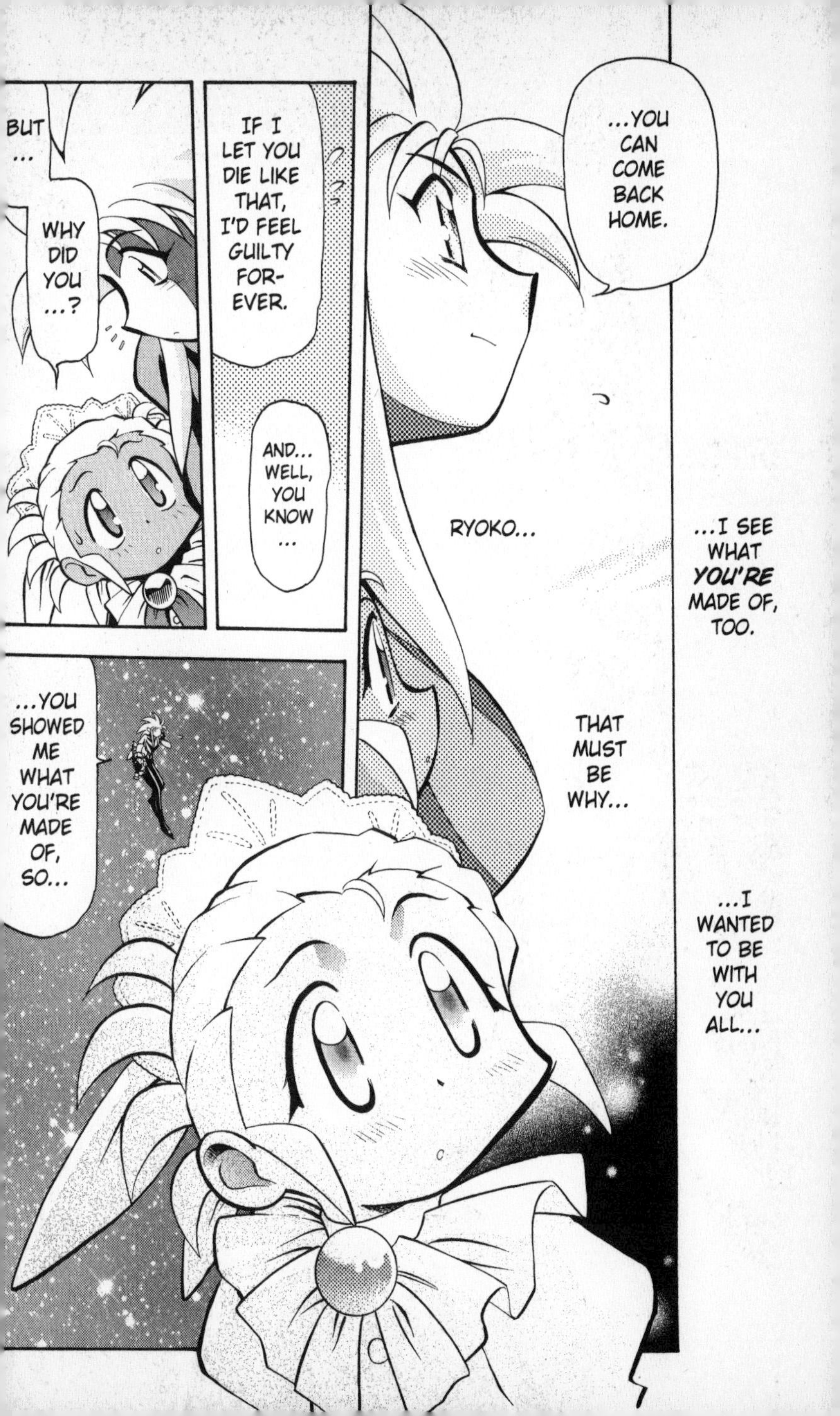
BUT ...
WHY DID YOU ...?
IF I LET YOU DIE LIKE THAT, I'D FEEL GUILTY FOR-EVER.
AND... WELL, YOU KNOW ...
...YOU SHOWED ME WHAT YOU'RE MADE OF, SO...
...YOU CAN COME BACK HOME.
RYOKO...
...I SEE WHAT ***YOU'RE*** MADE OF, TOO.
THAT MUST BE WHY...
...I WANTED TO BE WITH YOU ALL...

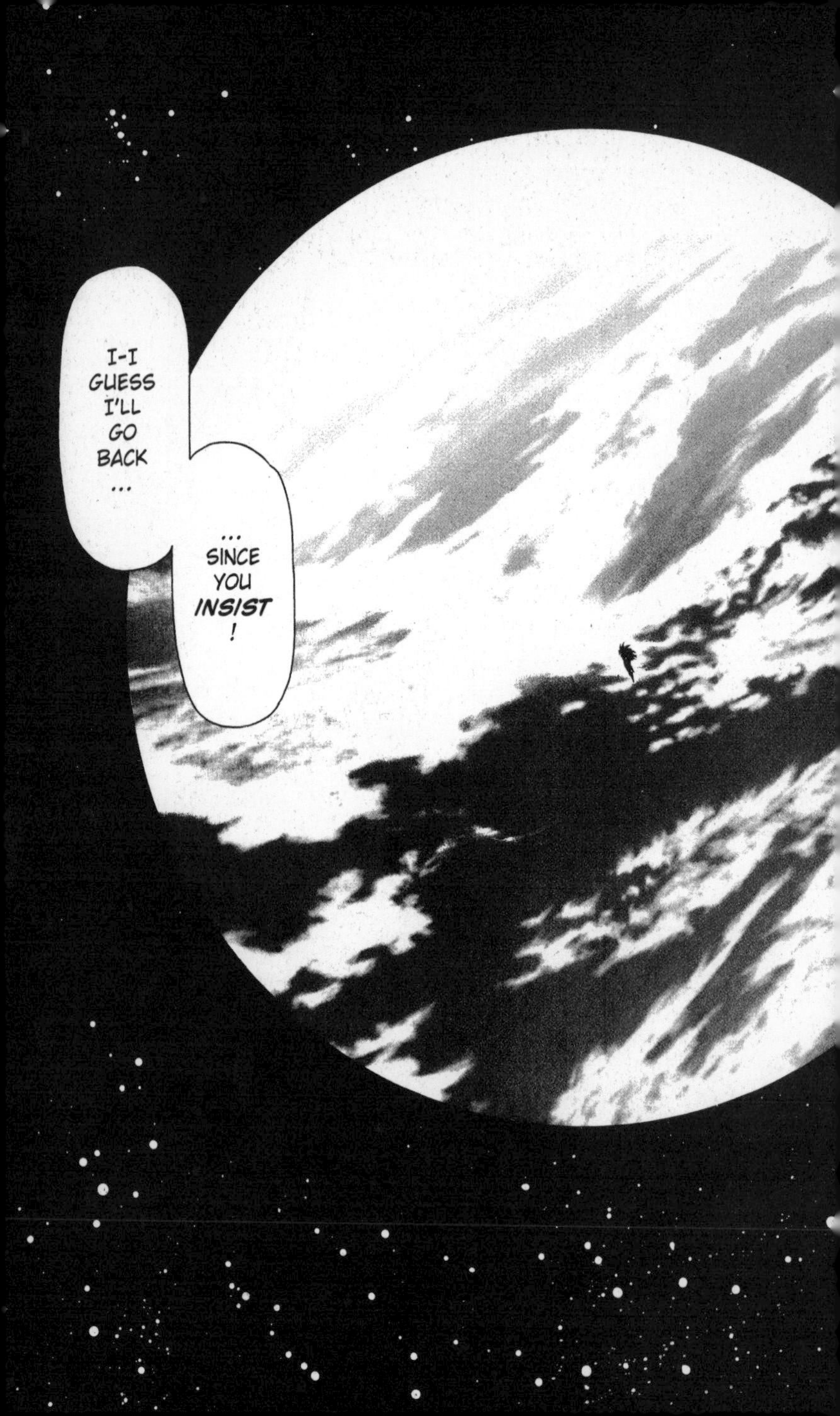
I-I GUESS I'LL GO BACK ...
... SINCE YOU *INSIST* !

I NEVER WANT TO LEAVE THEM AGAIN...
HMPH! YOU STILL SOUND LIKE DARK WASHU!
OR MAYBE MORE LIKE WASHU HERSELF.
I'M GLAD TO BE HOME...

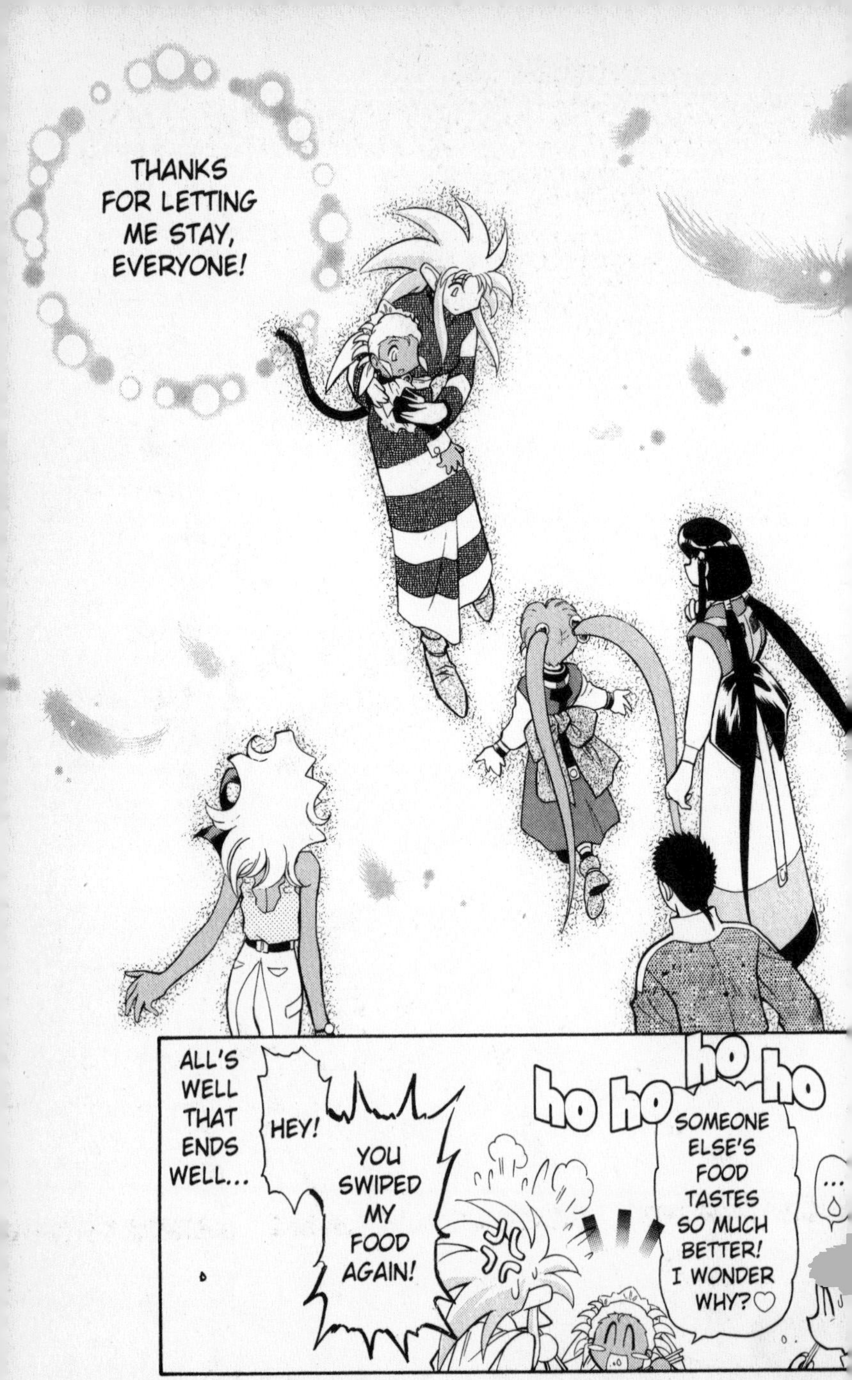
THANKS FOR LETTING ME STAY, EVERYONE!
ALL'S WELL THAT ENDS WELL...
HEY!
YOU SWIPED MY FOOD AGAIN!
ho ho ho ho
SOMEONE ELSE'S FOOD TASTES SO MUCH BETTER! I WONDER WHY?♡
...

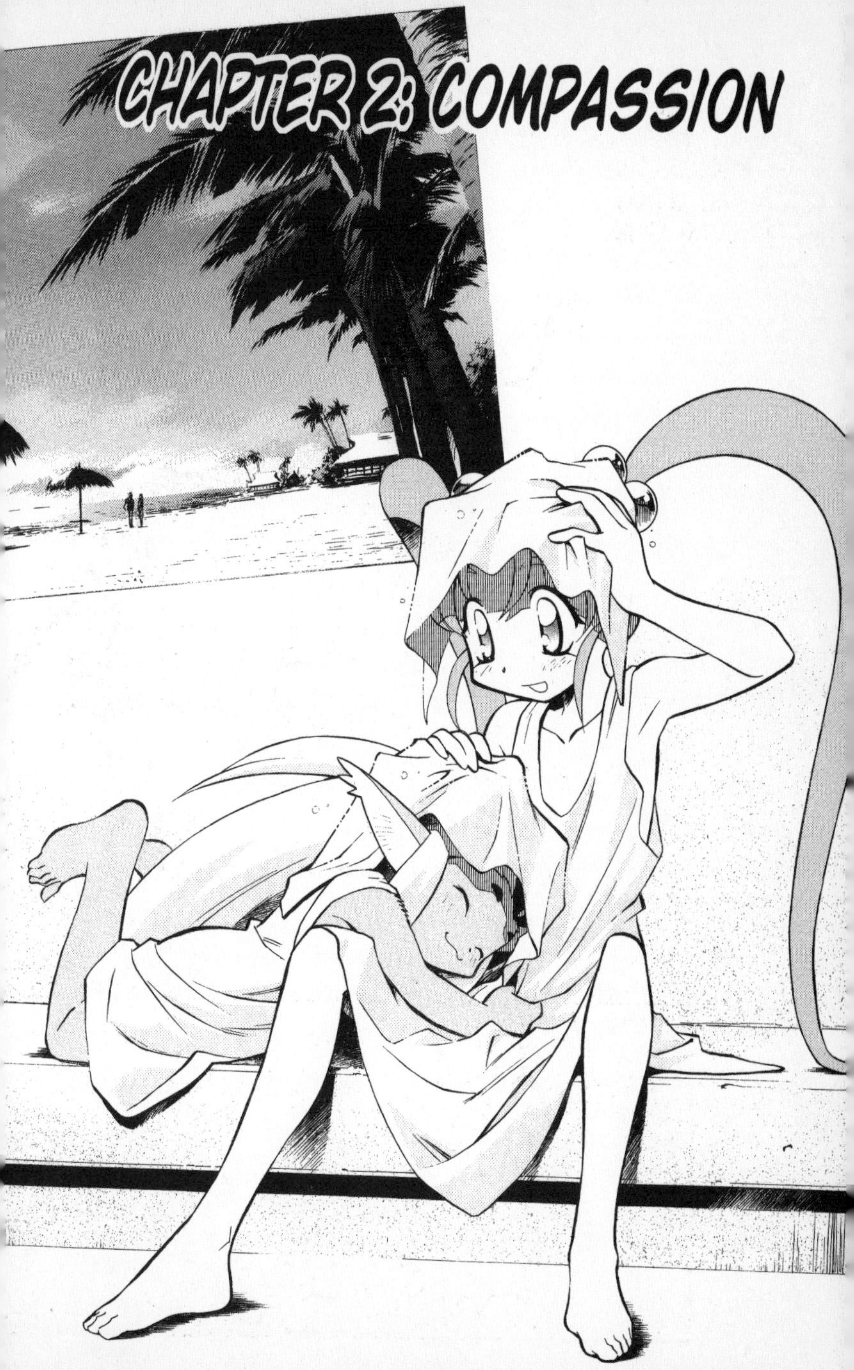
CHAPTER 2: COMPASSION

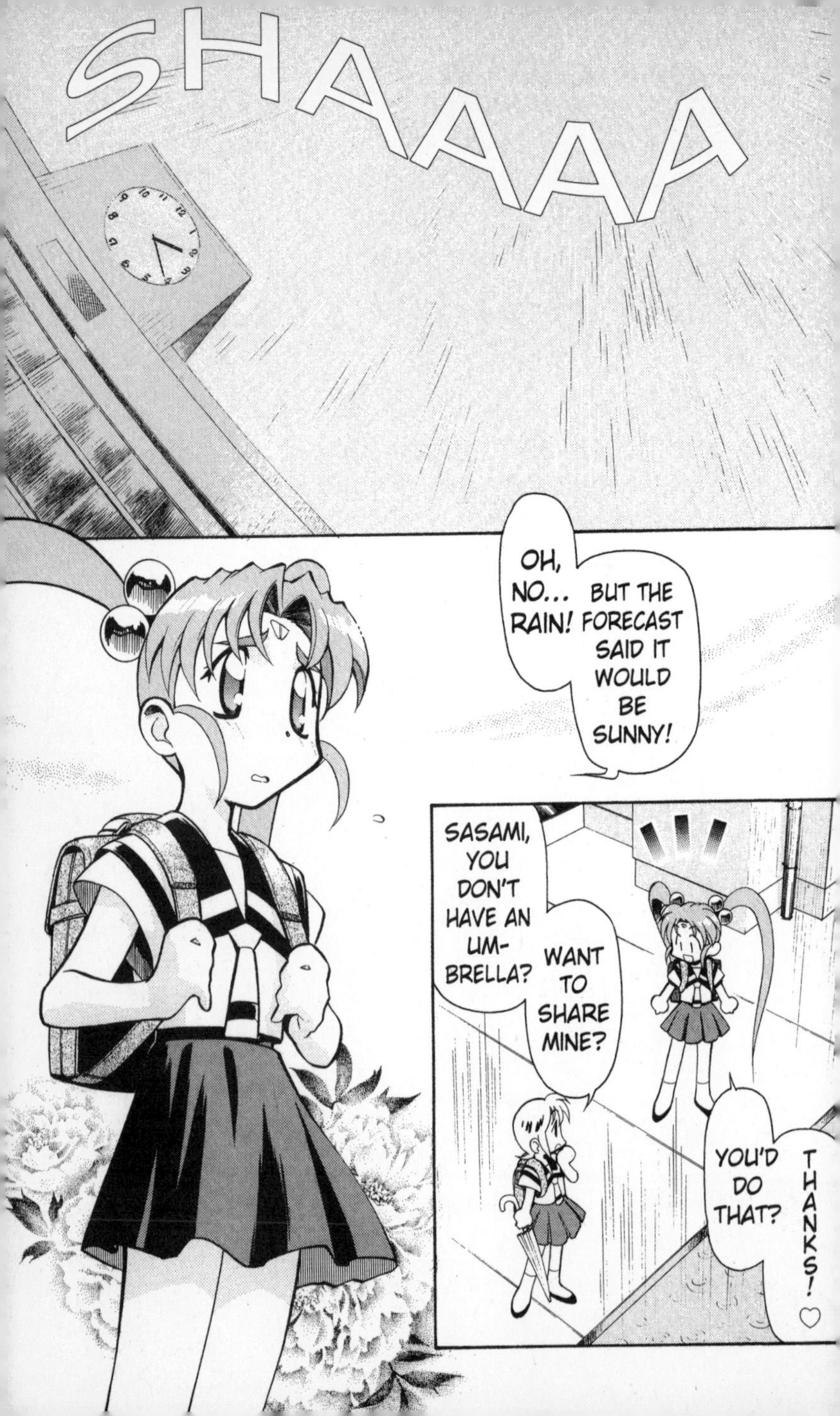
SHAAAAA
OH, NO... RAIN!
BUT THE FORECAST SAID IT WOULD BE SUNNY!
SASAMI, YOU DON'T HAVE AN UM-BRELLA?
WANT TO SHARE MINE?
YOU'D DO THAT?
THANKS! ♡

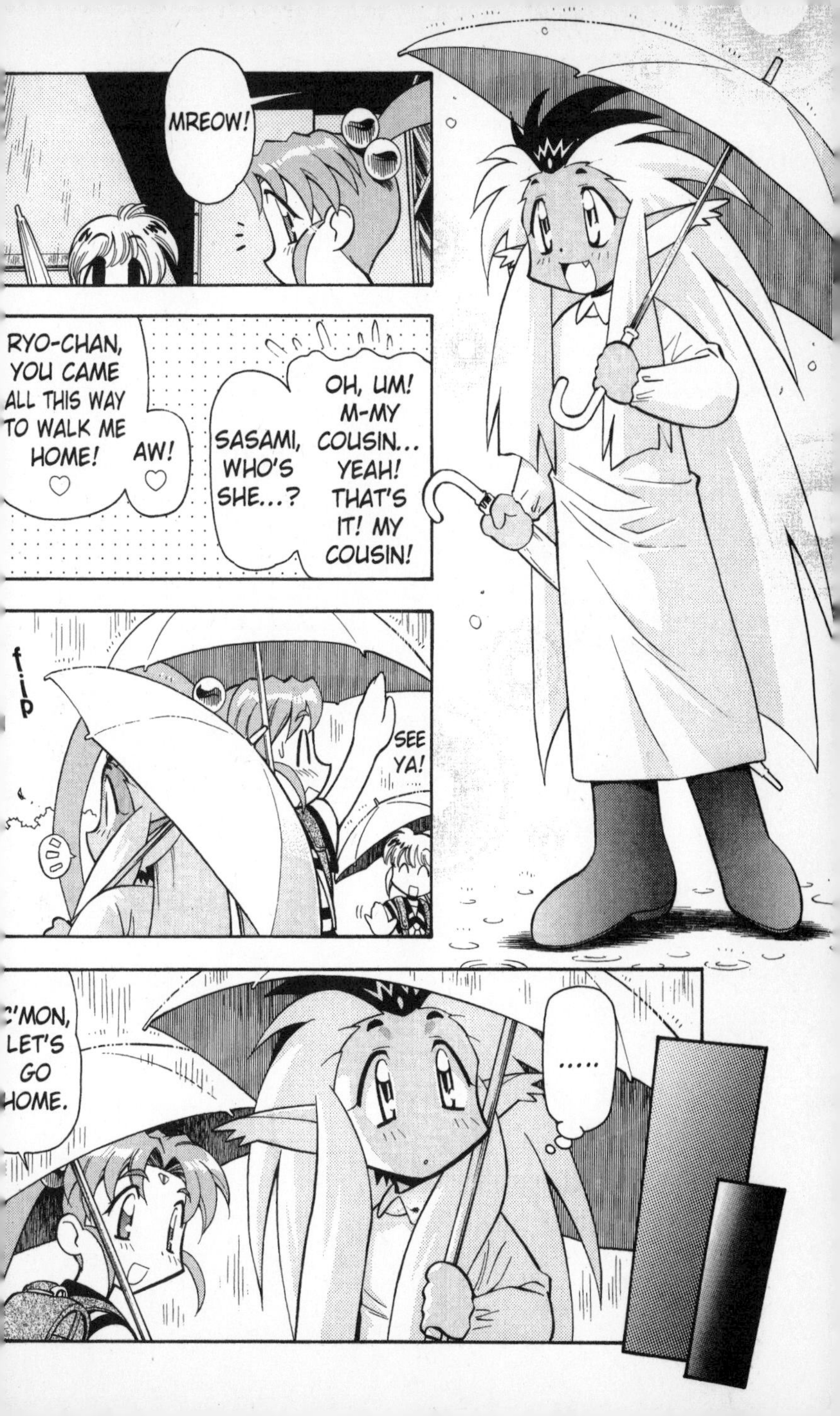

MREOW!
RYO-CHAN, YOU CAME ALL THIS WAY TO WALK ME HOME! ♡
AW! ♡
SASAMI, WHO'S SHE...?
OH, UM! M-MY COUSIN... YEAH! THAT'S IT! MY COUSIN!
flip
SEE YA!
C'MON, LET'S GO HOME.
.....

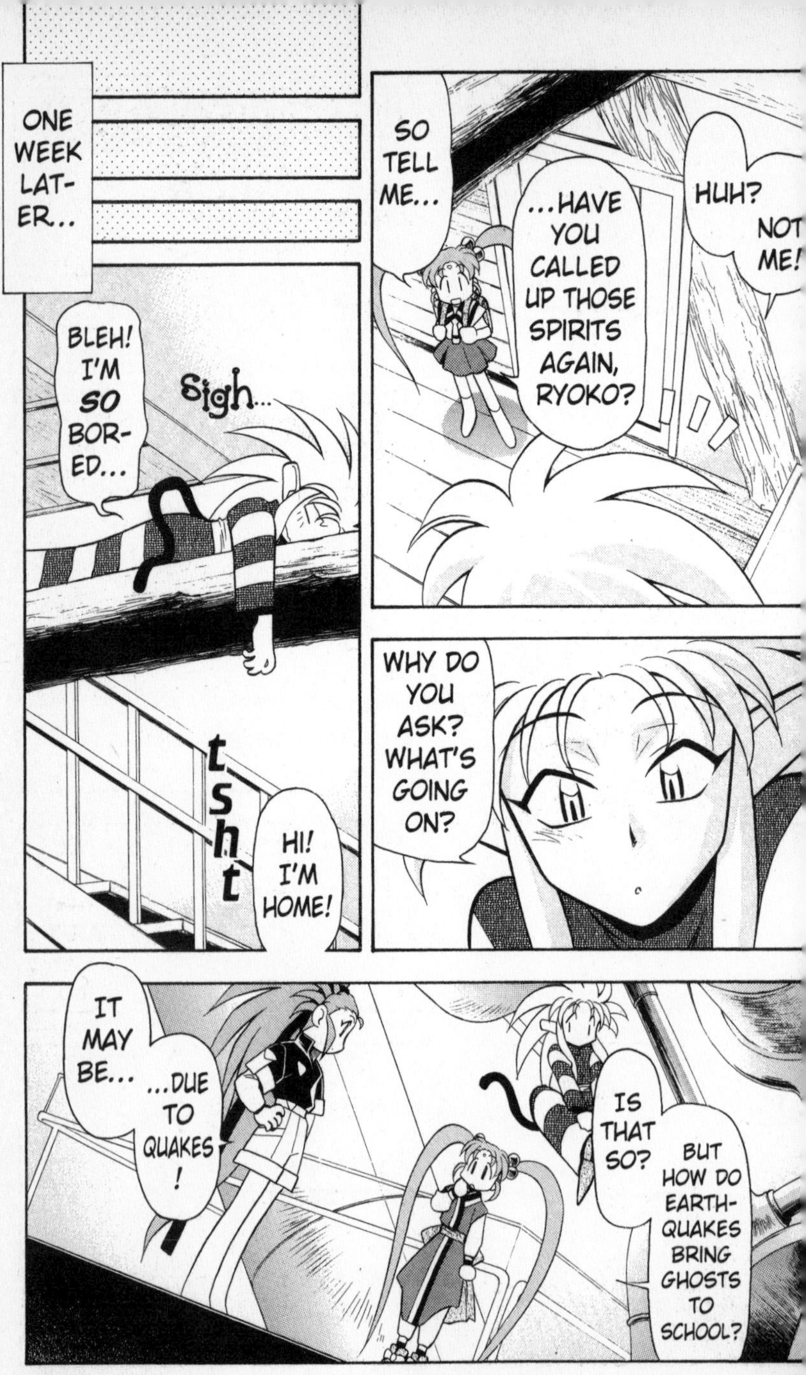
ONE WEEK LAT-ER...
BLEH! I'M *SO* BOR-ED...
Sigh...
tsht
HI! I'M HOME!
SO TELL ME...
...HAVE YOU CALLED UP THOSE SPIRITS AGAIN, RYOKO?
HUH?
NOT ME!
WHY DO YOU ASK? WHAT'S GOING ON?
IT MAY BE...
...DUE TO QUAKES!
IS THAT SO?
BUT HOW DO EARTH-QUAKES BRING GHOSTS TO SCHOOL?

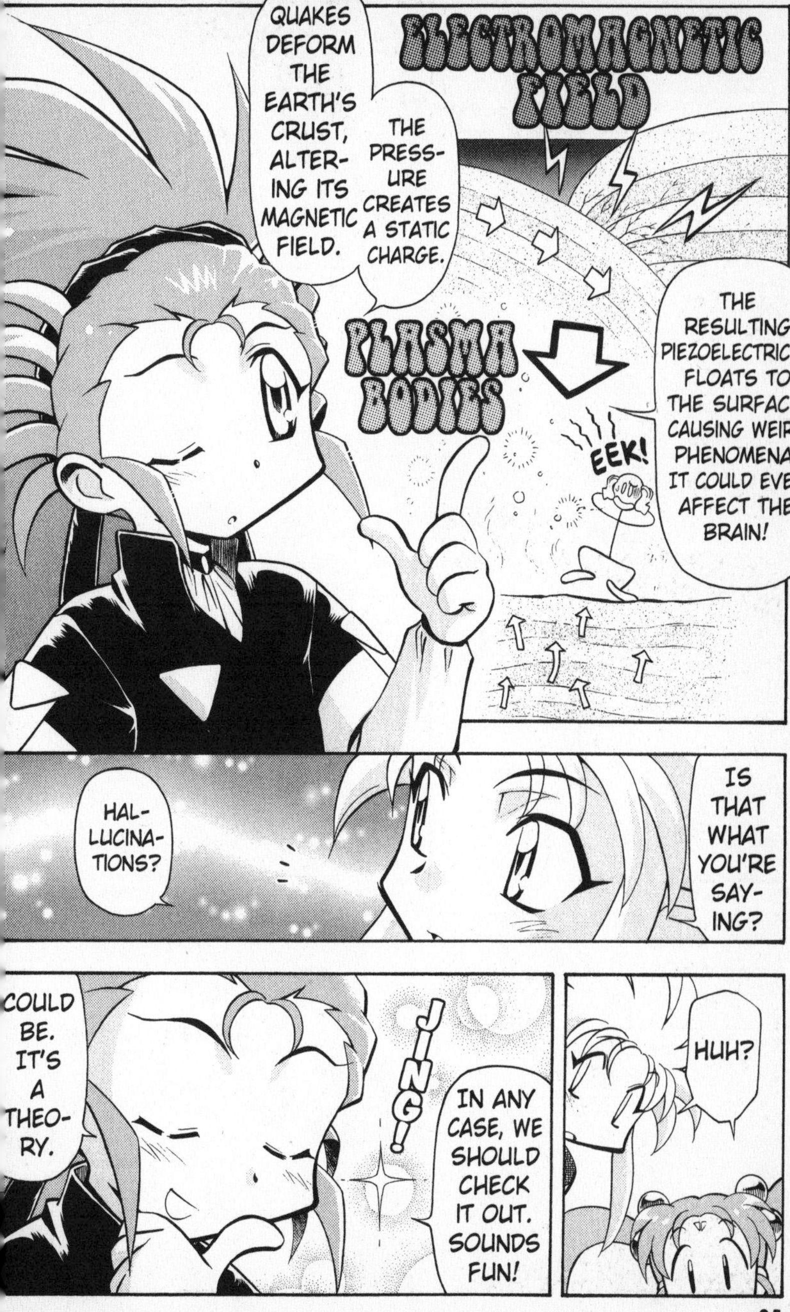
QUAKES DEFORM THE EARTH'S CRUST, ALTERING ITS MAGNETIC FIELD.
THE PRESSURE CREATES A STATIC CHARGE.
ELECTROMAGNETIC FIELD
PLASMA BODIES
EEK!
THE RESULTING PIEZOELECTRICITY FLOATS TO THE SURFACE, CAUSING WEIRD PHENOMENA. IT COULD EVEN AFFECT THE BRAIN!
HALLUCINATIONS?
IS THAT WHAT YOU'RE SAYING?
COULD BE. IT'S A THEORY.
JING!
IN ANY CASE, WE SHOULD CHECK IT OUT. SOUNDS FUN!
HUH?

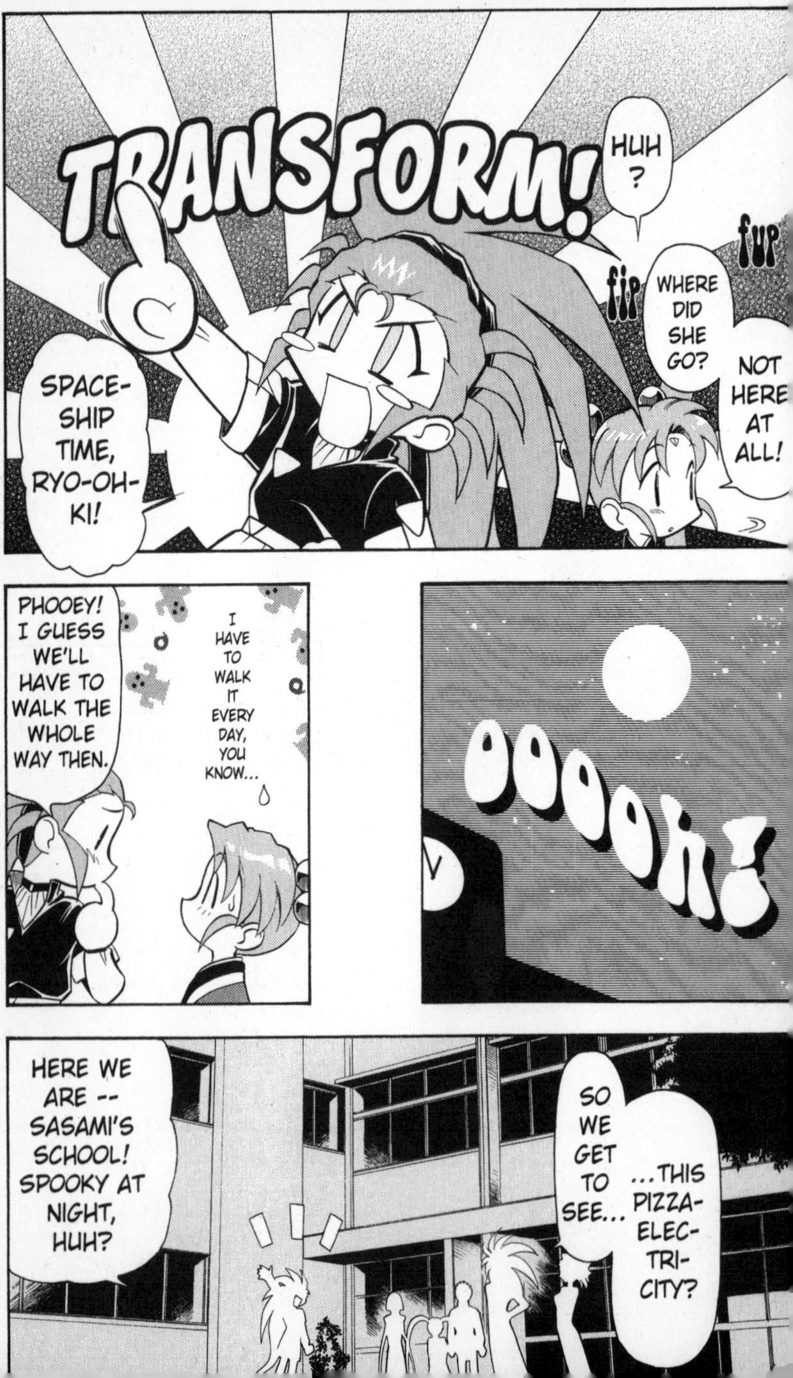

TRANSFORM!
SPACE-SHIP TIME, RYO-OH-KI!
HUH?
fip
fup
WHERE DID SHE GO?
NOT HERE AT ALL!
PHOOEY! I GUESS WE'LL HAVE TO WALK THE WHOLE WAY THEN.
I HAVE TO WALK IT EVERY DAY, YOU KNOW...
OOOOh!
HERE WE ARE -- SASAMI'S SCHOOL! SPOOKY AT NIGHT, HUH?
SO WE GET TO SEE...
...THIS PIZZA-ELEC-TRI-CITY?

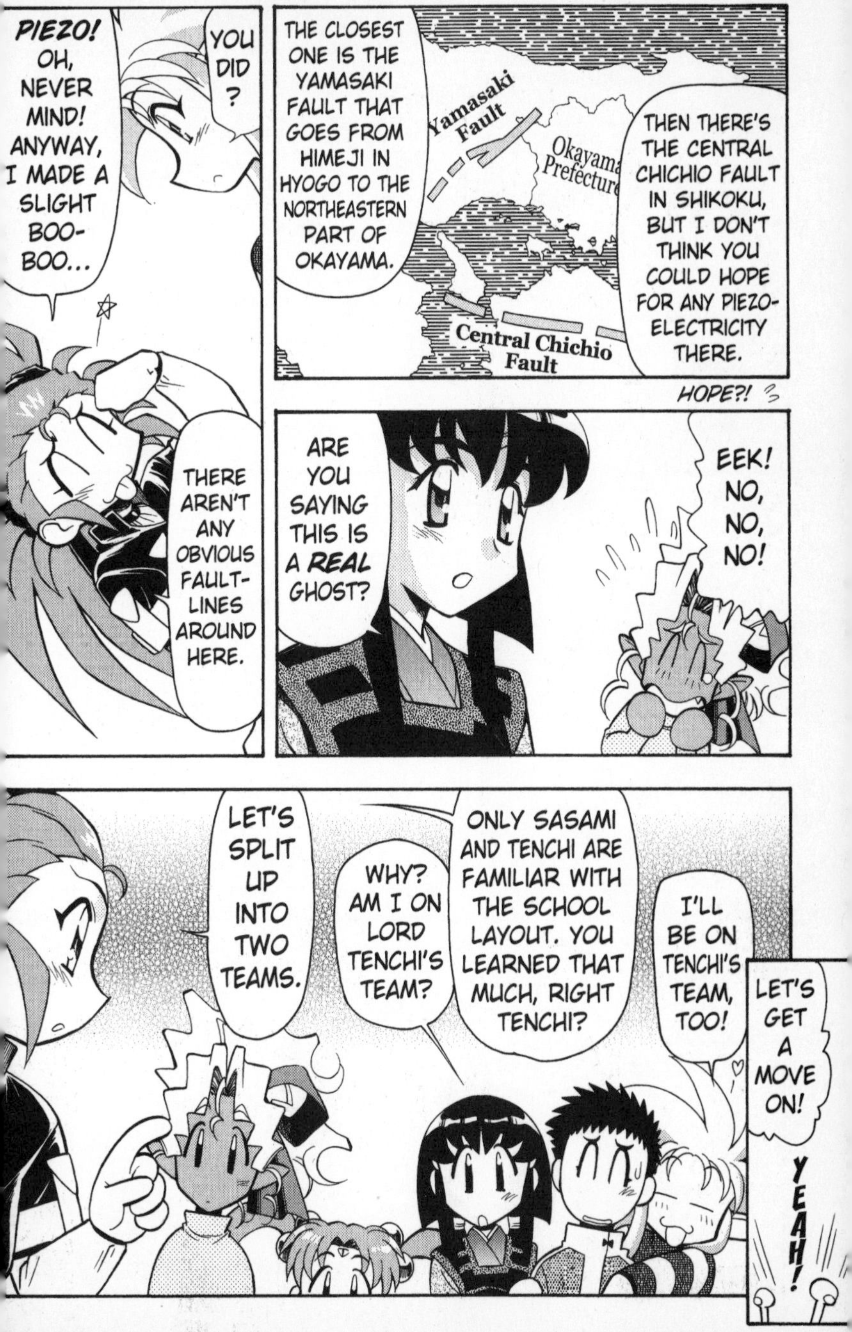
PIEZO! OH, NEVER MIND! ANYWAY, I MADE A SLIGHT BOO-BOO...
YOU DID?
THERE AREN'T ANY OBVIOUS FAULT-LINES AROUND HERE.
THE CLOSEST ONE IS THE YAMASAKI FAULT THAT GOES FROM HIMEJI IN HYOGO TO THE NORTHEASTERN PART OF OKAYAMA.
Yamasaki Fault
Okayama Prefecture
THEN THERE'S THE CENTRAL CHICHIO FAULT IN SHIKOKU, BUT I DON'T THINK YOU COULD HOPE FOR ANY PIEZO-ELECTRICITY THERE.
Central Chichio Fault
HOPE?!
ARE YOU SAYING THIS IS A *REAL* GHOST?
EEK! NO, NO, NO!
LET'S SPLIT UP INTO TWO TEAMS.
WHY? AM I ON LORD TENCHI'S TEAM?
ONLY SASAMI AND TENCHI ARE FAMILIAR WITH THE SCHOOL LAYOUT. YOU LEARNED THAT MUCH, RIGHT TENCHI?
I'LL BE ON TENCHI'S TEAM, TOO!
LET'S GET A MOVE ON!
YEAH!

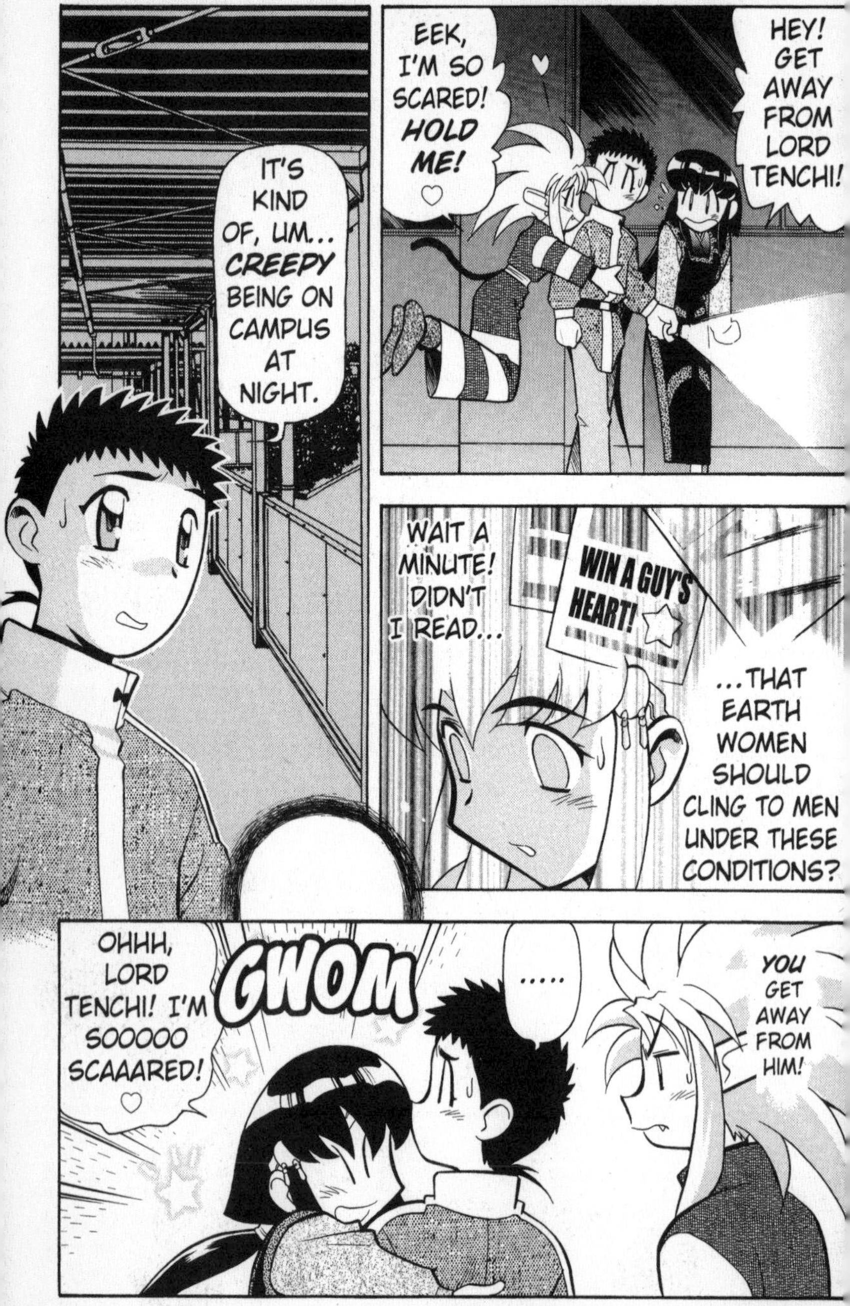
IT'S KIND OF, UM... CREEPY BEING ON CAMPUS AT NIGHT.
EEK, I'M SO SCARED! HOLD ME!
HEY! GET AWAY FROM LORD TENCHI!
WAIT A MINUTE! DIDN'T I READ...
WIN A GUY'S HEART!
...THAT EARTH WOMEN SHOULD CLING TO MEN UNDER THESE CONDITIONS?
OHHH, LORD TENCHI! I'M SOOOOO SCAAARED!
GWOM
.....
YOU GET AWAY FROM HIM!

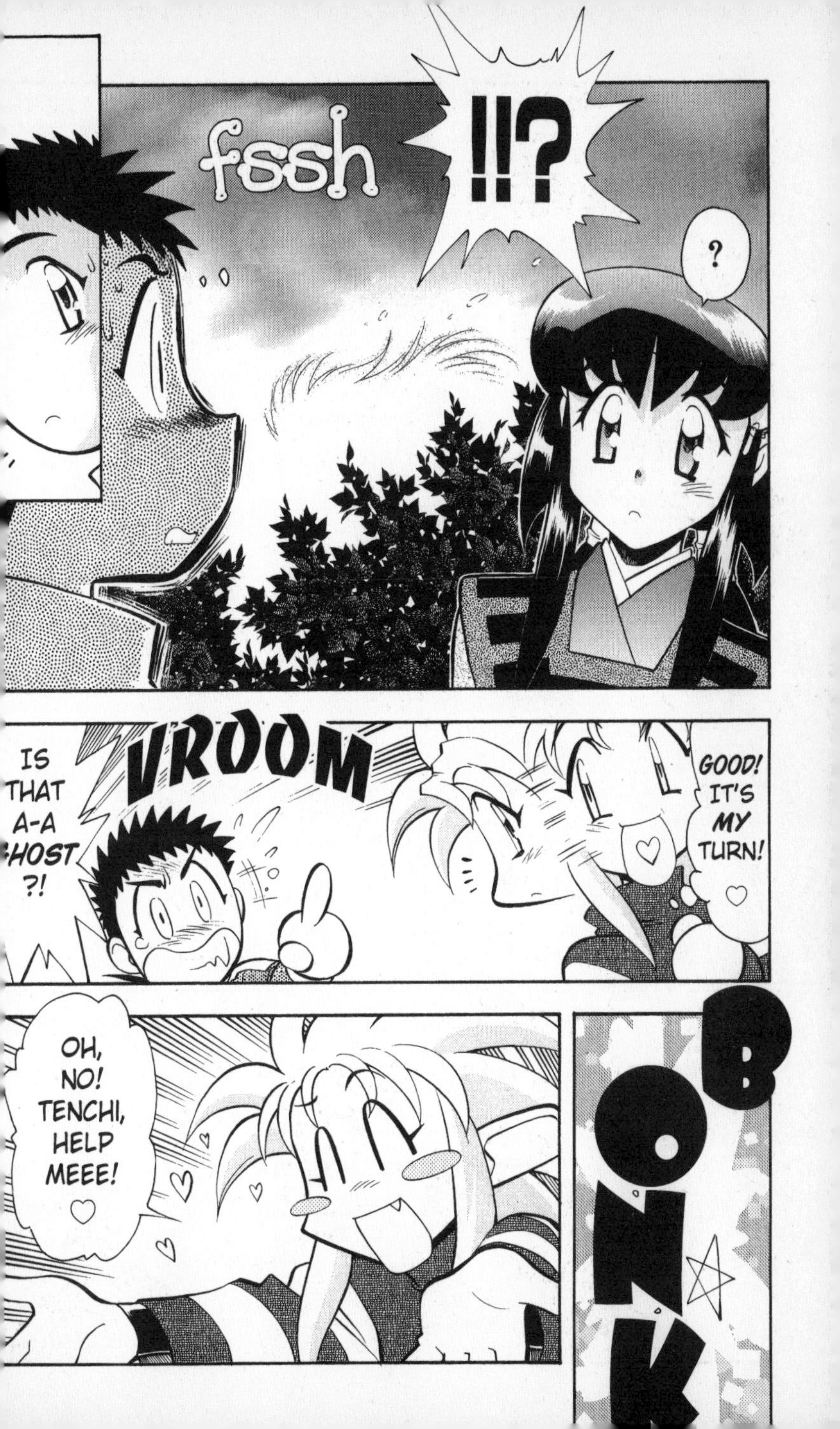
fssh
!!?
?
IS THAT A-A HOST ?!
VROOM
GOOD! IT'S MY TURN!
OH, NO! TENCHI, HELP MEEE!
BOINK

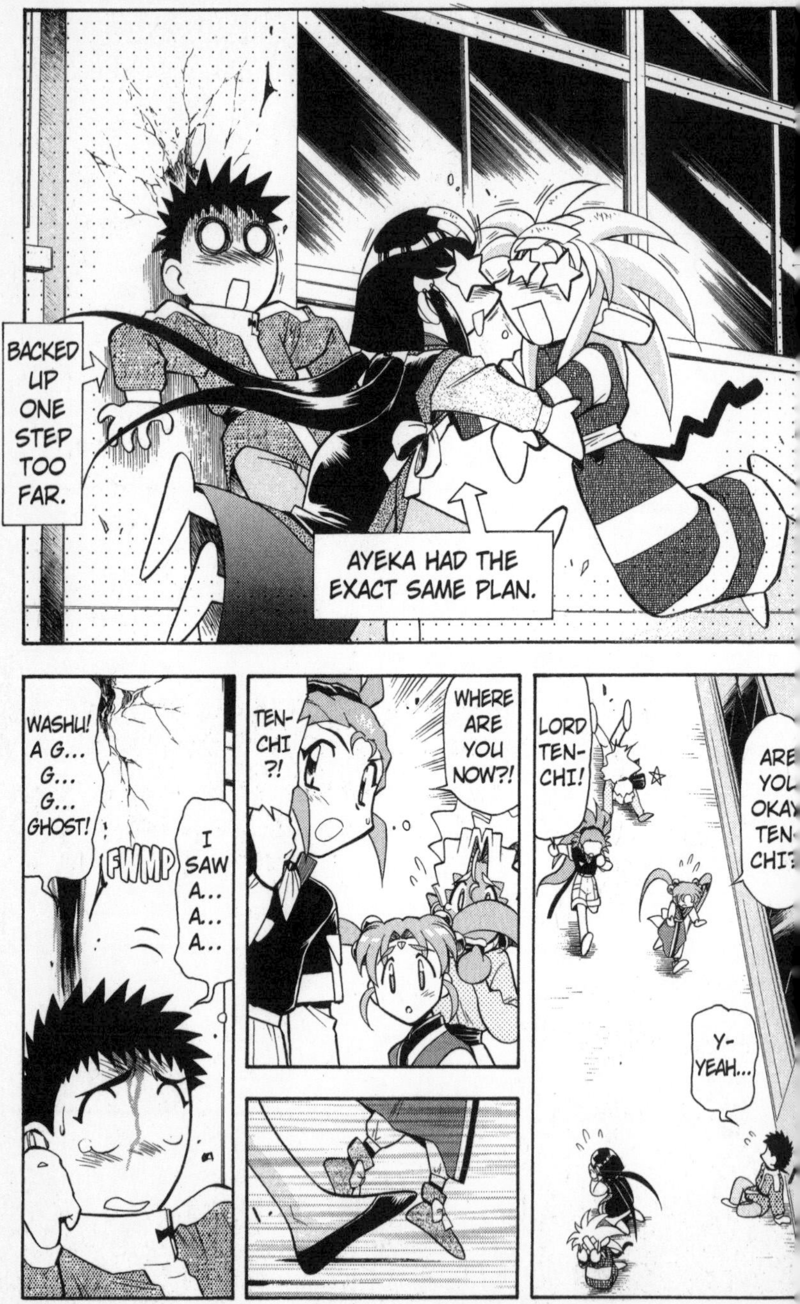
BACKED UP ONE STEP TOO FAR.
AYEKA HAD THE EXACT SAME PLAN.
WASHU! A G... G... G... GHOST!
FWMP
I SAW A... A... A...
TEN-CHI?!
WHERE ARE YOU NOW?!
LORD TEN-CHI!
ARE YOU OKAY TEN-CHI?
Y-YEAH...

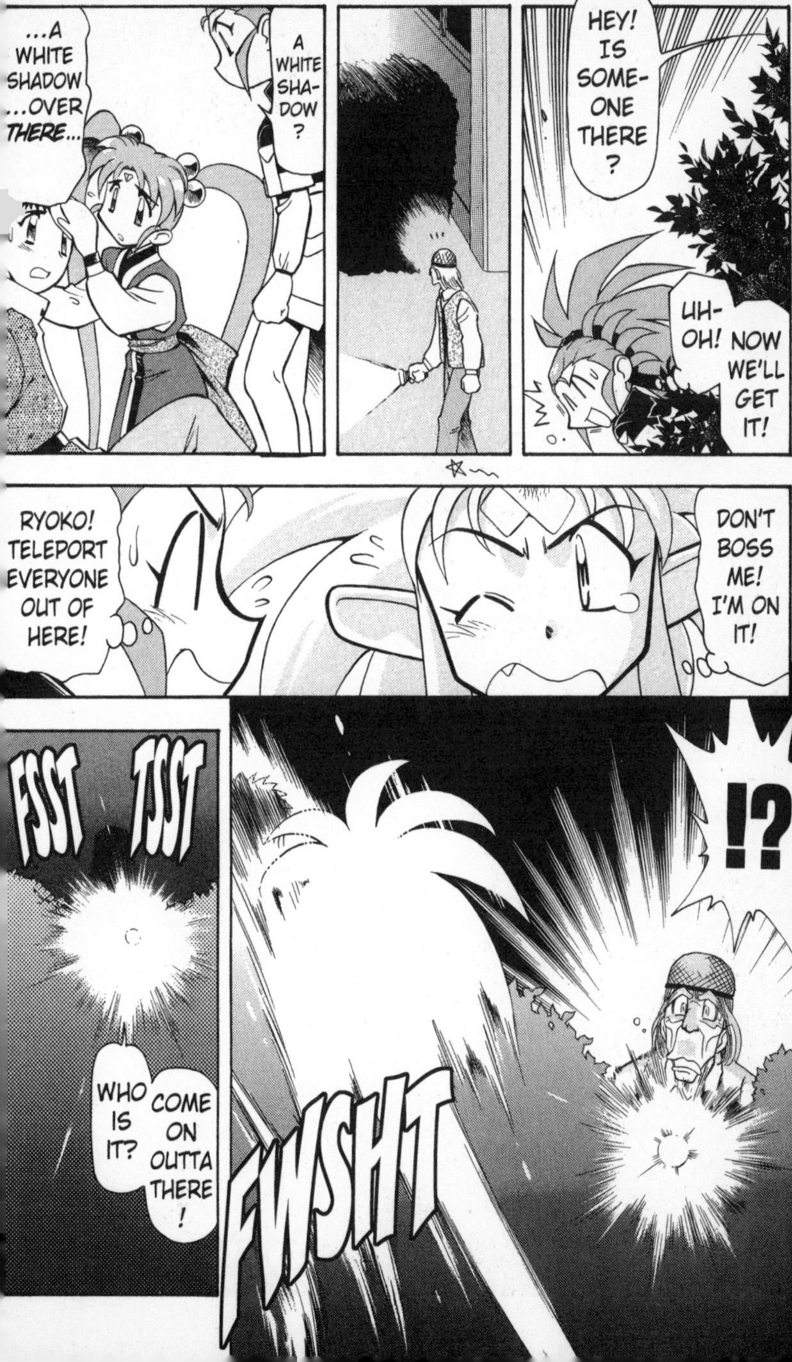

...A WHITE SHADOW ...OVER THERE...
A WHITE SHA-DOW?
HEY! IS SOME-ONE THERE?
UH-OH!
NOW WE'LL GET IT!
RYOKO! TELEPORT EVERYONE OUT OF HERE!
DON'T BOSS ME! I'M ON IT!
FSST
TSST
WHO IS IT?
COME ON OUTTA THERE!
FWSHT
!?

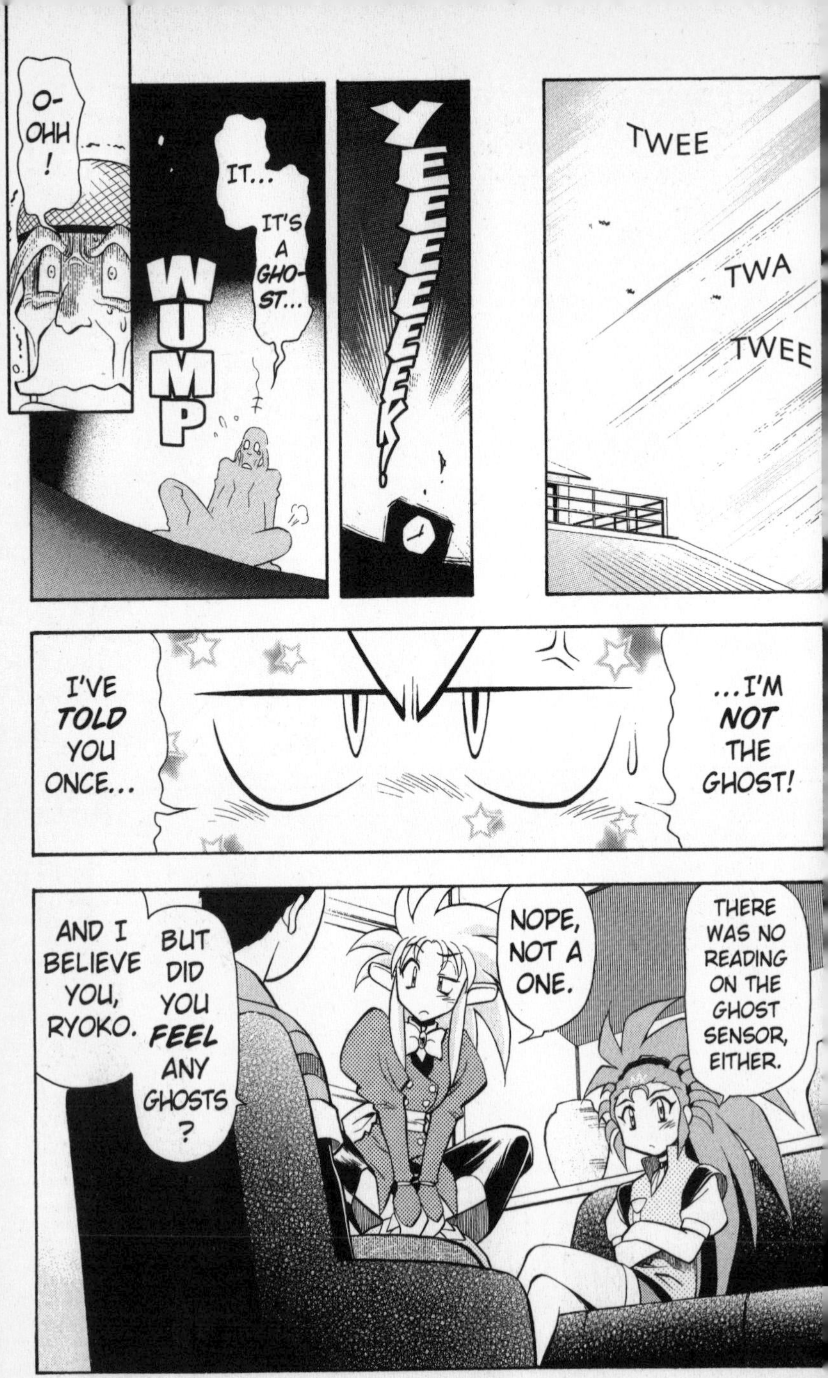
O-OHH!
IT... IT'S A GHO-ST...
WUMP
YEEEEEEK!
TWEE
TWA
TWEE
I'VE TOLD YOU ONCE...
...I'M NOT THE GHOST!
AND I BELIEVE YOU, RYOKO.
BUT DID YOU FEEL ANY GHOSTS?
NOPE, NOT A ONE.
THERE WAS NO READING ON THE GHOST SENSOR, EITHER.

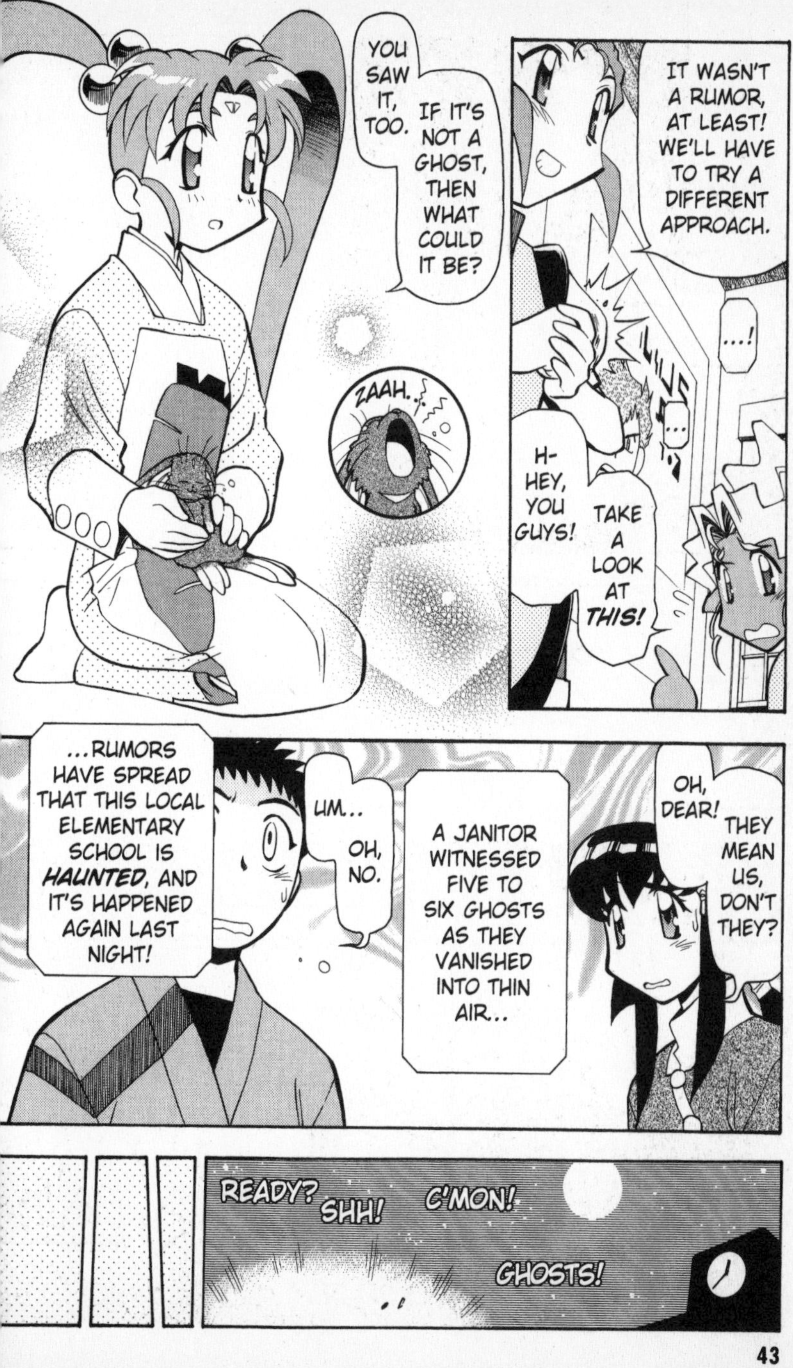
YOU SAW IT, TOO.
IF IT'S NOT A GHOST, THEN WHAT COULD IT BE?
ZAAH...
IT WASN'T A RUMOR, AT LEAST! WE'LL HAVE TO TRY A DIFFERENT APPROACH.
...!
...
H-HEY, YOU GUYS!
TAKE A LOOK AT *THIS!*
...RUMORS HAVE SPREAD THAT THIS LOCAL ELEMENTARY SCHOOL IS *HAUNTED*, AND IT'S HAPPENED AGAIN LAST NIGHT!
UM..
OH, NO.
A JANITOR WITNESSED FIVE TO SIX GHOSTS AS THEY VANISHED INTO THIN AIR...
OH, DEAR!
THEY MEAN US, DON'T THEY?
READY?
SHH!
C'MON!
GHOSTS!

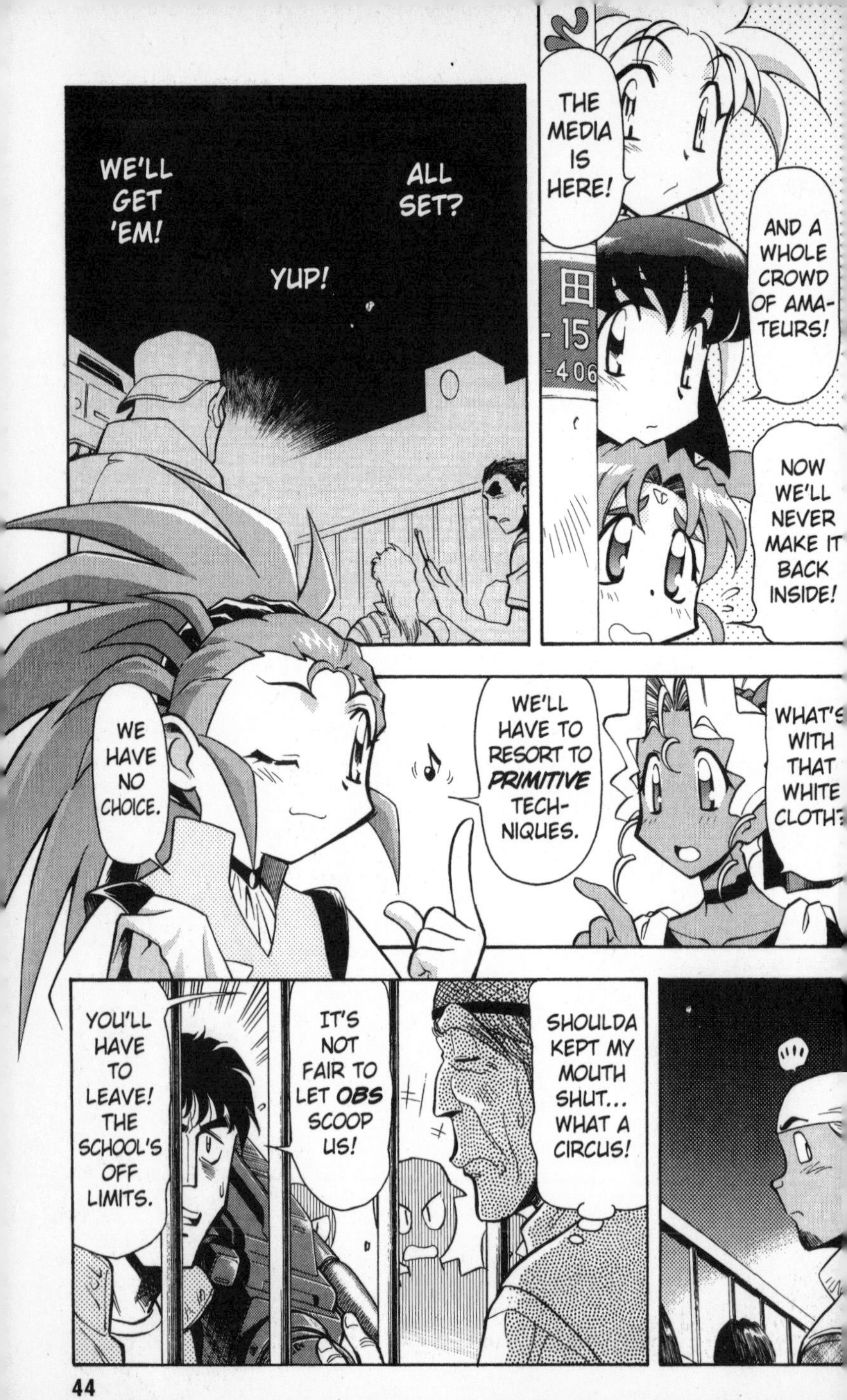
WE'LL GET 'EM!
ALL SET?
YUP!
THE MEDIA IS HERE!
AND A WHOLE CROWD OF AMA-TEURS!
NOW WE'LL NEVER MAKE IT BACK INSIDE!
WE HAVE NO CHOICE.
WE'LL HAVE TO RESORT TO *PRIMITIVE* TECH-NIQUES.
WHAT'S WITH THAT WHITE CLOTH?
YOU'LL HAVE TO LEAVE! THE SCHOOL'S OFF LIMITS.
IT'S NOT FAIR TO LET *OBS* SCOOP US!
SHOULDA KEPT MY MOUTH SHUT... WHAT A CIRCUS!

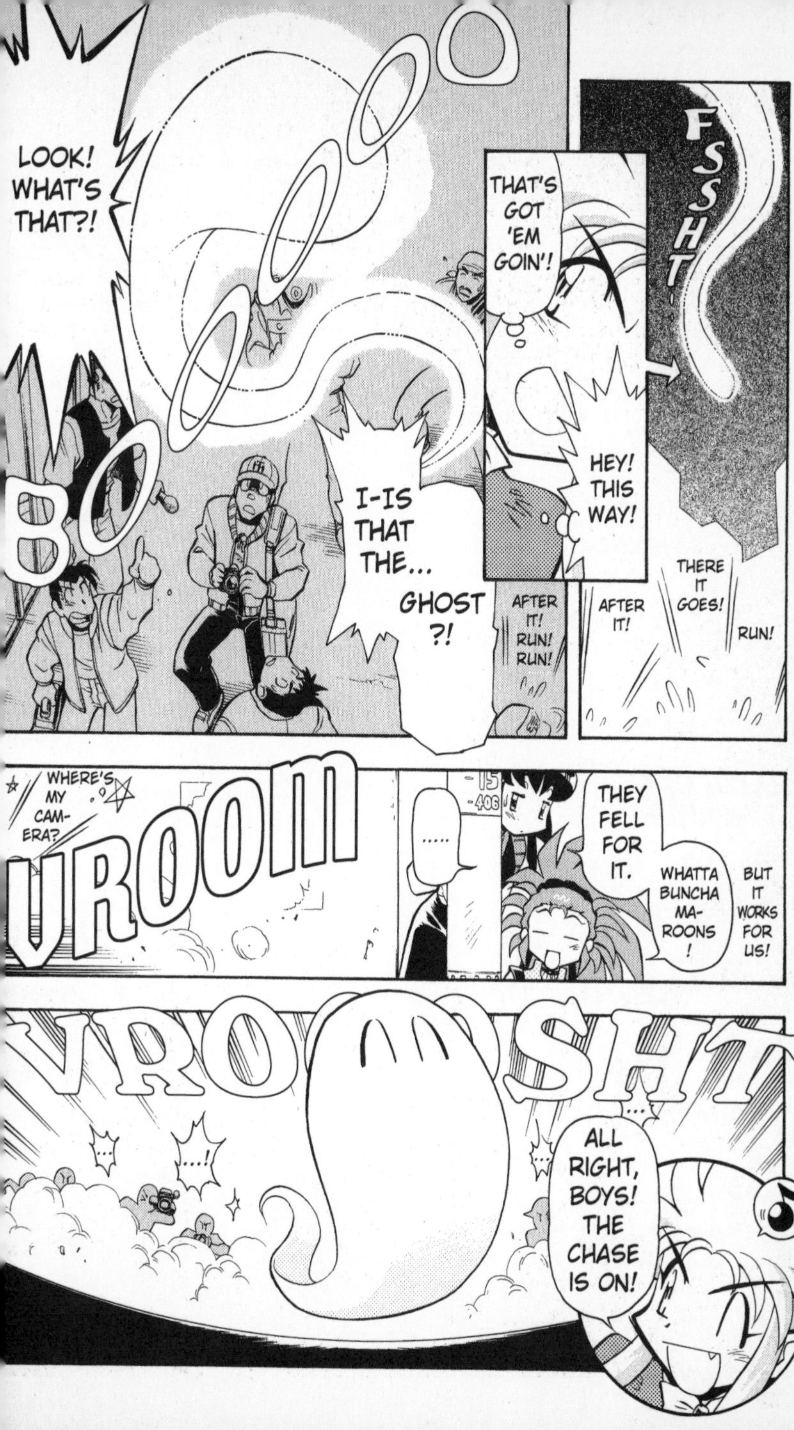
LOOK! WHAT'S THAT?!
BOOOOOOOO
I-IS THAT THE... GHOST?!
FSSHT
THAT'S GOT 'EM GOIN'!
HEY! THIS WAY!
AFTER IT! RUN! RUN!
AFTER IT!
THERE IT GOES!
RUN!
WHERE'S MY CAMERA?
VROOM
.....
15
-406
THEY FELL FOR IT.
WHATTA BUNCHA MAROONS!
BUT IT WORKS FOR US!
VROOSHT
...!
...!
...!
ALL RIGHT, BOYS! THE CHASE IS ON!

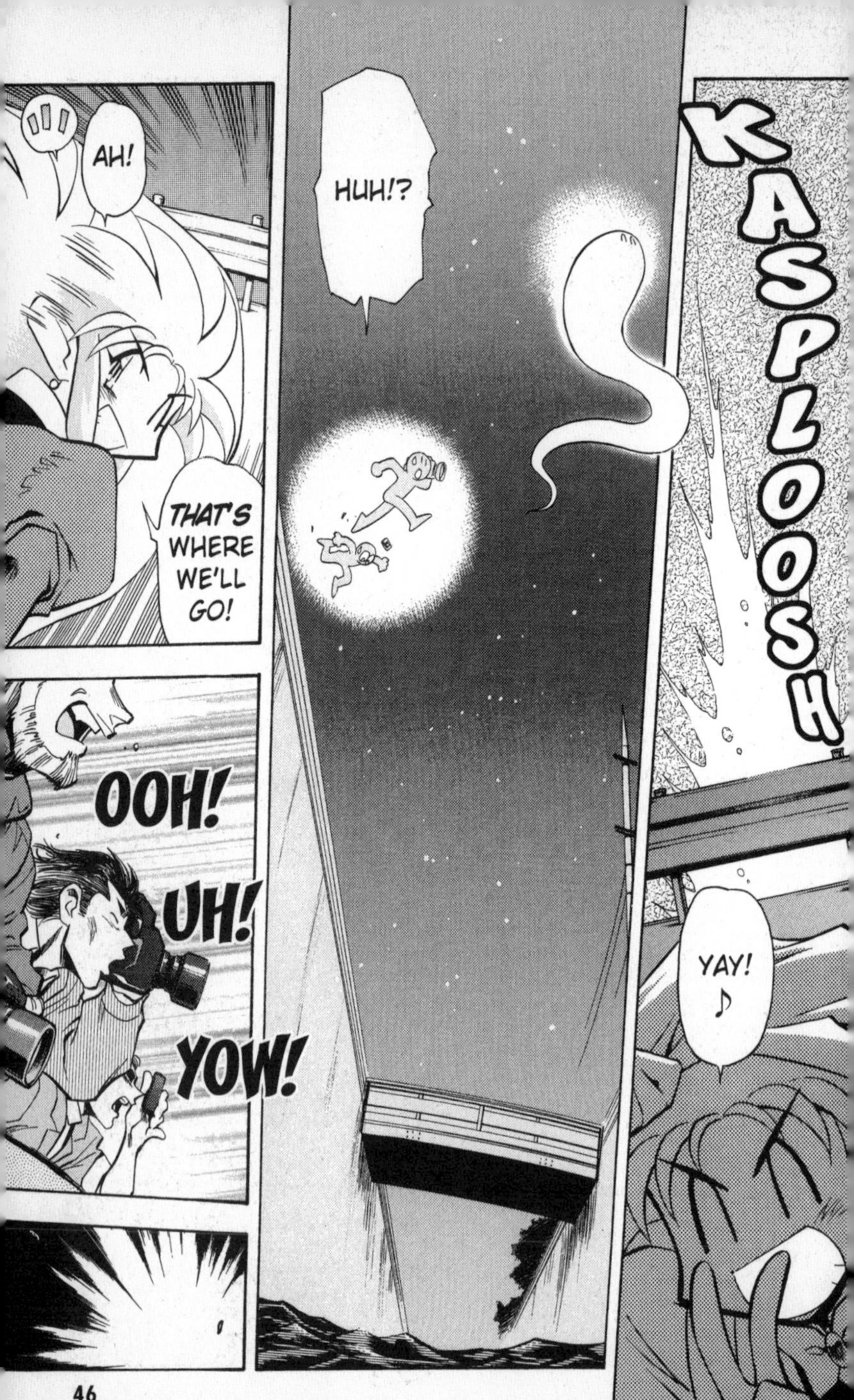

AH!
THAT'S WHERE WE'LL GO!
OOH!
UH!
YOW!
HUH!?
KASPLOOSH
YAY! ♪

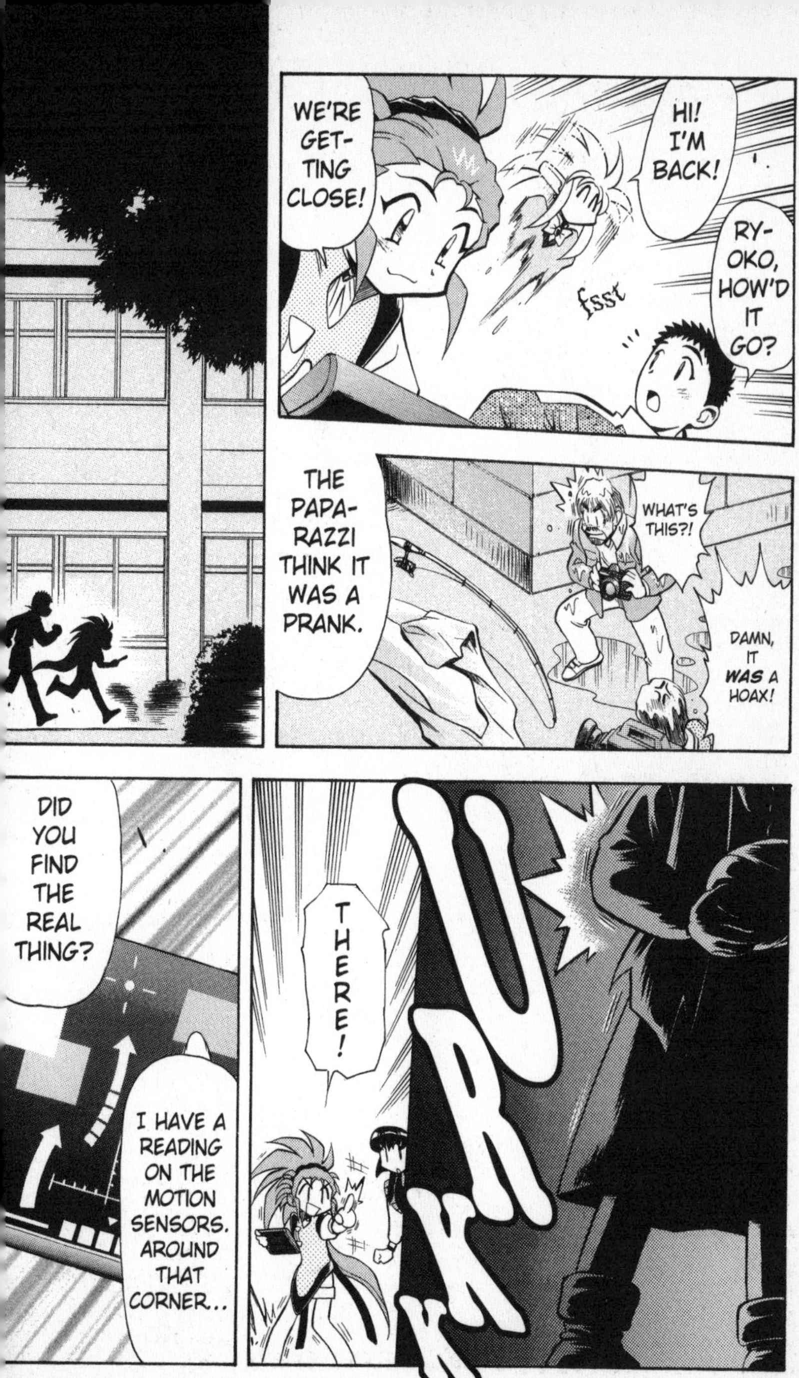
WE'RE GETTING CLOSE!
HI! I'M BACK!
fsst
RYOKO, HOW'D IT GO?
THE PAPARAZZI THINK IT WAS A PRANK.
WHAT'S THIS?!
DAMN, IT *WAS* A HOAX!
DID YOU FIND THE REAL THING?
I HAVE A READING ON THE MOTION SENSORS. AROUND THAT CORNER...
THERE!

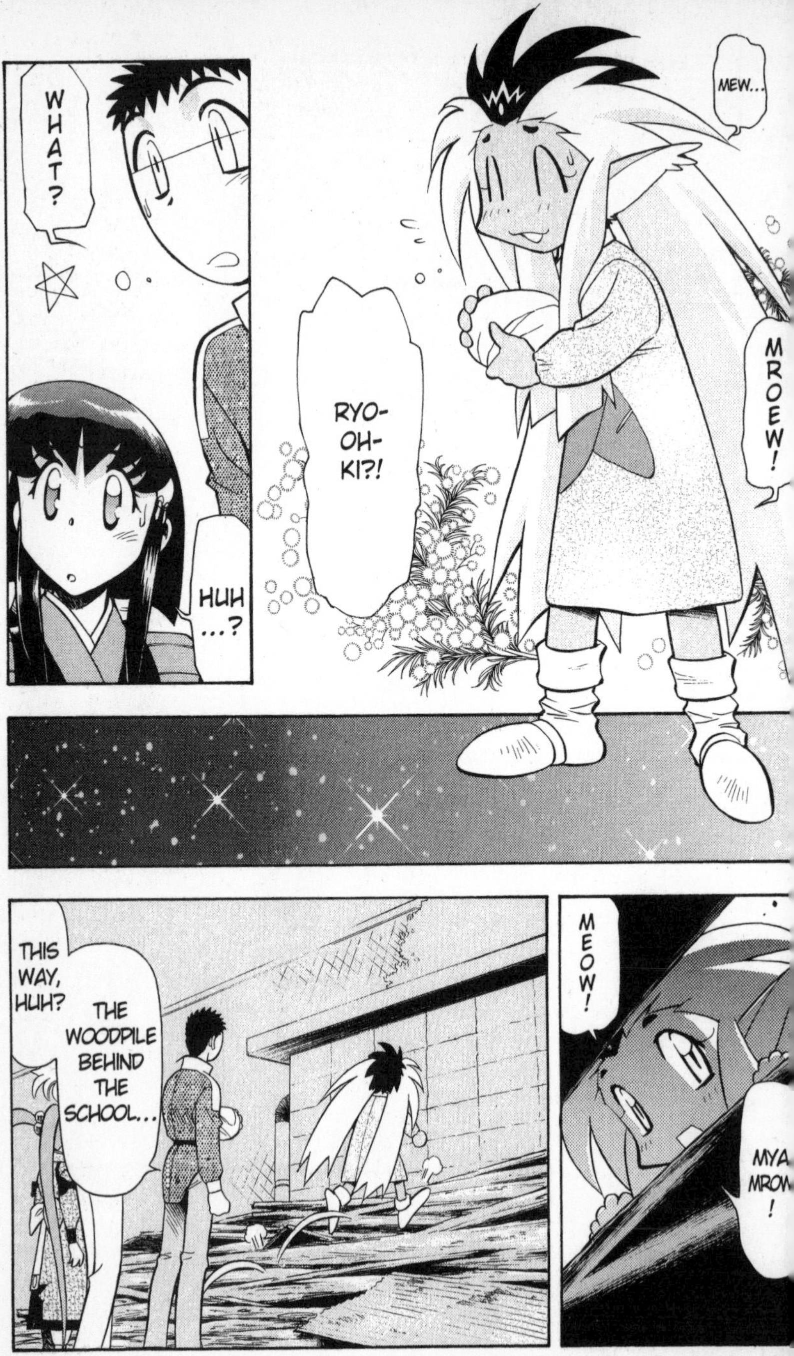
WHAT?
HUH...?
RYO-OH-KI?!
MEW...
MROEW!
THIS WAY, HUH?
THE WOODPILE BEHIND THE SCHOOL...
MEOW!
MYA MROW!

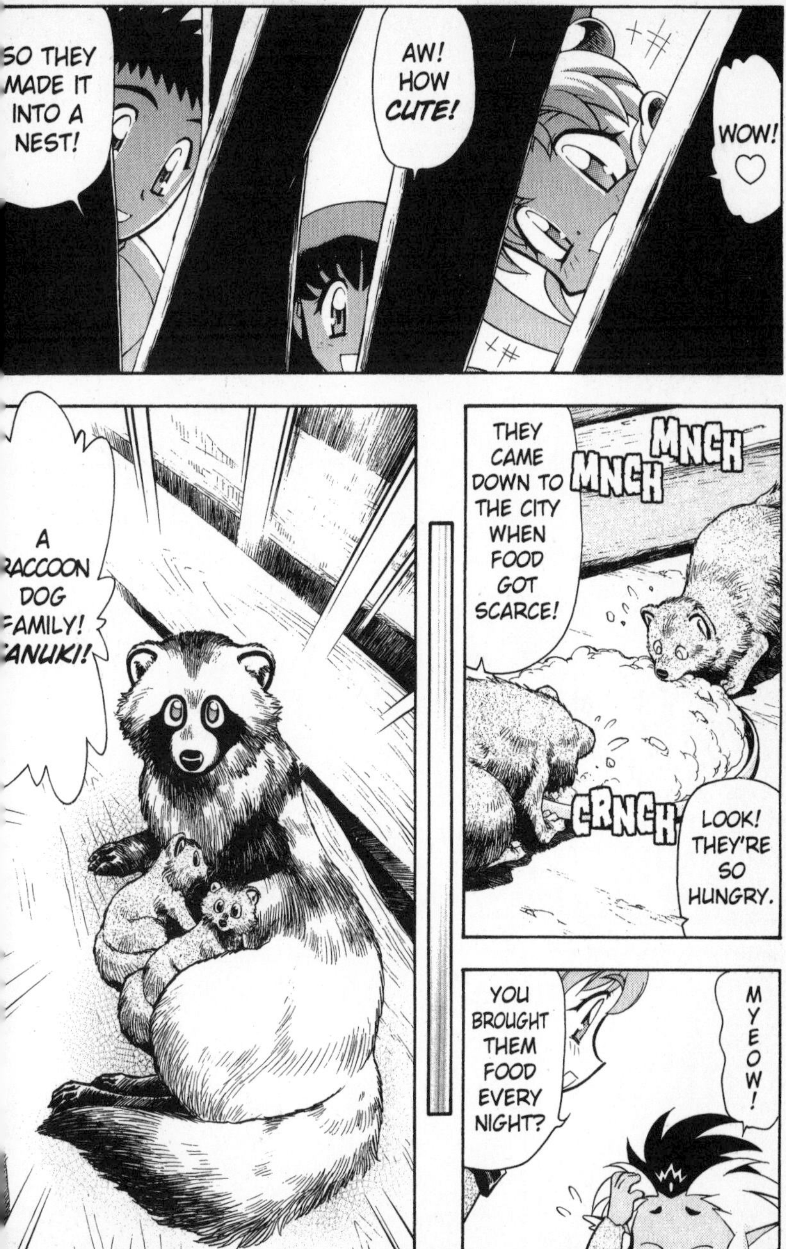

SO THEY MADE IT INTO A NEST!
AW! HOW CUTE!
WOW! ♡
A RACCOON DOG FAMILY! TANUKI!
THEY CAME DOWN TO THE CITY WHEN FOOD GOT SCARCE!
MNCH MNCH
CRNCH
LOOK! THEY'RE SO HUNGRY.
YOU BROUGHT THEM FOOD EVERY NIGHT?
MYEOW!

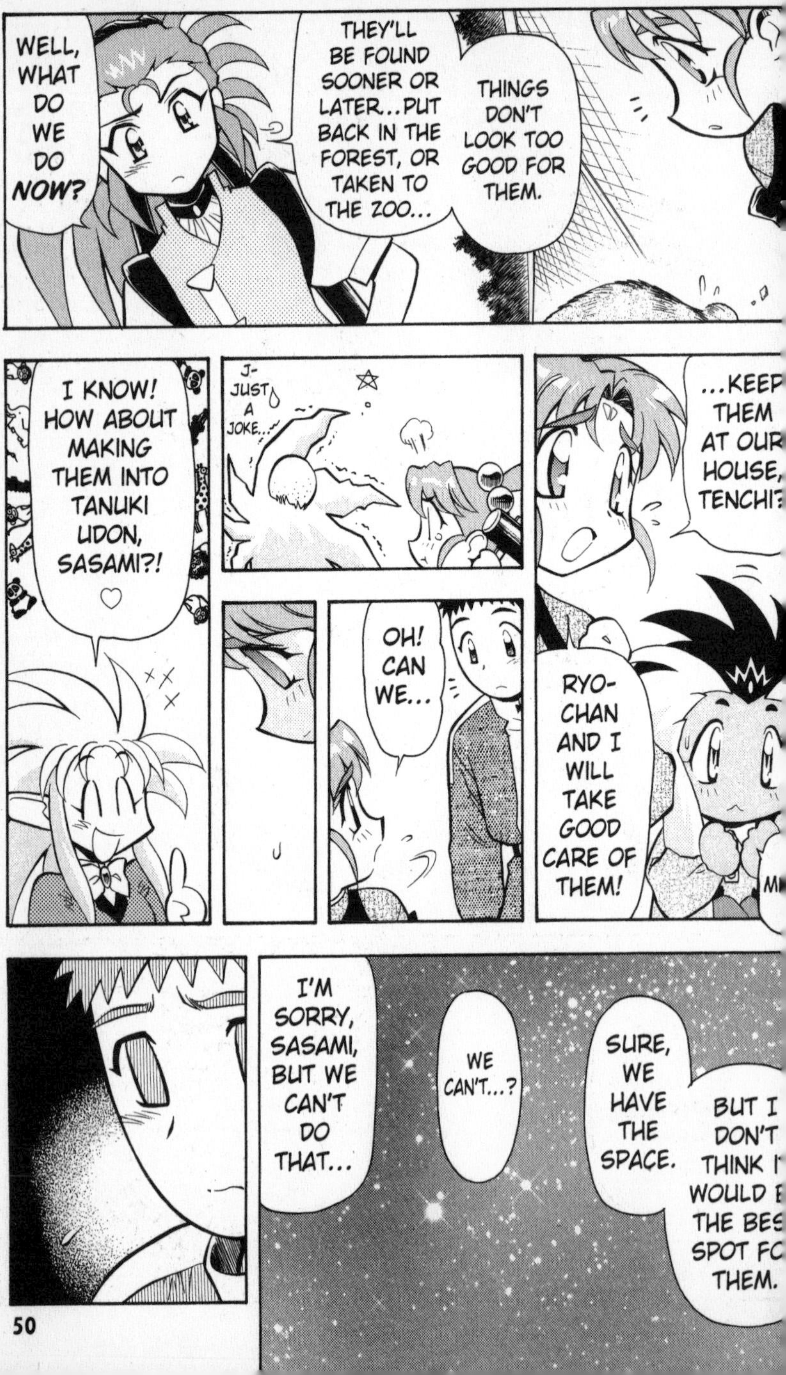
WELL, WHAT DO WE DO *NOW?*
THEY'LL BE FOUND SOONER OR LATER...PUT BACK IN THE FOREST, OR TAKEN TO THE ZOO...
THINGS DON'T LOOK TOO GOOD FOR THEM.
I KNOW! HOW ABOUT MAKING THEM INTO TANUKI UDON, SASAMI?! ♡
J-JUST A JOKE...
OH! CAN WE...
...KEEP THEM AT OUR HOUSE, TENCHI?
RYO-CHAN AND I WILL TAKE GOOD CARE OF THEM!
I'M SORRY, SASAMI, BUT WE CAN'T DO THAT...
WE CAN'T...?
SURE, WE HAVE THE SPACE.
BUT I DON'T THINK I' WOULD B THE BES SPOT FO THEM.

IF THEY CONTINUE TO DEPEND ON *PEOPLE* FOR FOOD, THEY WON'T EVER LEARN HOW TO FEND FOR THEMSELVES.

THEY'D NEVER BE ABLE TO GO BACK TO THE WILD.

I HOPE THAT YOU UNDERSTAND, SASAMI... RYO-OH-KI...

JUST BECAUSE THEY'RE CUTE, OR WE FEEL SORRY FOR THEM, DOESN'T MAKE IT RIGHT...

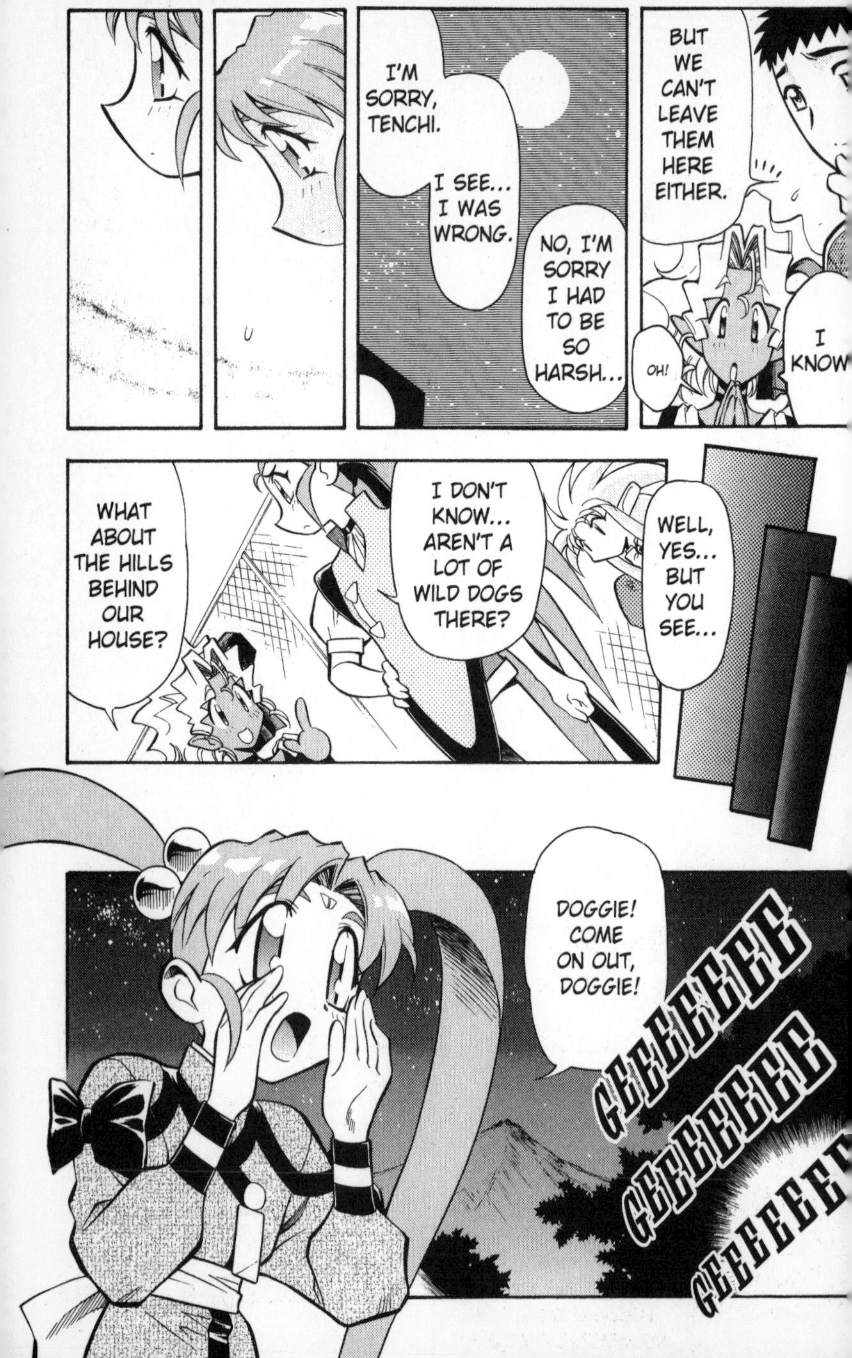
I'M SORRY, TENCHI.
I SEE... I WAS WRONG.
NO, I'M SORRY I HAD TO BE SO HARSH...
BUT WE CAN'T LEAVE THEM HERE EITHER.
OH!
I KNOW
WHAT ABOUT THE HILLS BEHIND OUR HOUSE?
I DON'T KNOW... AREN'T A LOT OF WILD DOGS THERE?
WELL, YES... BUT YOU SEE...
DOGGIE! COME ON OUT, DOGGIE!
GEEEEEEE
GEEEEEEE
GEEEEEE

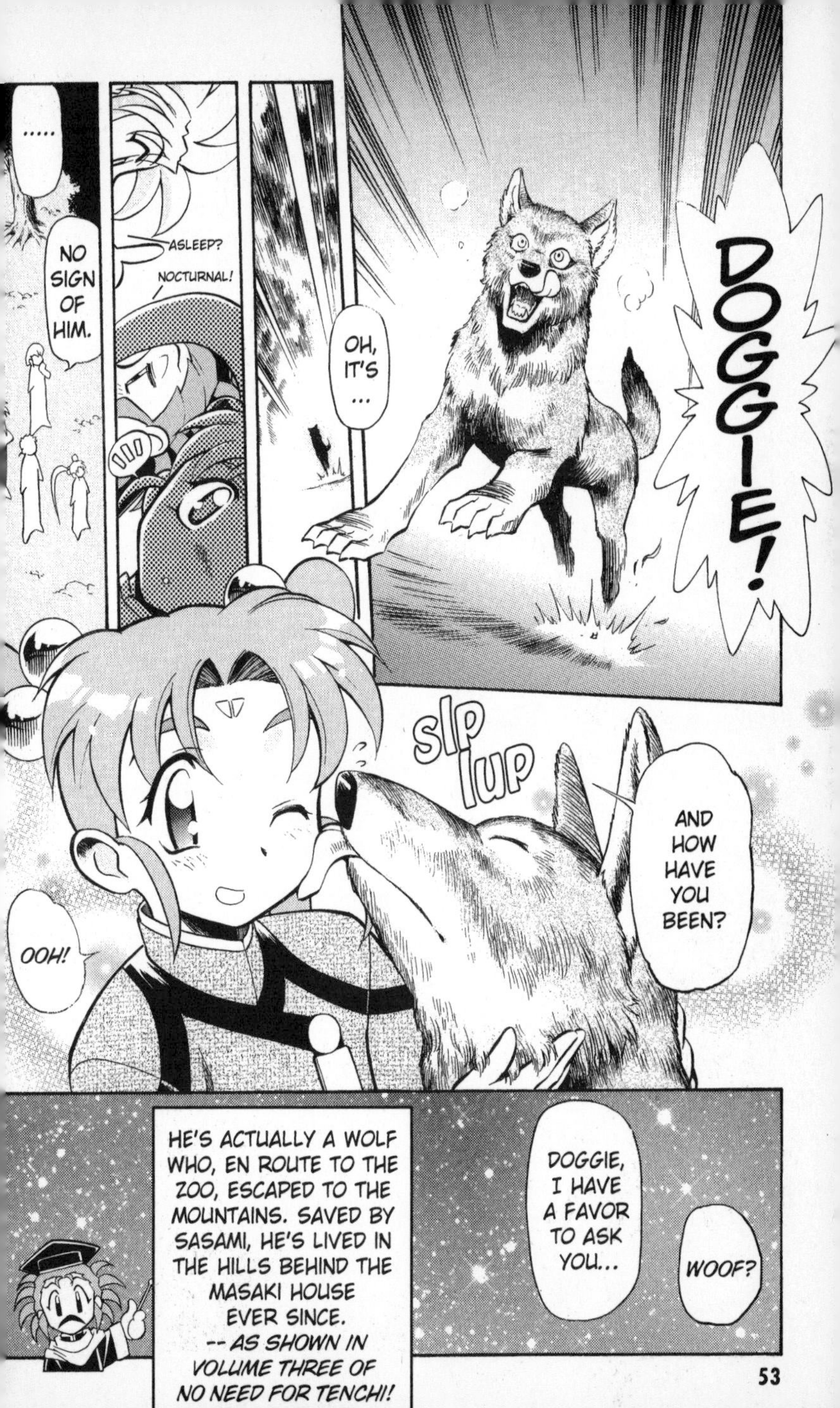

......
NO SIGN OF HIM.
ASLEEP?
NOCTURNAL!
OH, IT'S ...
DOGGIE!
slp lup
OOH!
AND HOW HAVE YOU BEEN?
HE'S ACTUALLY A WOLF WHO, EN ROUTE TO THE ZOO, ESCAPED TO THE MOUNTAINS. SAVED BY SASAMI, HE'S LIVED IN THE HILLS BEHIND THE MASAKI HOUSE EVER SINCE. -- AS SHOWN IN VOLUME THREE OF NO NEED FOR TENCHI!
DOGGIE, I HAVE A FAVOR TO ASK YOU...
WOOF?

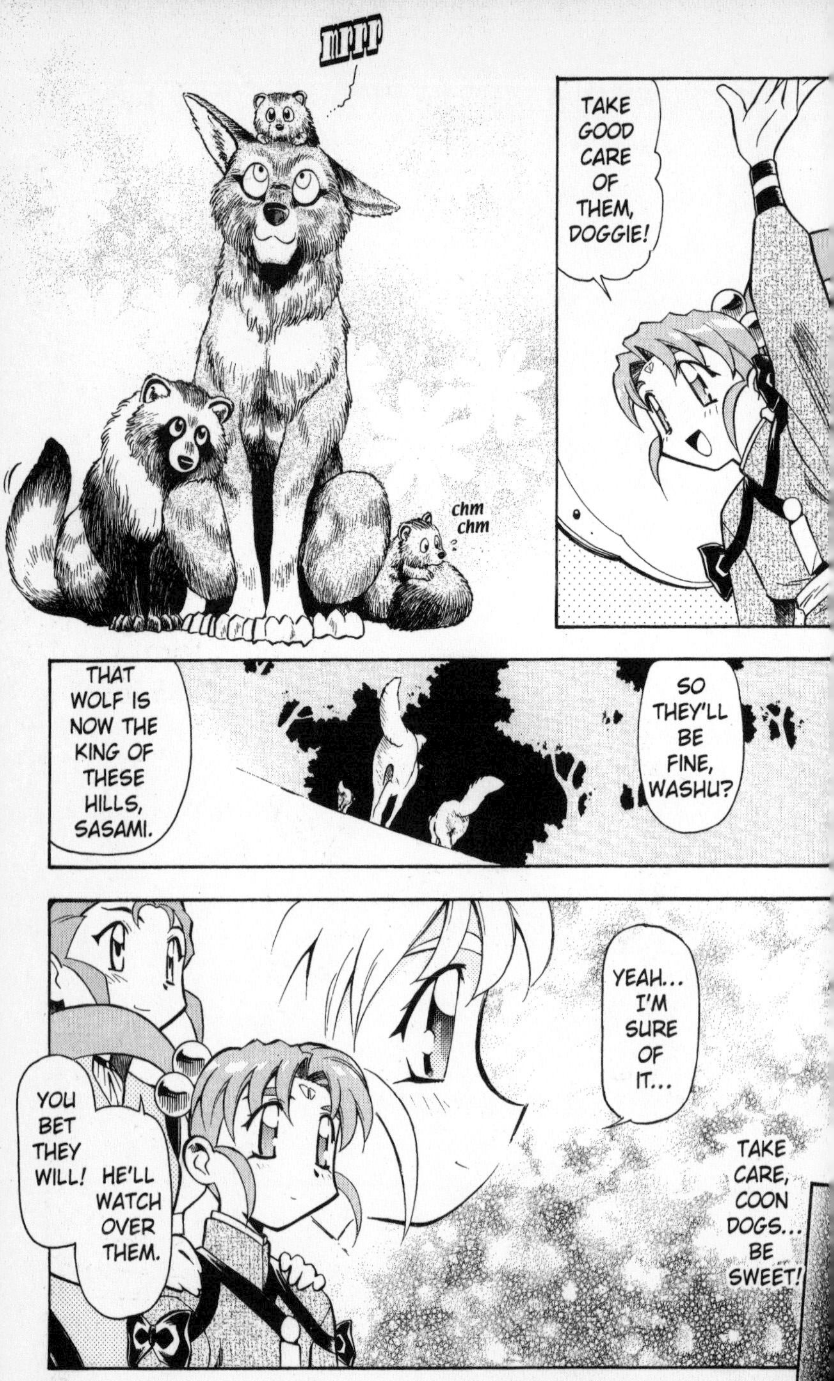
MRRR
chm chm
TAKE GOOD CARE OF THEM, DOGGIE!
THAT WOLF IS NOW THE KING OF THESE HILLS, SASAMI.
SO THEY'LL BE FINE, WASHU?
YOU BET THEY WILL!
HE'LL WATCH OVER THEM.
YEAH... I'M SURE OF IT...
TAKE CARE, COON DOGS... BE SWEET!

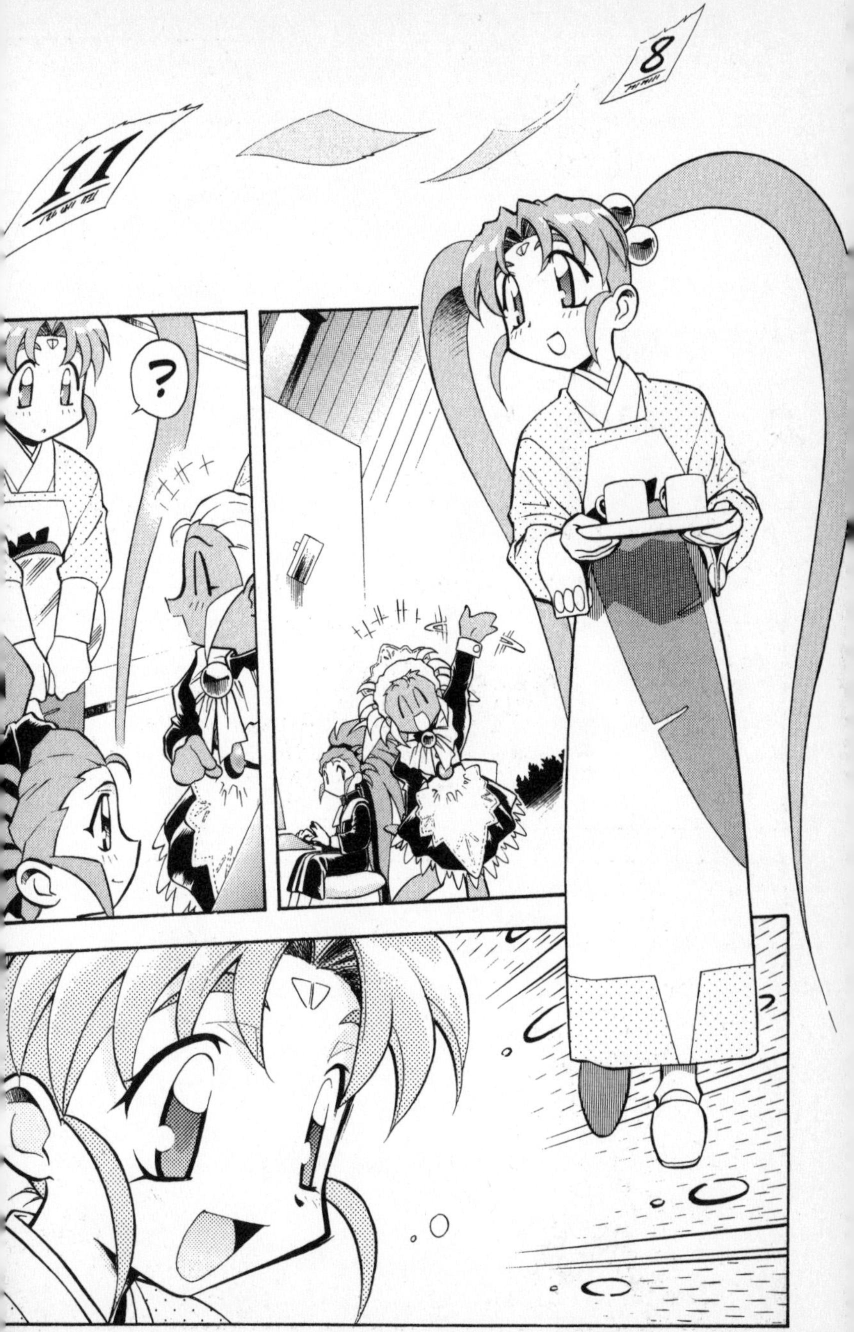

11
8
?

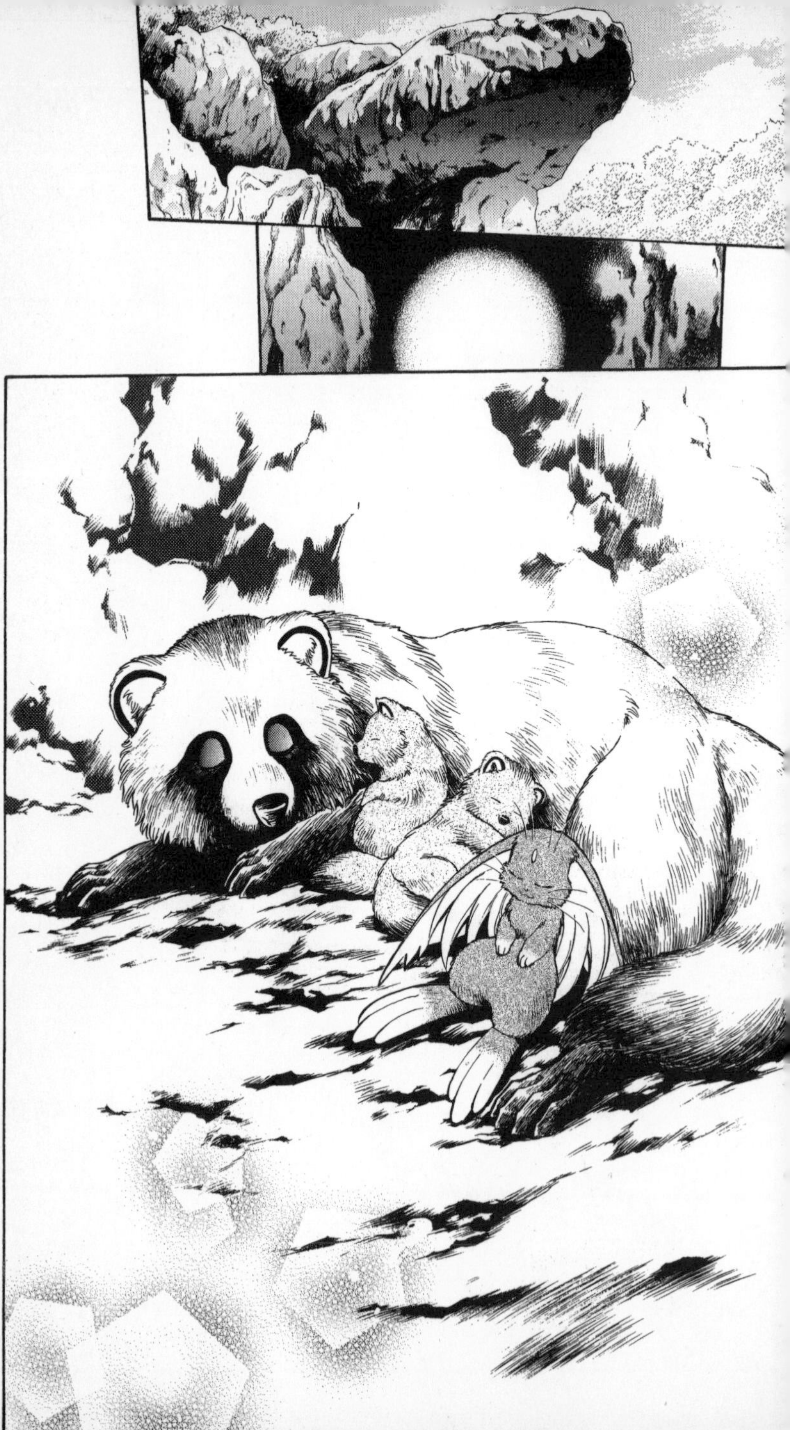

CHAPTER 3: METAMORPHOSIS

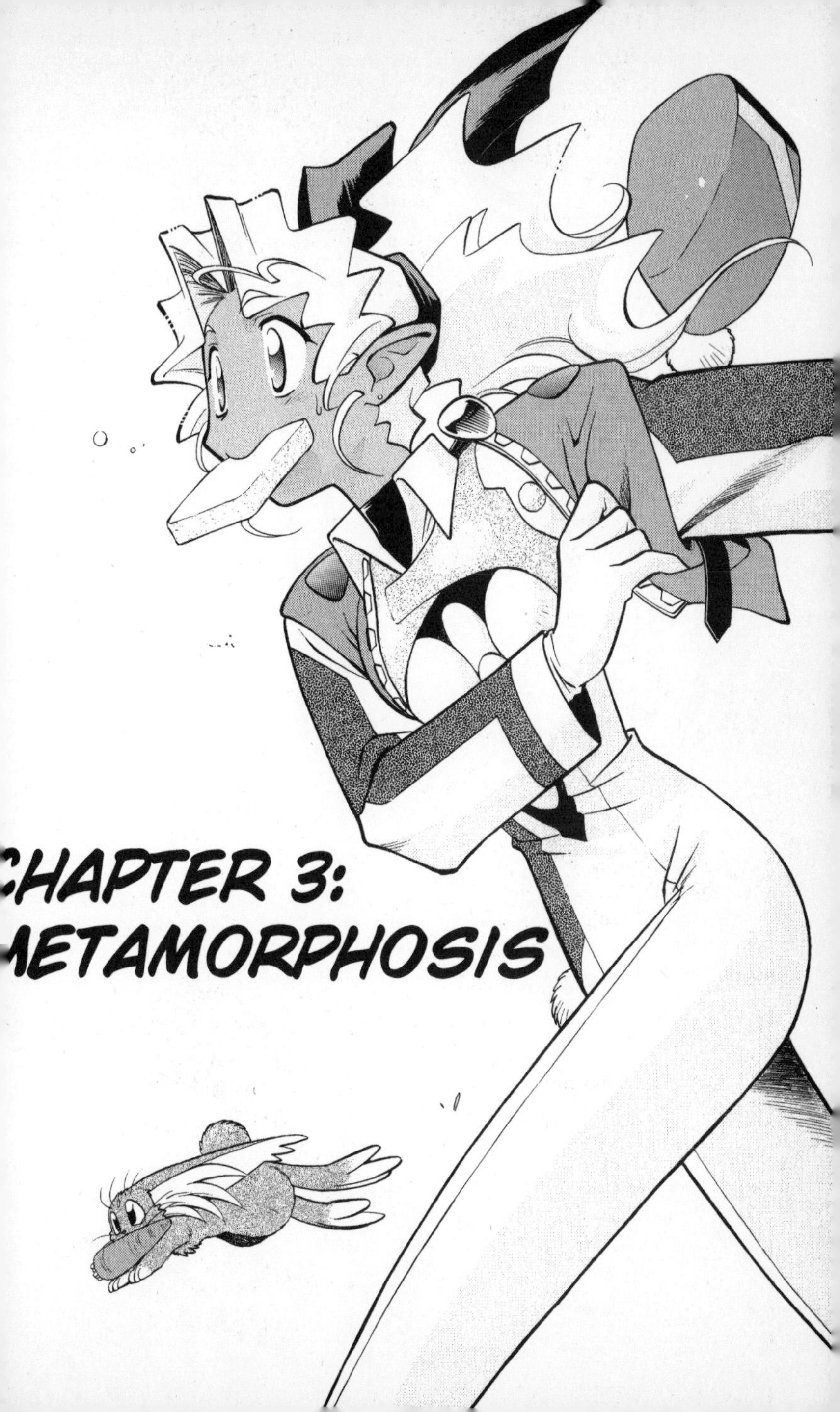

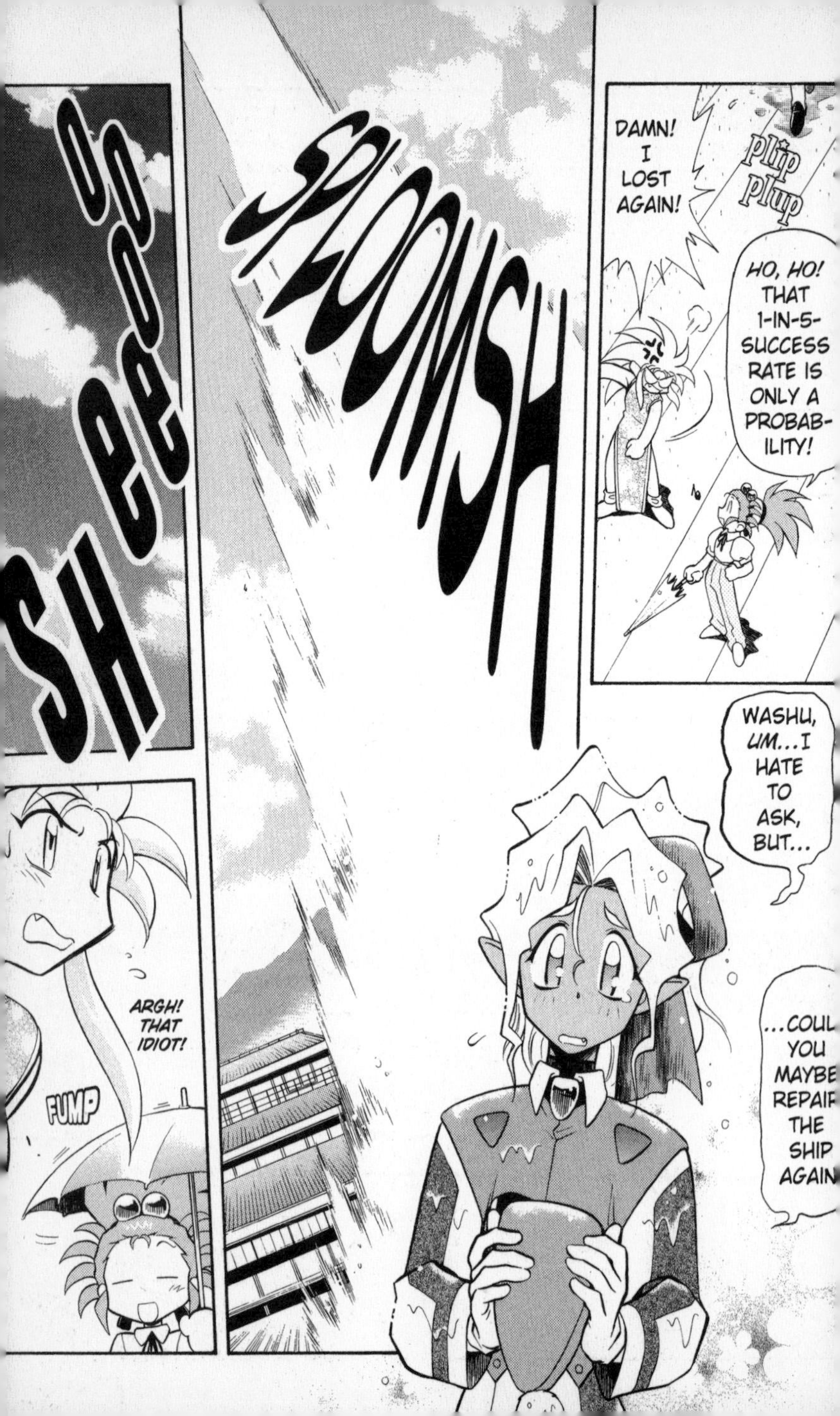
DAMN! I LOST AGAIN!
Plip plup
HO, HO! THAT 1-IN-5-SUCCESS RATE IS ONLY A PROBAB-ILITY!
SPLOOMSH
WASHU, UM...I HATE TO ASK, BUT...
...COUL YOU MAYBE REPAIR THE SHIP AGAIN
ARGH! THAT IDIOT!
FUMP

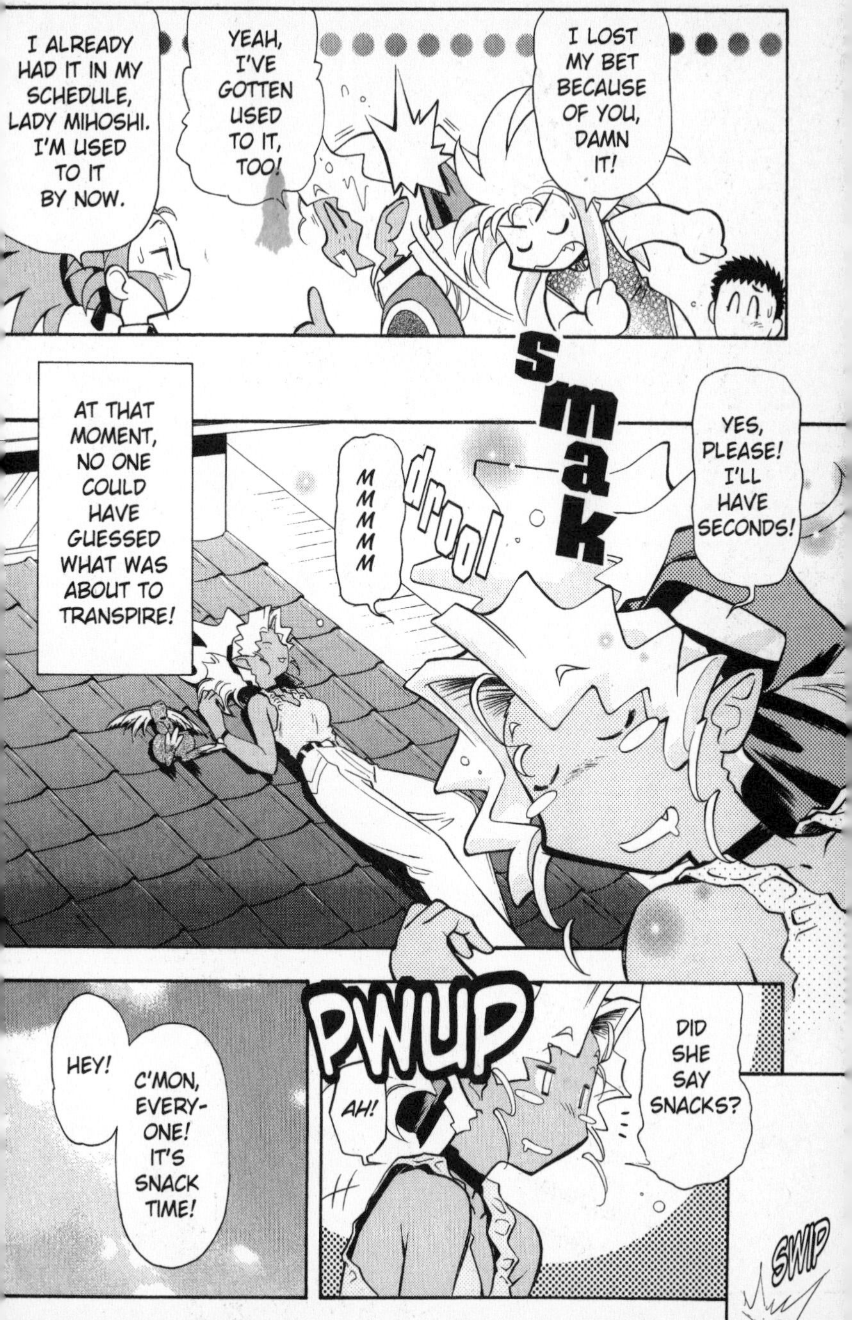
I ALREADY HAD IT IN MY SCHEDULE, LADY MIHOSHI. I'M USED TO IT BY NOW.
YEAH, I'VE GOTTEN USED TO IT, TOO!
I LOST MY BET BECAUSE OF YOU, DAMN IT!
AT THAT MOMENT, NO ONE COULD HAVE GUESSED WHAT WAS ABOUT TO TRANSPIRE!
MMMMMM
drool
smak
YES, PLEASE! I'LL HAVE SECONDS!
HEY!
C'MON, EVERY-ONE! IT'S SNACK TIME!
PWUP
AH!
DID SHE SAY SNACKS?
SWIP

FUP FUP

KRASH

?!

HUH? ?!

M-MIHOSHI! ARE YOU ALL RIGHT?!

SQUEEP...

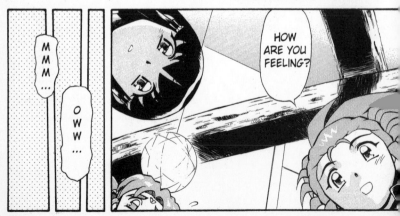

MMM...

OWW...

HOW ARE YOU FEELING?

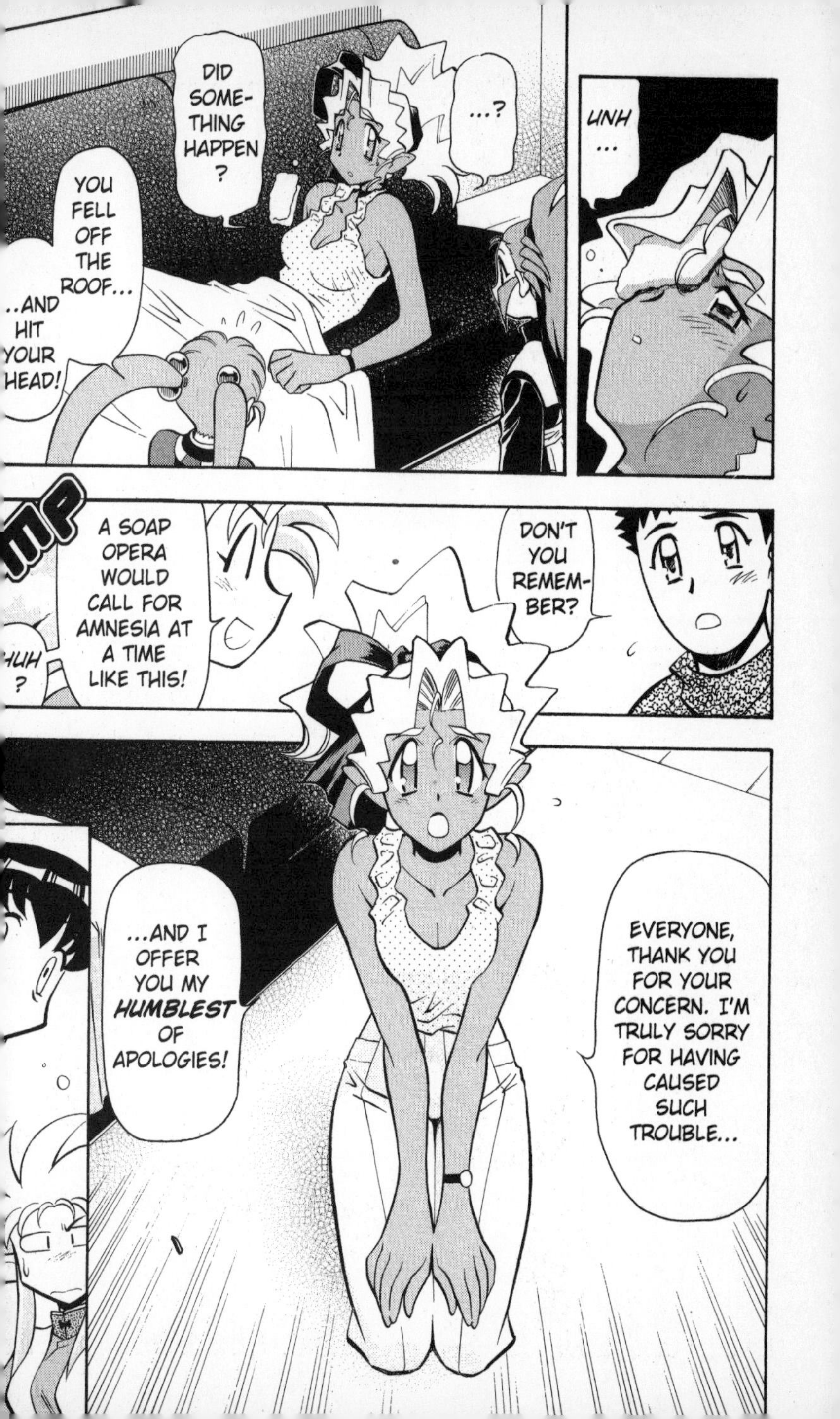
UNH ...
...?
DID SOME-THING HAPPEN ?
YOU FELL OFF THE ROOF...
..AND HIT YOUR HEAD!
DON'T YOU REMEM-BER?
A SOAP OPERA WOULD CALL FOR AMNESIA AT A TIME LIKE THIS!
HUH ?
MP
EVERYONE, THANK YOU FOR YOUR CONCERN. I'M TRULY SORRY FOR HAVING CAUSED SUCH TROUBLE...
...AND I OFFER YOU MY **HUMBLEST** OF APOLOGIES!

AS I REFLECT ON DAYS LONG PASSED...

...MY LIFE SEEMS A SERIES OF MISTAKES, BLUNDERS, AND INADEQUACIES.

PLEASE... YOU MUST ALLOW ME TO MAKE AMENDS!

FWUMSH

M-MIHOSHI!

I DON'T GET IT.

IS THIS TURN OF EVENTS GOOD OR BAD, WASHU?

WE'LL HAVE TO SEE.

AND SO THEY WENT TO BED, CURIOUS TO FIND OUT WHAT THEIR NEW MIHOSHI WOULD DO NEXT...

GOOD DAY TO YOU ALL!

SNAP!

I'M OFF TO DO MY DUTY AS A GALAXY POLICE INSPECTOR, FIRST CLASS.

UM... OKAY! H-HAVE A NICE DAY THEN...

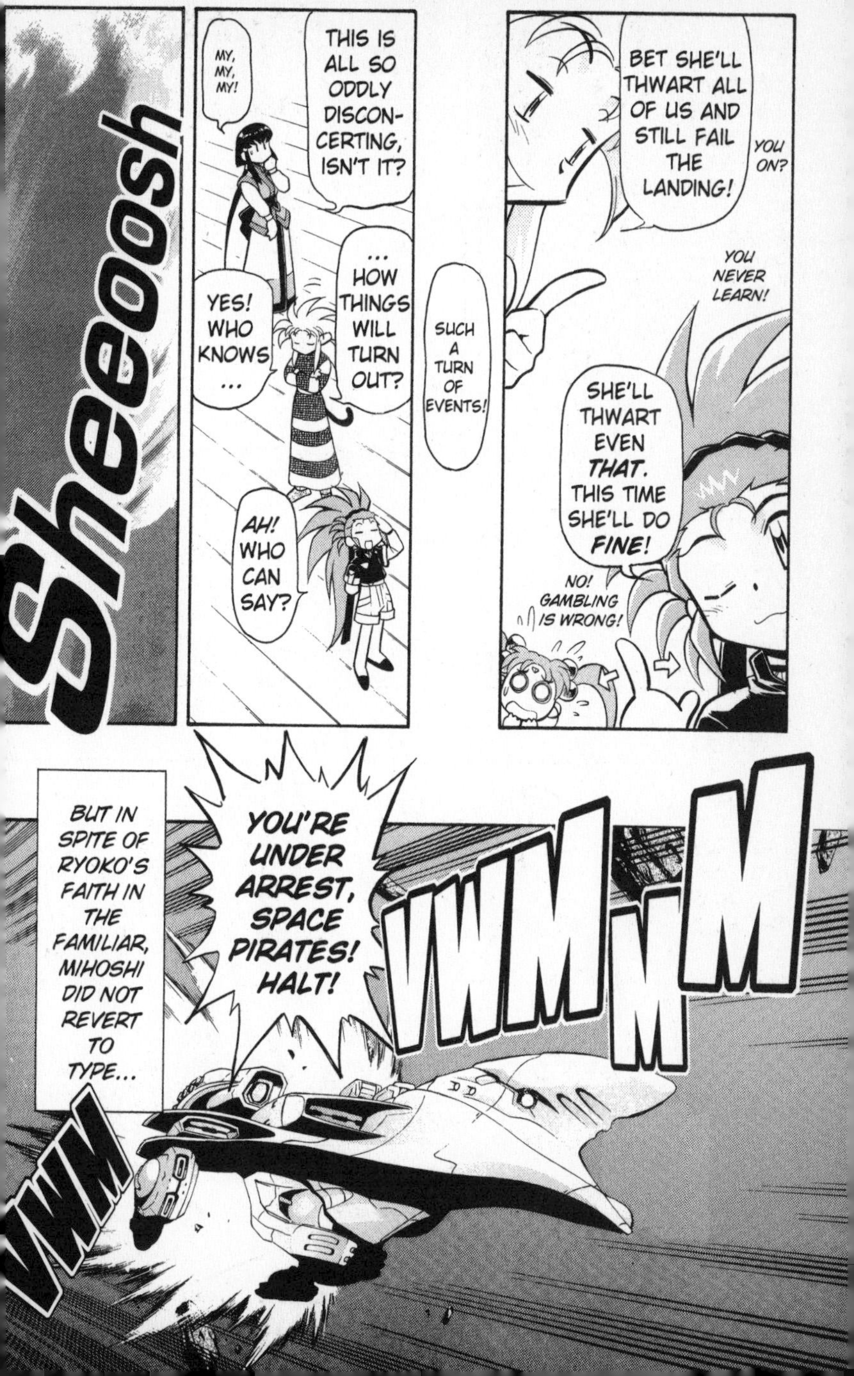
Sheeosh
MY, MY, MY!
THIS IS ALL SO ODDLY DISCONCERTING, ISN'T IT?
YES! WHO KNOWS ...
... HOW THINGS WILL TURN OUT?
SUCH A TURN OF EVENTS!
AH! WHO CAN SAY?
BET SHE'LL THWART ALL OF US AND STILL FAIL THE LANDING!
YOU ON?
YOU NEVER LEARN!
SHE'LL THWART EVEN THAT. THIS TIME SHE'LL DO FINE!
NO! GAMBLING IS WRONG!
BUT IN SPITE OF RYOKO'S FAITH IN THE FAMILIAR, MIHOSHI DID NOT REVERT TO TYPE...
YOU'RE UNDER ARREST, SPACE PIRATES! HALT!
VWMMM
VWM

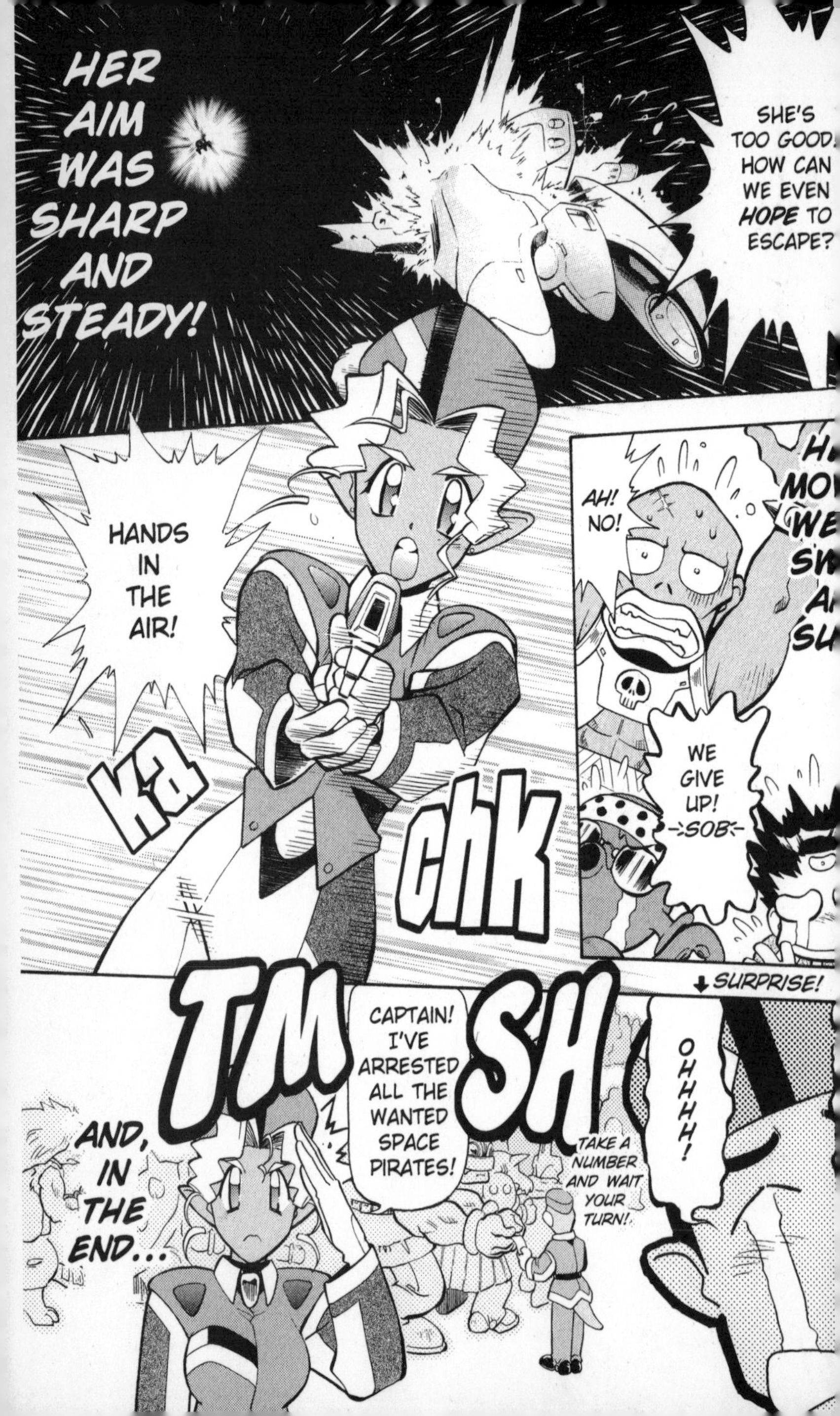
HER AIM WAS SHARP AND STEADY!
SHE'S TOO GOOD. HOW CAN WE EVEN HOPE TO ESCAPE?
HANDS IN THE AIR!
Ka chK
AH! NO!
WE GIVE UP! -SOB-
TMSH
AND, IN THE END...
CAPTAIN! I'VE ARRESTED ALL THE WANTED SPACE PIRATES!
TAKE A NUMBER AND WAIT YOUR TURN!
SURPRISE!
OHHHH!

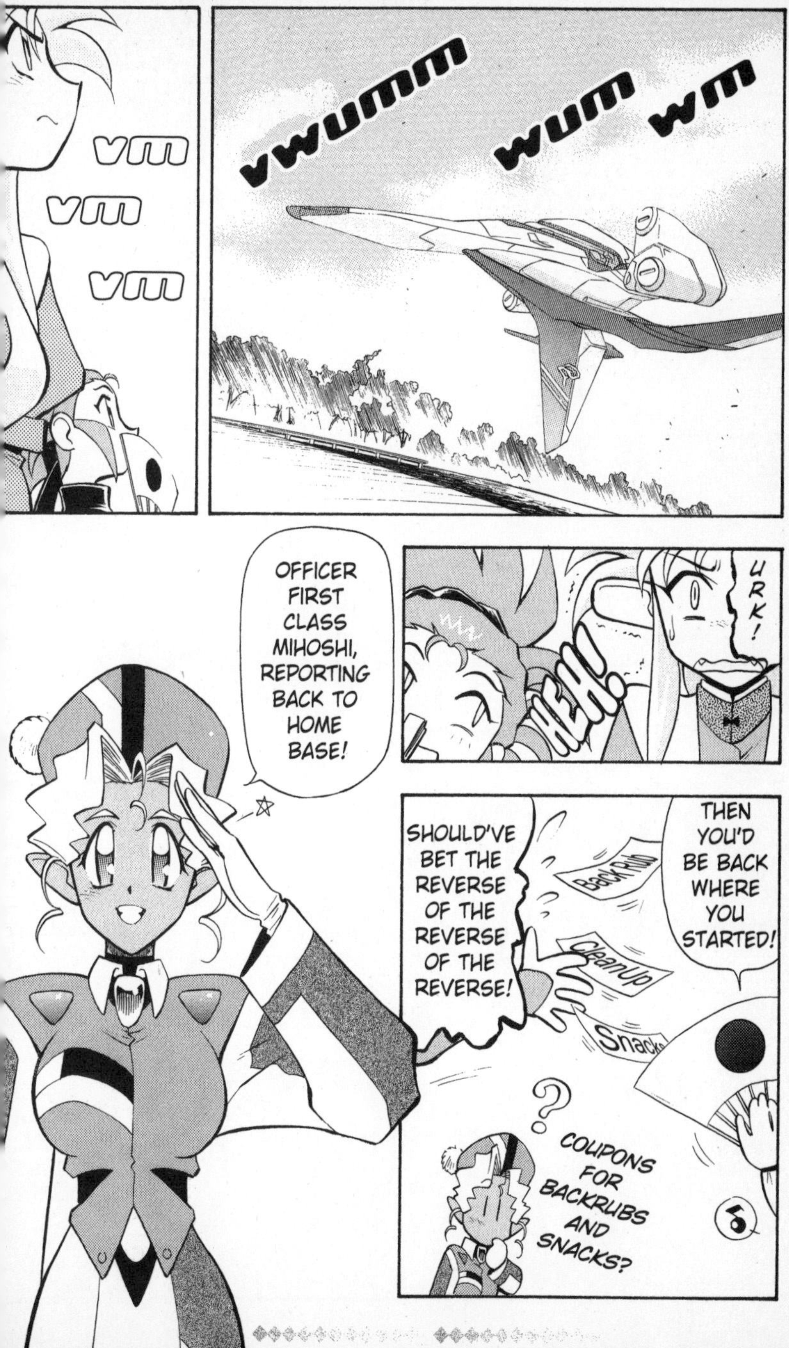
VM
VM
VM
VWUMMM
WUM
WM
OFFICER FIRST CLASS MIHOSHI, REPORTING BACK TO HOME BASE!
HEH?!
URK!
SHOULD'VE BET THE REVERSE OF THE REVERSE OF THE REVERSE!
THEN YOU'D BE BACK WHERE YOU STARTED!
Back Rub
Clean Up
Snacks
?
COUPONS FOR BACKRUBS AND SNACKS?

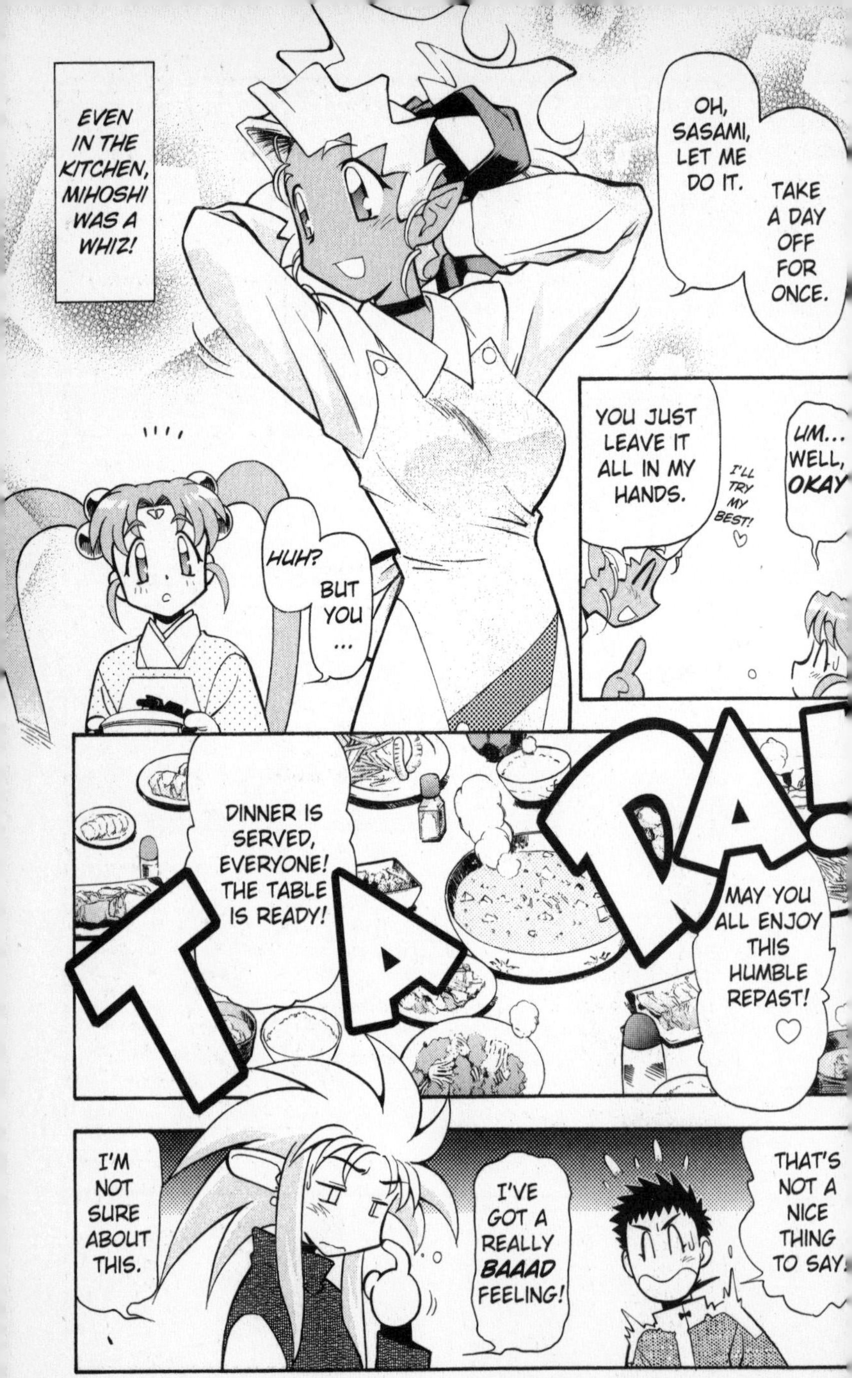
EVEN IN THE KITCHEN, MIHOSHI WAS A WHIZ!
OH, SASAMI, LET ME DO IT.
TAKE A DAY OFF FOR ONCE.
...
HUH? BUT YOU ...
YOU JUST LEAVE IT ALL IN MY HANDS.
I'LL TRY MY BEST! ♡
UM... WELL, OKAY
TA-DA!
DINNER IS SERVED, EVERYONE! THE TABLE IS READY!
MAY YOU ALL ENJOY THIS HUMBLE REPAST! ♡
I'M NOT SURE ABOUT THIS.
I'VE GOT A REALLY *BAAAD* FEELING!
THAT'S NOT A NICE THING TO SAY.

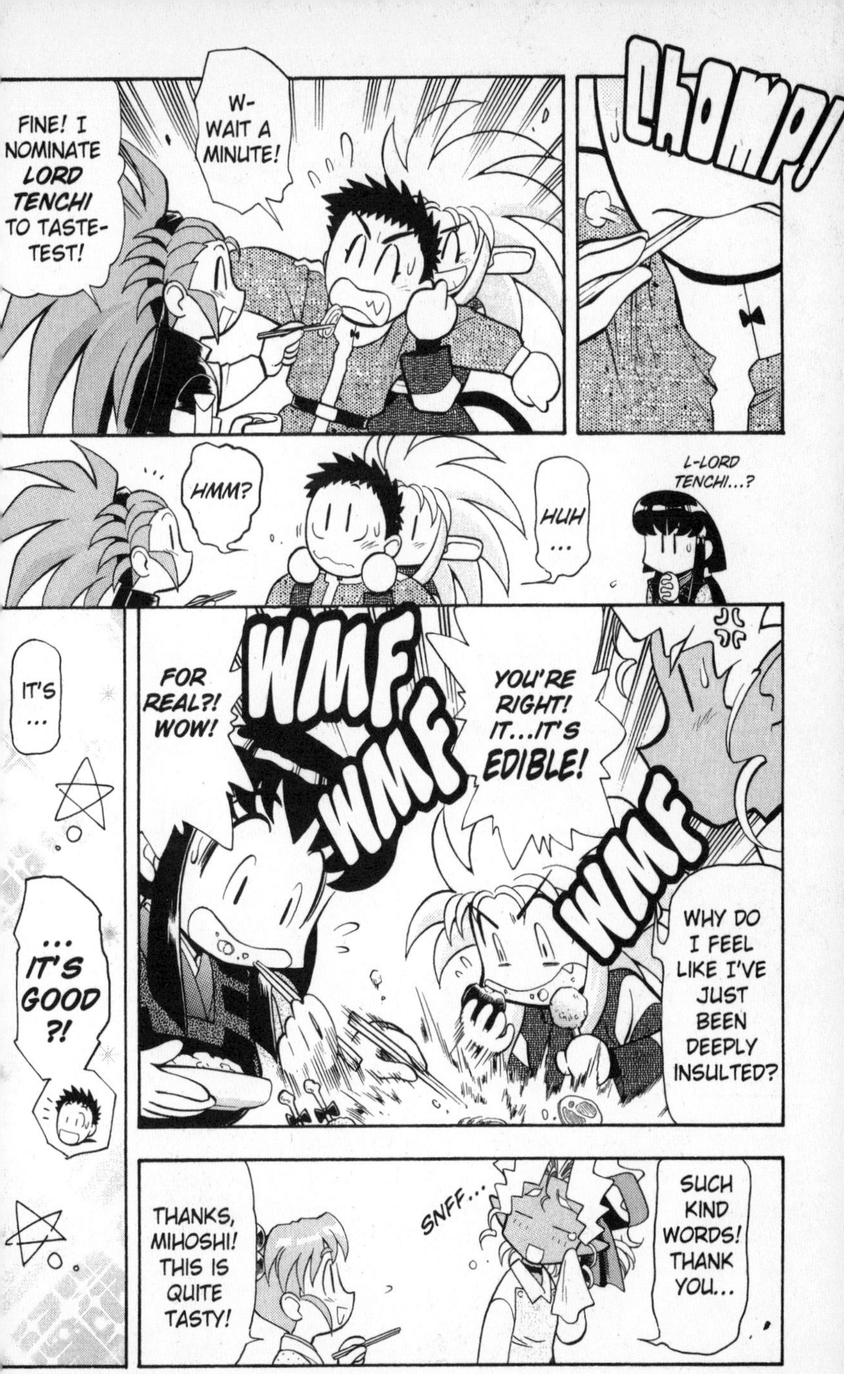
FINE! I NOMINATE LORD TENCHI TO TASTE-TEST!
W- WAIT A MINUTE!
CHOMP!
...
HMM?
HUH ...
L-LORD TENCHI...?
IT'S ...
... IT'S GOOD ?!
FOR REAL?! WOW!
WMF
WMF
YOU'RE RIGHT! IT...IT'S EDIBLE!
WMF
WHY DO I FEEL LIKE I'VE JUST BEEN DEEPLY INSULTED?
THANKS, MIHOSHI! THIS IS QUITE TASTY!
SNFF...
SUCH KIND WORDS! THANK YOU...

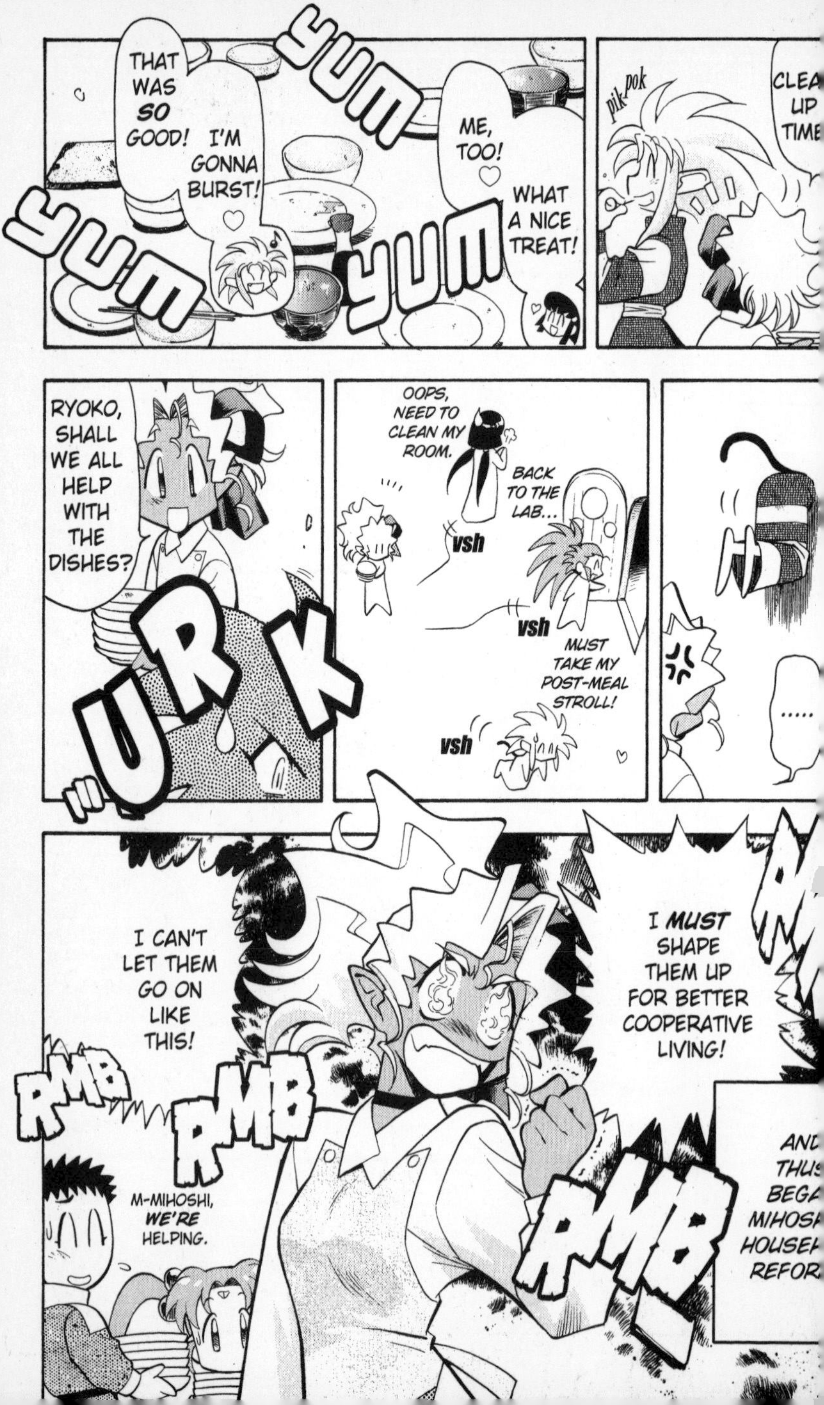
YUM
THAT WAS SO GOOD! I'M GONNA BURST!
ME, TOO! WHAT A NICE TREAT!
YUM
YUM
pik pok
CLEA UP TIME
RYOKO, SHALL WE ALL HELP WITH THE DISHES?
URK
OOPS, NEED TO CLEAN MY ROOM.
vsh
BACK TO THE LAB...
vsh
MUST TAKE MY POST-MEAL STROLL!
vsh
.....
I CAN'T LET THEM GO ON LIKE THIS!
RMB
RMB
M-MIHOSHI, WE'RE HELPING.
I MUST SHAPE THEM UP FOR BETTER COOPERATIVE LIVING!
RMB
AND THUS BEGA MIHOSH HOUSEH REFOR

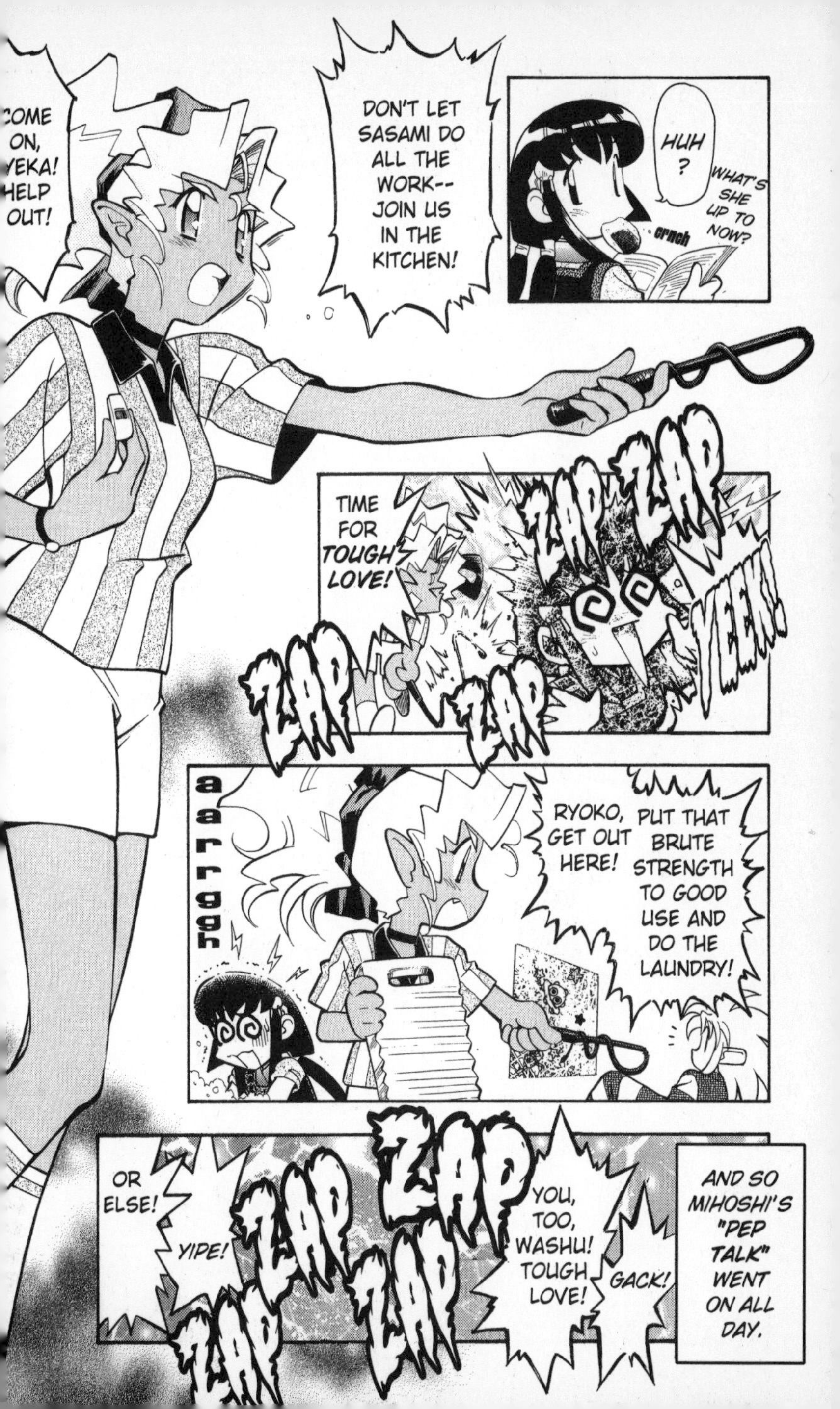

COME ON, YEKA! HELP OUT!
DON'T LET SASAMI DO ALL THE WORK-- JOIN US IN THE KITCHEN!
HUH?
WHAT'S SHE UP TO NOW?
crnch
TIME FOR TOUGH LOVE!
ZAP ZAP
ZAP
ZAP
YEEK!!
aarrggh
RYOKO, GET OUT HERE!
PUT THAT BRUTE STRENGTH TO GOOD USE AND DO THE LAUNDRY!
OR ELSE!
YIPE!
ZAP
ZAP
ZAP
ZAP
YOU, TOO, WASHU! TOUGH LOVE!
GACK!
AND SO MIHOSHI'S "PEP TALK" WENT ON ALL DAY.

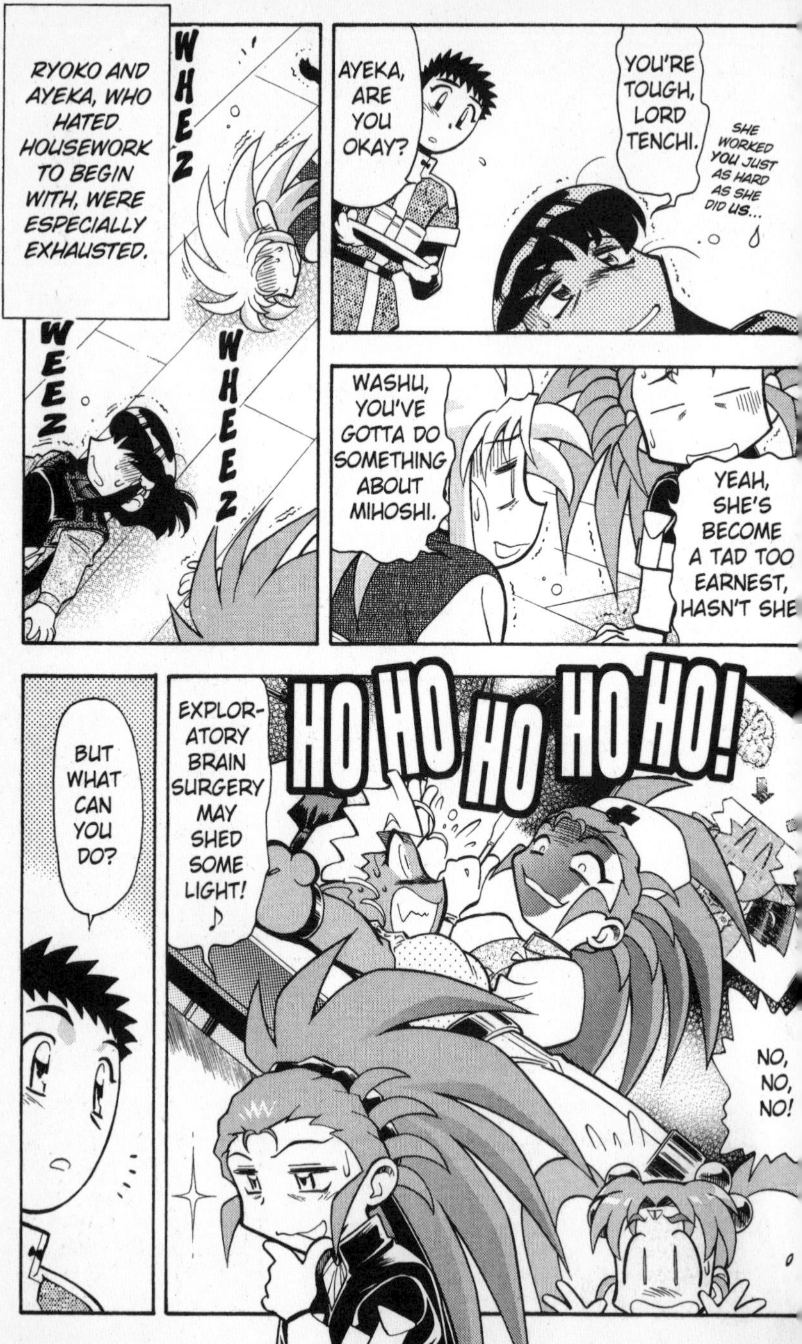
RYOKO AND AYEKA, WHO HATED HOUSEWORK TO BEGIN WITH, WERE ESPECIALLY EXHAUSTED.
WHEZ
WEEZ
WHEEZ
AYEKA, ARE YOU OKAY?
YOU'RE TOUGH, LORD TENCHI.
SHE WORKED YOU JUST AS HARD AS SHE DID US...
WASHU, YOU'VE GOTTA DO SOMETHING ABOUT MIHOSHI.
YEAH, SHE'S BECOME A TAD TOO EARNEST, HASN'T SHE
BUT WHAT CAN YOU DO?
EXPLOR-ATORY BRAIN SURGERY MAY SHED SOME LIGHT! ♪
HO HO HO HO HO!
NO, NO, NO!

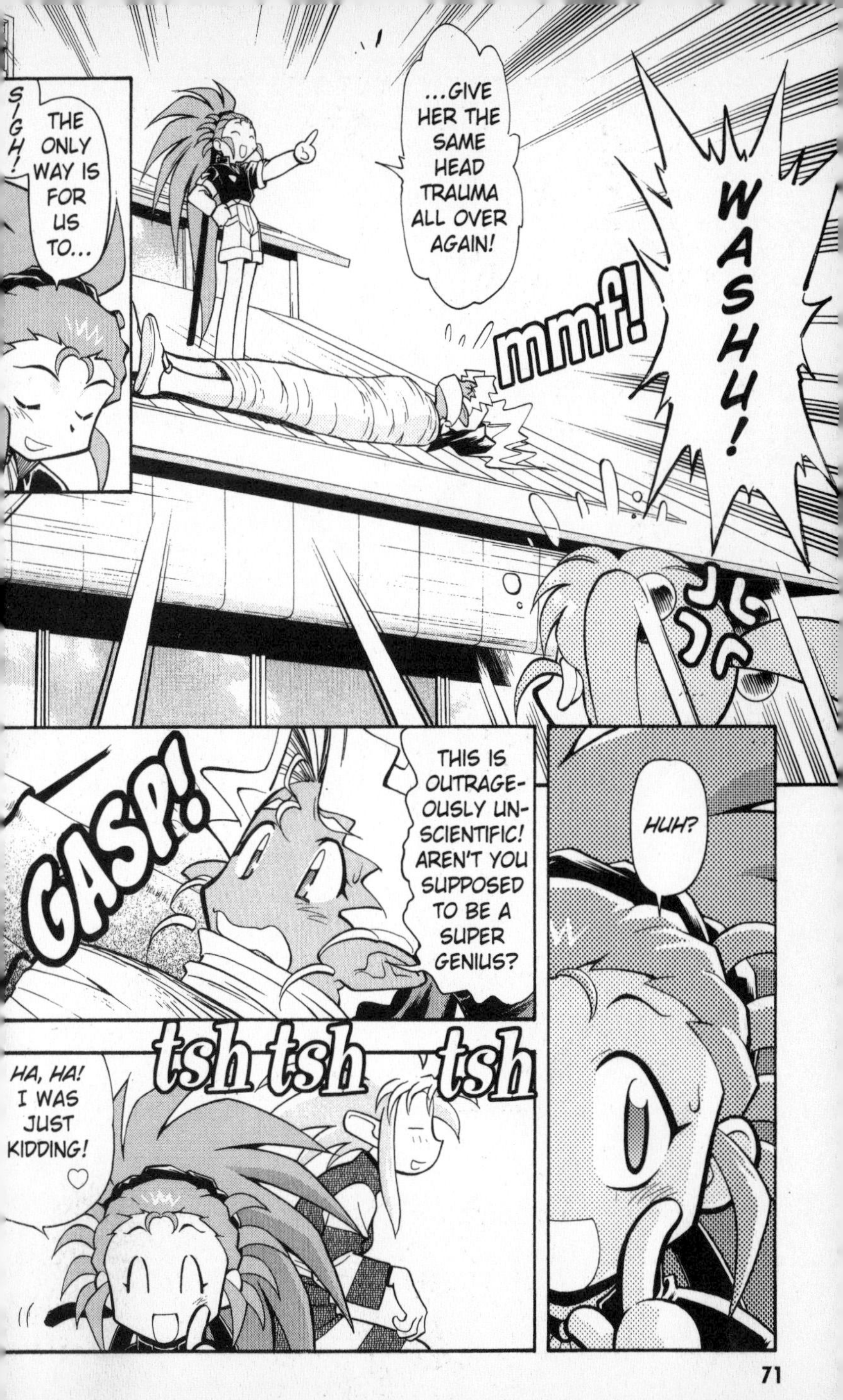
SIGH!
THE ONLY WAY IS FOR US TO...
...GIVE HER THE SAME HEAD TRAUMA ALL OVER AGAIN!
mmf!
WASHU!
GASP!
THIS IS OUTRAGEOUSLY UNSCIENTIFIC! AREN'T YOU SUPPOSED TO BE A SUPER GENIUS?
tsh tsh tsh
HA, HA! I WAS JUST KIDDING! ♡
HUH?

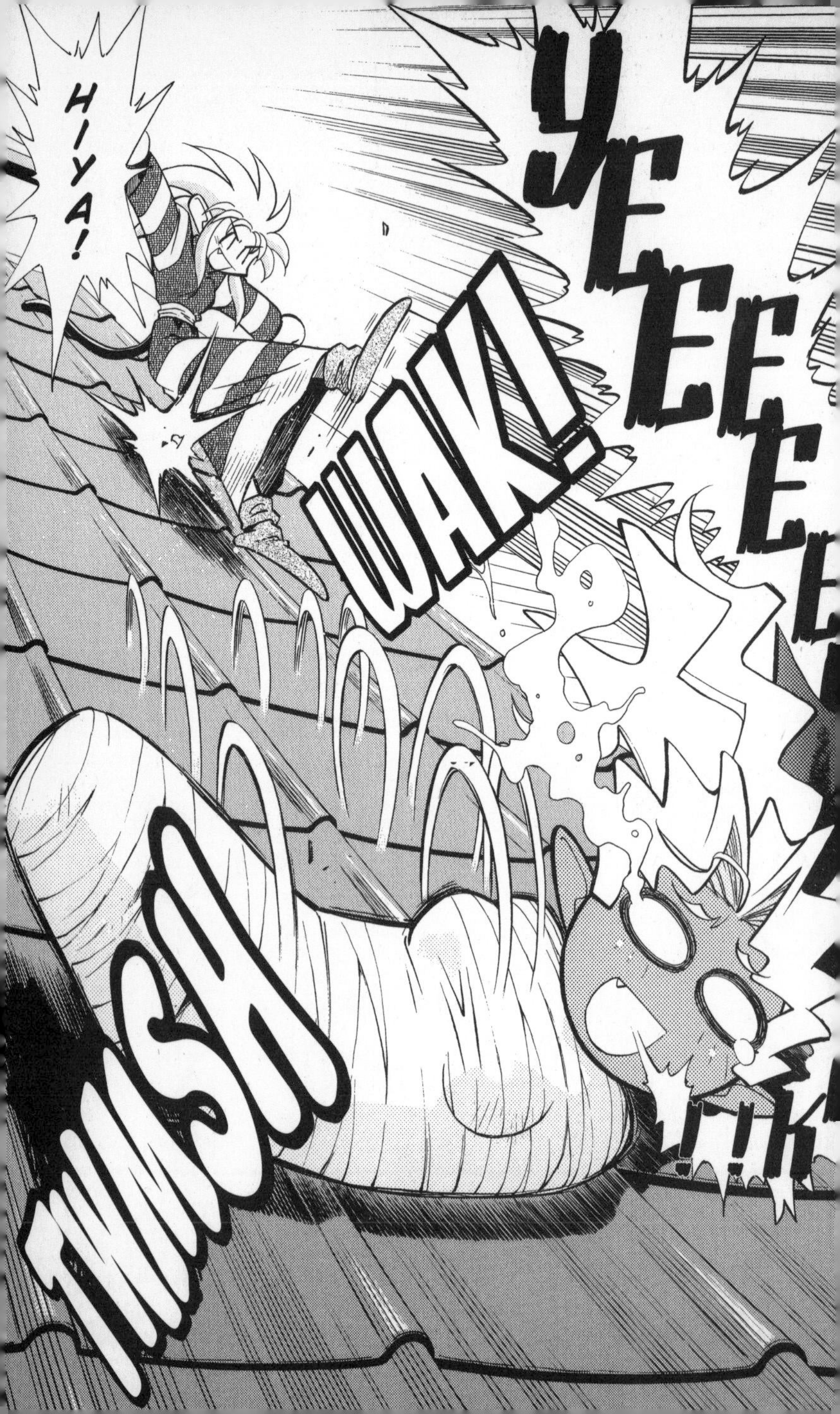

HIYA!
YEEEEE
WAK!
THWSH

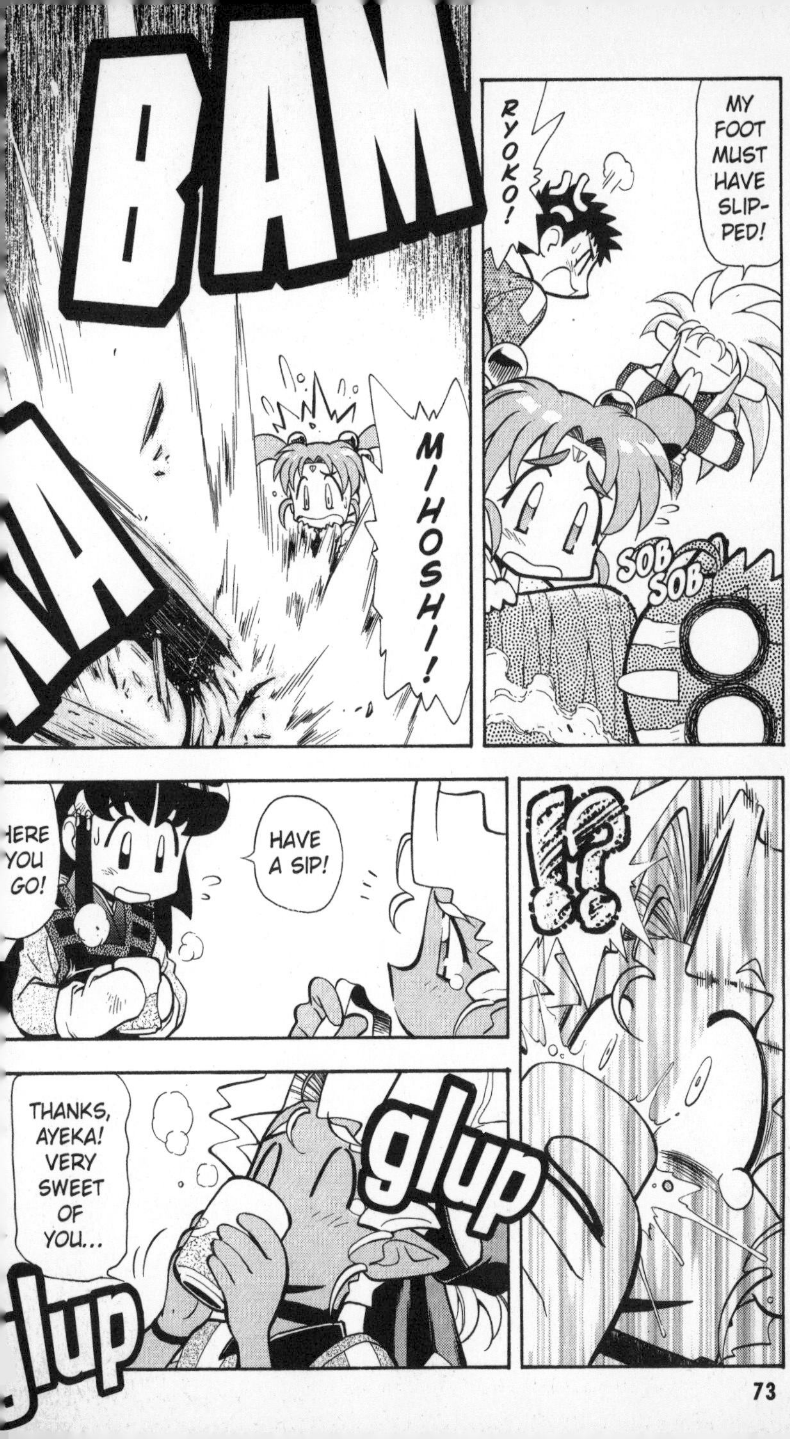
BAM
MIHOSHI!
RYOKO!
MY FOOT MUST HAVE SLIP-PED!
SOB SOB
HERE YOU GO!
HAVE A SIP!
THANKS, AYEKA! VERY SWEET OF YOU...
glup
glup
!?

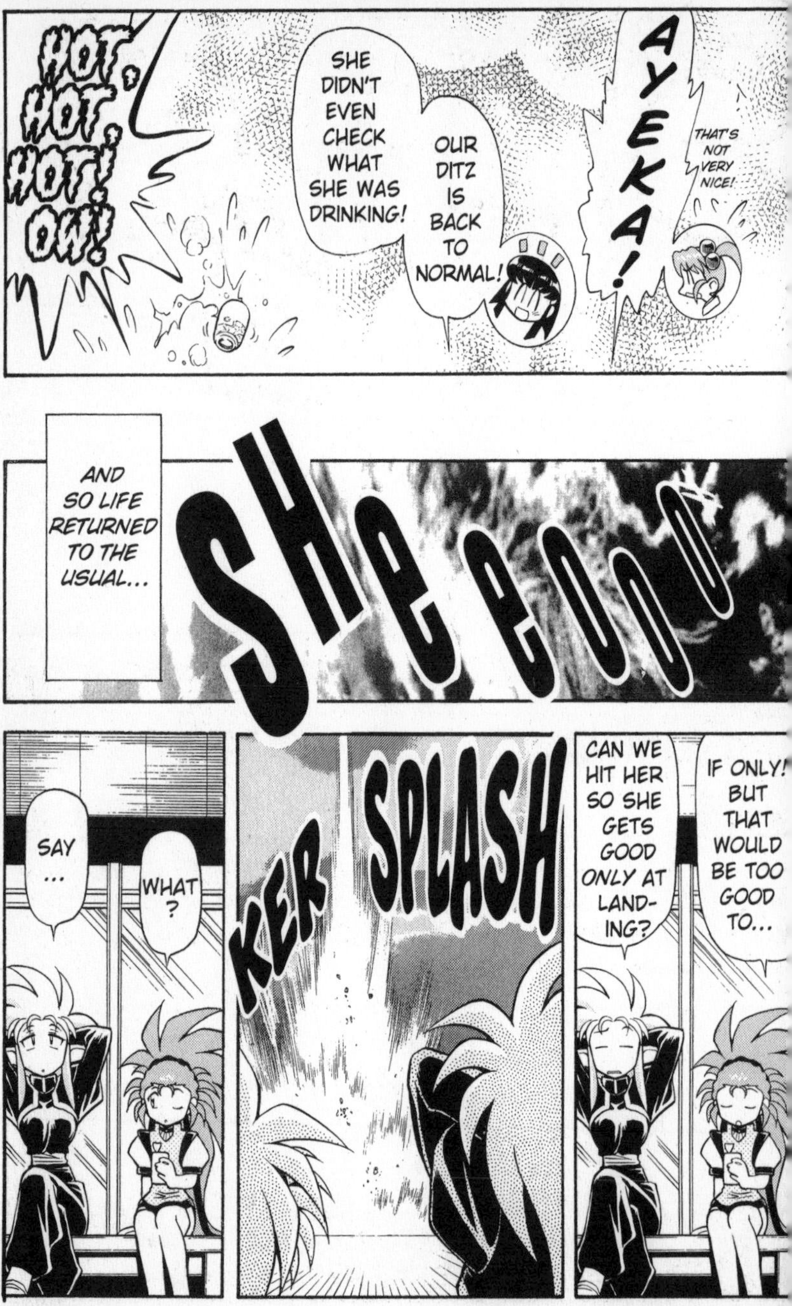
HOT, HOT, HOT! OW!
SHE DIDN'T EVEN CHECK WHAT SHE WAS DRINKING!
OUR DITZ IS BACK TO NORMAL!
AYEKA!
THAT'S NOT VERY NICE!
AND SO LIFE RETURNED TO THE USUAL...
SHEOOO
SAY ...
WHAT ?
KER SPLASH
CAN WE HIT HER SO SHE GETS GOOD ONLY AT LAND-ING?
IF ONLY! BUT THAT WOULD BE TOO GOOD TO...

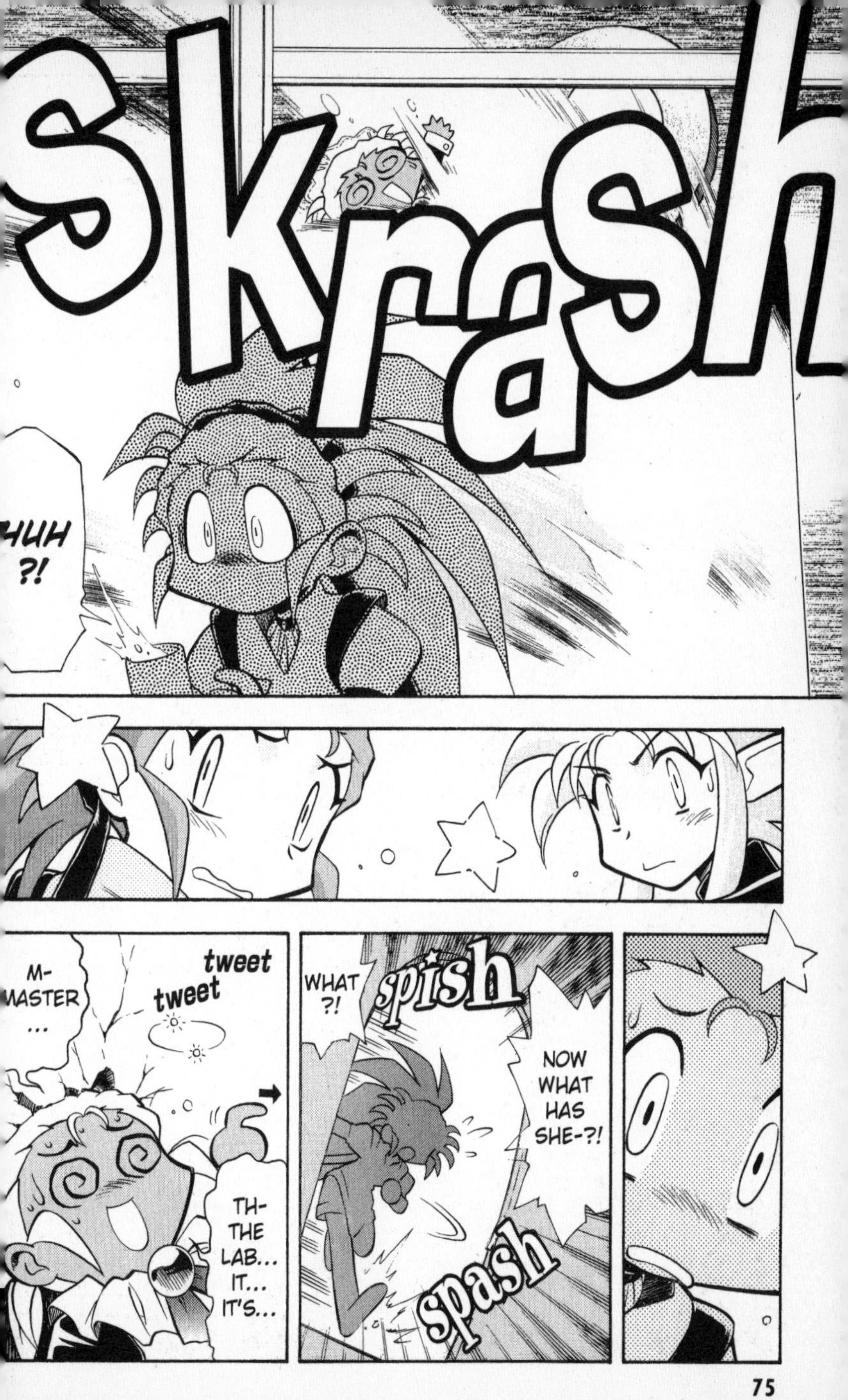
skrash
HUH ?!
M- MASTER ...
tweet
tweet
TH- THE LAB... IT... IT'S...
WHAT ?!
spish
NOW WHAT HAS SHE-?!
spash

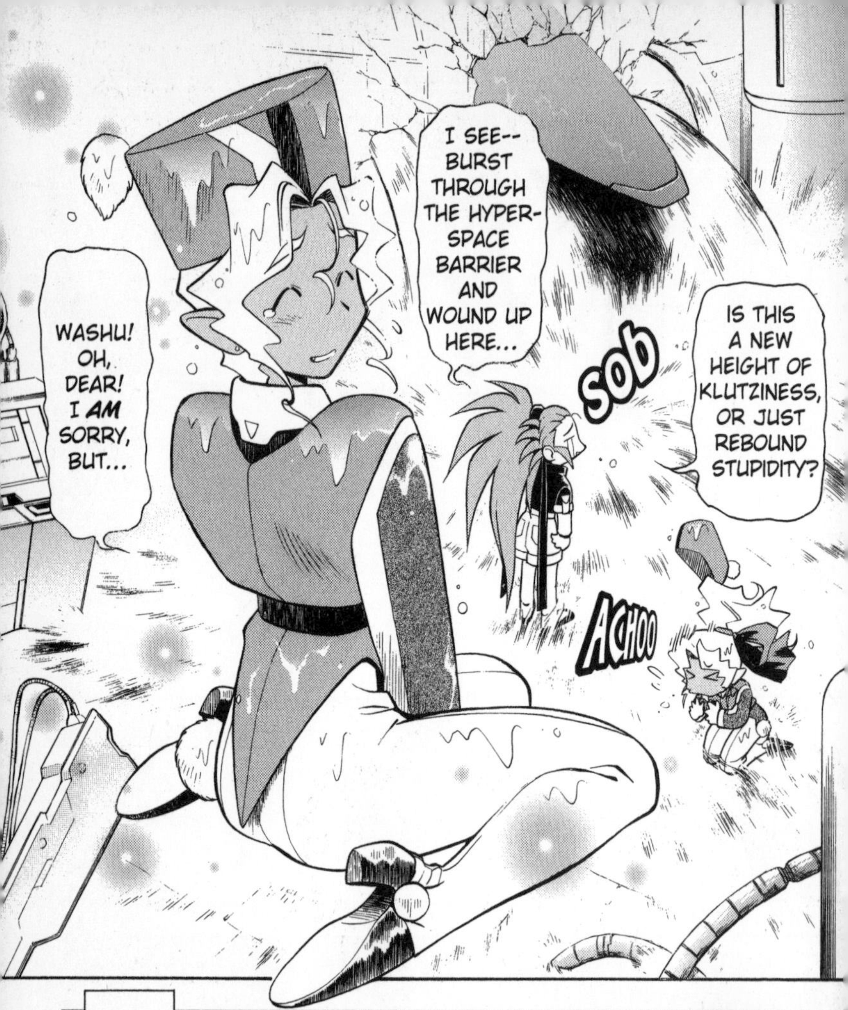
WASHU! OH, DEAR! I *AM* SORRY, BUT...
I SEE-- BURST THROUGH THE HYPER-SPACE BARRIER AND WOUND UP HERE...
SOB
IS THIS A NEW HEIGHT OF KLUTZINESS, OR JUST REBOUND STUPIDITY?
ACHOO

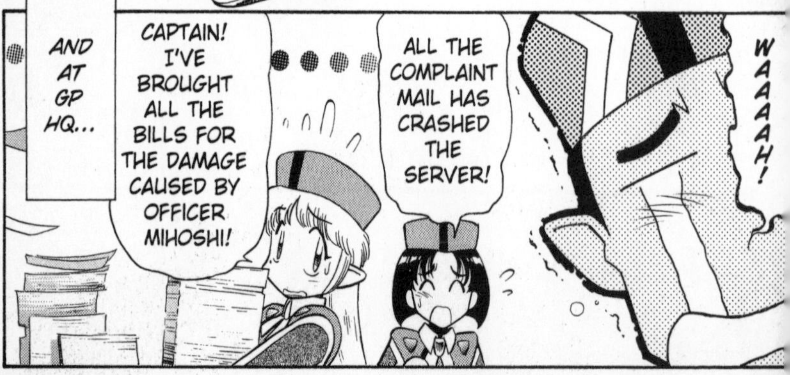
AND AT GP HQ...
CAPTAIN! I'VE BROUGHT ALL THE BILLS FOR THE DAMAGE CAUSED BY OFFICER MIHOSHI!
ALL THE COMPLAINT MAIL HAS CRASHED THE SERVER!
WAAAAH!

CHAPTER 4: GIVING THANKS

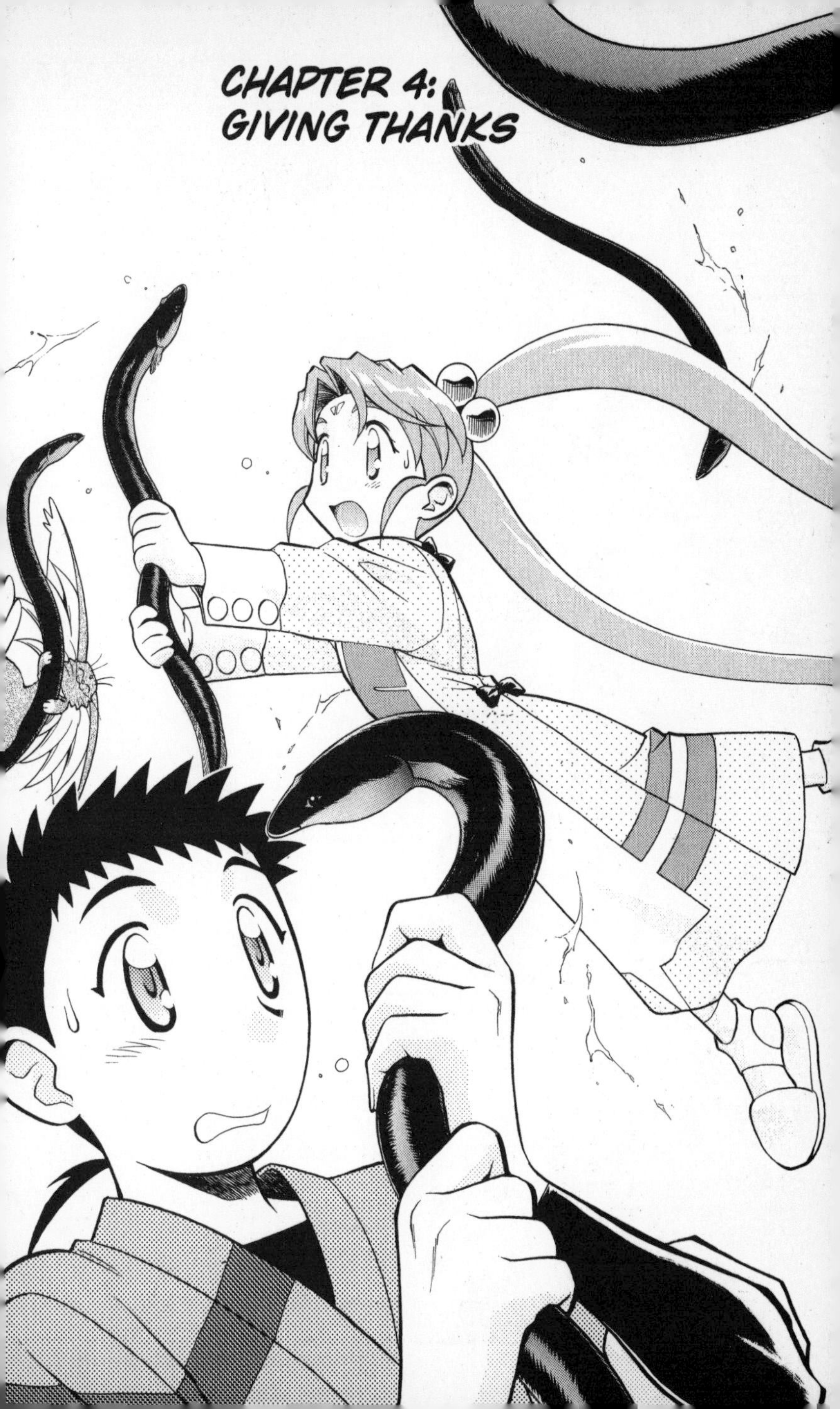

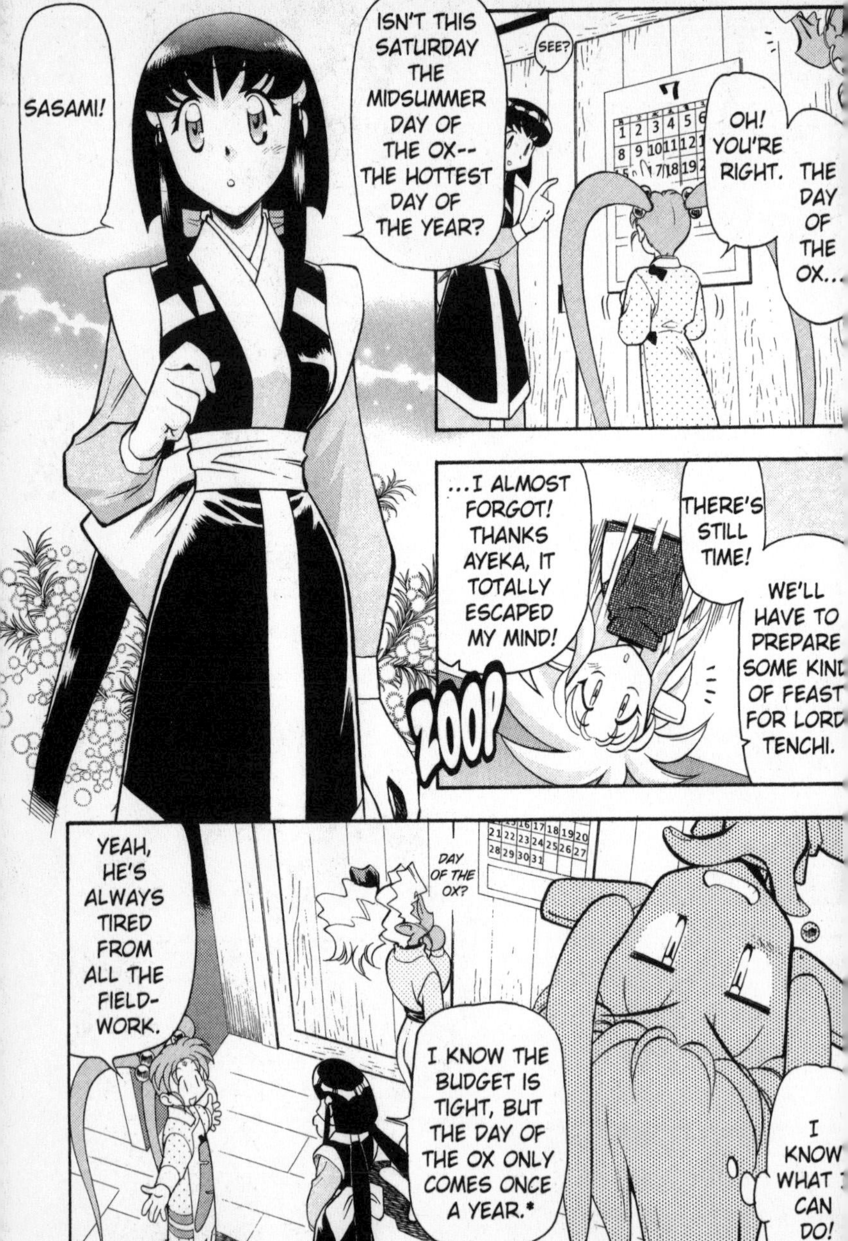
SASAMI!
ISN'T THIS SATURDAY THE MIDSUMMER DAY OF THE OX-- THE HOTTEST DAY OF THE YEAR?
SEE?
OH! YOU'RE RIGHT.
THE DAY OF THE OX...
...I ALMOST FORGOT! THANKS AYEKA, IT TOTALLY ESCAPED MY MIND!
ZOOP
THERE'S STILL TIME!
WE'LL HAVE TO PREPARE SOME KIND OF FEAST FOR LORD TENCHI.
YEAH, HE'S ALWAYS TIRED FROM ALL THE FIELD-WORK.
DAY OF THE OX?
I KNOW THE BUDGET IS TIGHT, BUT THE DAY OF THE OX ONLY COMES ONCE A YEAR.*
I KNOW WHAT I CAN DO!

*NO, LADY AYEKA, IT OCCURS EVERY 12 DAY

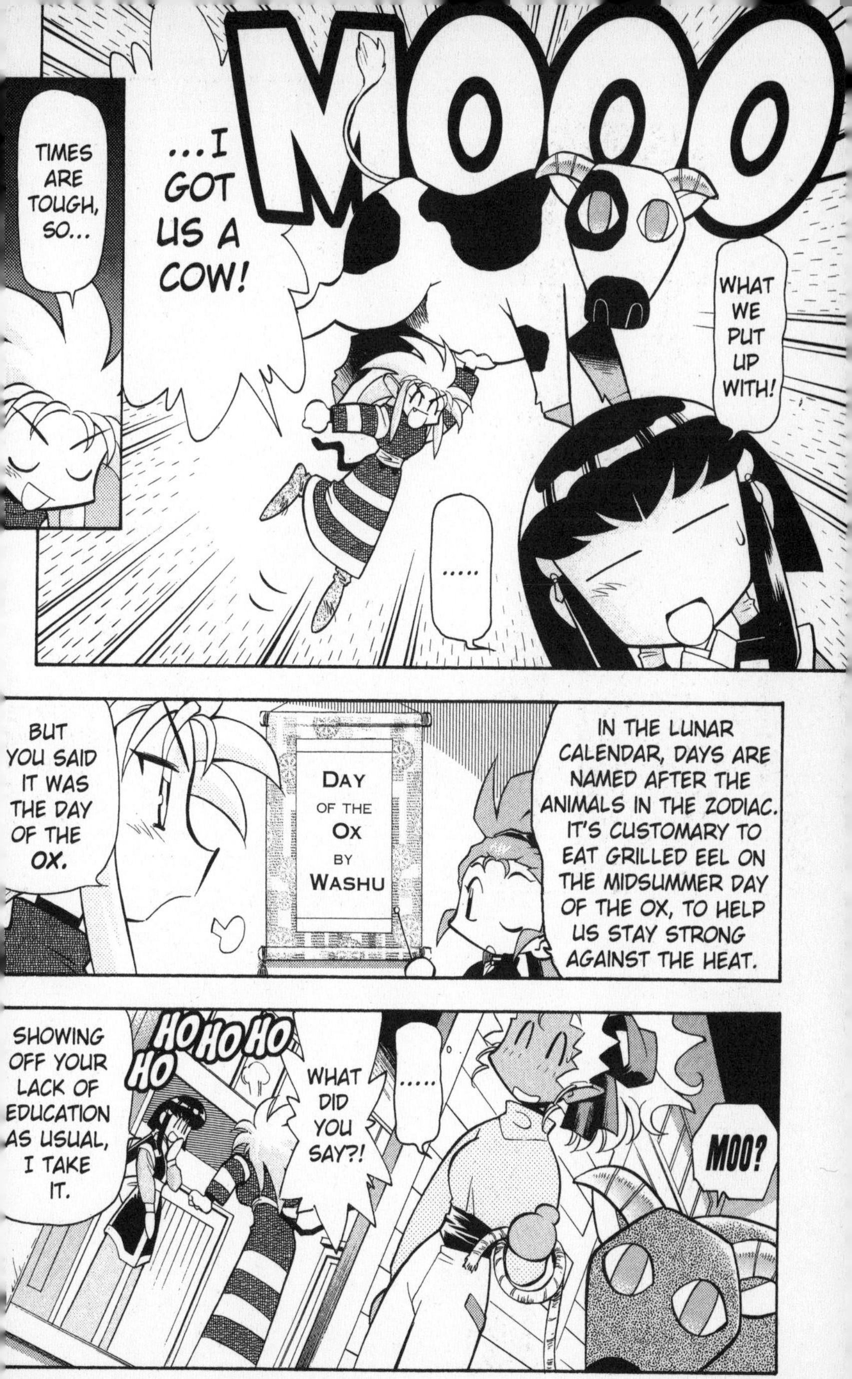
TIMES ARE TOUGH, SO...
...I GOT US A COW!
MOOO
WHAT WE PUT UP WITH!
.....
BUT YOU SAID IT WAS THE DAY OF THE OX.
DAY OF THE OX BY WASHU
IN THE LUNAR CALENDAR, DAYS ARE NAMED AFTER THE ANIMALS IN THE ZODIAC. IT'S CUSTOMARY TO EAT GRILLED EEL ON THE MIDSUMMER DAY OF THE OX, TO HELP US STAY STRONG AGAINST THE HEAT.
SHOWING OFF YOUR LACK OF EDUCATION AS USUAL, I TAKE IT.
HO HO HO HO
WHAT DID YOU SAY?!
.....
MOO?

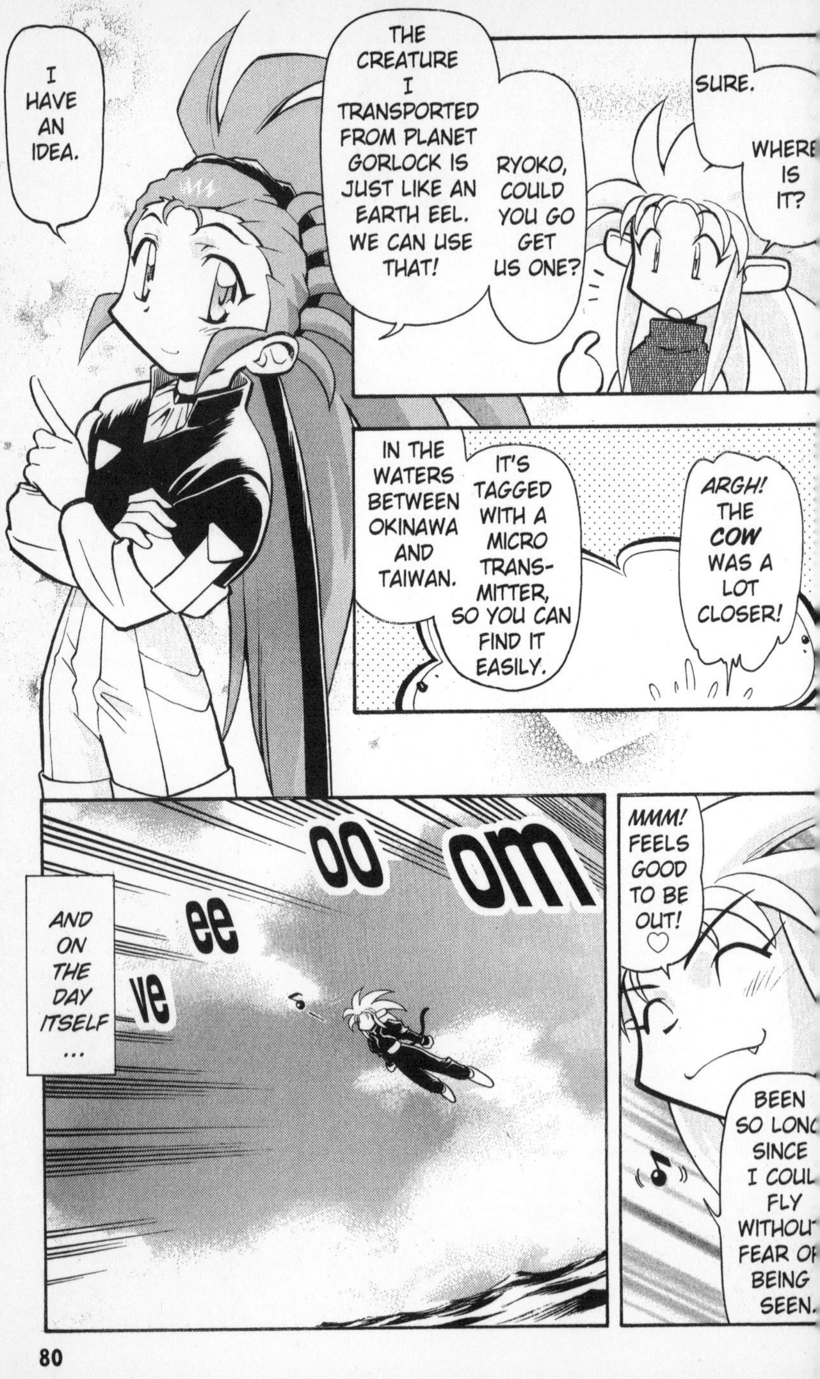
I HAVE AN IDEA.
THE CREATURE I TRANSPORTED FROM PLANET GORLOCK IS JUST LIKE AN EARTH EEL. WE CAN USE THAT!
RYOKO, COULD YOU GO GET US ONE?
SURE.
WHERE IS IT?
IN THE WATERS BETWEEN OKINAWA AND TAIWAN.
IT'S TAGGED WITH A MICRO TRANS-MITTER, SO YOU CAN FIND IT EASILY.
ARGH! THE COW WAS A LOT CLOSER!
AND ON THE DAY ITSELF...
ve
ee
oo
om
MMM! FEELS GOOD TO BE OUT! ♡
BEEN SO LON SINCE I COUL FLY WITHOU FEAR O BEING SEEN.

SO, LADY WASHU, HOW IS THIS *PSEUDO* EEL...

...ANY DIFFERENT FROM A REGULAR EARTH EEL?

IT TASTES JUST AS GOOD! BUT IT'S MUCH, MUCH, MUCH, MUCH BIGGER!

GURK

MUCH, MUCH, MUCH, MUCH? JUST *HOW* BIG IS IT?

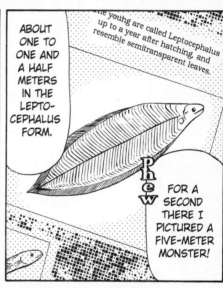

ABOUT ONE TO ONE AND A HALF METERS IN THE LEPTO-CEPHALUS FORM.

The young are called Leptocephalus up to a year after hatching, and resemble semitransparent leaves.

Phew

FOR A SECOND THERE I PICTURED A FIVE-METER MONSTER!

AND WHAT'S THIS *LEPTO* THING YOU'RE TALKING ABOUT?

JUST THE NAME FOR THEIR JUVENILE FORM.

EARTH ONES ARE ONLY FIVE TO SEVEN CENTI-METERS LONG.

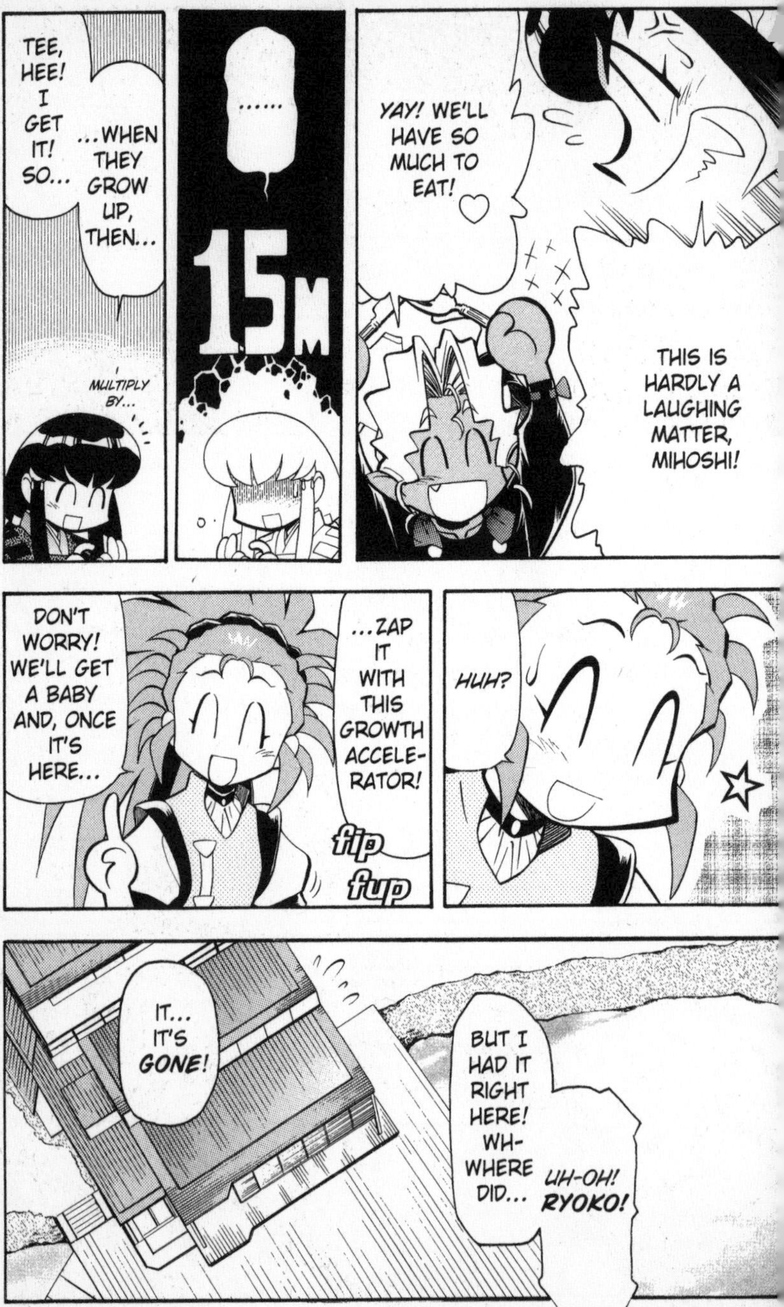

TEE, HEE! I GET IT! SO...
...WHEN THEY GROW UP, THEN...
I MULTIPLY BY...
......
15M
YAY! WE'LL HAVE SO MUCH TO EAT! ♡
THIS IS HARDLY A LAUGHING MATTER, MIHOSHI!
DON'T WORRY! WE'LL GET A BABY AND, ONCE IT'S HERE...
...ZAP IT WITH THIS GROWTH ACCELE-RATOR!
fip
fup
HUH?
IT... IT'S GONE!
BUT I HAD IT RIGHT HERE! WH-WHERE DID...
UH-OH! RYOKO!

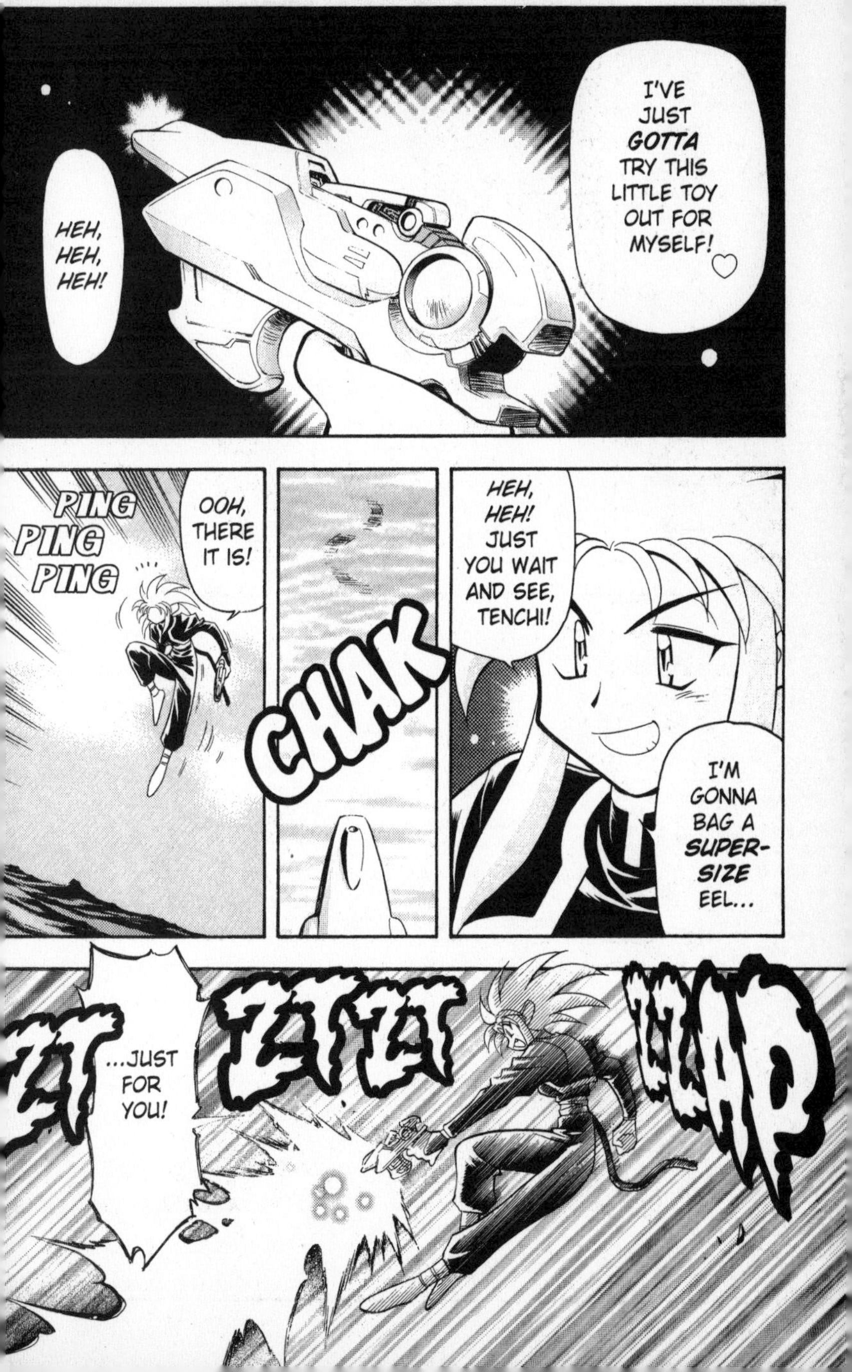
HEH, HEH, HEH!
I'VE JUST *GOTTA* TRY THIS LITTLE TOY OUT FOR MYSELF! ♡
PING PING PING
OOH, THERE IT IS!
CHAK
HEH, HEH! JUST YOU WAIT AND SEE, TENCHI!
I'M GONNA BAG A *SUPER-SIZE* EEL...
...JUST FOR YOU!
ZT ZTZT
ZZAP

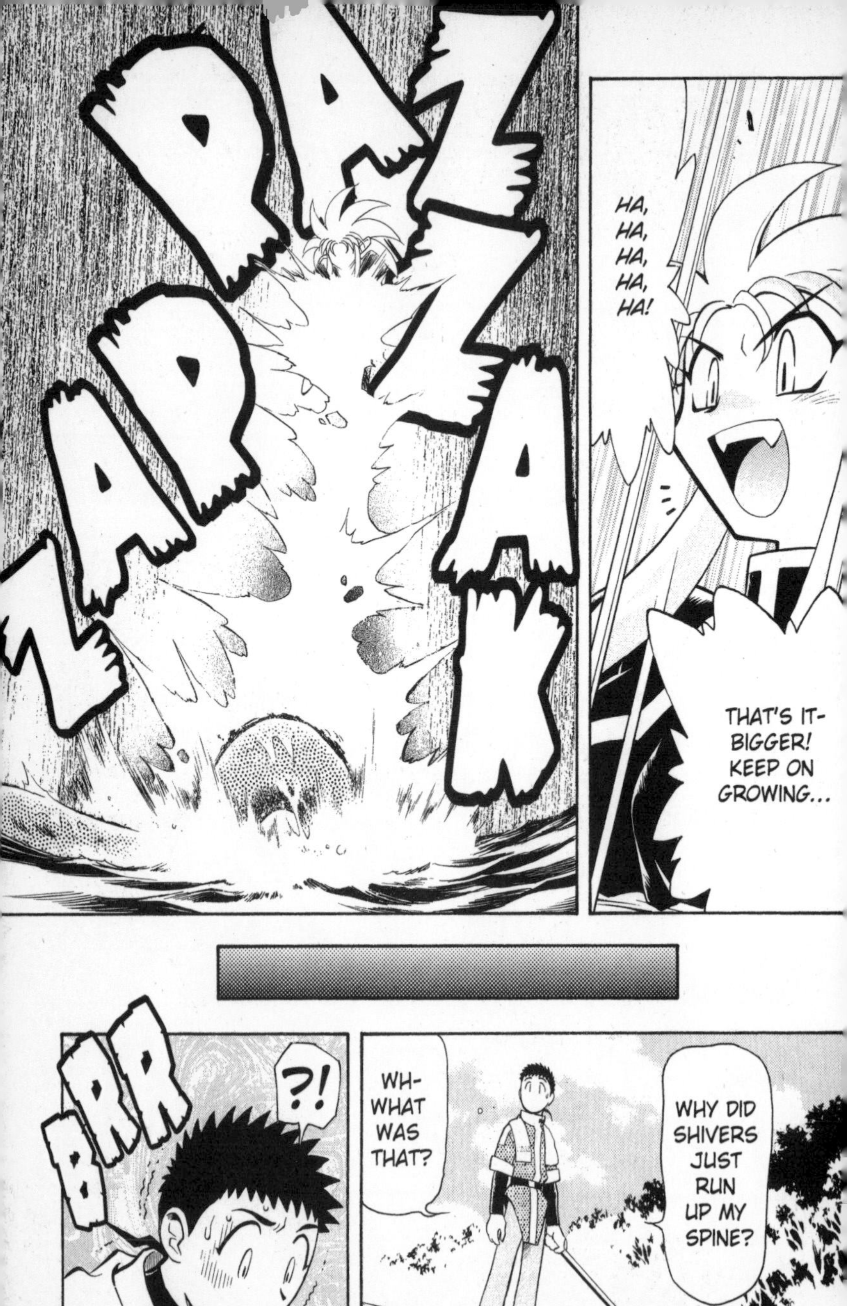
ZAPPAZZAK
HA, HA, HA, HA, HA!
THAT'S IT- BIGGER! KEEP ON GROWING...
BRR
?!
WH- WHAT WAS THAT?
WHY DID SHIVERS JUST RUN UP MY SPINE?

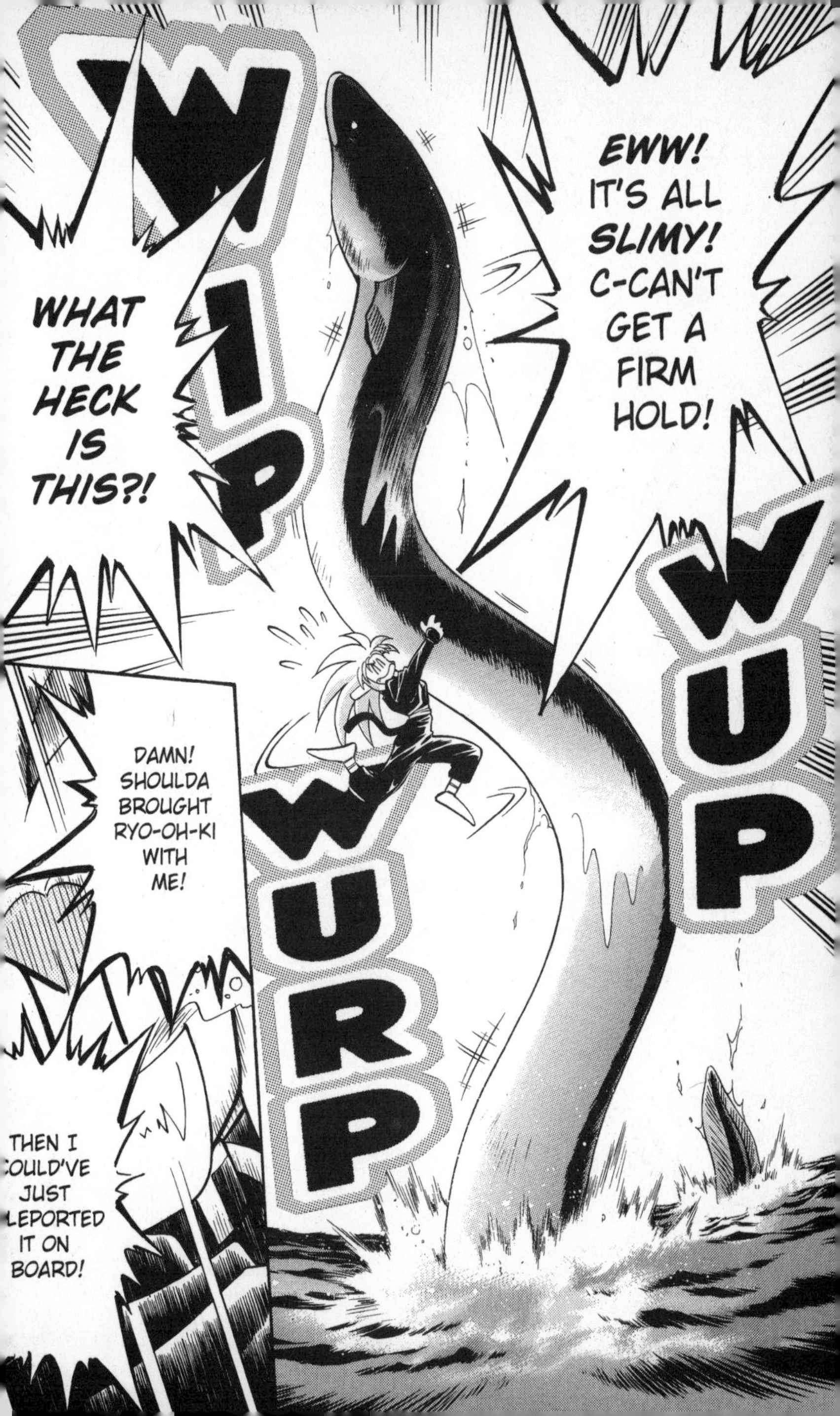

WIP
WHAT THE HECK IS THIS?!
EWW! IT'S ALL SLIMY! C-CAN'T GET A FIRM HOLD!
WUP
WURP
DAMN! SHOULDA BROUGHT RYO-OH-KI WITH ME!
THEN I OULD'VE JUST LEPORTED IT ON BOARD!

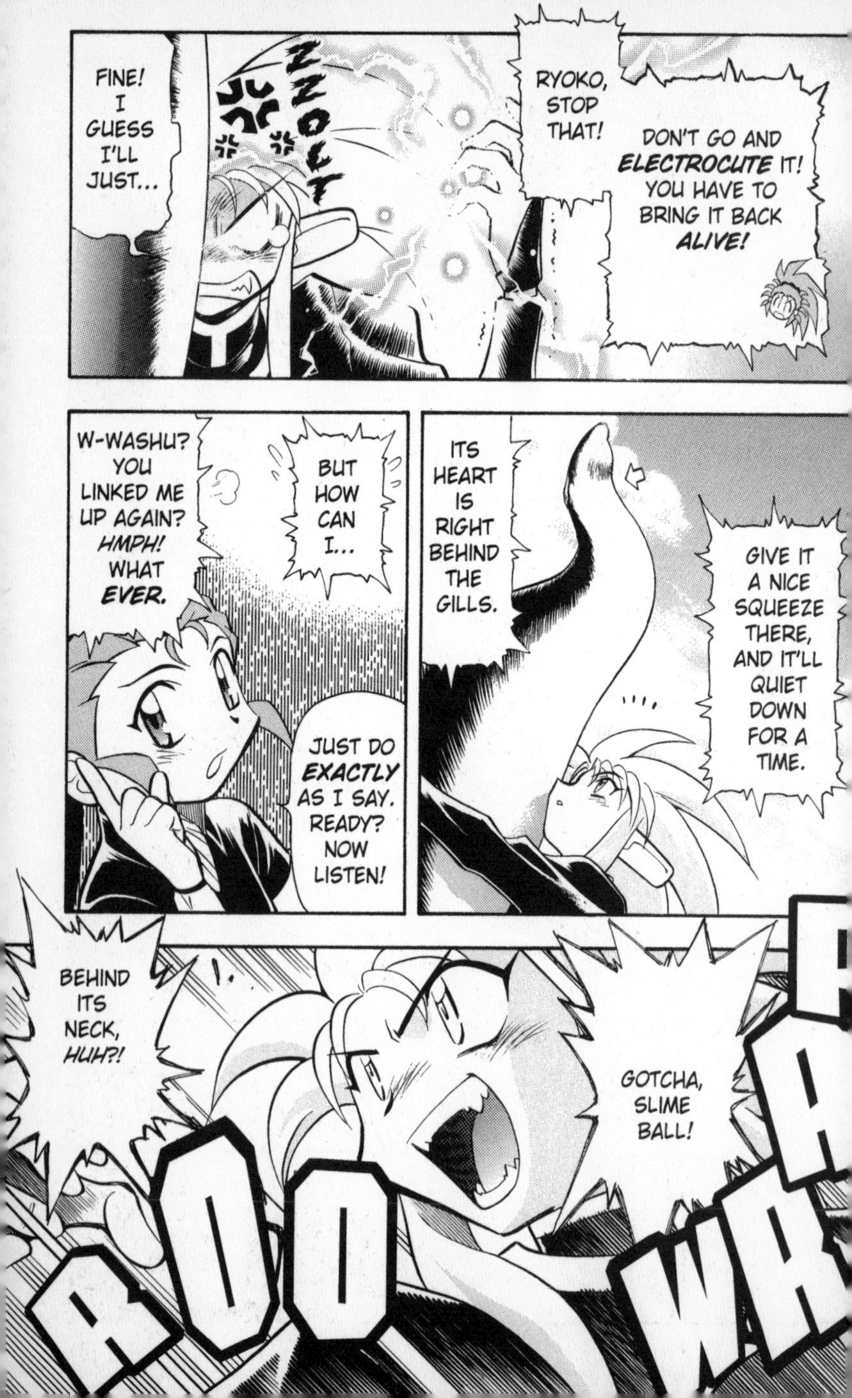

FINE! I GUESS I'LL JUST...
RYOKO, STOP THAT!
DON'T GO AND *ELECTROCUTE* IT! YOU HAVE TO BRING IT BACK *ALIVE!*
W-WASHU? YOU LINKED ME UP AGAIN? *HMPH!* WHAT *EVER.*
BUT HOW CAN I...
JUST DO *EXACTLY* AS I SAY. READY? NOW LISTEN!
ITS HEART IS RIGHT BEHIND THE GILLS.
GIVE IT A NICE SQUEEZE THERE, AND IT'LL QUIET DOWN FOR A TIME.
BEHIND ITS NECK, *HUH?!*
GOTCHA, SLIME BALL!

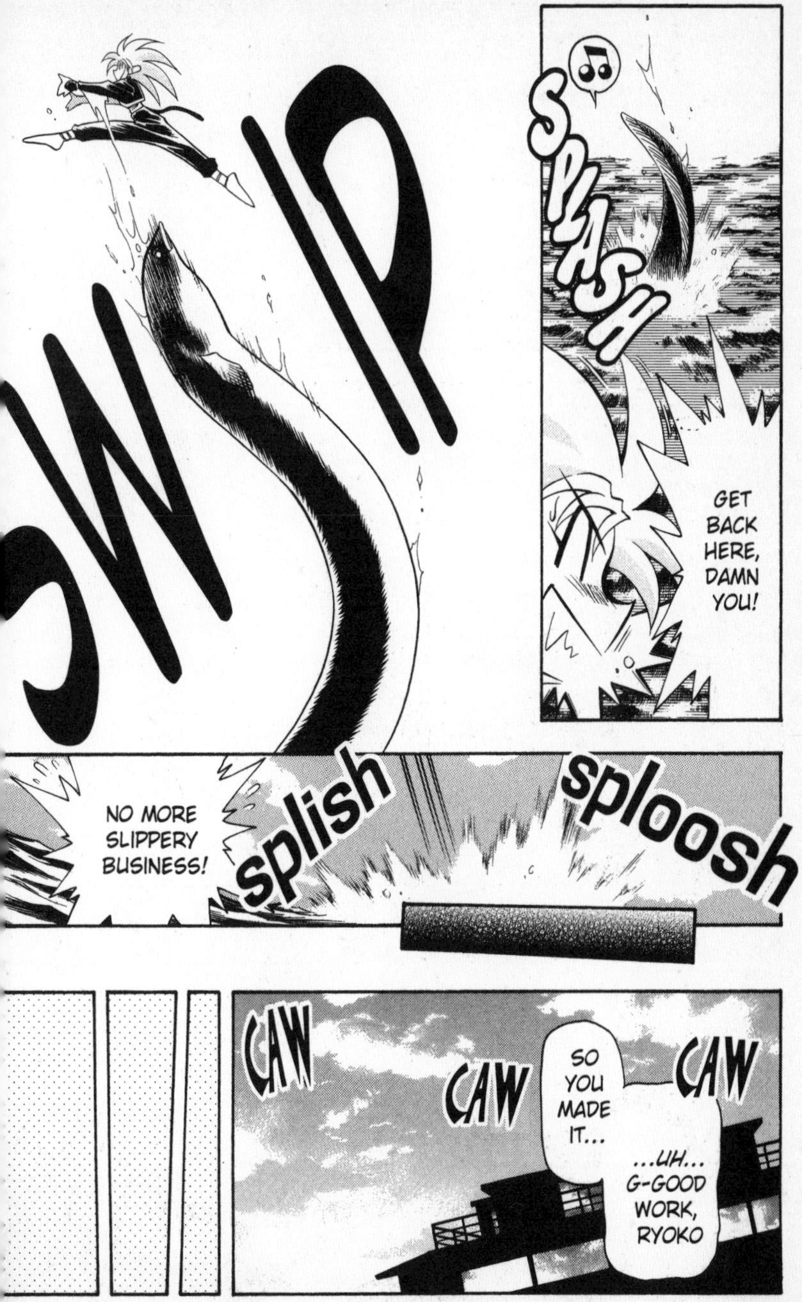
SWIP
SPLASH
GET BACK HERE, DAMN YOU!
NO MORE SLIPPERY BUSINESS!
splish
sploosh
CAW
CAW
SO YOU MADE IT...
CAW
...UH... G-GOOD WORK, RYOKO

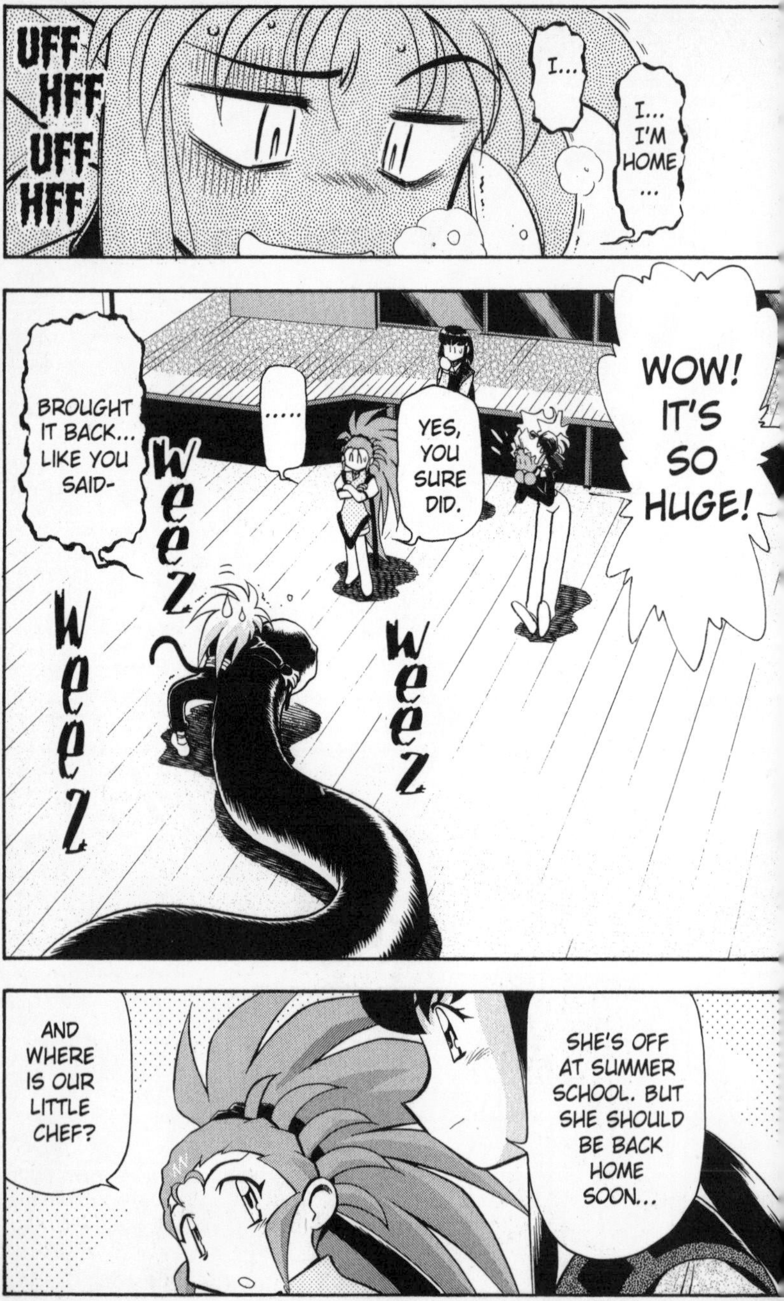
UFF HFF UFF HFF
I...
I... I'M HOME ...
BROUGHT IT BACK... LIKE YOU SAID-
weez
weez
.....
YES, YOU SURE DID.
weez
WOW! IT'S SO HUGE!
AND WHERE IS OUR LITTLE CHEF?
SHE'S OFF AT SUMMER SCHOOL. BUT SHE SHOULD BE BACK HOME SOON...

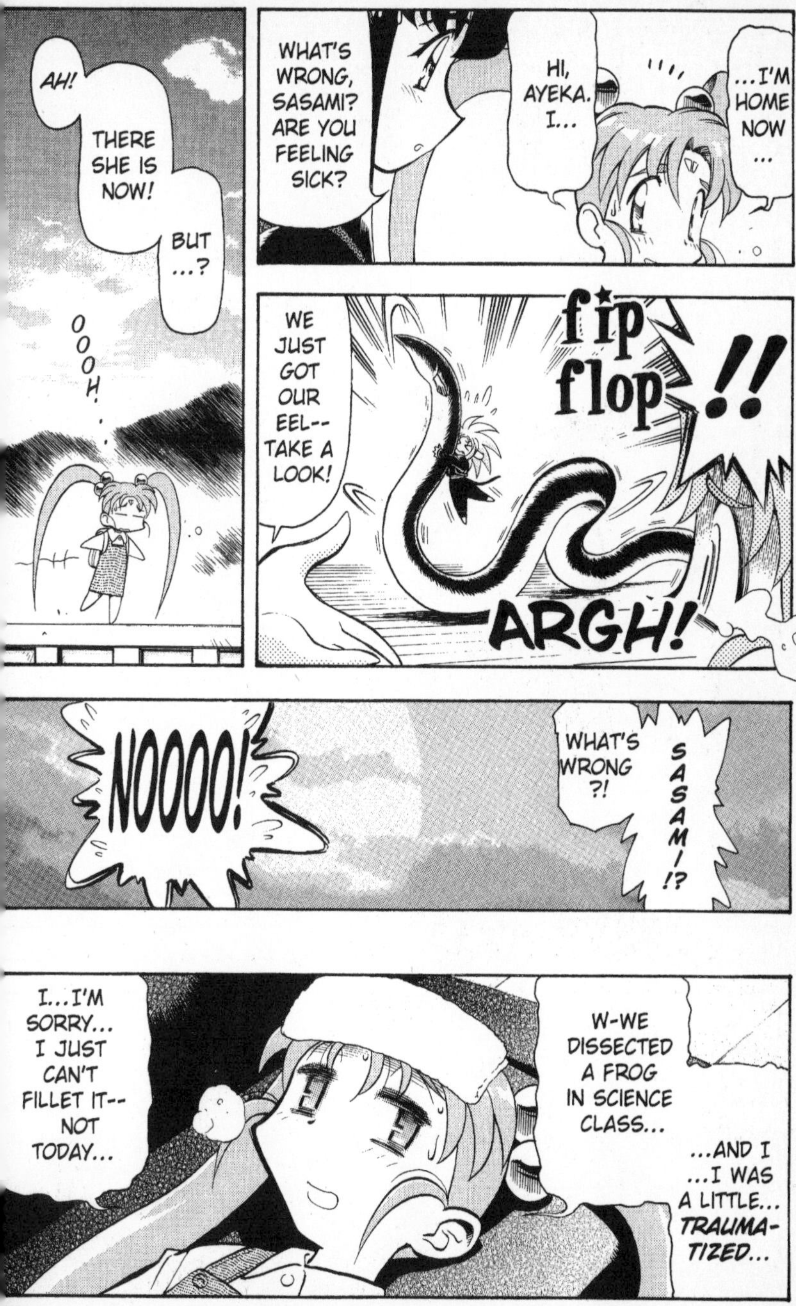
AH!
THERE SHE IS NOW!
BUT ...?
OOOH . . .
WHAT'S WRONG, SASAMI? ARE YOU FEELING SICK?
HI, AYEKA. I...
...I'M HOME NOW ...
WE JUST GOT OUR EEL-- TAKE A LOOK!
fip flop !!
ARGH!
NOOOO!
WHAT'S WRONG ?!
SASAMI!?
I...I'M SORRY... I JUST CAN'T FILLET IT-- NOT TODAY...
W-WE DISSECTED A FROG IN SCIENCE CLASS...
...AND I ...I WAS A LITTLE... TRAUMATIZED...

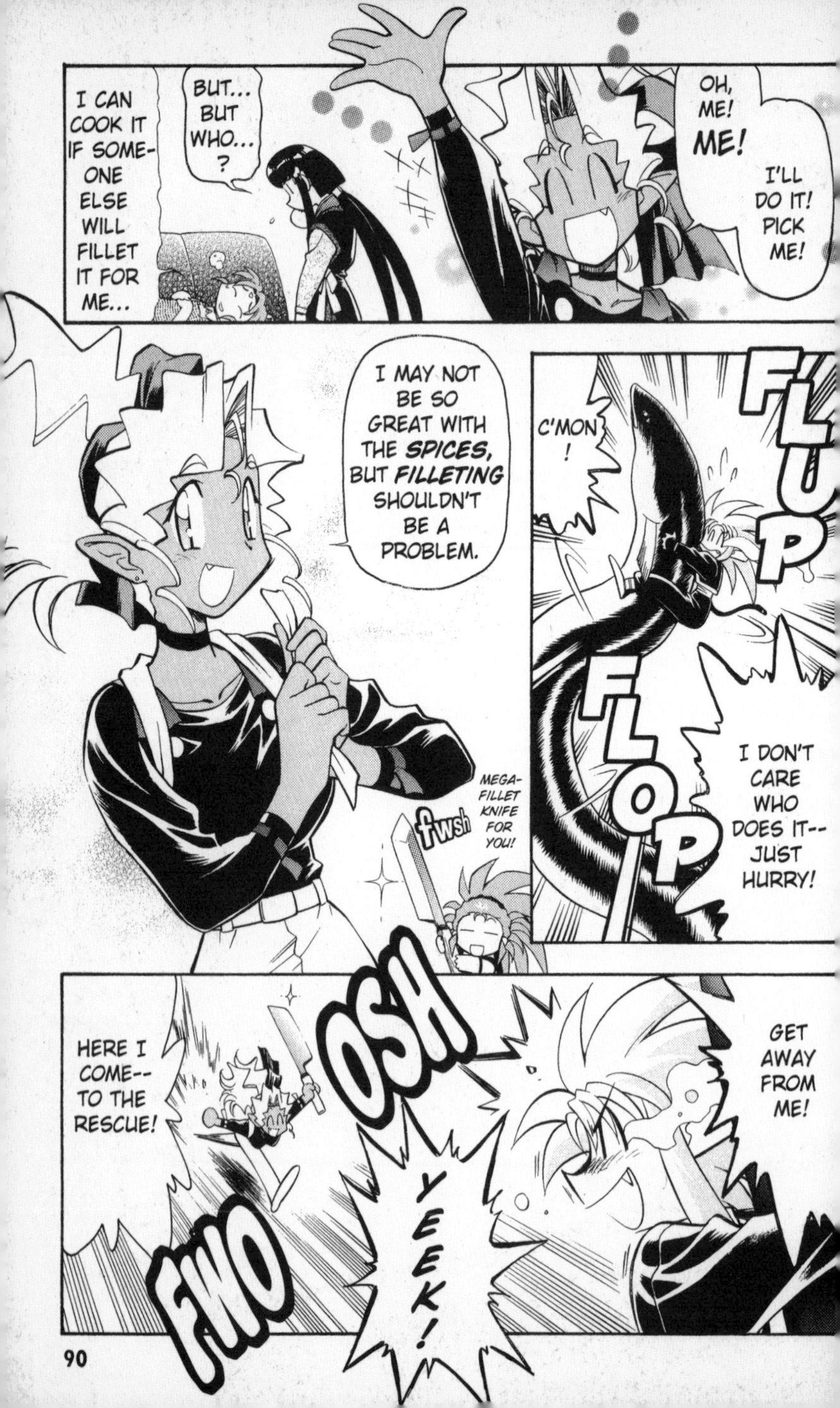
I CAN COOK IT IF SOME-ONE ELSE WILL FILLET IT FOR ME...
BUT... BUT WHO...?
OH, ME! ME!
I'LL DO IT! PICK ME!
I MAY NOT BE SO GREAT WITH THE SPICES, BUT FILLETING SHOULDN'T BE A PROBLEM.
fwsh
MEGA-FILLET KNIFE FOR YOU!
F'LUP
C'MON!
FLOP
I DON'T CARE WHO DOES IT-- JUST HURRY!
HERE I COME-- TO THE RESCUE!
FWOOSH
YEEK!
GET AWAY FROM ME!

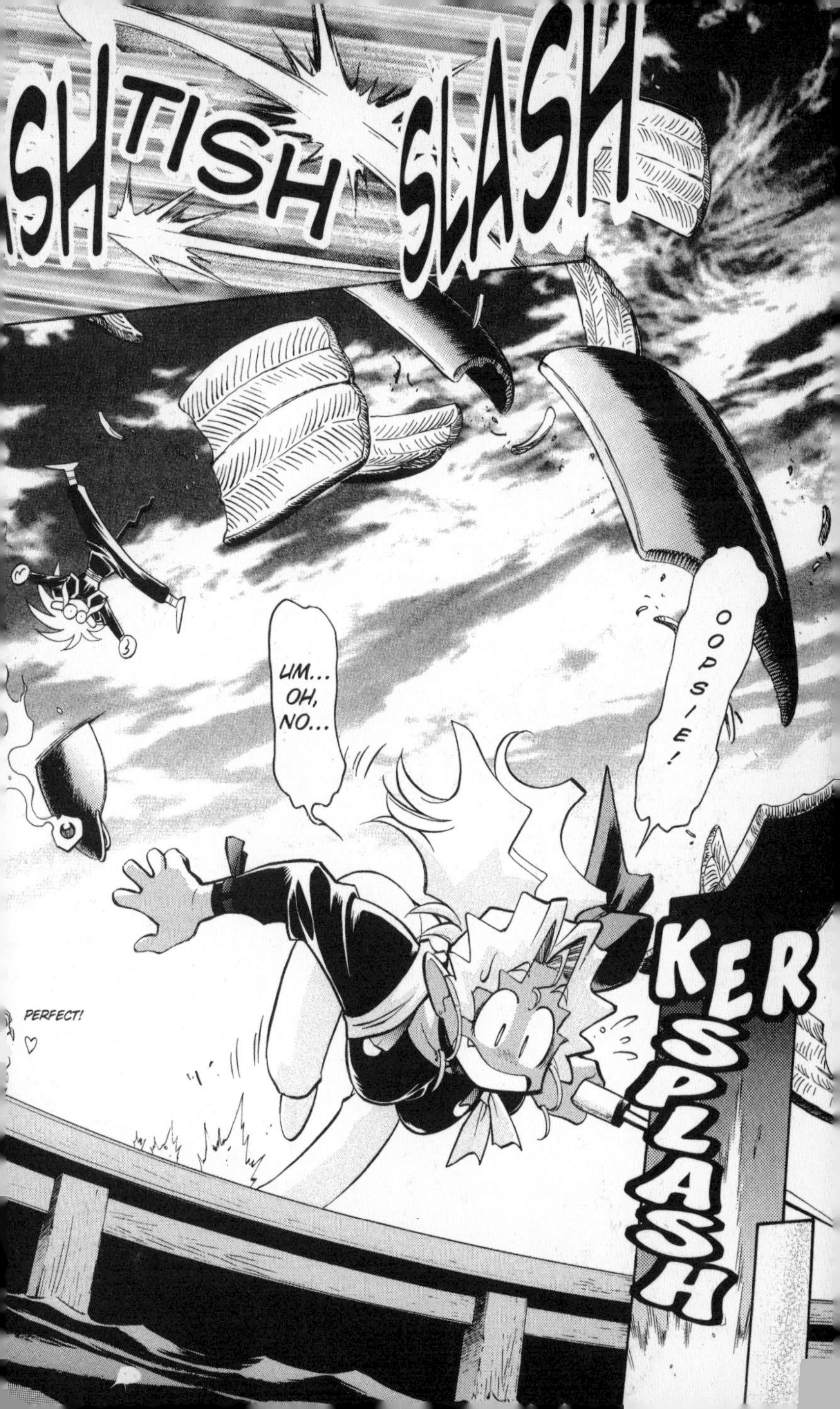
SH
TISH
SLASH
UM... OH, NO...
OOPSIE!
PERFECT! ♥
KER SPLASH

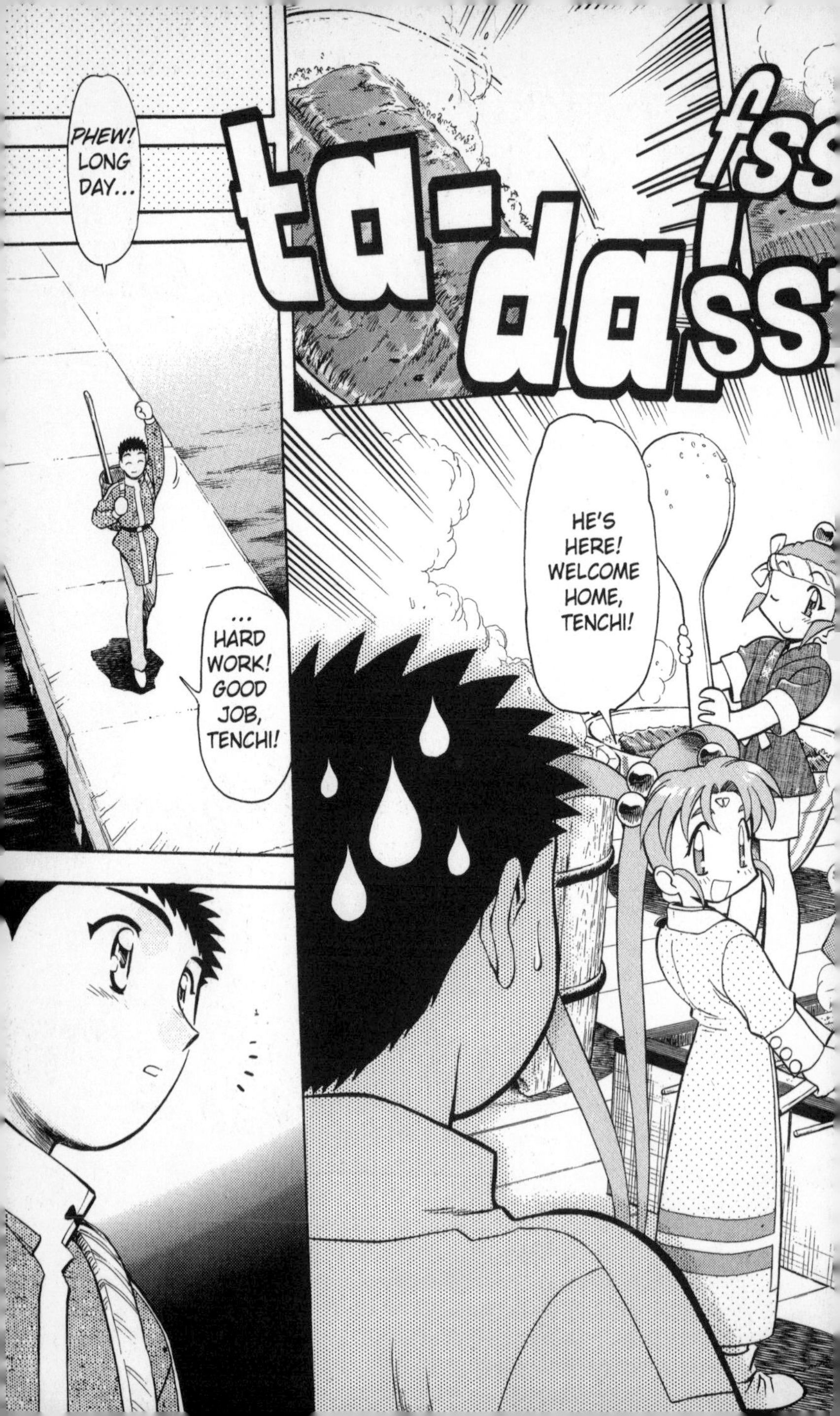
PHEW! LONG DAY...
...HARD WORK! GOOD JOB, TENCHI!
ta-da!
fss
ss
HE'S HERE! WELCOME HOME, TENCHI!

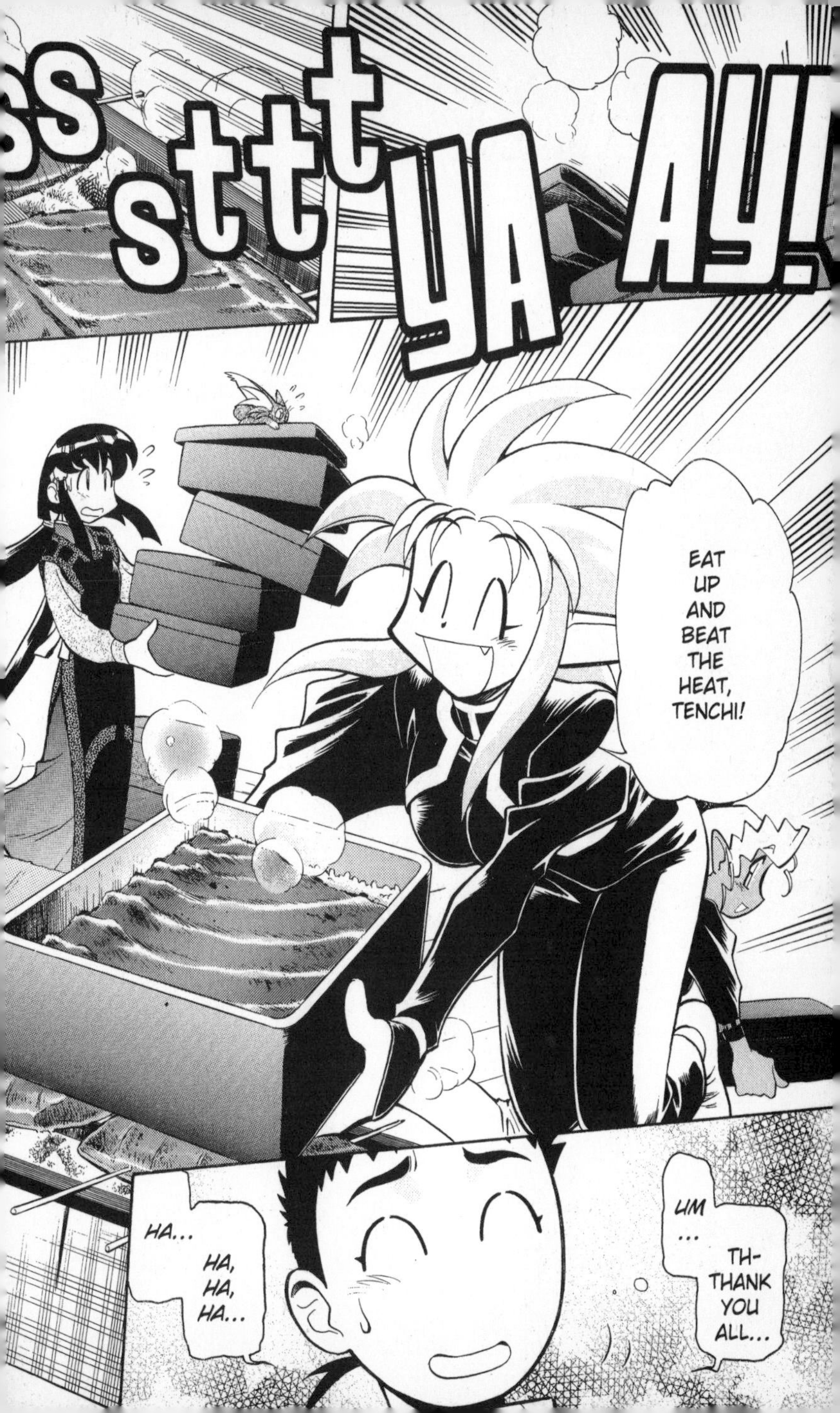
SSSTTTT
YAAY!
EAT UP AND BEAT THE HEAT, TENCHI!
HA... HA, HA, HA...
UM... TH-THANK YOU ALL...

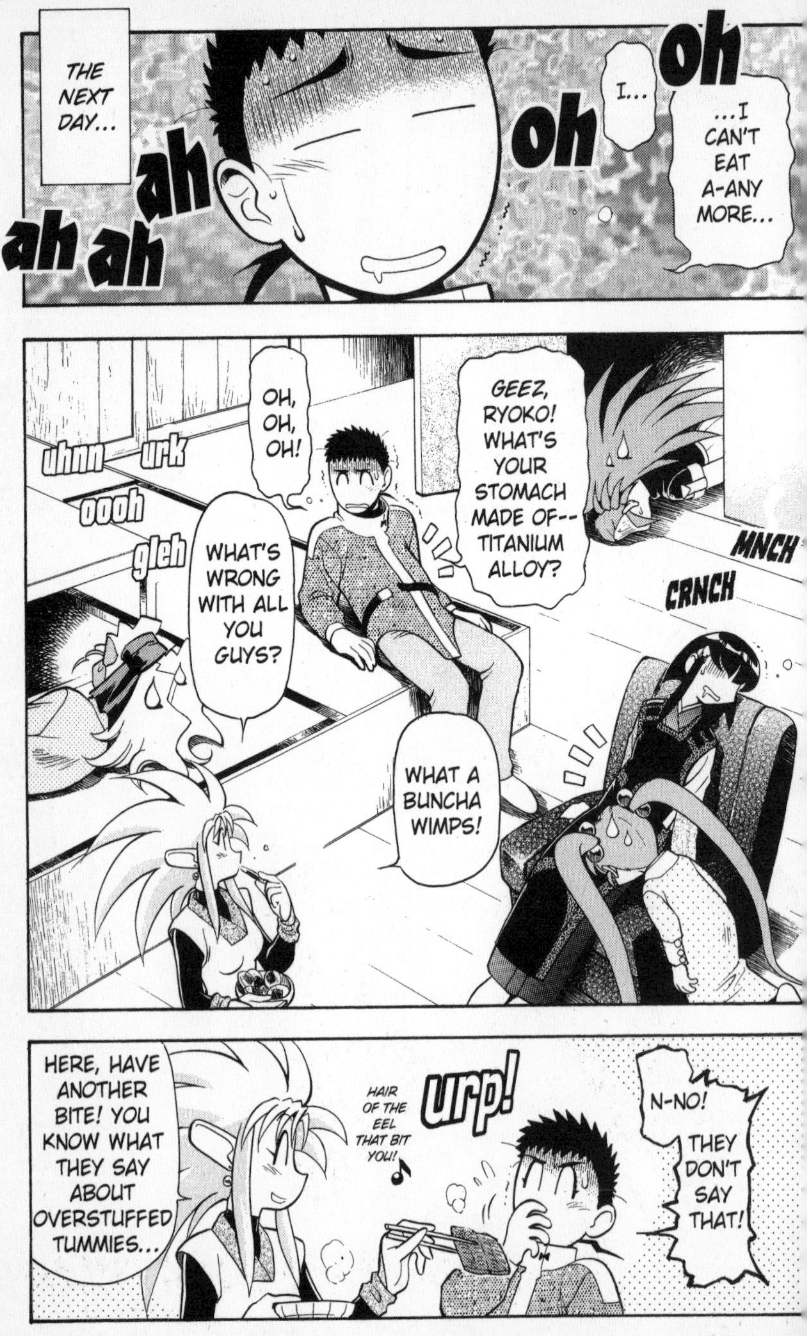

THE NEXT DAY...
ah ah ah
oh oh
I...
...I CAN'T EAT A-ANY MORE...
uhnn urk
oooh
gleh
OH, OH, OH!
WHAT'S WRONG WITH ALL YOU GUYS?
GEEZ, RYOKO! WHAT'S YOUR STOMACH MADE OF--TITANIUM ALLOY?
MNCH
CRNCH
WHAT A BUNCHA WIMPS!
HERE, HAVE ANOTHER BITE! YOU KNOW WHAT THEY SAY ABOUT OVERSTUFFED TUMMIES...
HAIR OF THE EEL THAT BIT YOU! ♪
urp!
N-NO!
THEY DON'T SAY THAT!

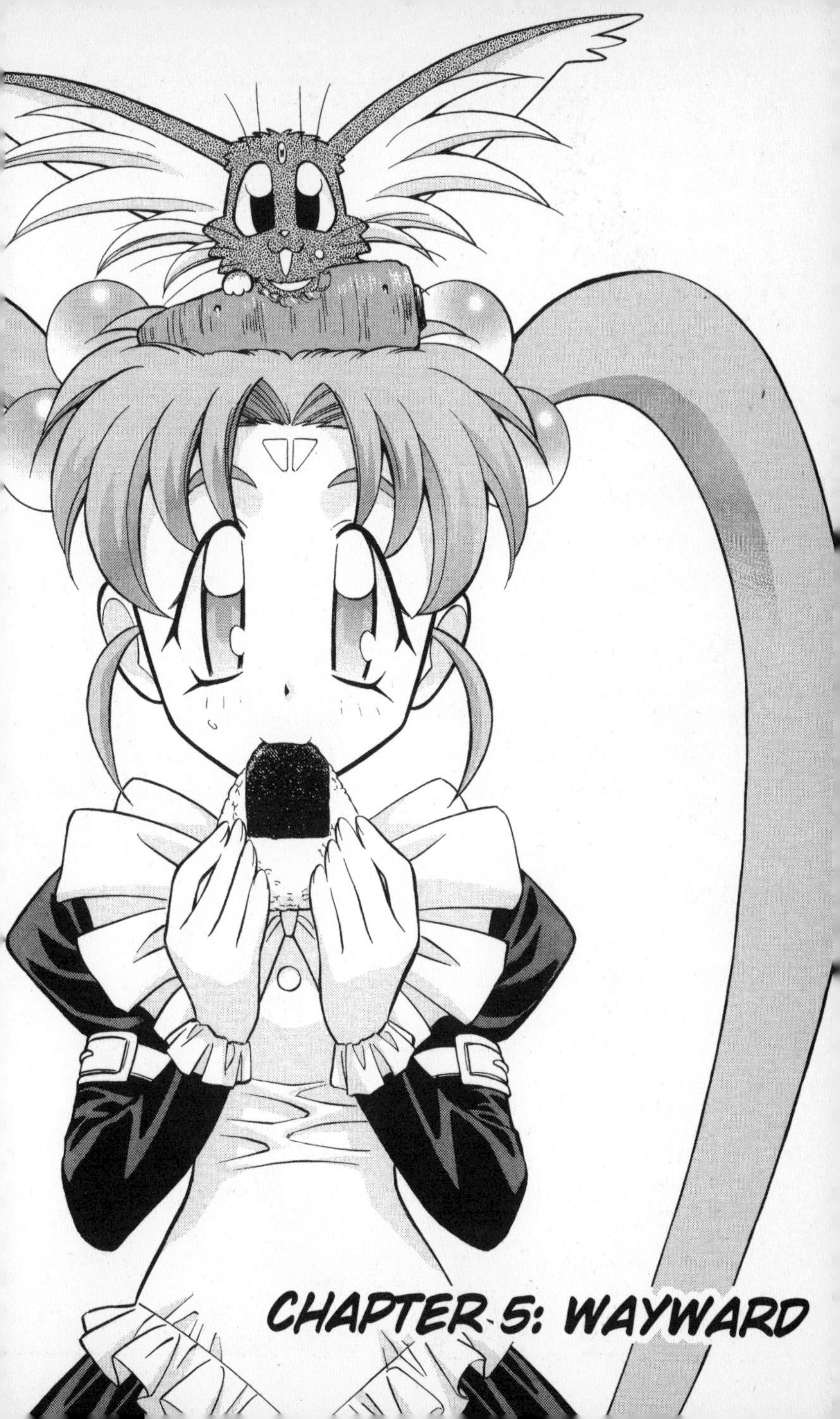
CHAPTER 5: WAYWARD

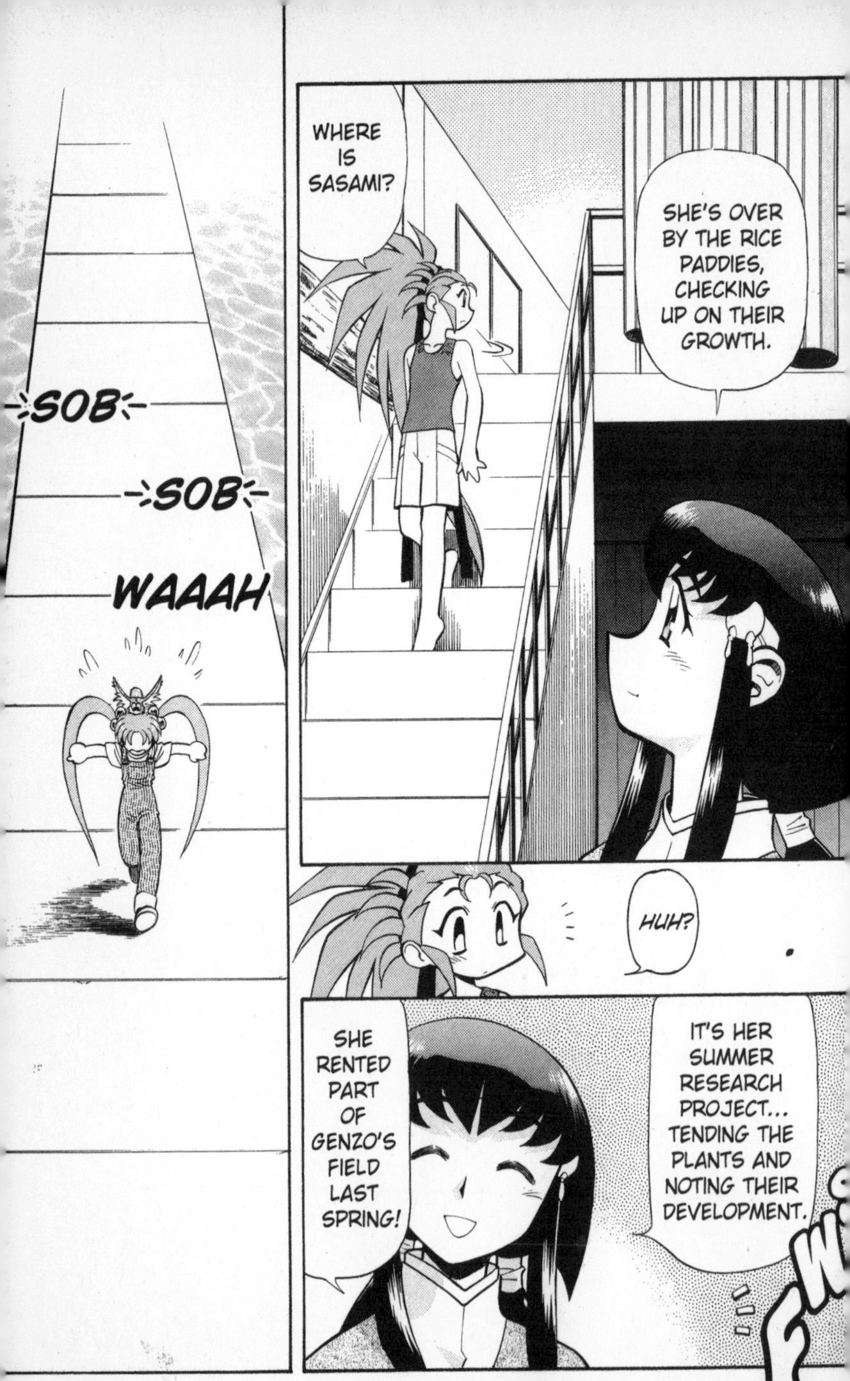
SOB
SOB
WAAAH
WHERE IS SASAMI?
SHE'S OVER BY THE RICE PADDIES, CHECKING UP ON THEIR GROWTH.
HUH?
SHE RENTED PART OF GENZO'S FIELD LAST SPRING!
IT'S HER SUMMER RESEARCH PROJECT... TENDING THE PLANTS AND NOTING THEIR DEVELOPMENT.

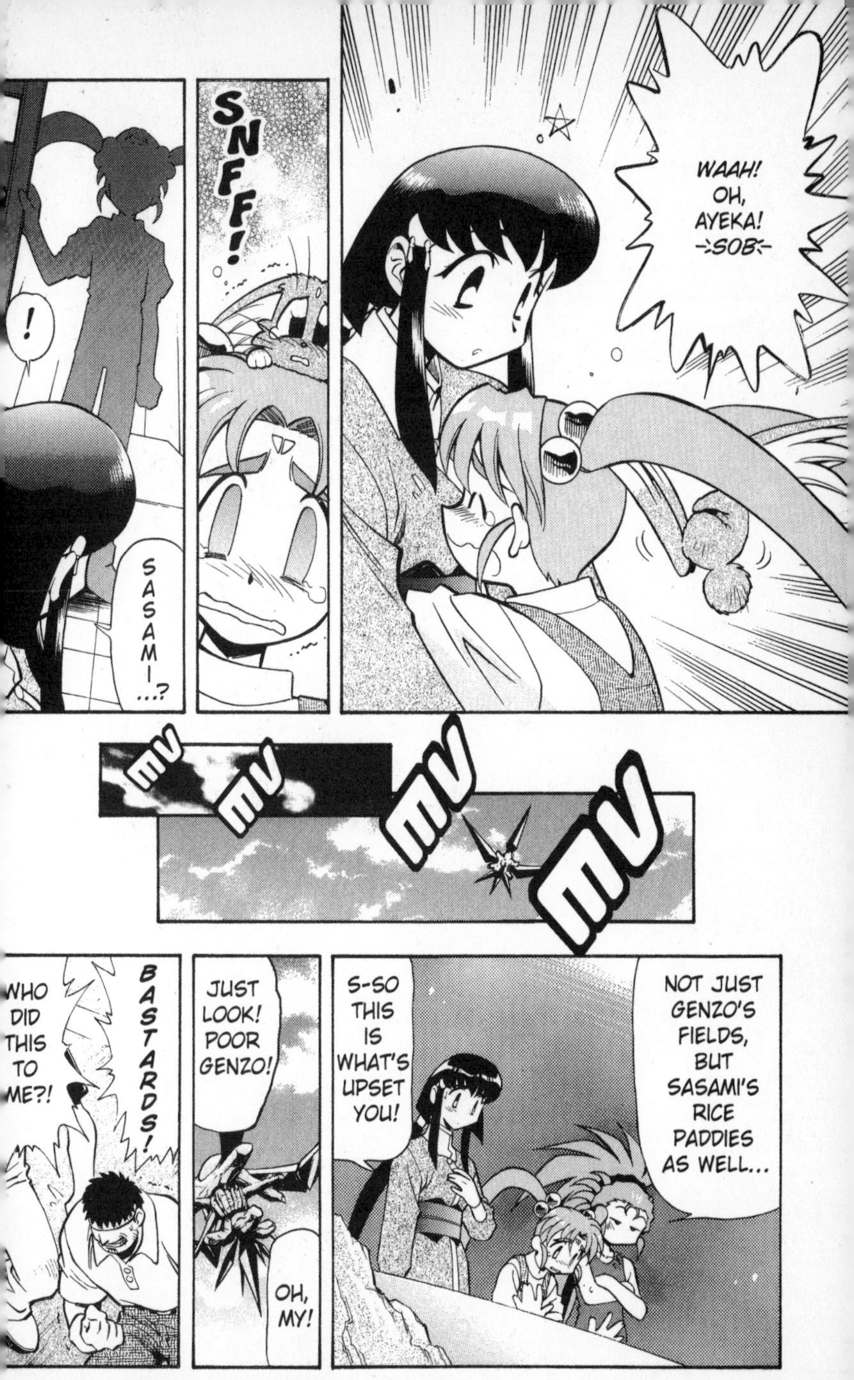
WAAH! OH, AYEKA! SOB
SNFF!
!
SASAMI...?
NOT JUST GENZO'S FIELDS, BUT SASAMI'S RICE PADDIES AS WELL...
S-SO THIS IS WHAT'S UPSET YOU!
JUST LOOK! POOR GENZO!
OH, MY!
BASTARDS!
WHO DID THIS TO ME?!

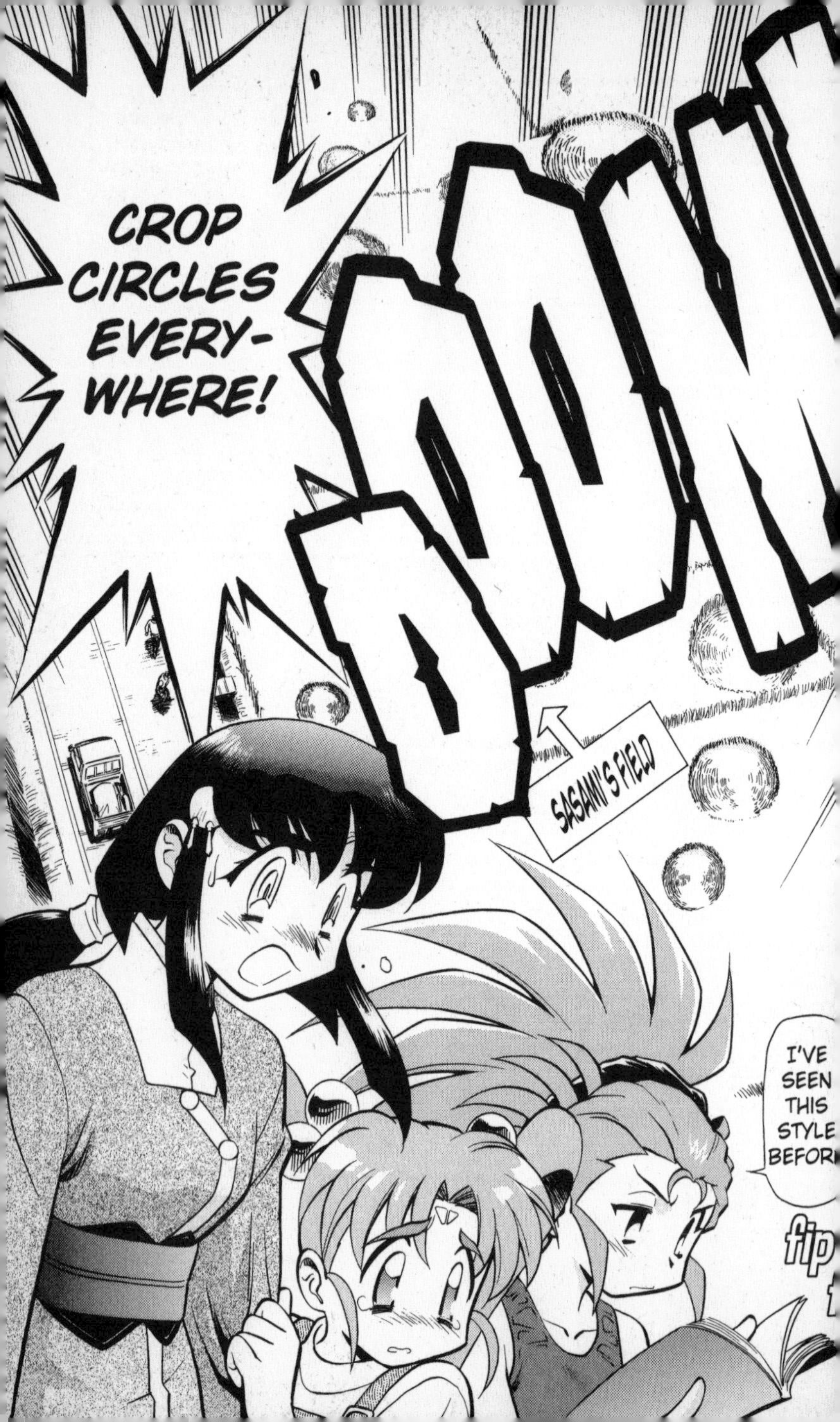
CROP CIRCLES EVERY-WHERE!
BOOM
SASAMI'S FIELD
I'VE SEEN THIS STYLE BEFOR
flip

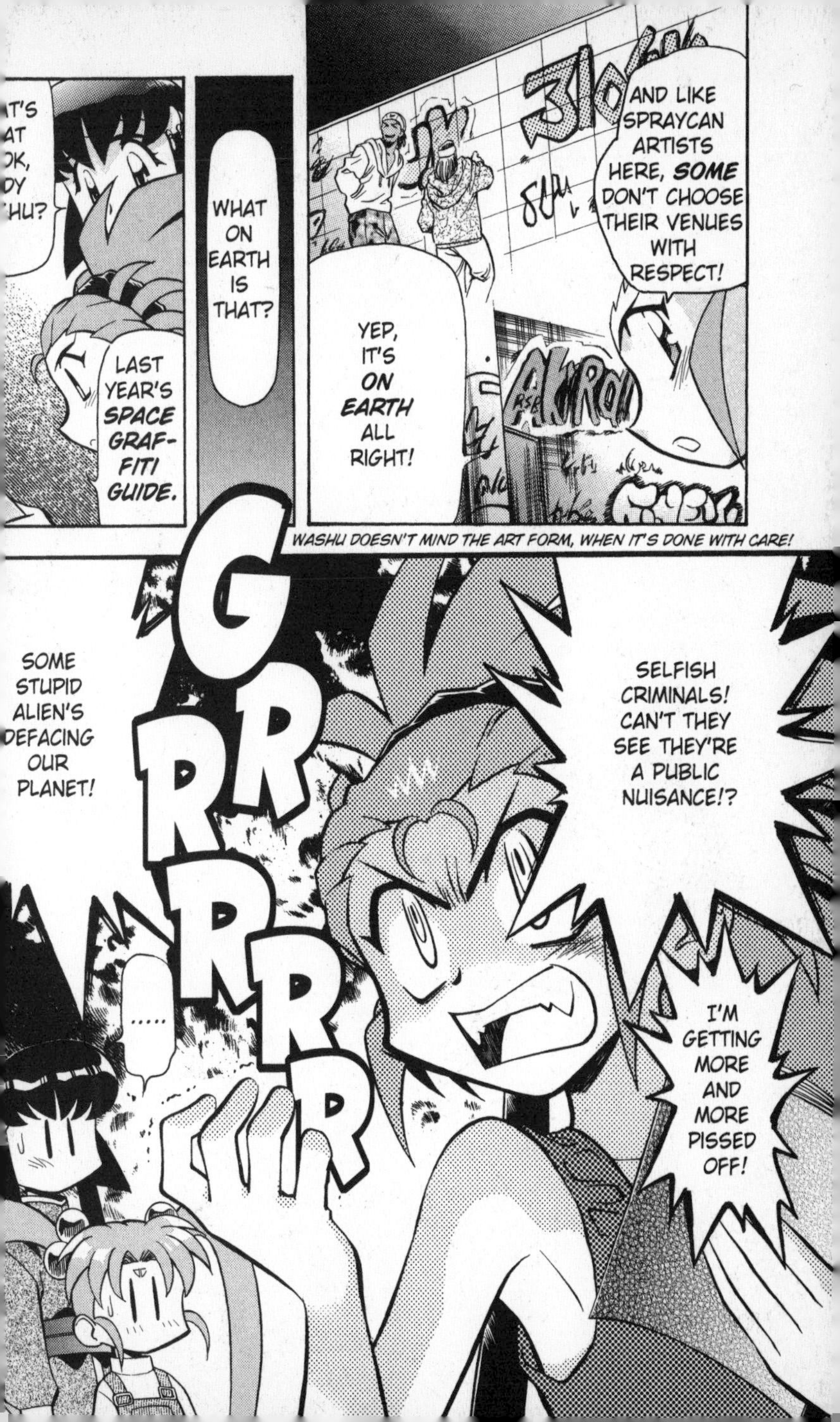
T'S AT OK, DY HU?
LAST YEAR'S SPACE GRAF-FITI GUIDE.
WHAT ON EARTH IS THAT?
YEP, IT'S ON EARTH ALL RIGHT!
AND LIKE SPRAYCAN ARTISTS HERE, SOME DON'T CHOOSE THEIR VENUES WITH RESPECT!
WASHU DOESN'T MIND THE ART FORM, WHEN IT'S DONE WITH CARE!
SOME STUPID ALIEN'S DEFACING OUR PLANET!
GRRRRR
SELFISH CRIMINALS! CAN'T THEY SEE THEY'RE A PUBLIC NUISANCE!?
.....
I'M GETTING MORE AND MORE PISSED OFF!

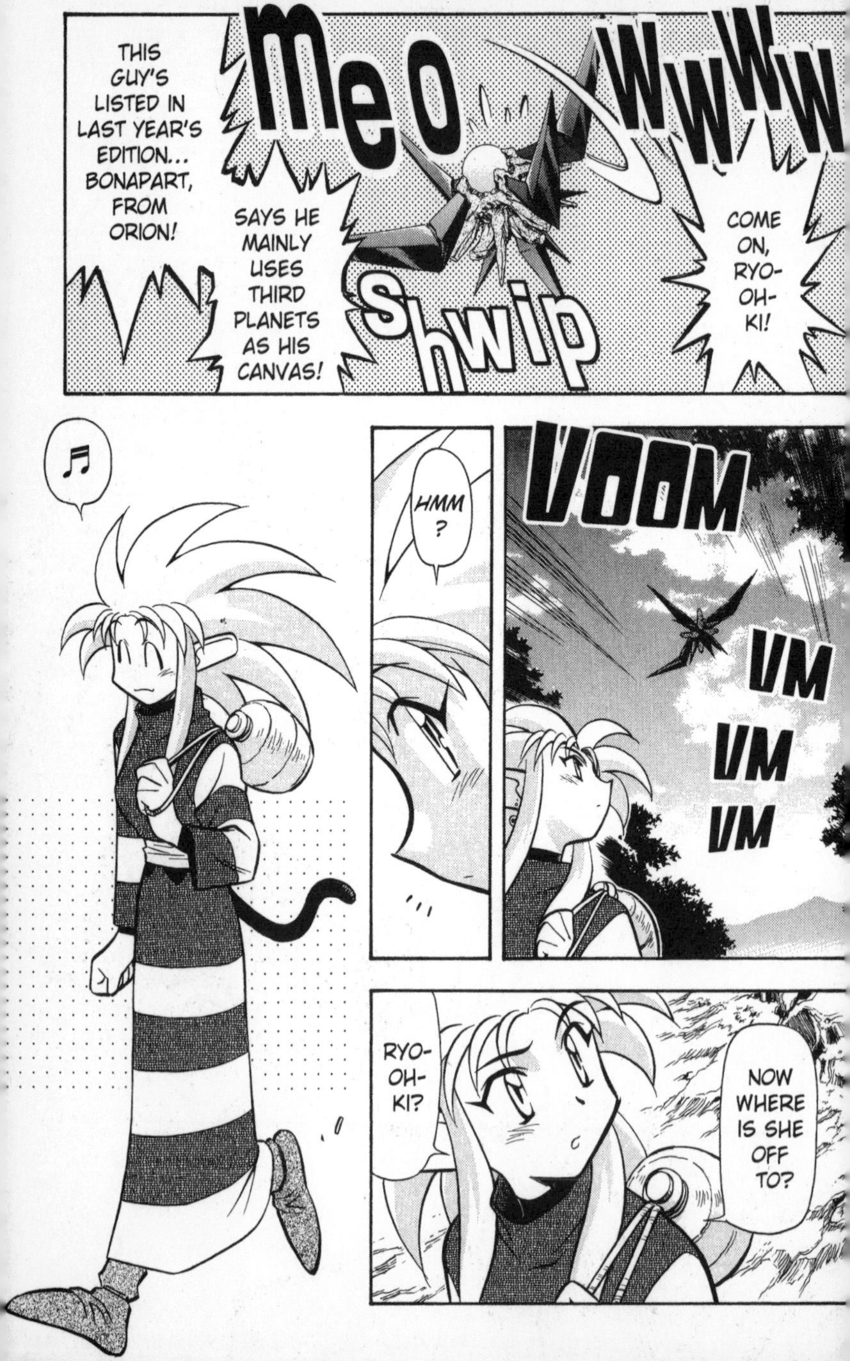
THIS GUY'S LISTED IN LAST YEAR'S EDITION... BONAPART, FROM ORION!
MEOWWWW
SAYS HE MAINLY USES THIRD PLANETS AS HIS CANVAS!
SHWIP
COME ON, RYO-OH-KI!
♬
HMM ?
VOOM
VM
VM
VM
RYO-OH-KI?
NOW WHERE IS SHE OFF TO?

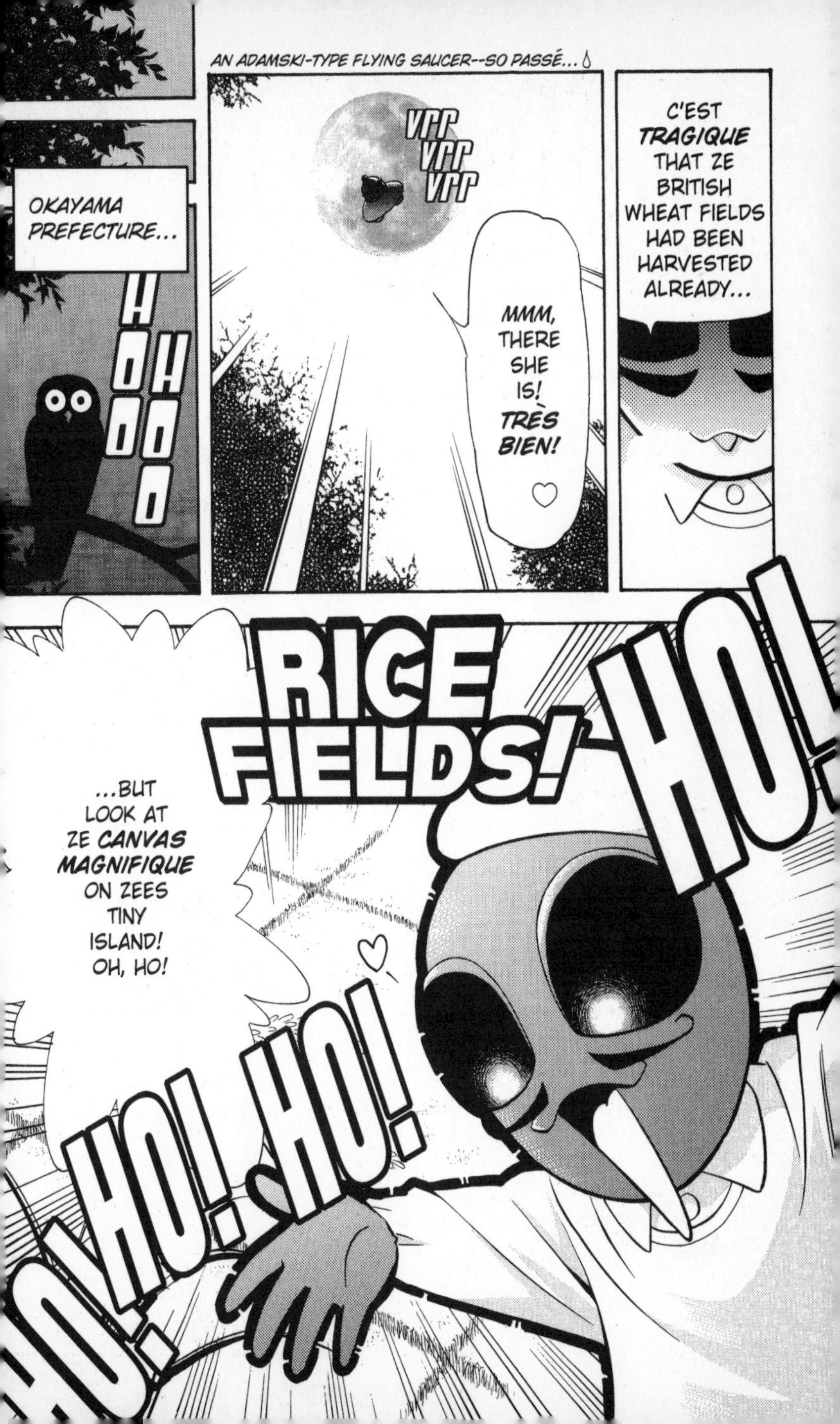
OKAYAMA PREFECTURE...
HOOOO HOOOO
AN ADAMSKI-TYPE FLYING SAUCER--SO PASSÉ...
VRR VRR VRR
MMM, THERE SHE IS! TRÈS BIEN!
C'EST TRAGIQUE THAT ZE BRITISH WHEAT FIELDS HAD BEEN HARVESTED ALREADY...
...BUT LOOK AT ZE CANVAS MAGNIFIQUE ON ZEES TINY ISLAND! OH, HO!
RICE FIELDS!
HO! HO! HO! HO!

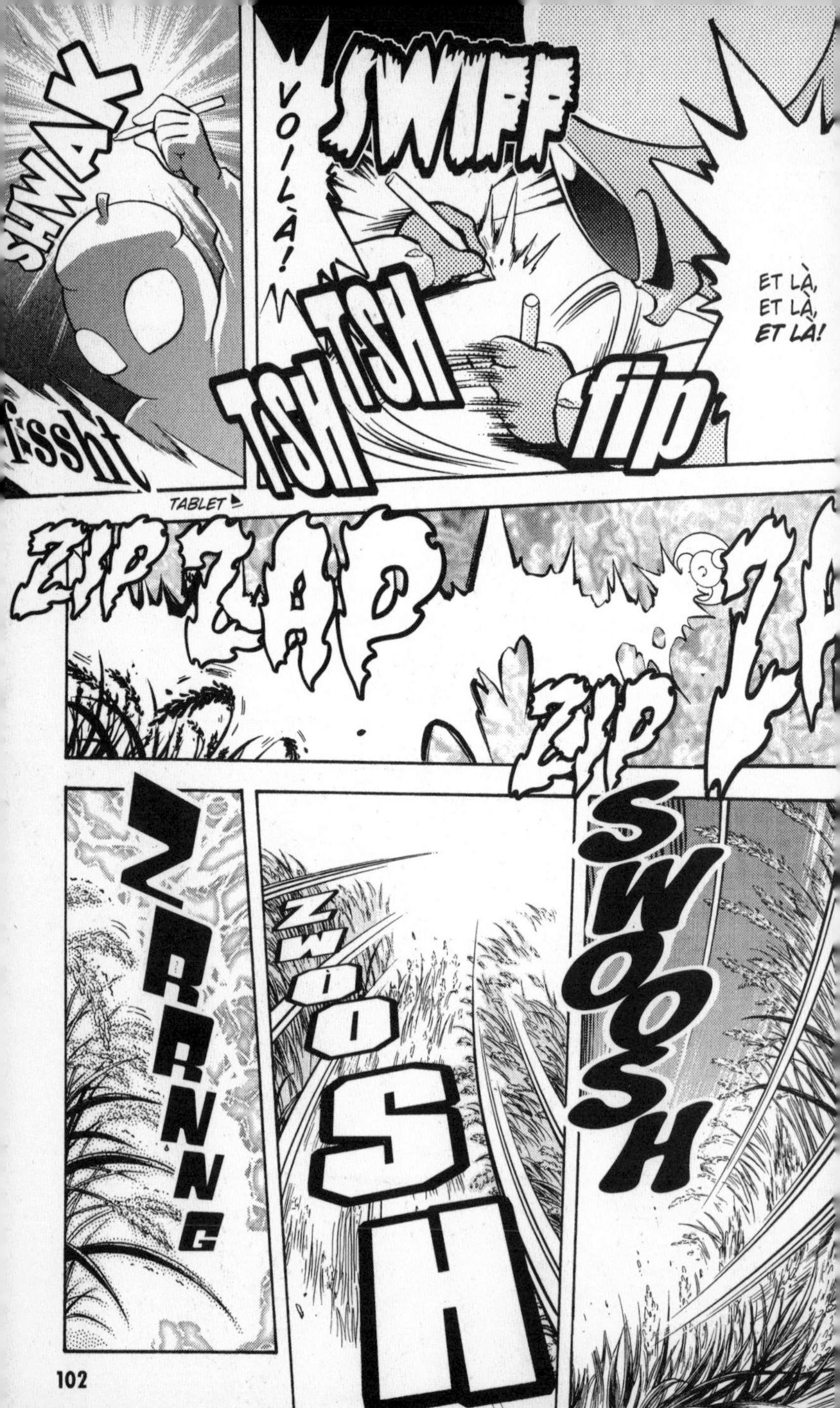
SHWAK
fissht
VOILÀ!
SWIFF
TSH TSH
TSH
fip
ET LÀ,
ET LÀ,
ET LÀ!
TABLET
ZIP ZAP
ZIP
ZIP
ZRRRNNG
ZWOOSH
SH
SWOOSH

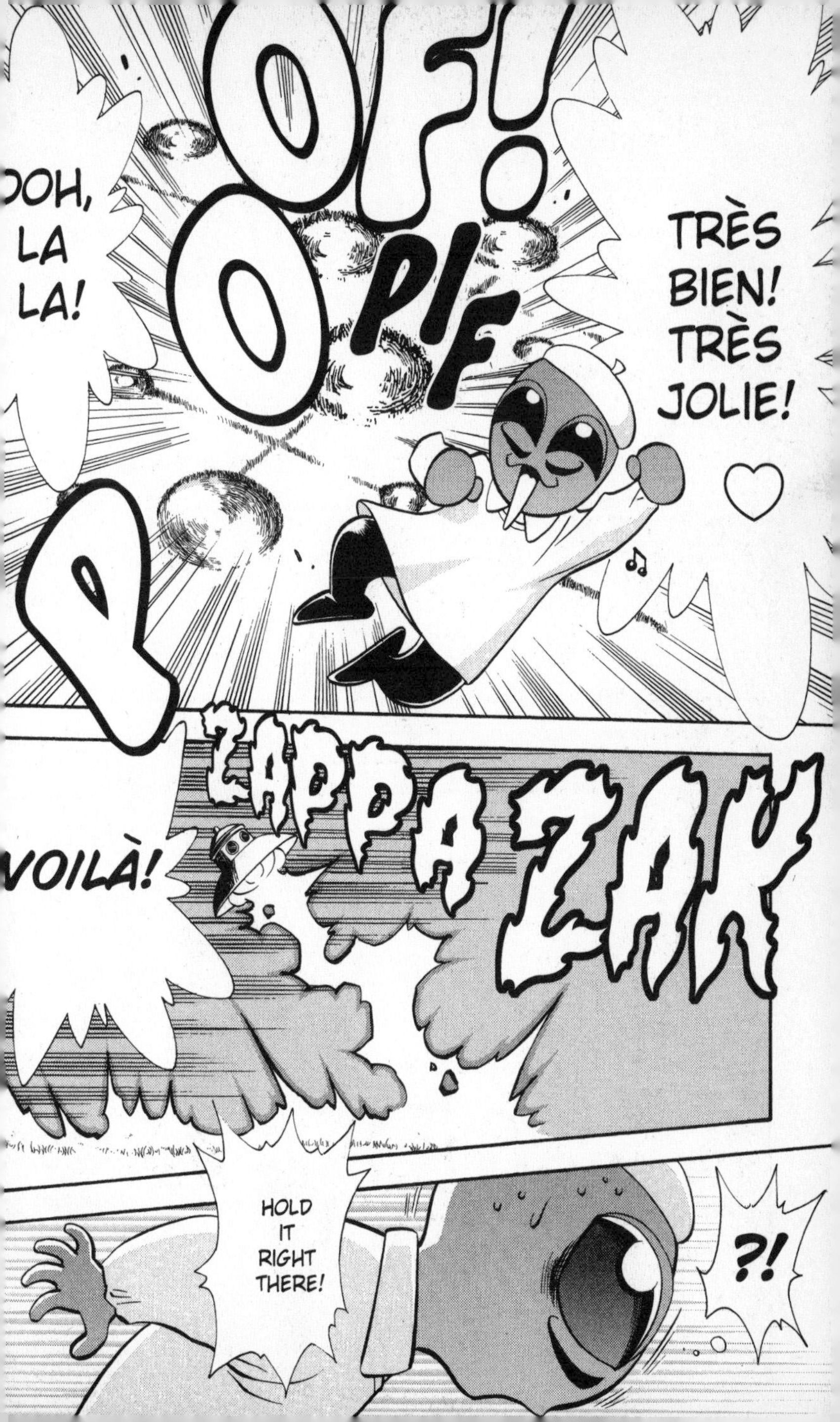
OOH, LA LA!
TRÈS BIEN! TRÈS JOLIE!
VOILÀ!
ZAPPA ZAK
HOLD IT RIGHT THERE!
?!

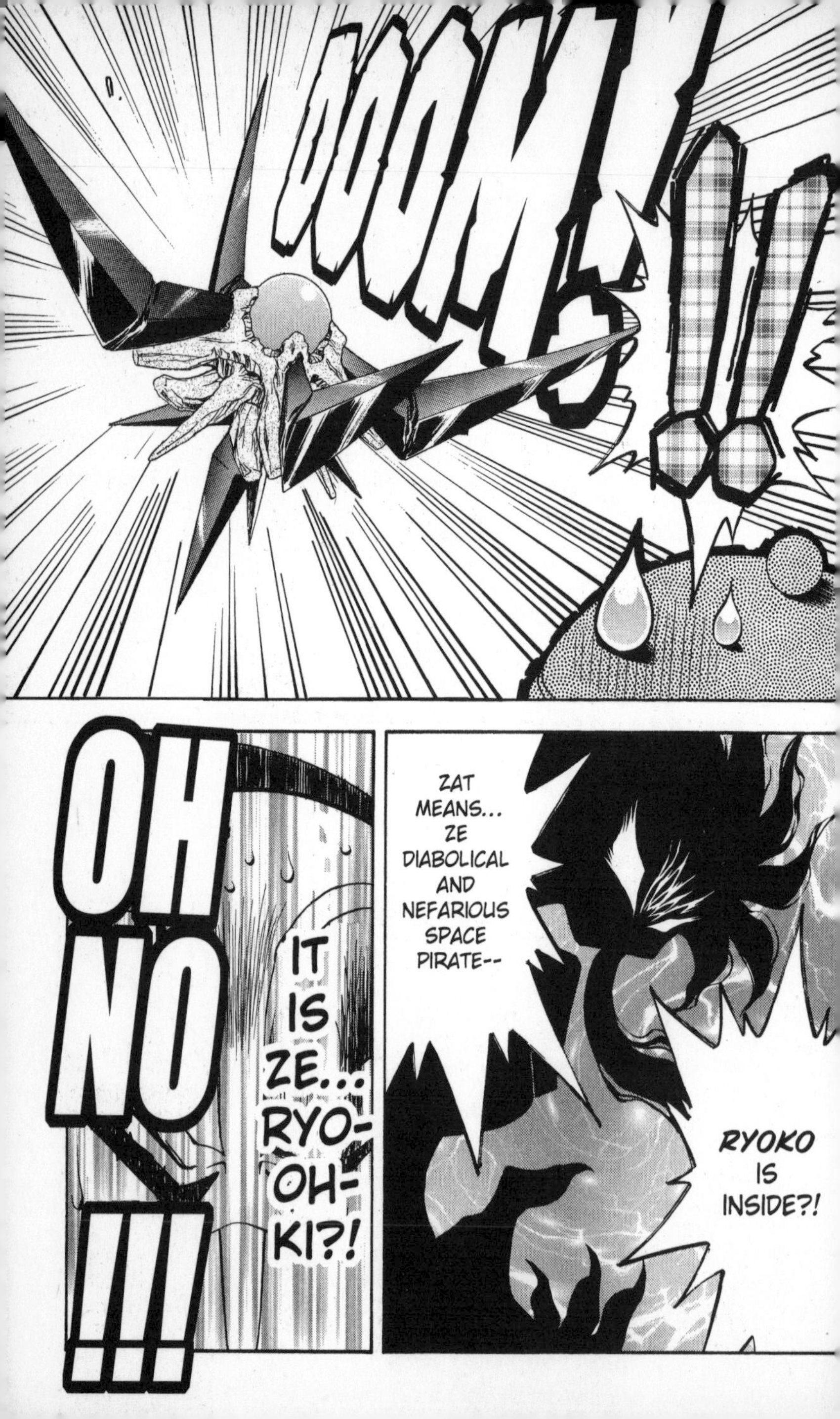

OH NO!!!!
IT IS ZE... RYO-OH-KI?!
ZAT MEANS... ZE DIABOLICAL AND NEFARIOUS SPACE PIRATE--
RYOKO IS INSIDE?!

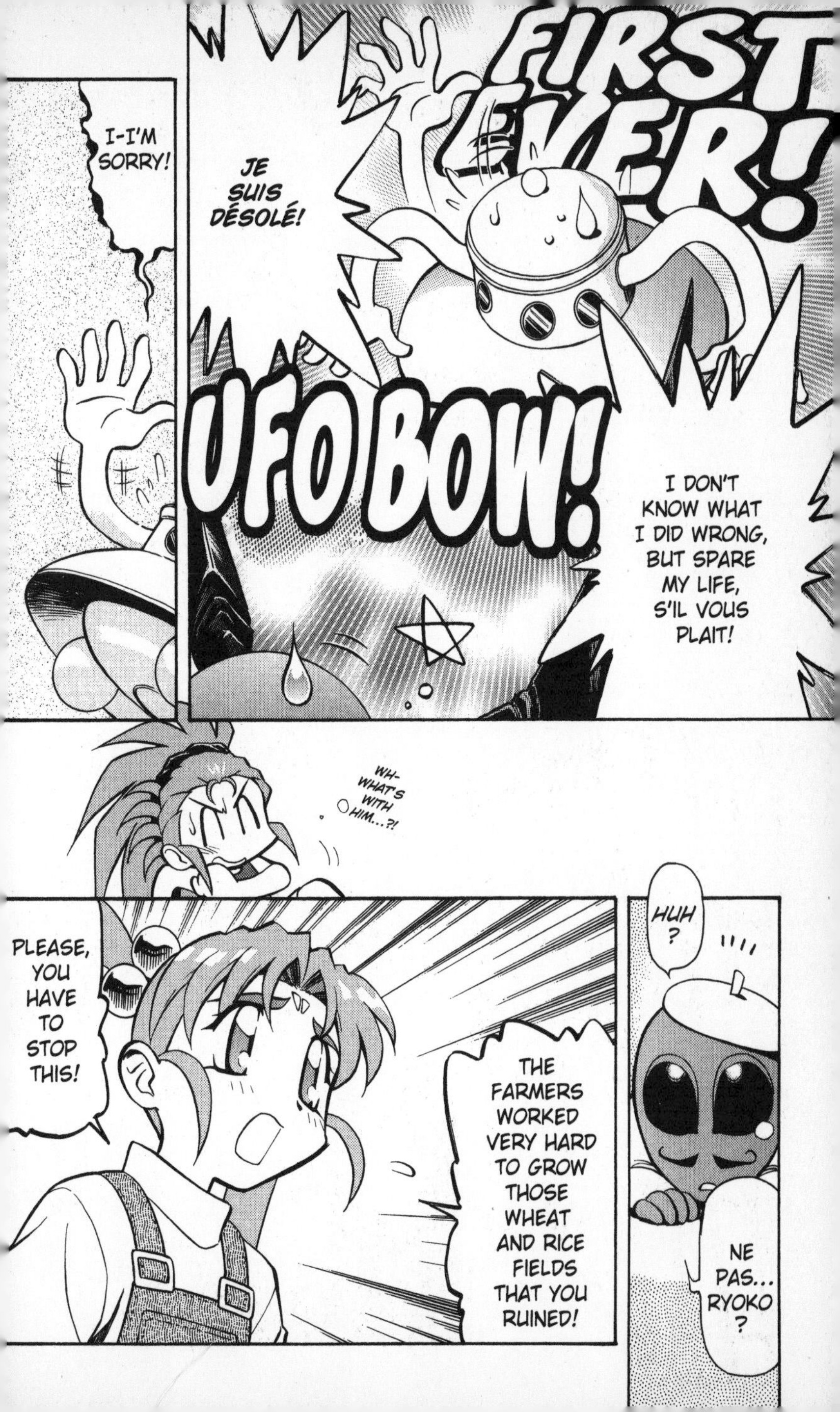
I-I'M SORRY!
JE SUIS DÉSOLÉ!
FIRST EVER!
UFO BOW!
I DON'T KNOW WHAT I DID WRONG, BUT SPARE MY LIFE, S'IL VOUS PLAIT!
WH-WHAT'S WITH HIM...?!
PLEASE, YOU HAVE TO STOP THIS!
THE FARMERS WORKED VERY HARD TO GROW THOSE WHEAT AND RICE FIELDS THAT YOU RUINED!
HUH?
NE PAS... RYOKO?

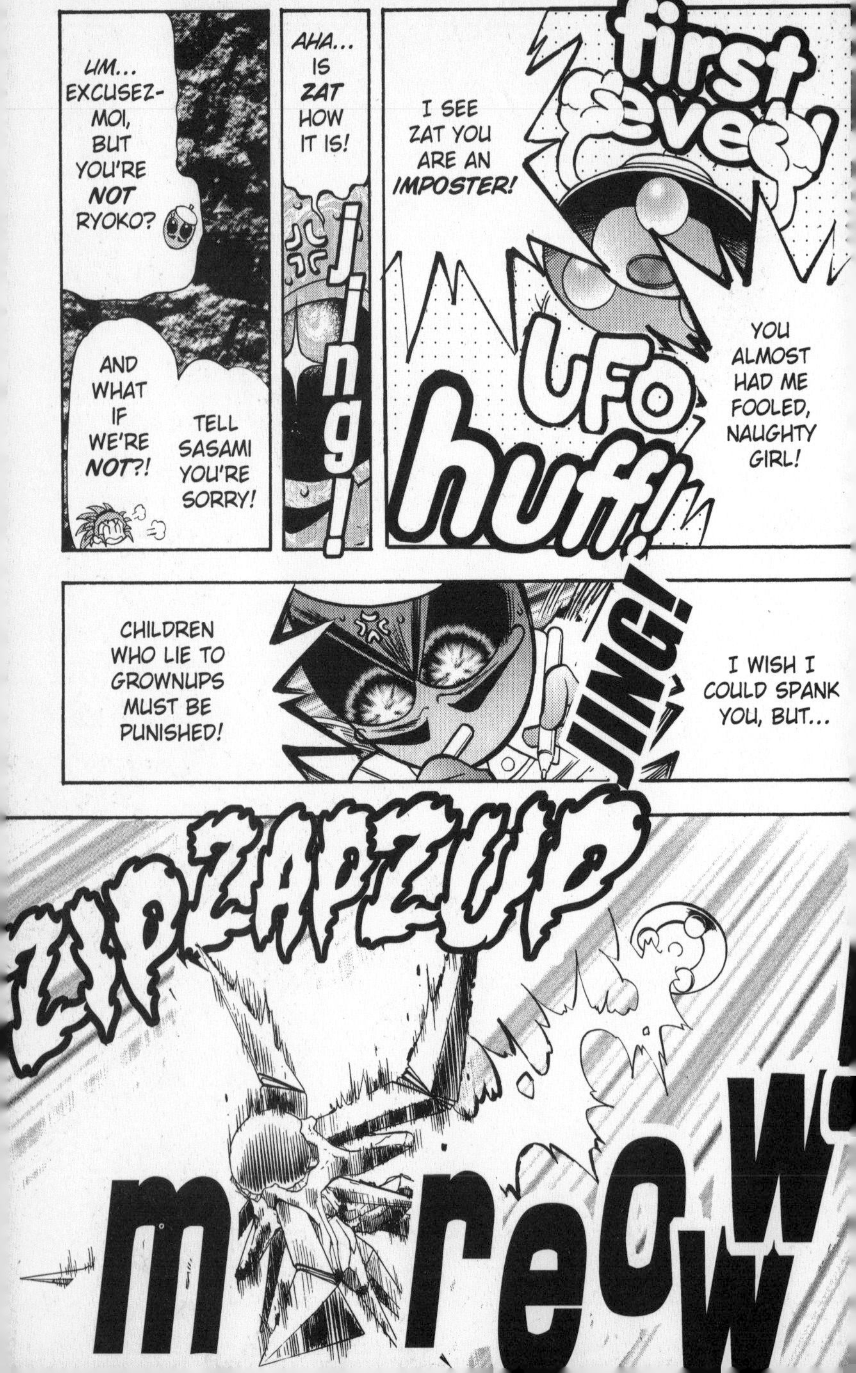
UM... EXCUSEZ-MOI, BUT YOU'RE NOT RYOKO?
AND WHAT IF WE'RE NOT?!
TELL SASAMI YOU'RE SORRY!
AHA... IS ZAT HOW IT IS!
jing!
I SEE ZAT YOU ARE AN IMPOSTER!
first eve
UFO huff!
YOU ALMOST HAD ME FOOLED, NAUGHTY GIRL!
CHILDREN WHO LIE TO GROWNUPS MUST BE PUNISHED!
JING!
I WISH I COULD SPANK YOU, BUT...
ZIPZAPZUP
m reow

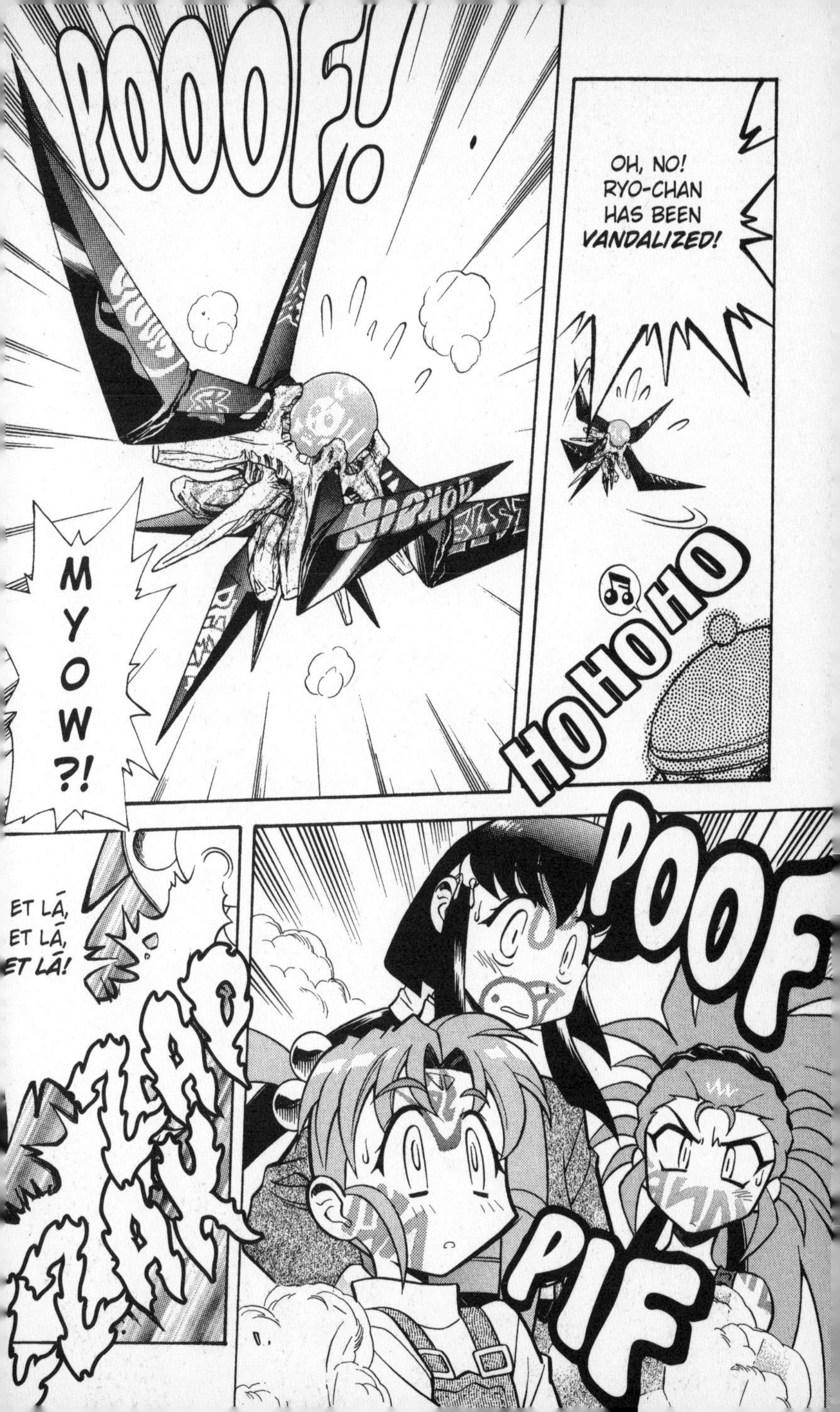
POOOF!
MYOW?!
OH, NO! RYO-CHAN HAS BEEN VANDALIZED!
HOHOHO
ET LÀ, ET LÀ, ET LÀ!
POOF
PIF

H-HEY, WHAT THE HECK IS THIS?!
OH, NO! IT'S NOT COMING OFF!
HOHOHOHO
thb thb
SILLY!
MADEMOISELLE, ZAT WAS A SLIP OF YOUR TONGUE! I AM NO VANDAL! ZAT'S WHAT YOU DESERVE!
I HAVE MADE YOU ZE WORK OF ART!
IT IS QUITE ZE HONOR TO BE CHOSEN AS MY CANVAS!
GRRR
WIPE THIS OFF US, YOU STUPID JERK!

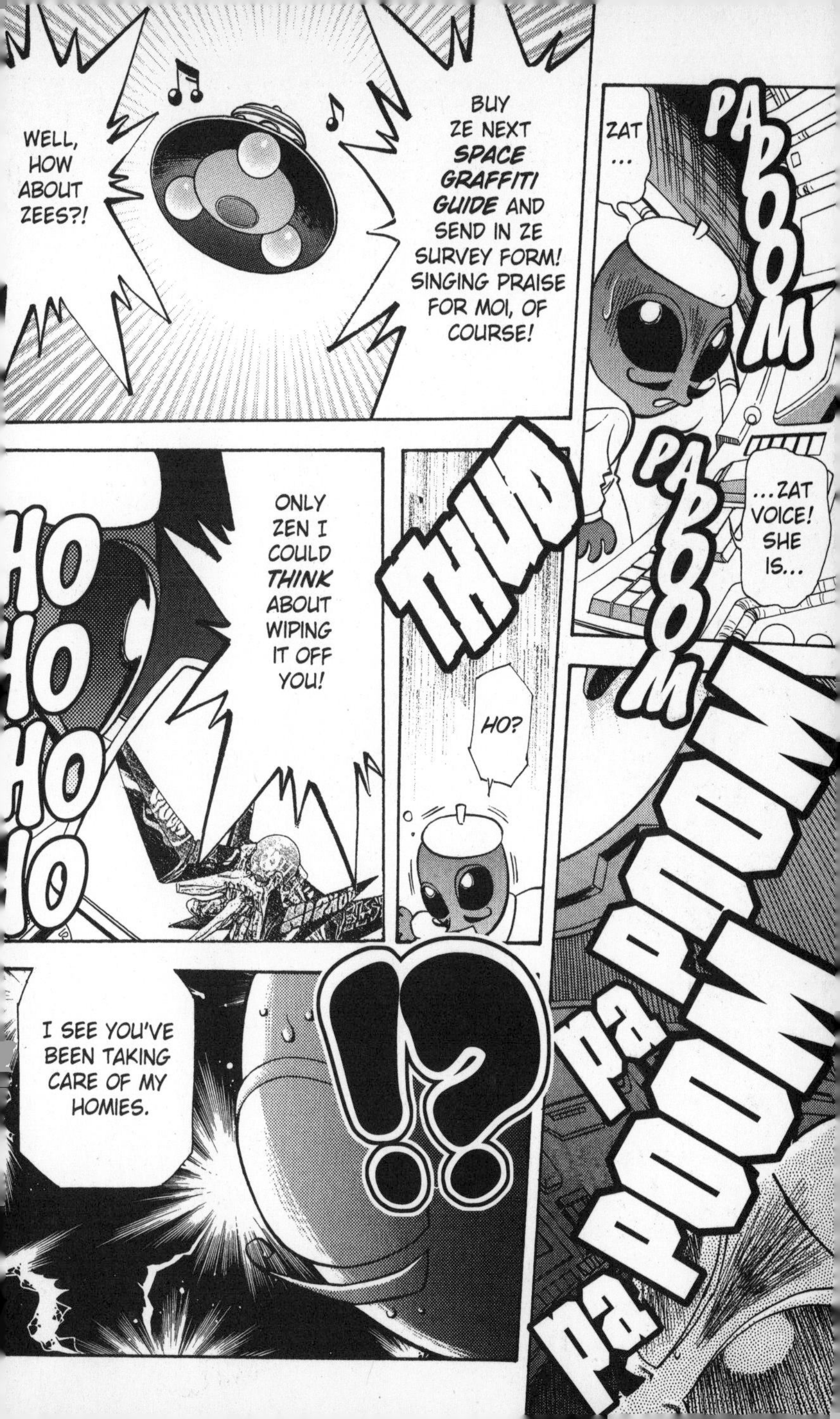
WELL, HOW ABOUT ZEES?!
BUY ZE NEXT SPACE GRAFFITI GUIDE AND SEND IN ZE SURVEY FORM! SINGING PRAISE FOR MOI, OF COURSE!
ZAT ...
PABOOM
PABOOM
...ZAT VOICE! SHE IS...
HO HO HO HO
ONLY ZEN I COULD THINK ABOUT WIPING IT OFF YOU!
THUD
HO?
I SEE YOU'VE BEEN TAKING CARE OF MY HOMIES.
!?
paBOOM
paBOOM

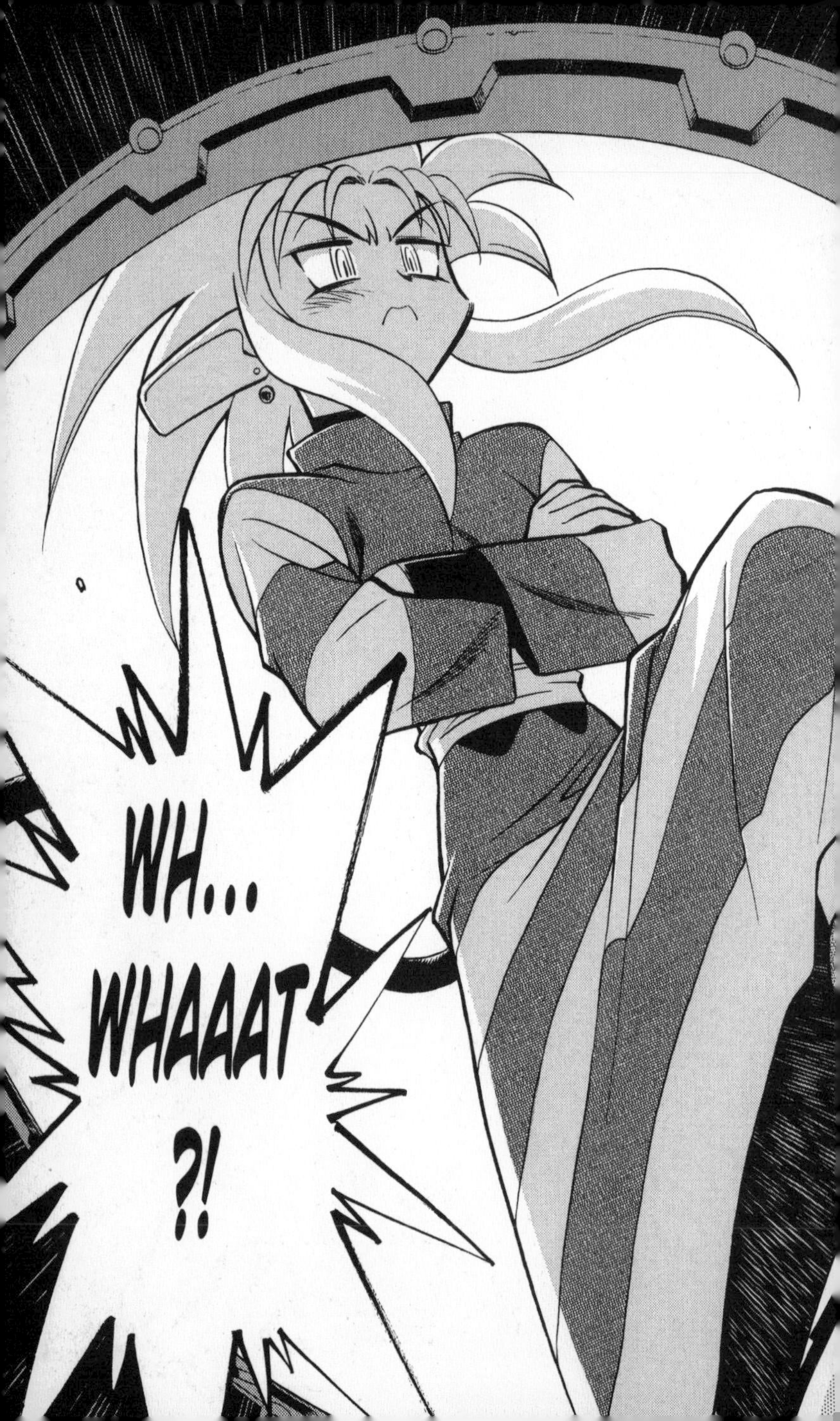
WH... WHAAAT?!

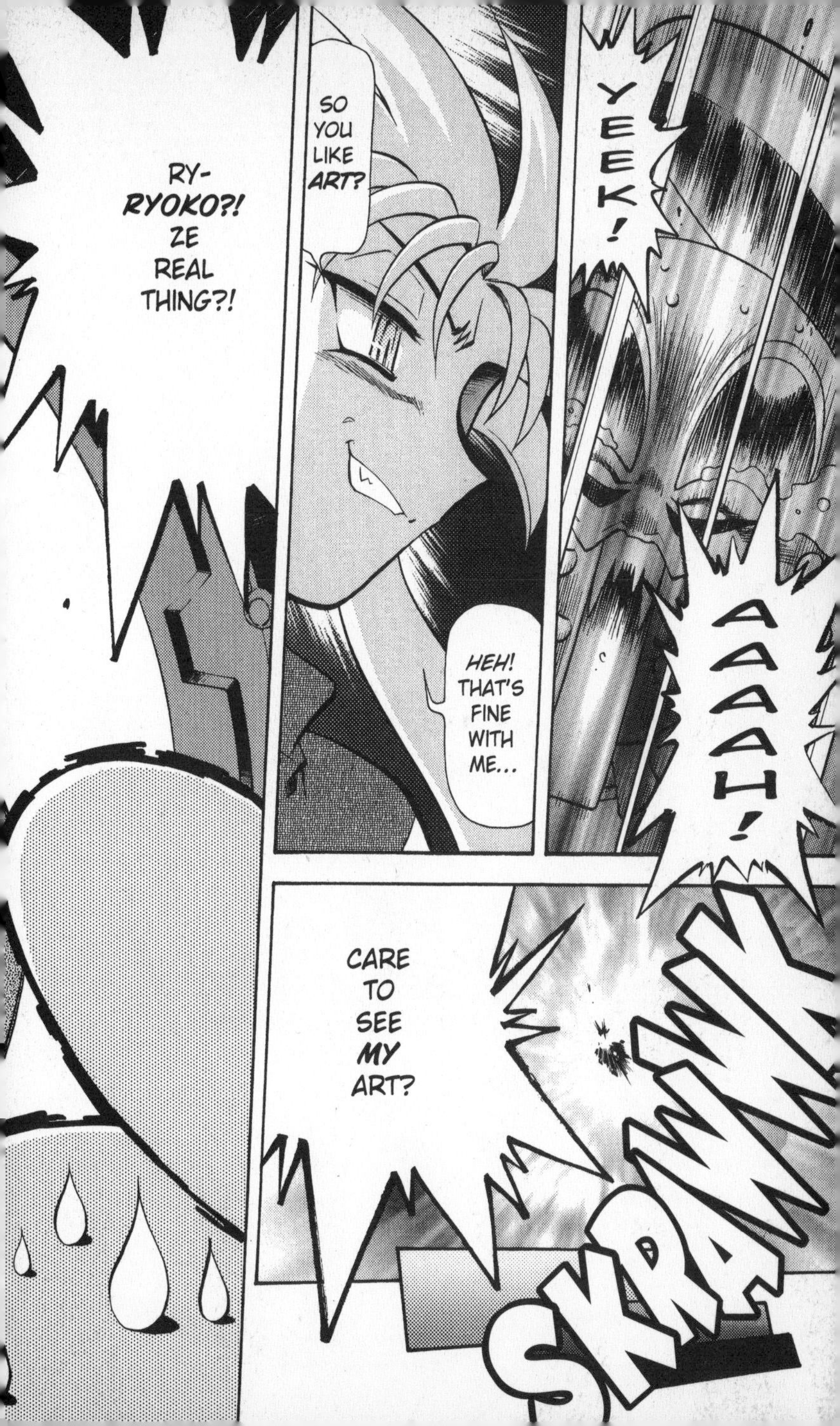
RY- *RYOKO?!* ZE REAL THING?!
SO YOU LIKE *ART?*
HEH! THAT'S FINE WITH ME...
YEEK!
AAAAH!
CARE TO SEE *MY* ART?
SKRA

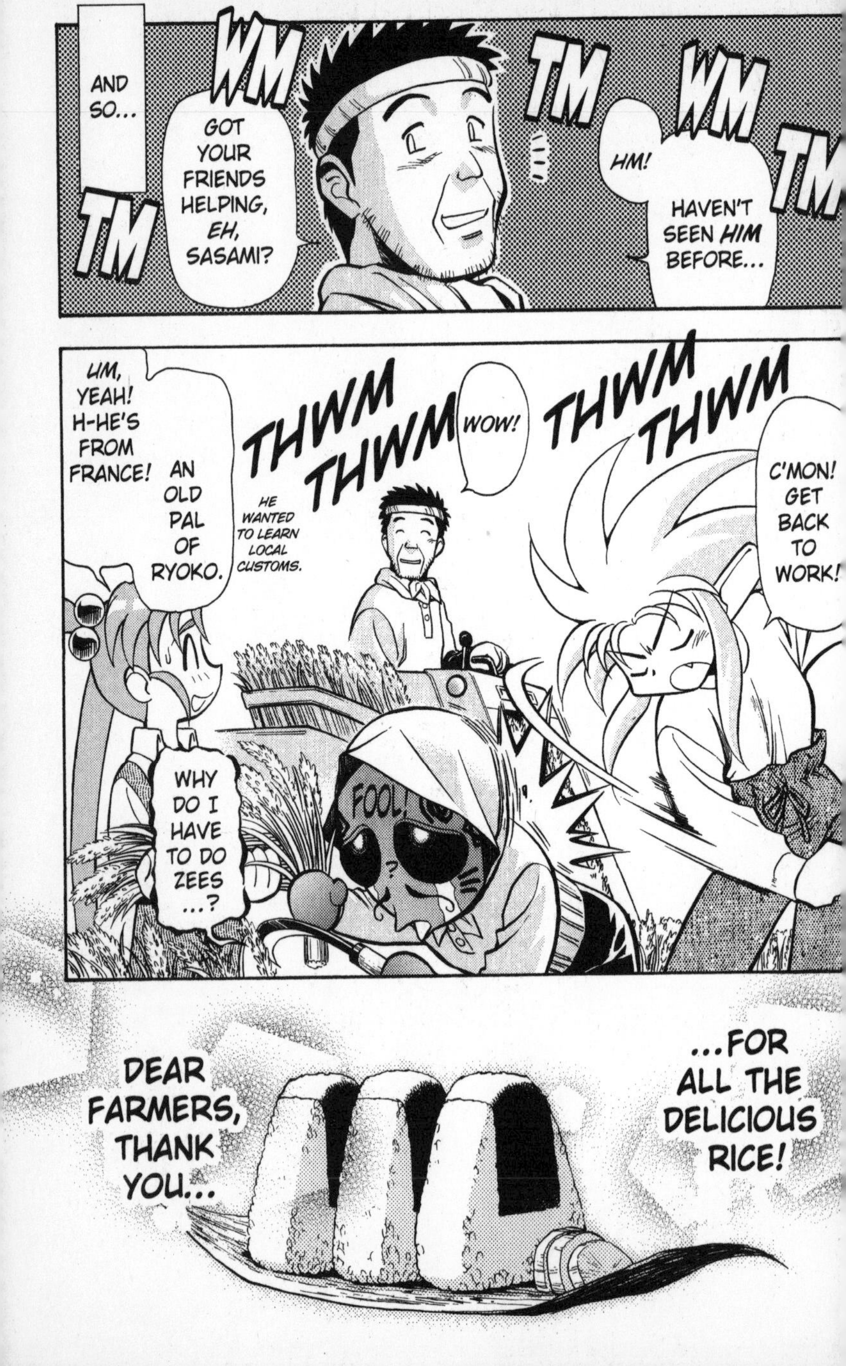
AND SO...
WM
GOT YOUR FRIENDS HELPING, EH, SASAMI?
TM
TM
WM
HM!
HAVEN'T SEEN HIM BEFORE...
TM
UM, YEAH! H-HE'S FROM FRANCE!
AN OLD PAL OF RYOKO.
HE WANTED TO LEARN LOCAL CUSTOMS.
THWM THWM
WOW!
THWM THWM
C'MON! GET BACK TO WORK!
WHY DO I HAVE TO DO ZEES ...?
FOOL!
DEAR FARMERS, THANK YOU...
...FOR ALL THE DELICIOUS RICE!

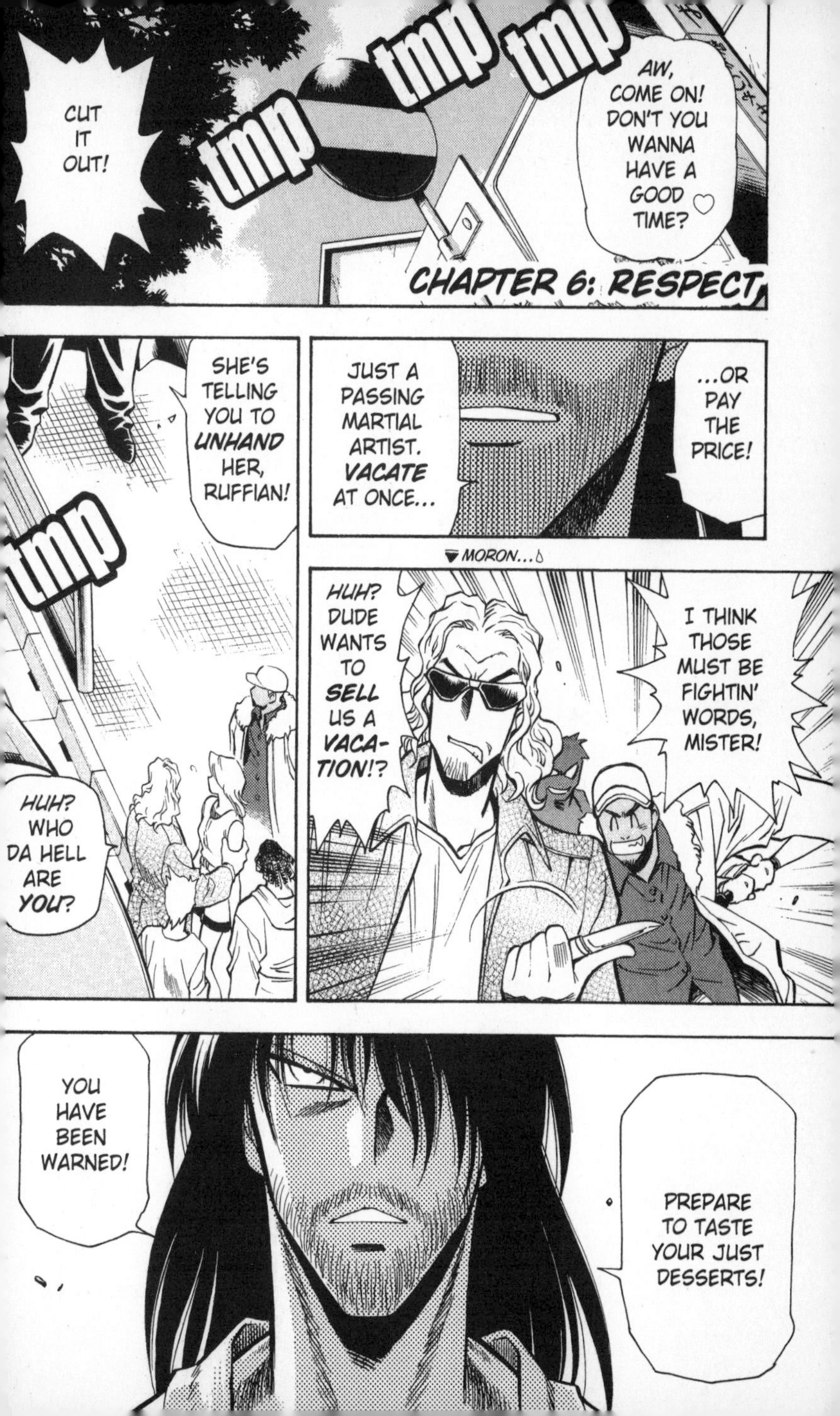
CUT IT OUT!
tmp tmp tmp tmp
AW, COME ON! DON'T YOU WANNA HAVE A GOOD TIME? ♡
CHAPTER 6: RESPECT
SHE'S TELLING YOU TO UNHAND HER, RUFFIAN!
tmp
HUH? WHO DA HELL ARE YOU?
JUST A PASSING MARTIAL ARTIST. VACATE AT ONCE...
...OR PAY THE PRICE!
MORON...
HUH? DUDE WANTS TO SELL US A VACA-TION!?
I THINK THOSE MUST BE FIGHTIN' WORDS, MISTER!
YOU HAVE BEEN WARNED!
PREPARE TO TASTE YOUR JUST DESSERTS!

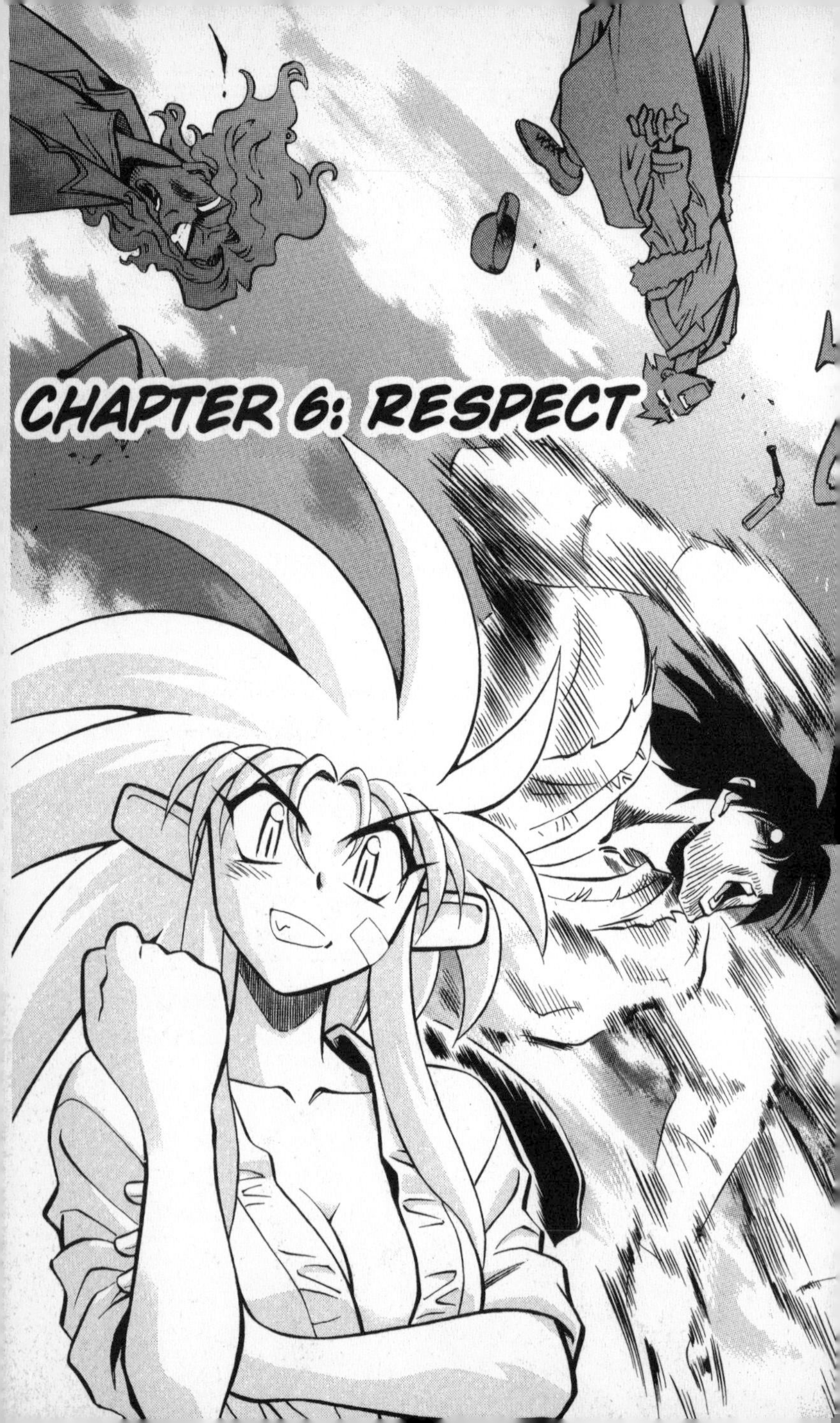
CHAPTER 6: RESPECT

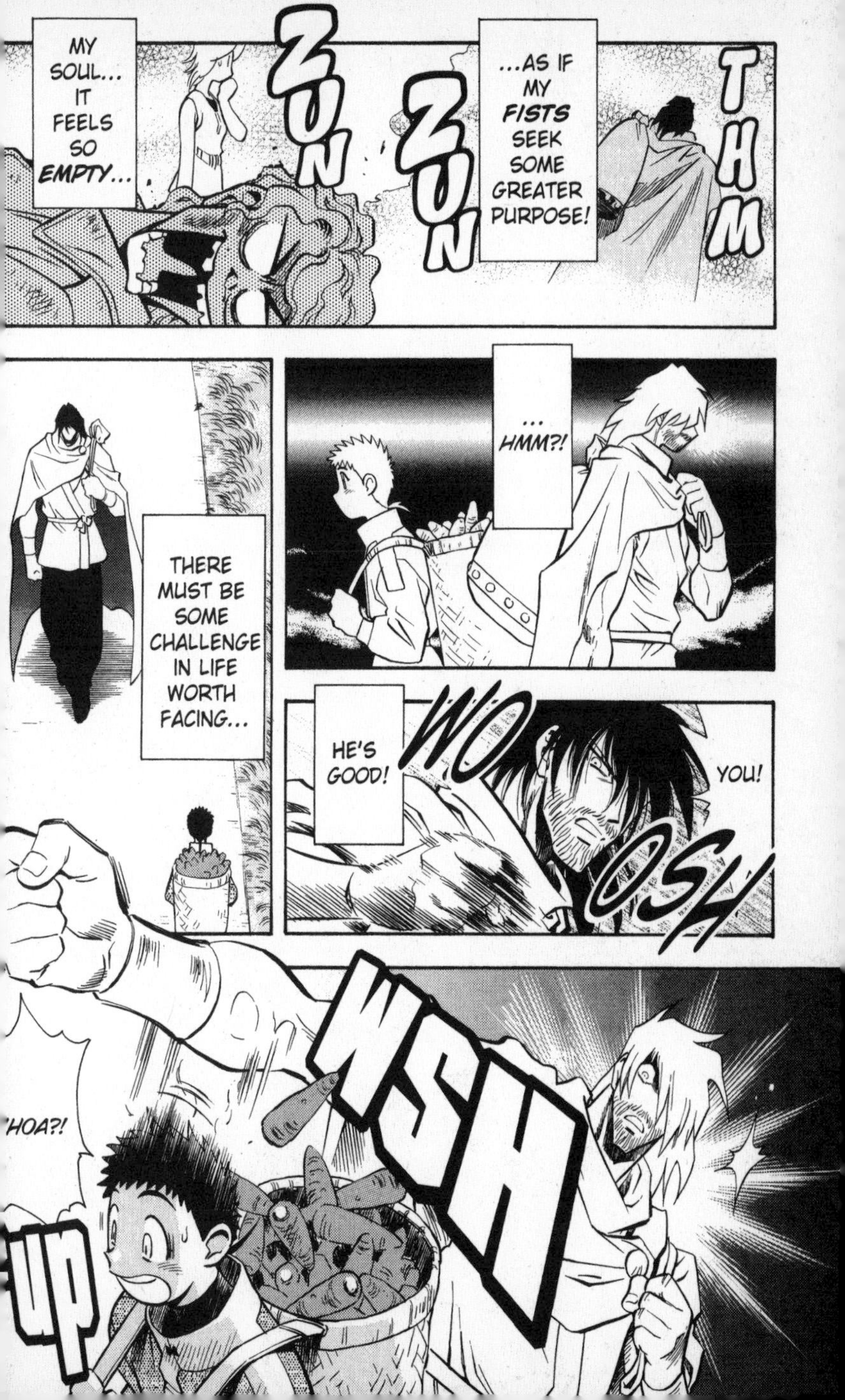

MY SOUL... IT FEELS SO EMPTY...
ZUN ZUN
...AS IF MY FISTS SEEK SOME GREATER PURPOSE!
THM
THERE MUST BE SOME CHALLENGE IN LIFE WORTH FACING...
... HMM?!
HE'S GOOD!
WOOSH
YOU!
HOA?!
WSH
up

HE... HE DODGED MY FIST!?

TENCHI, TENCHI, I LOVE YOOOU!!

WHAT'S UP DOWN THERE?!

FAP

FAP

WHAT DID I DO TO YOU?!

FUHFUH FUHFUH FUHFUH FUH!

ka FAP

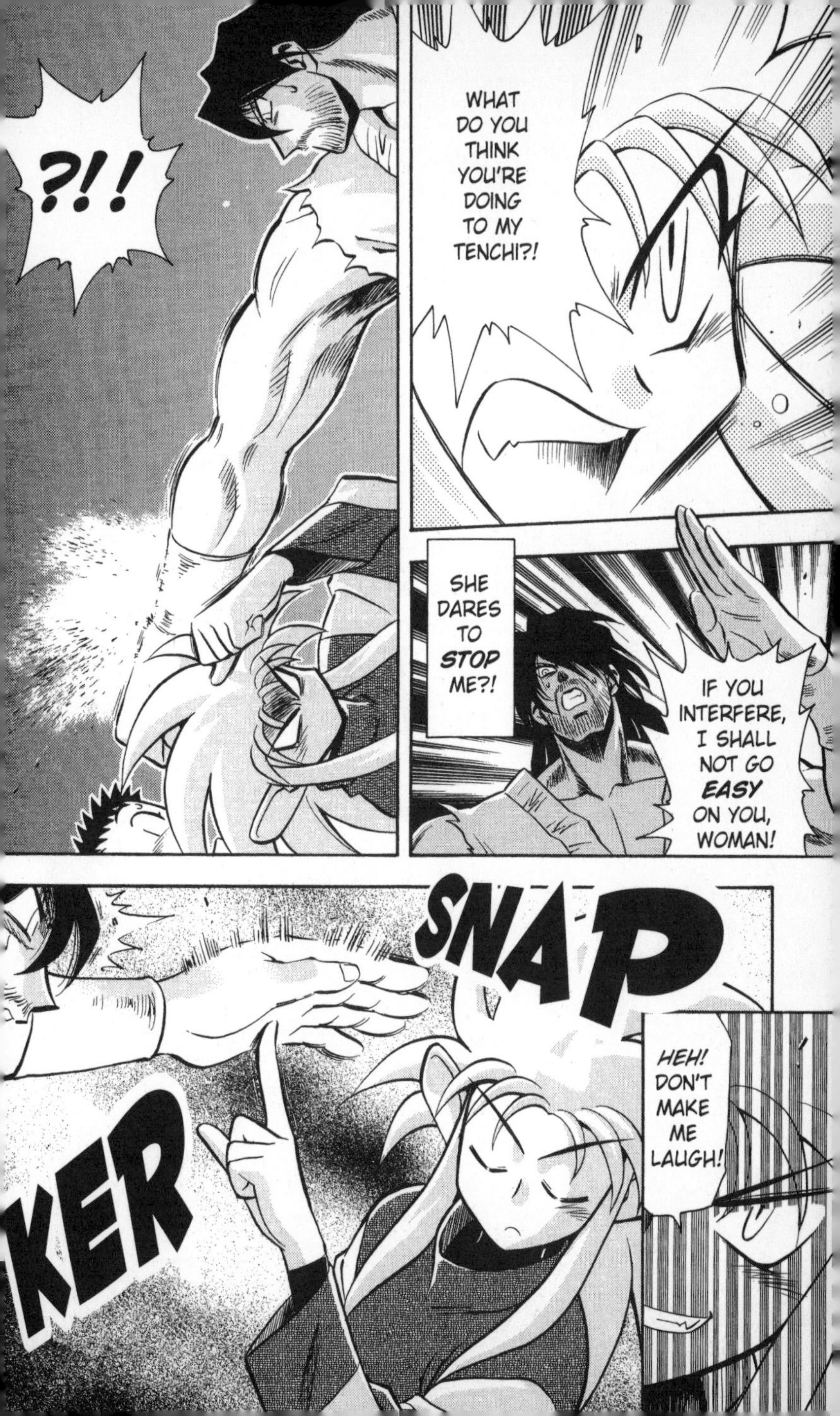
?!!
WHAT DO YOU THINK YOU'RE DOING TO MY TENCHI?!
SHE DARES TO STOP ME?!
IF YOU INTERFERE, I SHALL NOT GO EASY ON YOU, WOMAN!
SNAP
KER
HEH! DON'T MAKE ME LAUGH!

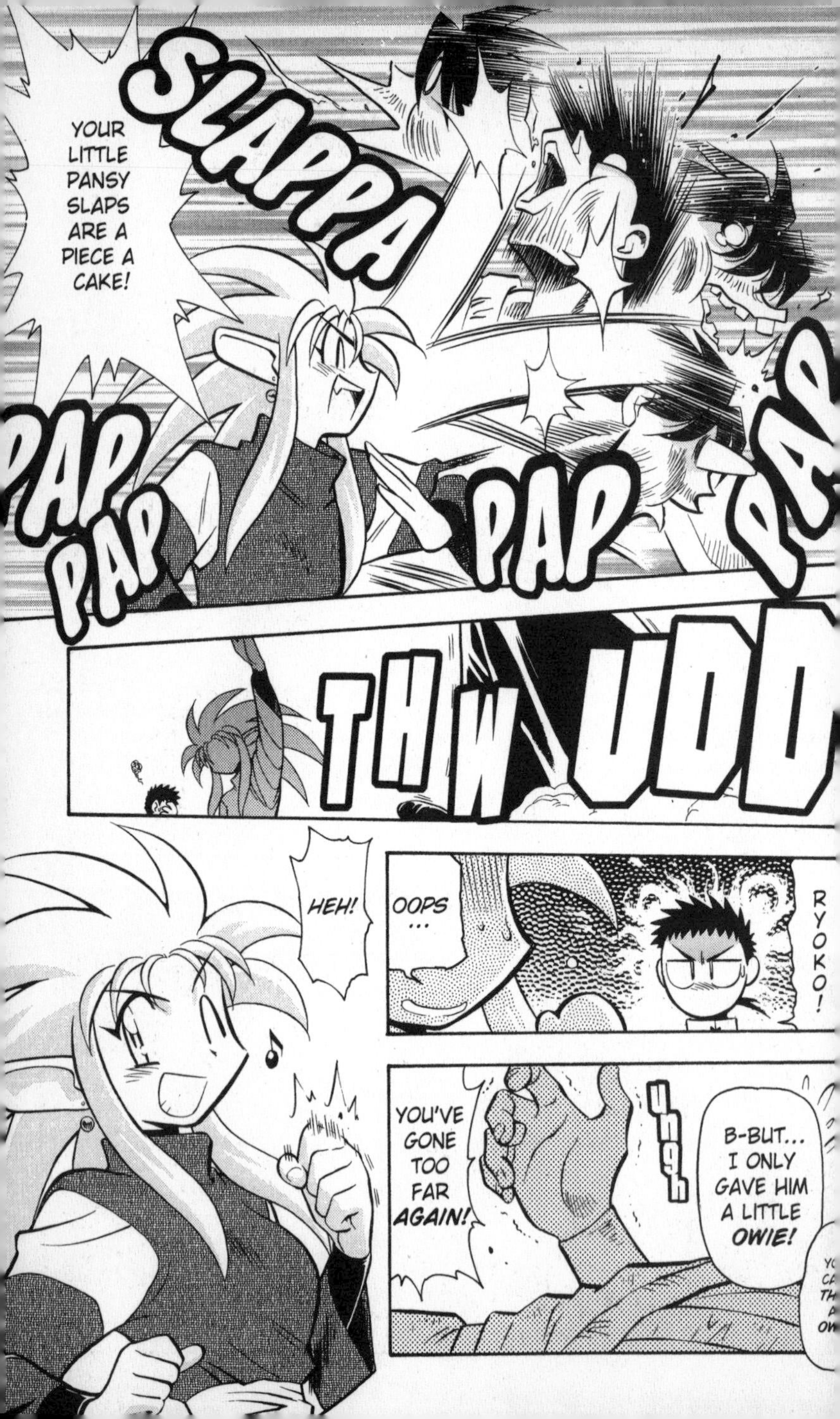
SLAPPA
YOUR LITTLE PANSY SLAPS ARE A PIECE A CAKE!
PAP PAP
PAP
PAP
THWUDD
HEH!
OOPS ...
RYOKO!
YOU'VE GONE TOO FAR AGAIN!
ungh
B-BUT... I ONLY GAVE HIM A LITTLE OWIE!

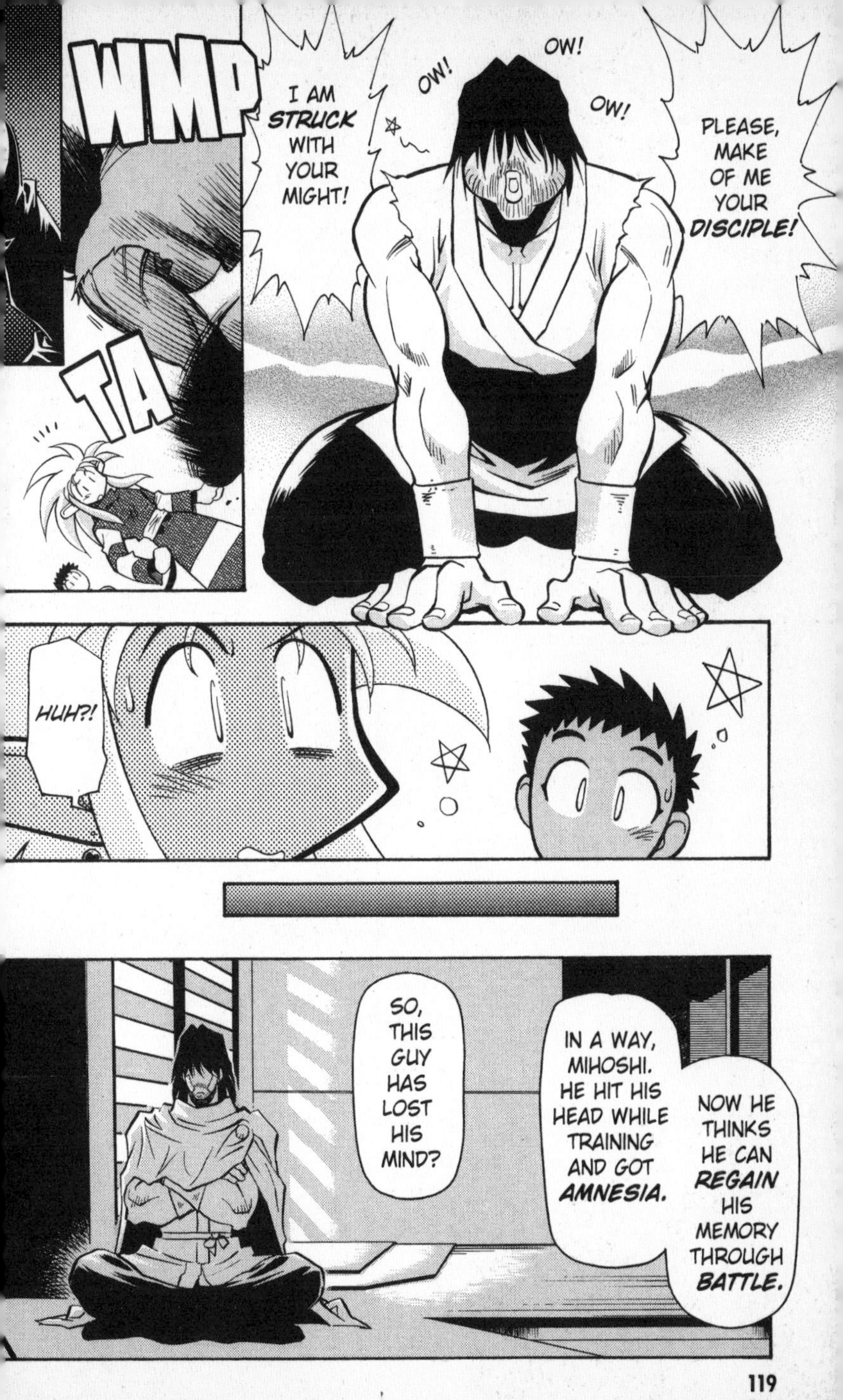
WMP
TA
I AM STRUCK WITH YOUR MIGHT!
OW!
OW!
OW!
PLEASE, MAKE OF ME YOUR DISCIPLE!
HUH?!
SO, THIS GUY HAS LOST HIS MIND?
IN A WAY, MIHOSHI. HE HIT HIS HEAD WHILE TRAINING AND GOT AMNESIA.
NOW HE THINKS HE CAN REGAIN HIS MEMORY THROUGH BATTLE.

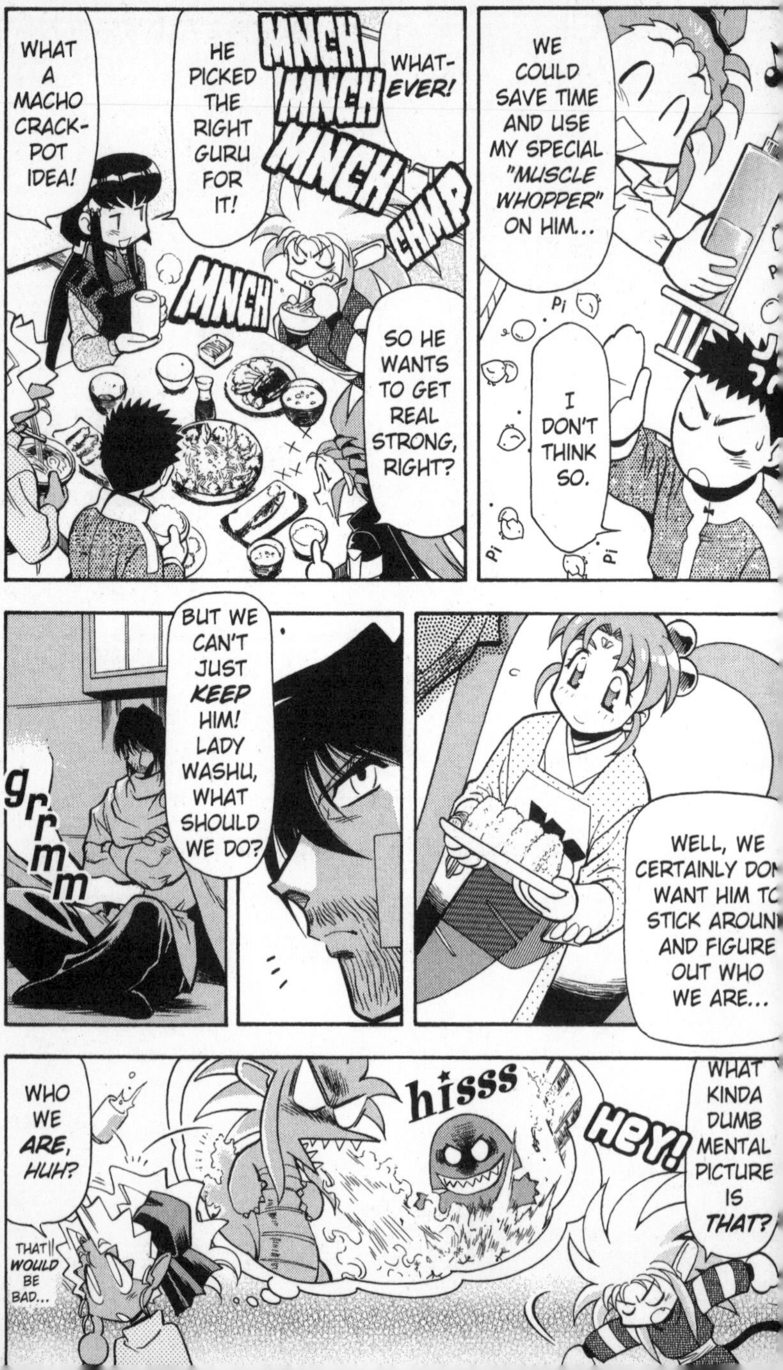
WHAT A MACHO CRACK-POT IDEA!
HE PICKED THE RIGHT GURU FOR IT!
MNCH MNCH MNCH
WHAT-EVER!
CHMP
MNCH
SO HE WANTS TO GET REAL STRONG, RIGHT?
WE COULD SAVE TIME AND USE MY SPECIAL "MUSCLE WHOPPER" ON HIM...
Pi
I DON'T THINK SO.
Pi
Pi
grrmm
BUT WE CAN'T JUST KEEP HIM! LADY WASHU, WHAT SHOULD WE DO?
WELL, WE CERTAINLY DON WANT HIM TO STICK AROUN AND FIGURE OUT WHO WE ARE...
WHO WE ARE, HUH?
THAT WOULD BE BAD...
hisss
HEY!
WHAT KINDA DUMB MENTAL PICTURE IS THAT?

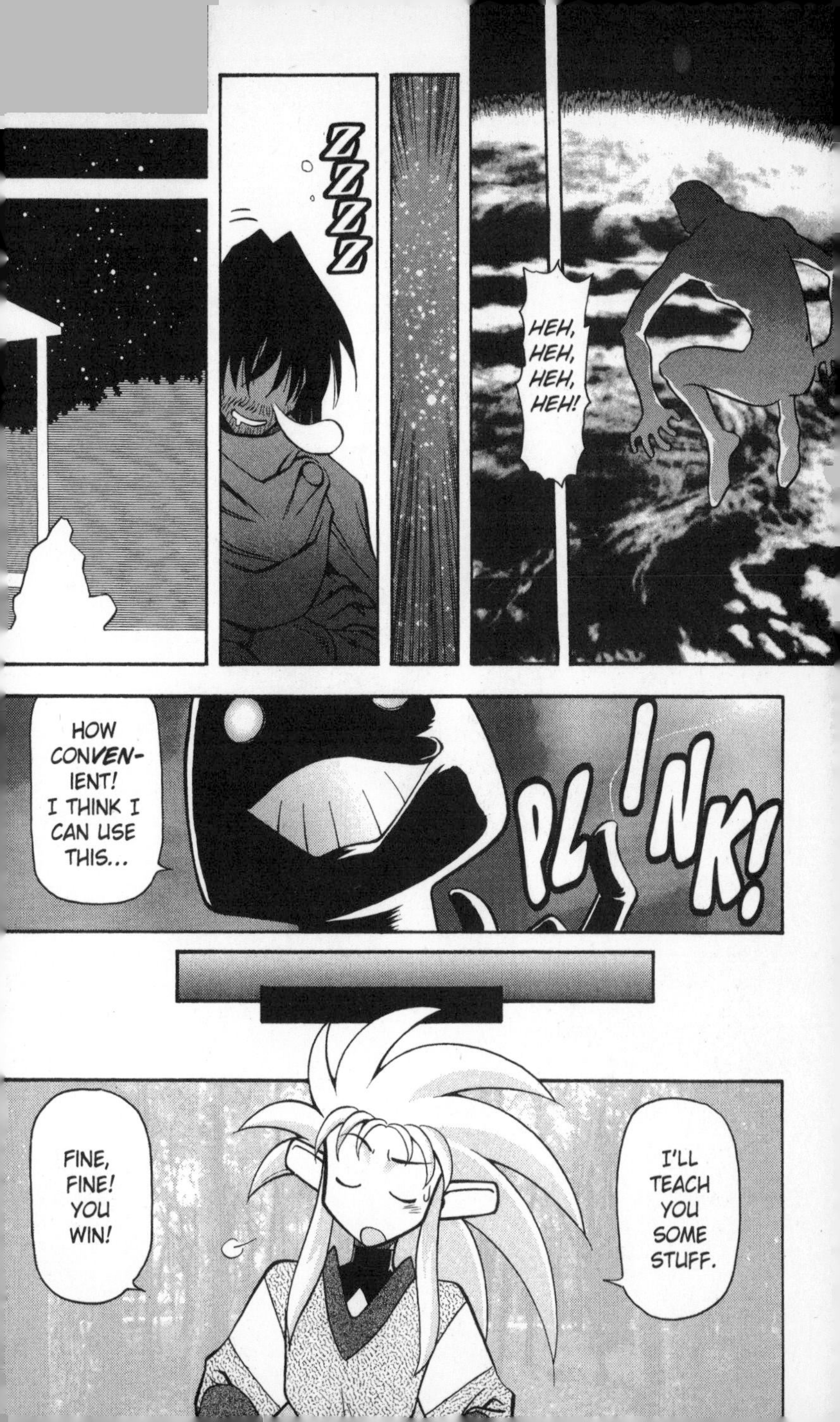
ZZZZZ
HEH, HEH, HEH, HEH!
HOW CONVEN-IENT! I THINK I CAN USE THIS...
PLINK!
FINE, FINE! YOU WIN!
I'LL TEACH YOU SOME STUFF.

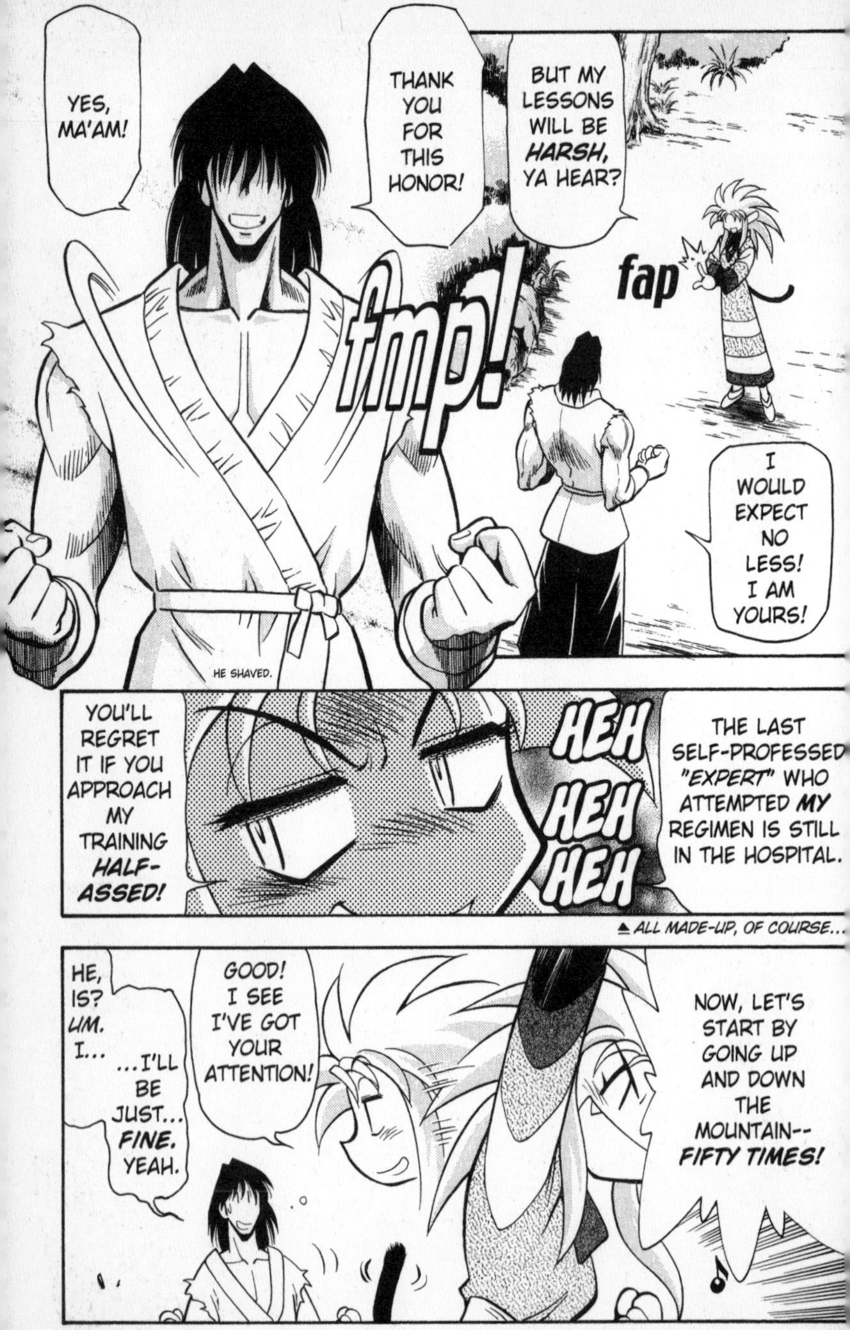
YES, MA'AM!
THANK YOU FOR THIS HONOR!
fmp!
HE SHAVED.
BUT MY LESSONS WILL BE *HARSH,* YA HEAR?
fap
I WOULD EXPECT NO LESS! I AM YOURS!
YOU'LL REGRET IT IF YOU APPROACH MY TRAINING *HALF-ASSED!*
HEH HEH HEH
THE LAST SELF-PROFESSED "*EXPERT*" WHO ATTEMPTED *MY* REGIMEN IS STILL IN THE HOSPITAL.
▲ALL MADE-UP, OF COURSE...
HE, IS? *UM.* I...
...I'LL BE JUST... *FINE.* YEAH.
GOOD! I SEE I'VE GOT YOUR ATTENTION!
NOW, LET'S START BY GOING UP AND DOWN THE MOUNTAIN-- *FIFTY TIMES!*

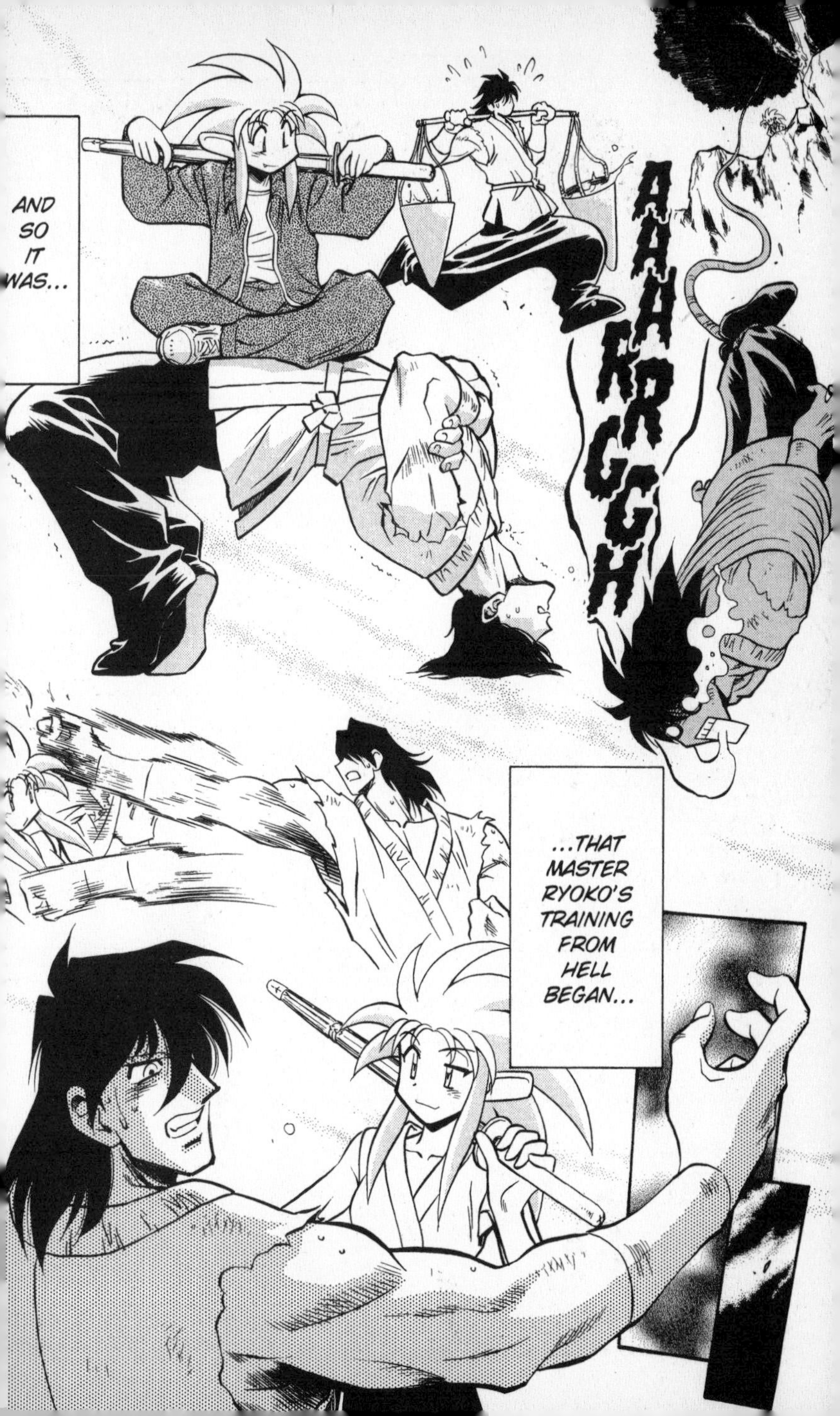
AND SO IT WAS...
AAAARRGGH
...THAT MASTER RYOKO'S TRAINING FROM HELL BEGAN...

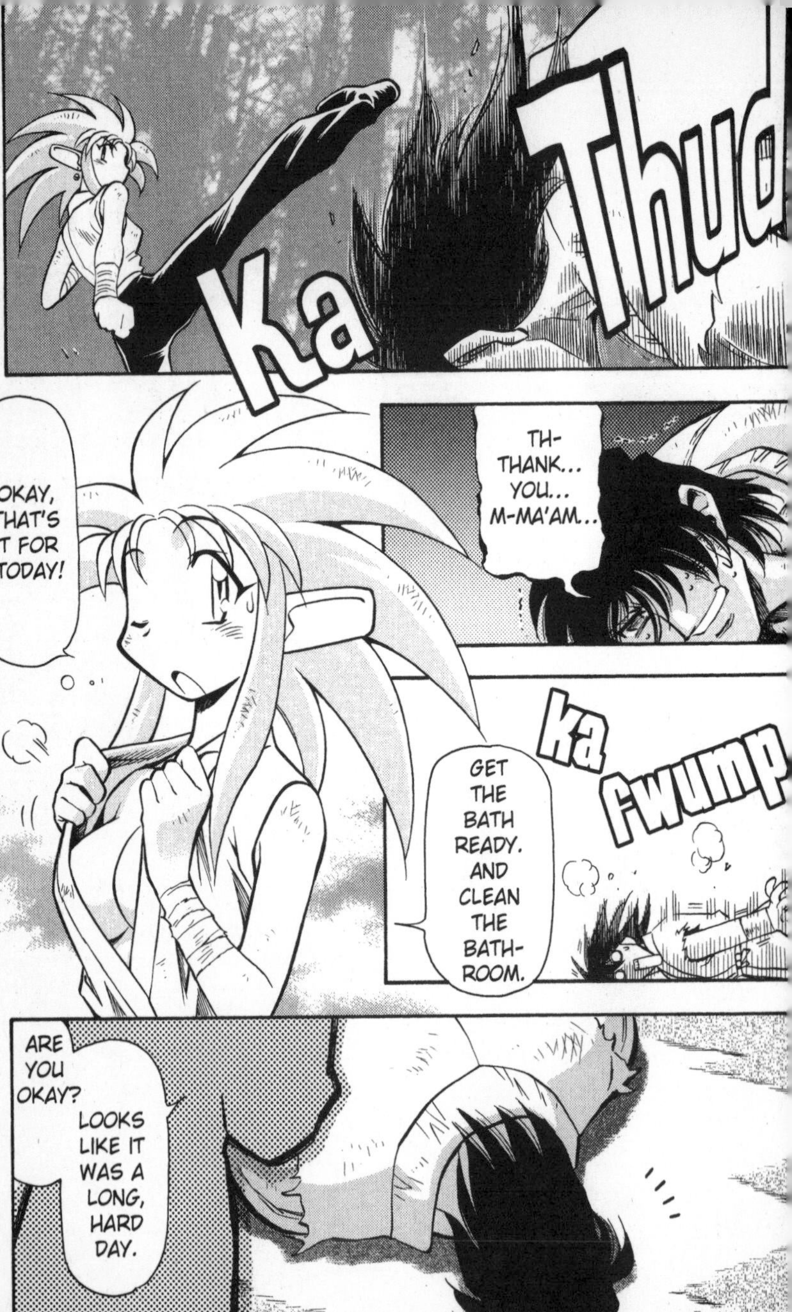
Ka
Thud
OKAY, THAT'S IT FOR TODAY!
TH- THANK... YOU... M-MA'AM...
GET THE BATH READY. AND CLEAN THE BATH-ROOM.
ka
fwump
ARE YOU OKAY?
LOOKS LIKE IT WAS A LONG, HARD DAY.

BET YOU'D LIKE A BITE TO EAT!

MNCH

CRNCH

SCRF

GULP

URK!

DON'T WOLF IT DOWN SO FAST! HERE... HAVE SOME TEA!

GLUG

THANK YOU, LADY SASAMI. MOST KIND...

ahh

IN ONE GULP

BUT WHO *AM* I...?

HMMM.

I THINK I MIGHT *ALMOST* REMEMBER SOMETHING, YET IT REMAINS ELUSIVE...

...JUST OUT OF REACH.

GUESS IT WON'T BE SO EASY...

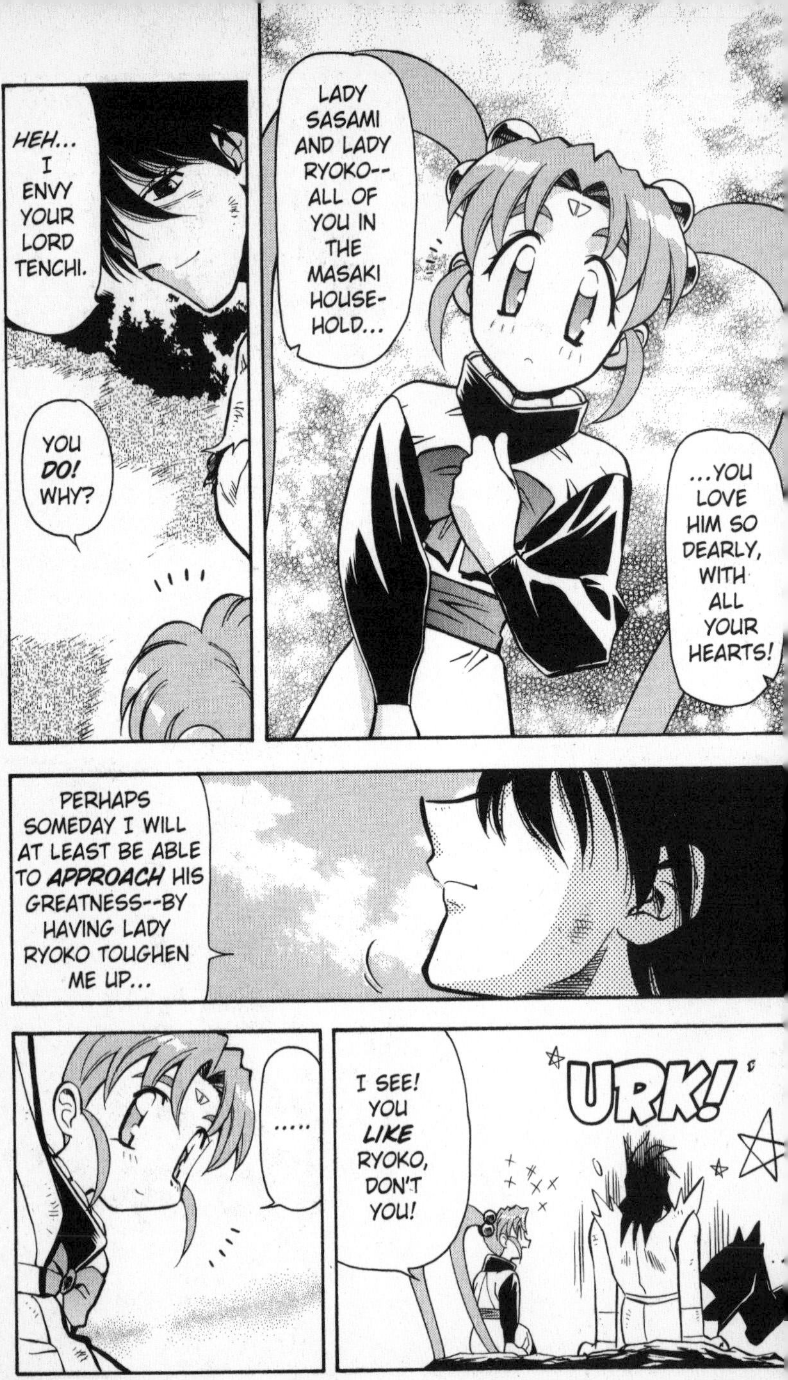
HEH... I ENVY YOUR LORD TENCHI.
YOU DO! WHY?
LADY SASAMI AND LADY RYOKO--ALL OF YOU IN THE MASAKI HOUSE-HOLD...
...YOU LOVE HIM SO DEARLY, WITH ALL YOUR HEARTS!
PERHAPS SOMEDAY I WILL AT LEAST BE ABLE TO APPROACH HIS GREATNESS--BY HAVING LADY RYOKO TOUGHEN ME UP...
.....
I SEE! YOU LIKE RYOKO, DON'T YOU!
URK!

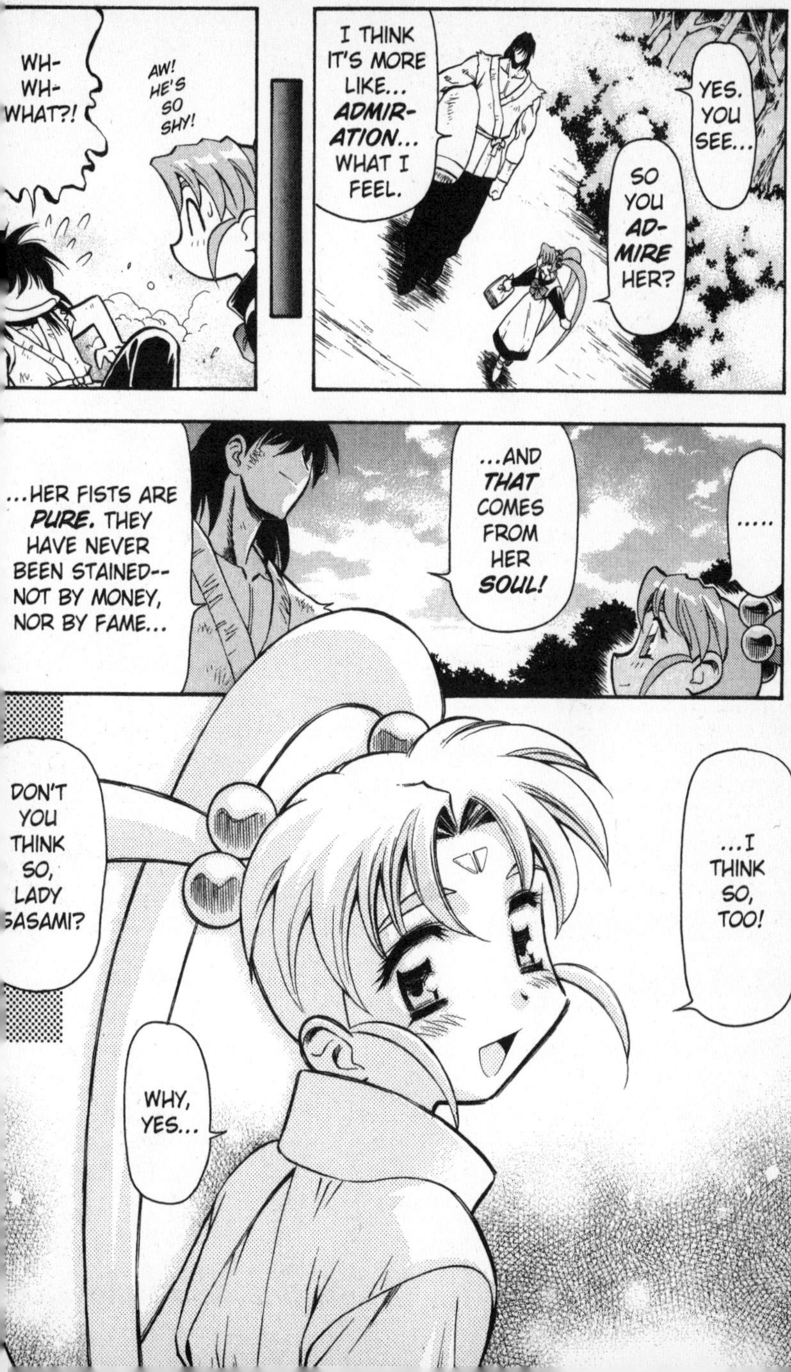
WH- WH- WHAT?!
AW! HE'S SO SHY!
I THINK IT'S MORE LIKE... ADMIR-ATION... WHAT I FEEL.
YES. YOU SEE...
SO YOU AD-MIRE HER?
...HER FISTS ARE PURE. THEY HAVE NEVER BEEN STAINED-- NOT BY MONEY, NOR BY FAME...
...AND THAT COMES FROM HER SOUL!
.....
DON'T YOU THINK SO, LADY SASAMI?
WHY, YES...
...I THINK SO, TOO!

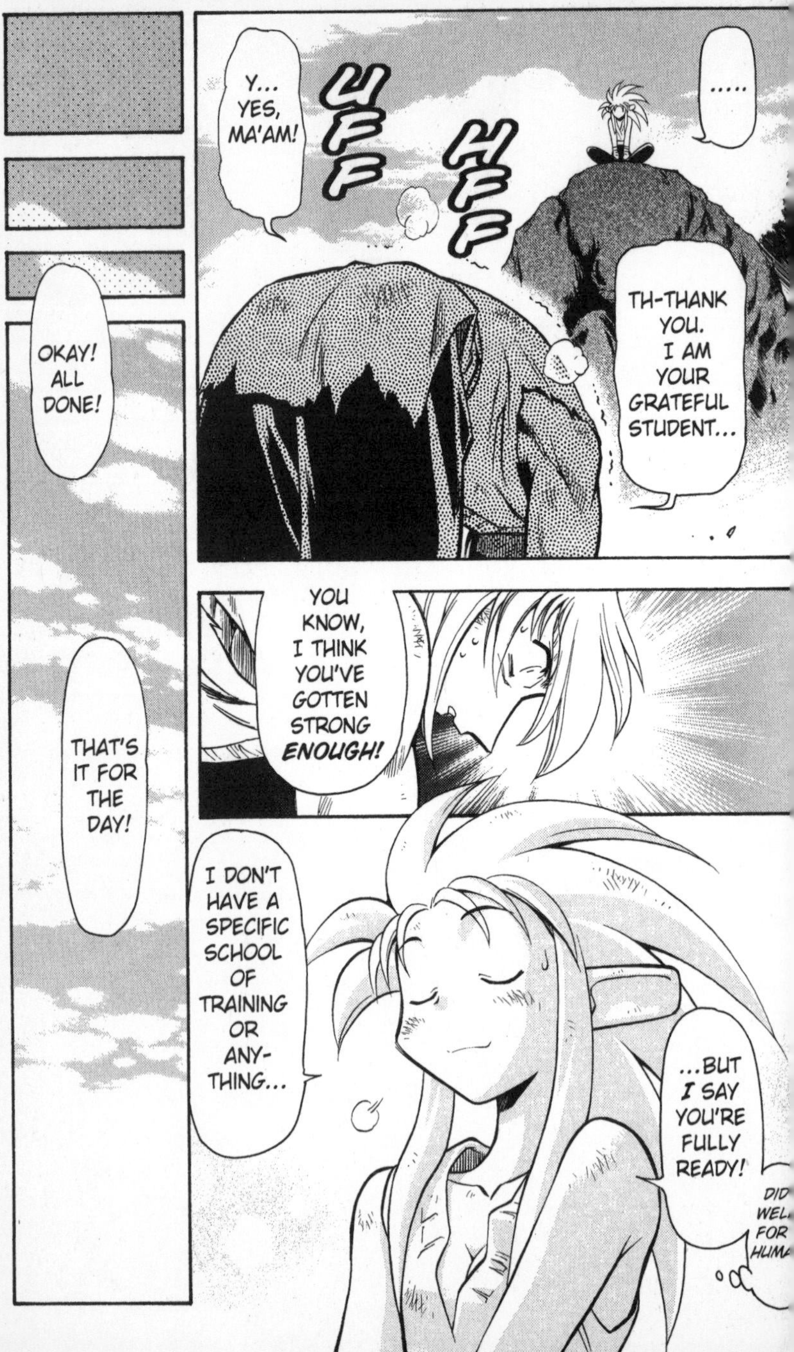
OKAY! ALL DONE!
THAT'S IT FOR THE DAY!
Y... YES, MA'AM!
UFF
HFF
.....
TH-THANK YOU. I AM YOUR GRATEFUL STUDENT...
YOU KNOW, I THINK YOU'VE GOTTEN STRONG *ENOUGH!*
I DON'T HAVE A SPECIFIC SCHOOL OF TRAINING OR ANY-THING...
...BUT *I* SAY YOU'RE FULLY READY!

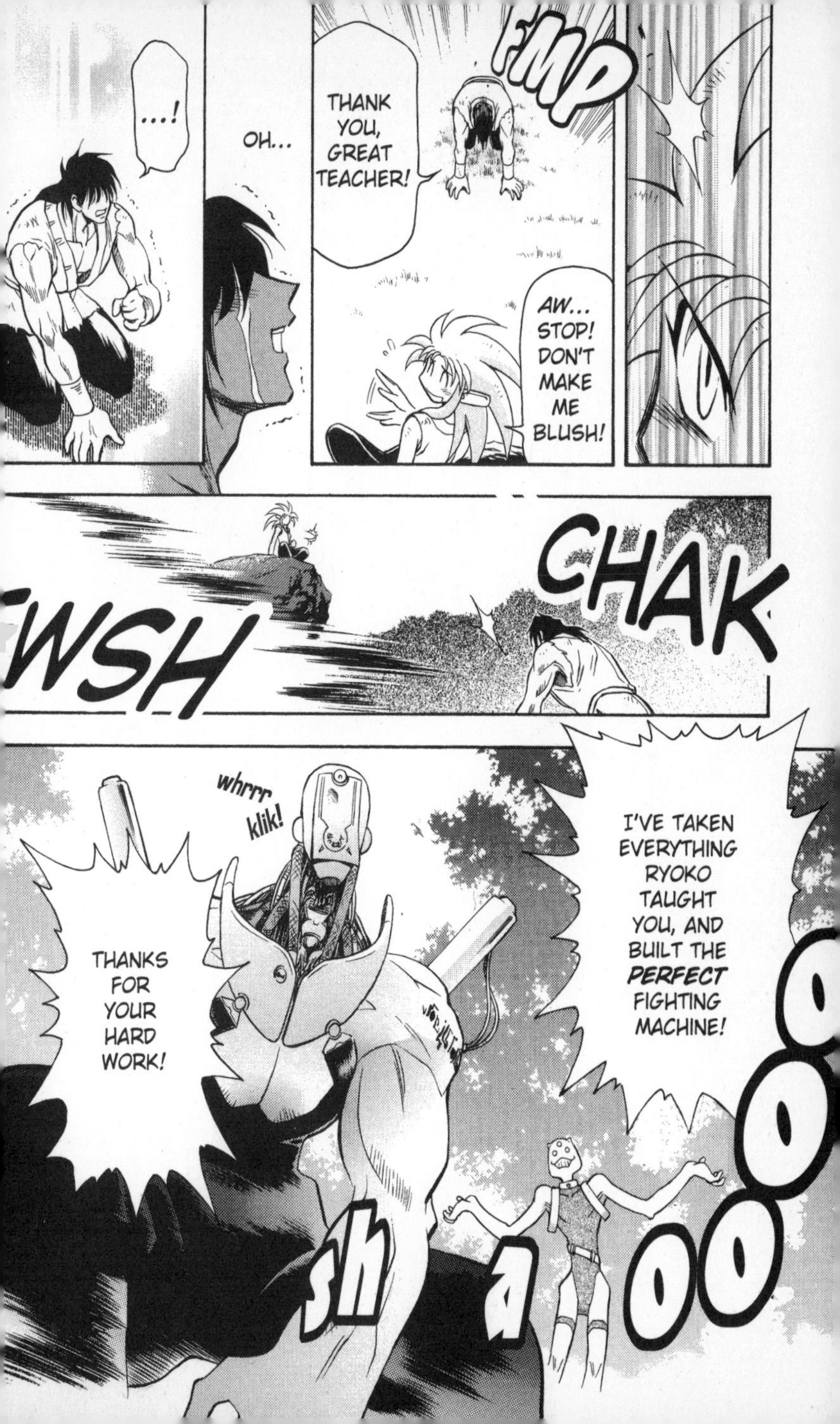
...!
OH...
THANK YOU, GREAT TEACHER!
FMP
AW... STOP! DON'T MAKE ME BLUSH!
FWSH
CHAK
whrrr klik!
THANKS FOR YOUR HARD WORK!
I'VE TAKEN EVERYTHING RYOKO TAUGHT YOU, AND BUILT THE ***PERFECT*** FIGHTING MACHINE!
sh a OOOOO

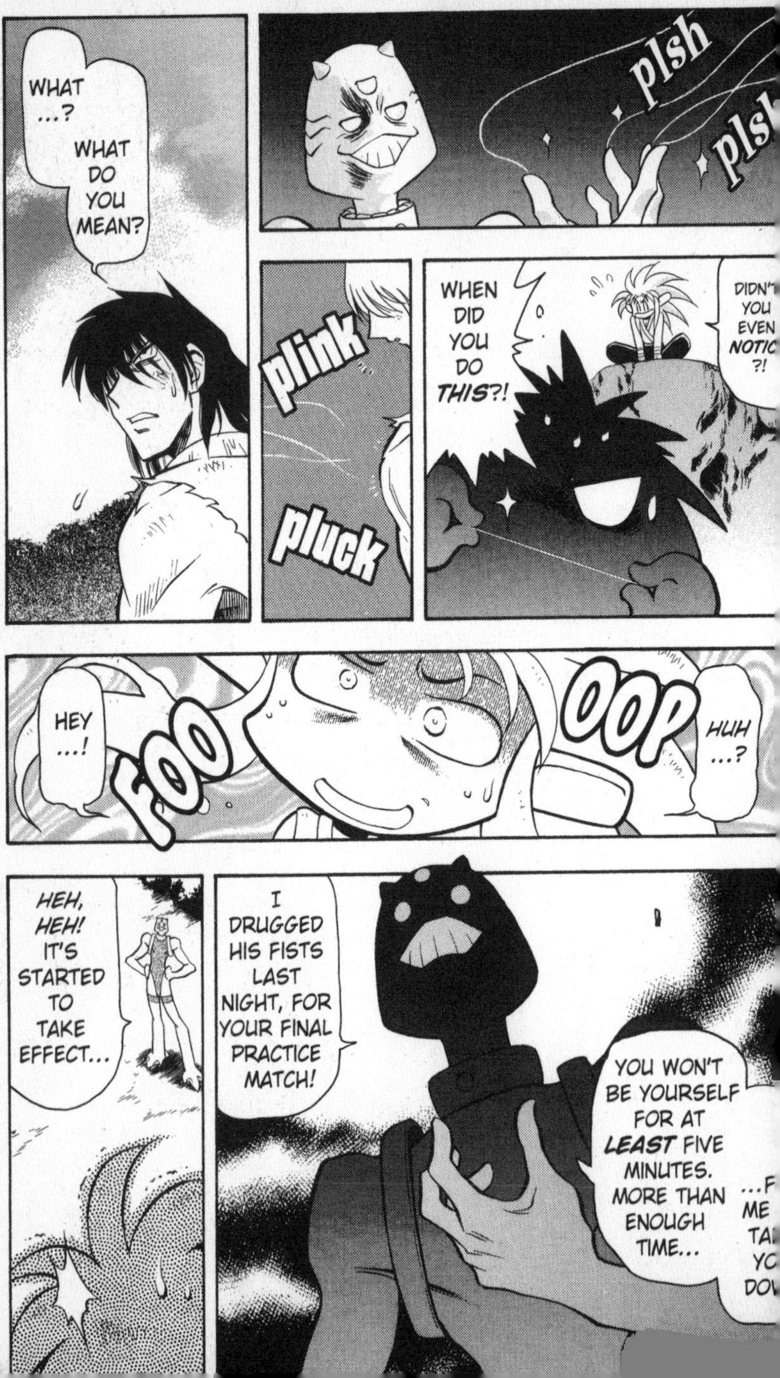
WHAT ...? WHAT DO YOU MEAN?
plsh
plsh
plink
pluck
WHEN DID YOU DO THIS?!
DIDN'T YOU EVEN NOTIC ?!
HEY ...!
FOO
OOP
HUH ...?
HEH, HEH! IT'S STARTED TO TAKE EFFECT...
I DRUGGED HIS FISTS LAST NIGHT, FOR YOUR FINAL PRACTICE MATCH!
YOU WON'T BE YOURSELF FOR AT LEAST FIVE MINUTES. MORE THAN ENOUGH TIME...
...F ME TA YO DOW

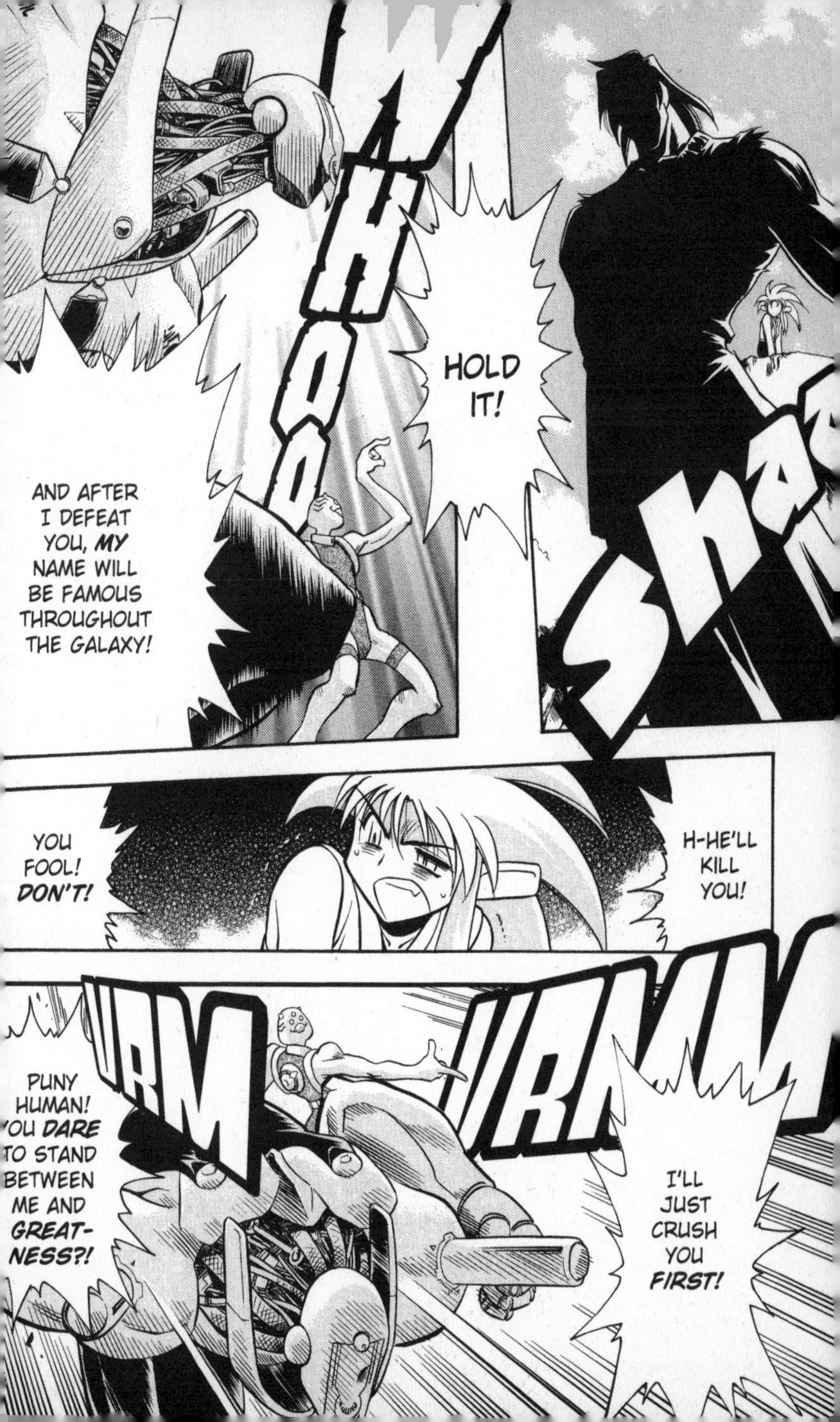
AND AFTER I DEFEAT YOU, **MY** NAME WILL BE FAMOUS THROUGHOUT THE GALAXY!
HOLD IT!
YOU FOOL! **DON'T!**
H-HE'LL KILL YOU!
URM
PUNY HUMAN! 'OU **DARE** TO STAND BETWEEN ME AND **GREATNESS?!**
I'LL JUST CRUSH YOU **FIRST!**

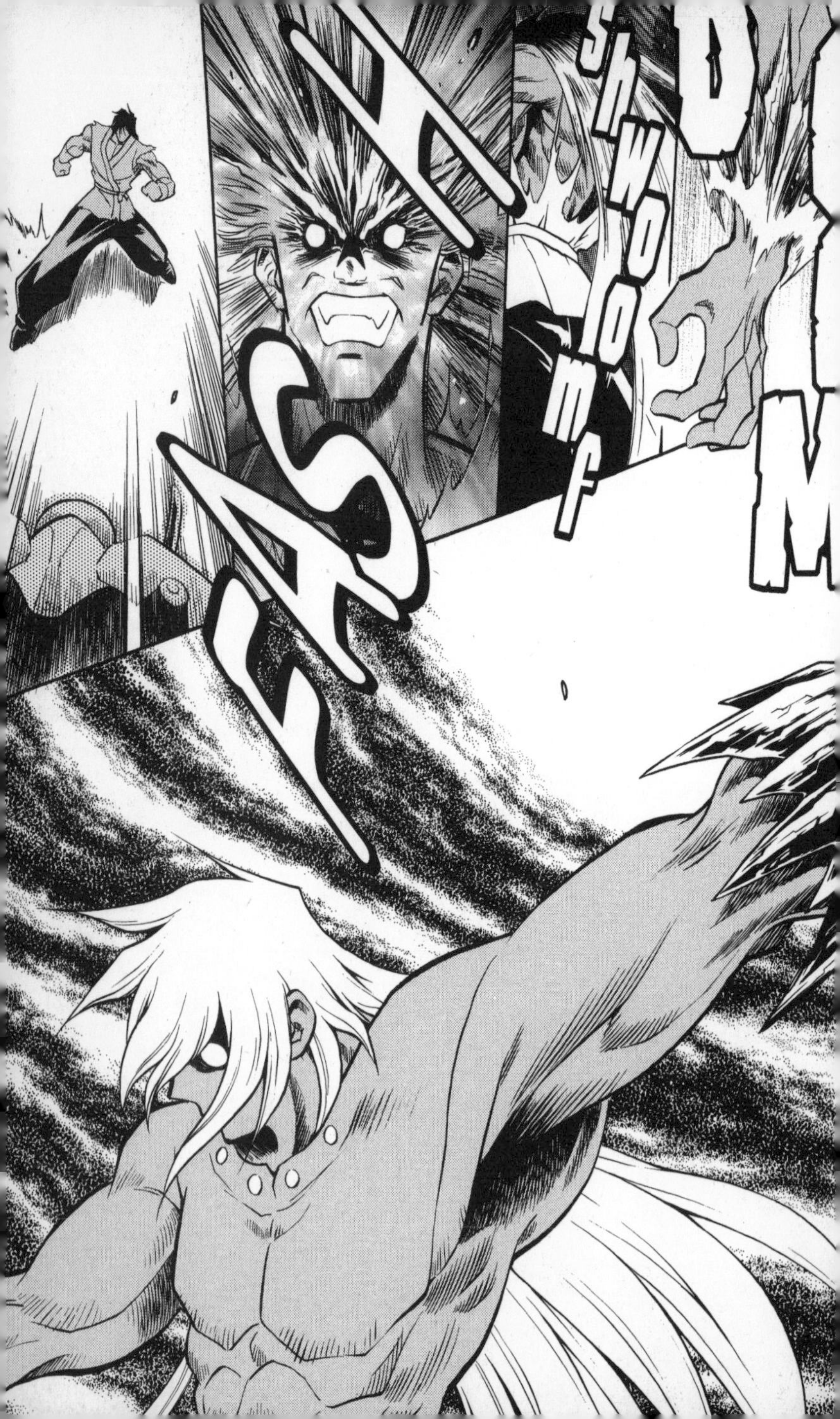
ShWOOOMf

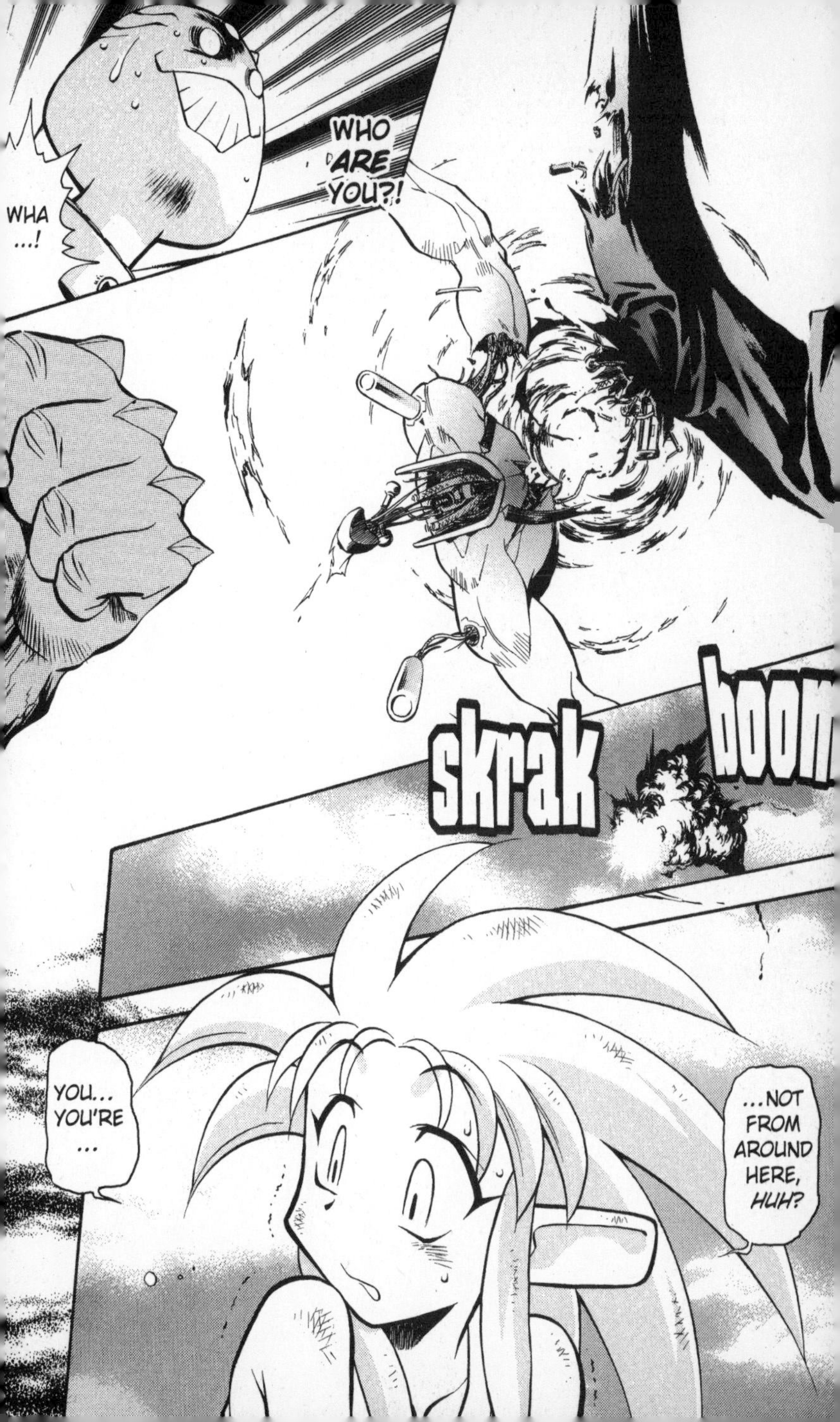
WHA ...!
WHO ARE YOU?!
skrak
boom
YOU... YOU'RE ...
...NOT FROM AROUND HERE, HUH?

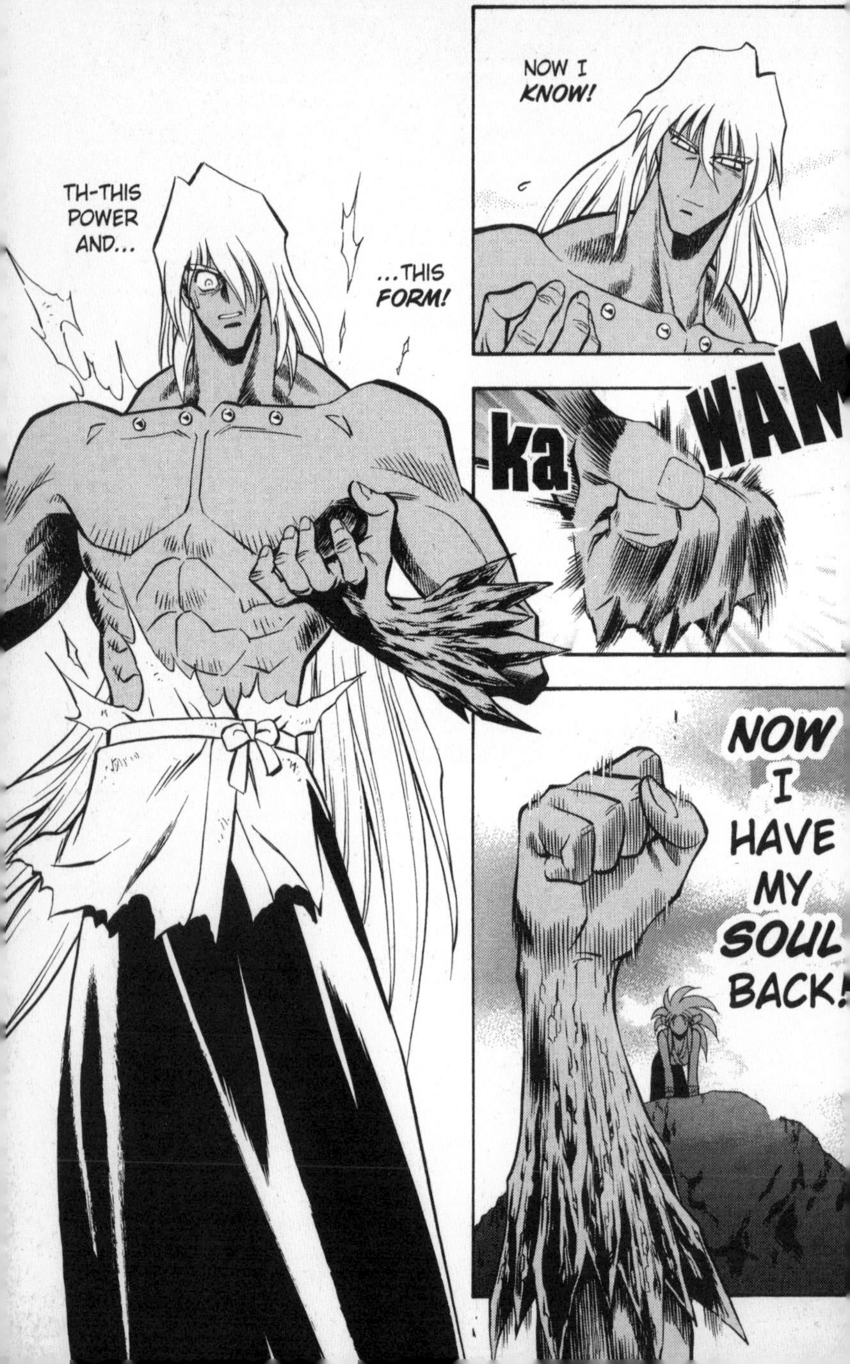
TH-THIS POWER AND...
...THIS FORM!
NOW I KNOW!
ka
WAM
NOW I HAVE MY SOUL BACK!

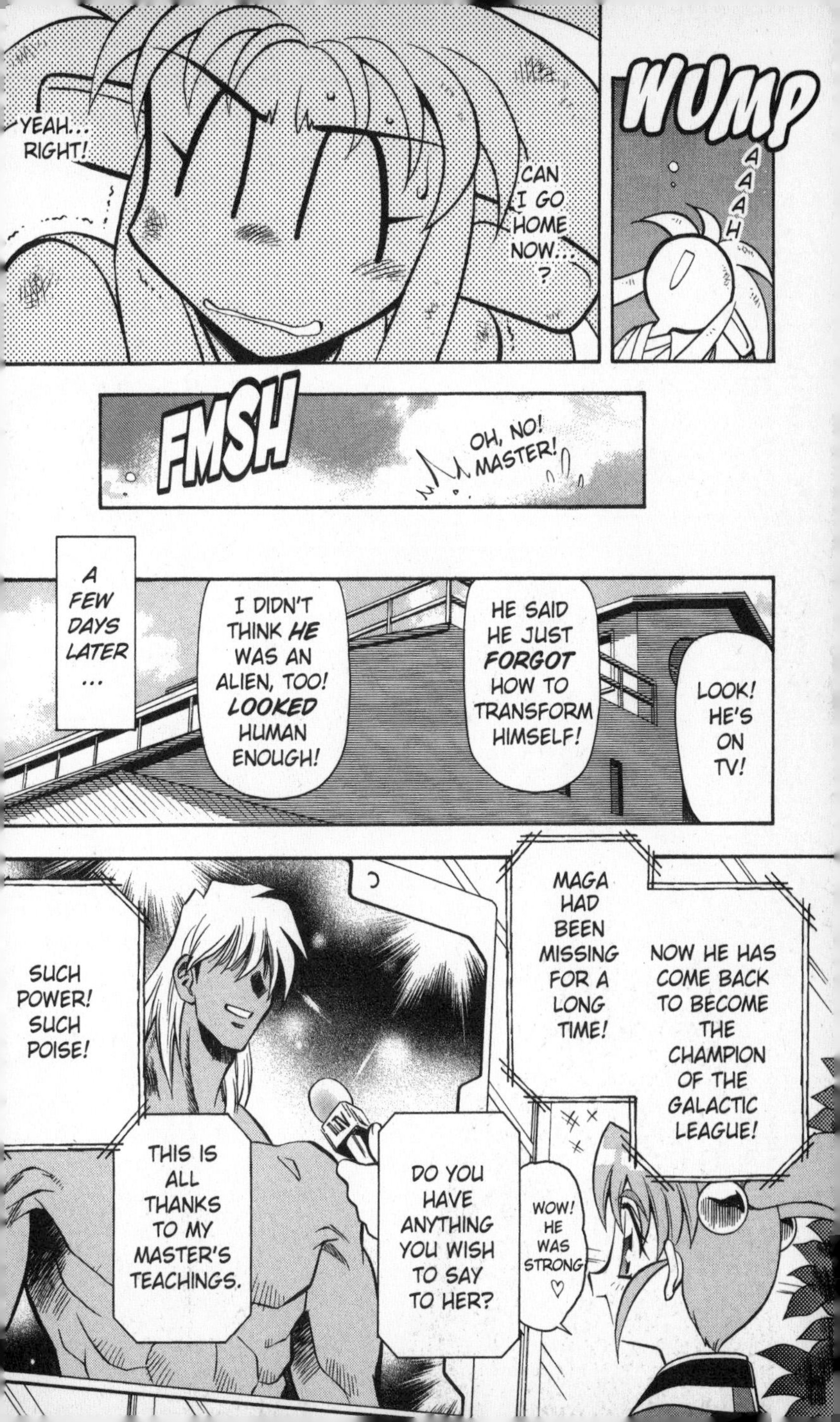
YEAH... RIGHT!
CAN I GO HOME NOW...?
WUMP
AAAAH
FMSH
OH, NO! MASTER!
A FEW DAYS LATER...
I DIDN'T THINK HE WAS AN ALIEN, TOO! LOOKED HUMAN ENOUGH!
HE SAID HE JUST FORGOT HOW TO TRANSFORM HIMSELF!
LOOK! HE'S ON TV!
SUCH POWER! SUCH POISE!
MAGA HAD BEEN MISSING FOR A LONG TIME!
NOW HE HAS COME BACK TO BECOME THE CHAMPION OF THE GALACTIC LEAGUE!
THIS IS ALL THANKS TO MY MASTER'S TEACHINGS.
DO YOU HAVE ANYTHING YOU WISH TO SAY TO HER?
WOW! HE WAS STRONG ♡

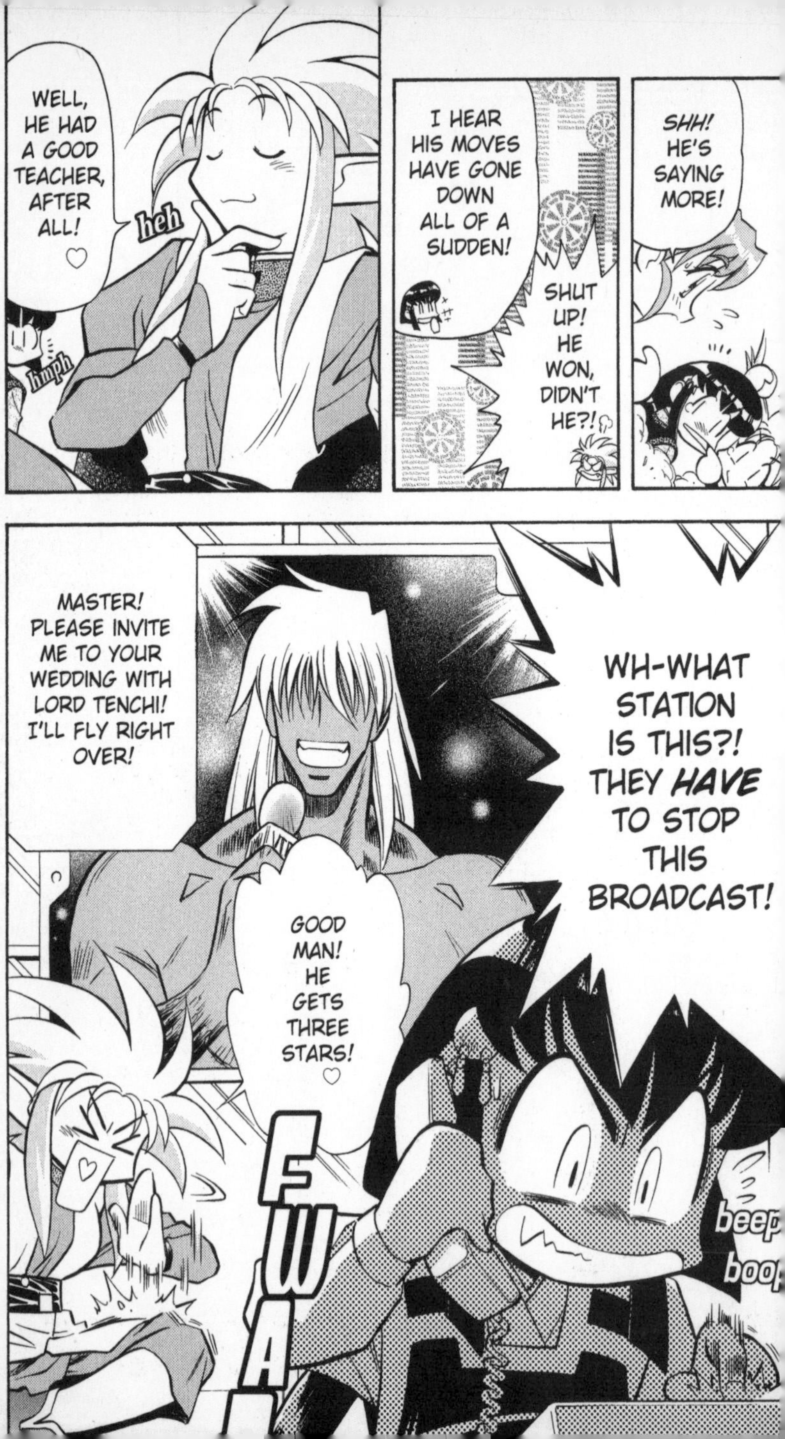
WELL, HE HAD A GOOD TEACHER, AFTER ALL! ♡
heh
hmph
I HEAR HIS MOVES HAVE GONE DOWN ALL OF A SUDDEN!
SHUT UP! HE WON, DIDN'T HE?!
SHH! HE'S SAYING MORE!
MASTER! PLEASE INVITE ME TO YOUR WEDDING WITH LORD TENCHI! I'LL FLY RIGHT OVER!
GOOD MAN! HE GETS THREE STARS! ♡
WH-WHAT STATION IS THIS?! THEY ***HAVE*** TO STOP THIS BROADCAST!
FWA
beep
boo

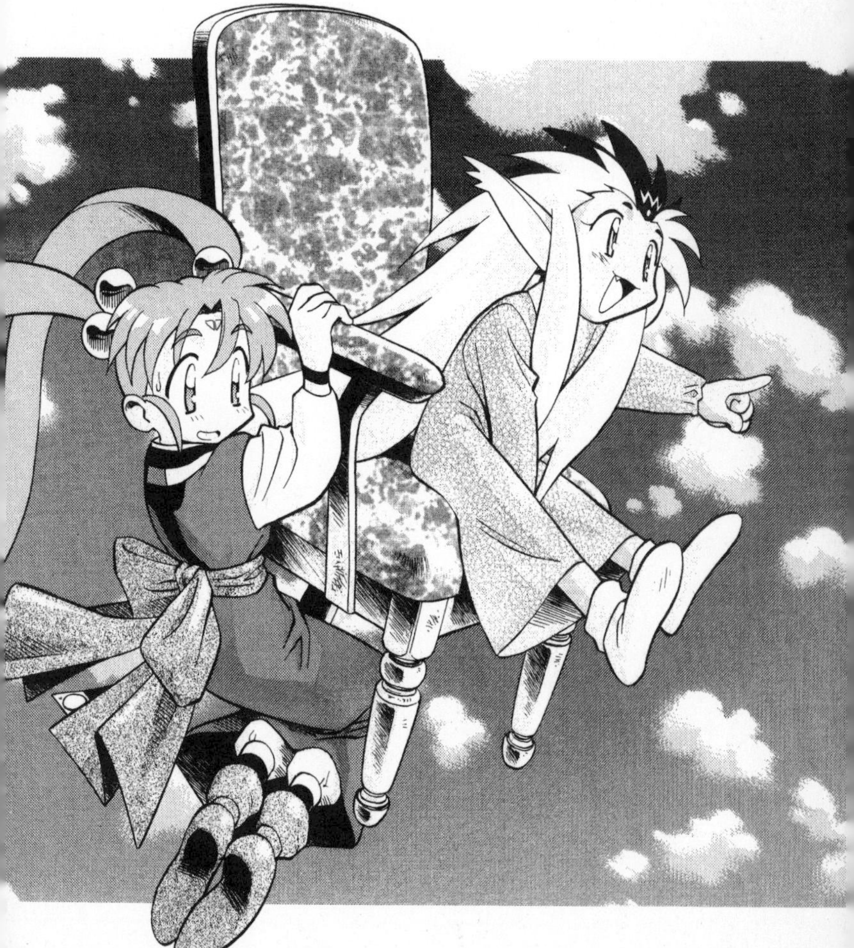

CHAPTER 7: REGRET

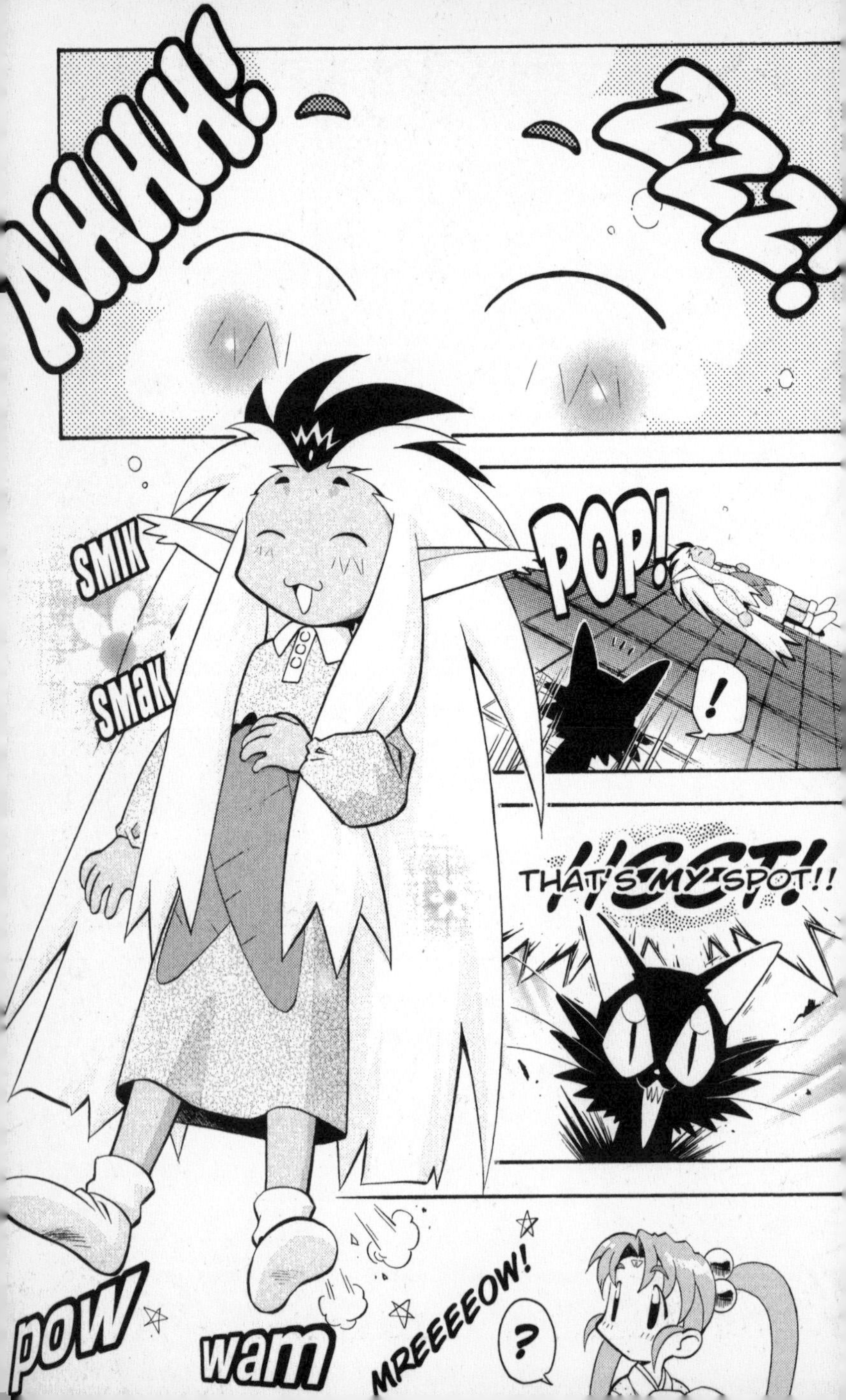
AHHH!
ZZZ!
SMIK
SMAK
pow
wam
POP!
!
THAT'S MY SPOT!!
MREEEEOW!
?

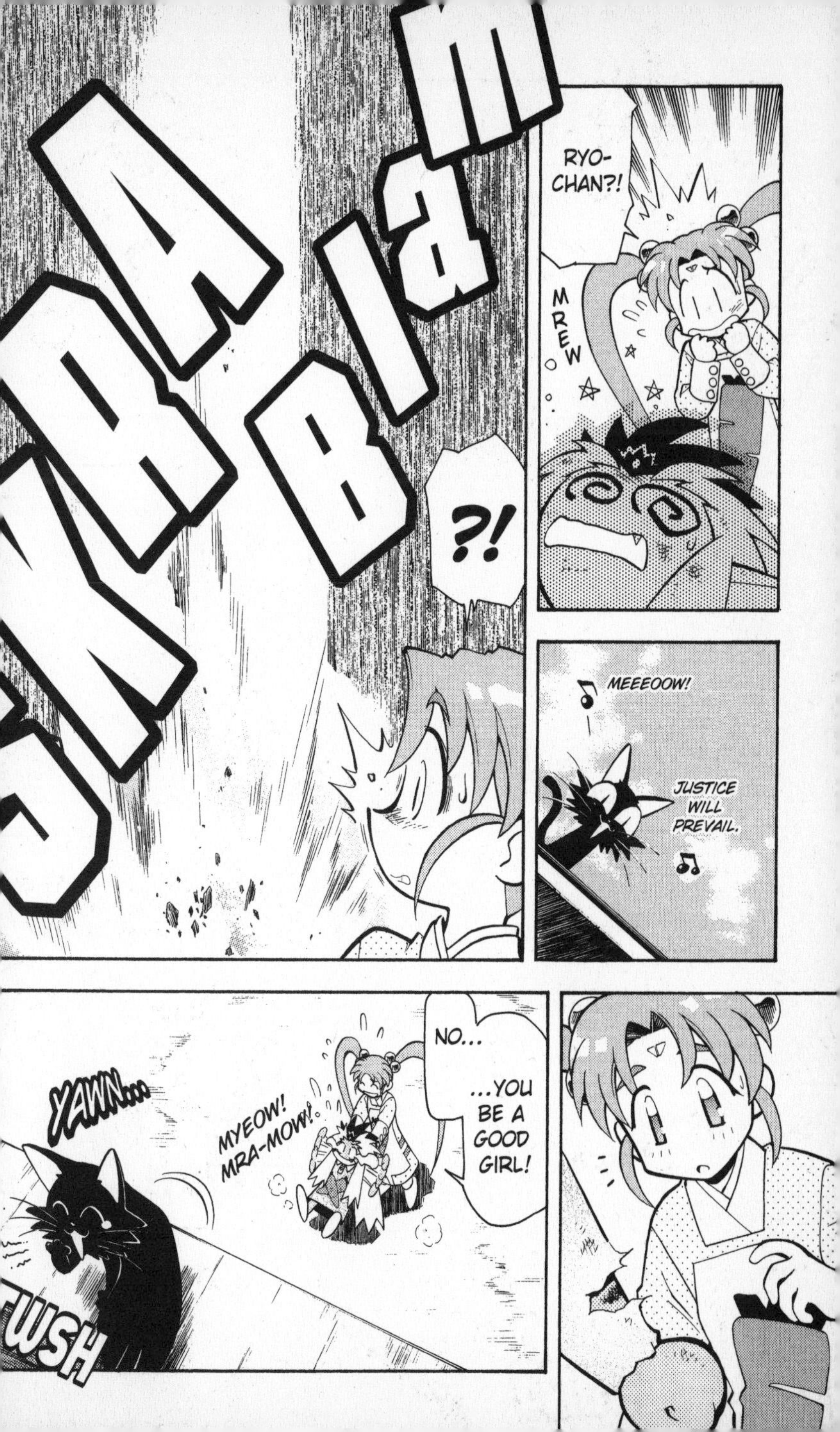
?!
RYO-CHAN?!
MREW
MEEEOOW!
JUSTICE WILL PREVAIL.
YAWN...
MYEOW! MRA-MOW!
NO...
...YOU BE A GOOD GIRL!

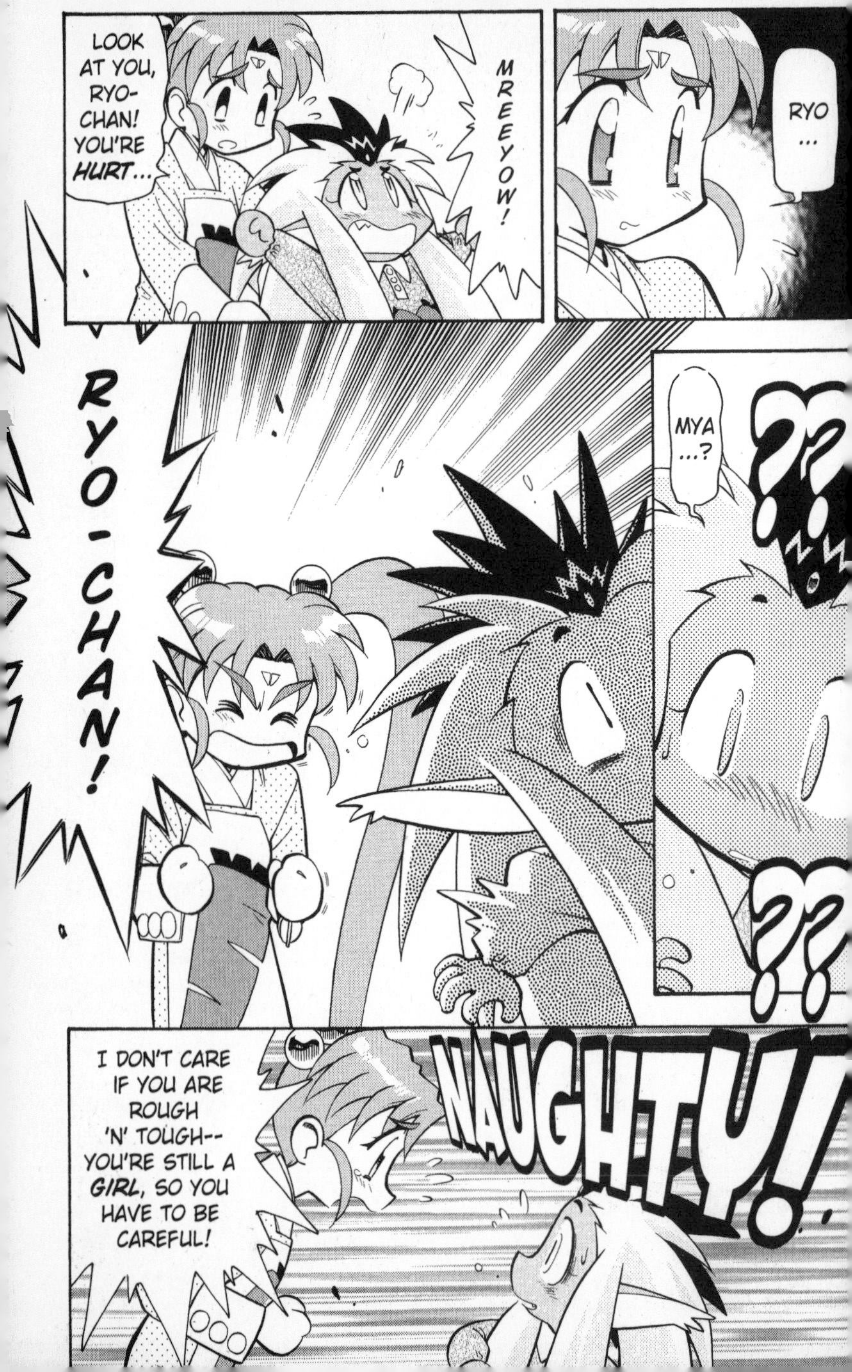
LOOK AT YOU, RYO-CHAN! YOU'RE HURT...
MREEYOW!
RYO...
RYO-CHAN!
MYA ...?
??
??
I DON'T CARE IF YOU ARE ROUGH 'N' TOUGH-- YOU'RE STILL A GIRL, SO YOU HAVE TO BE CAREFUL!
NAUGHTY!!

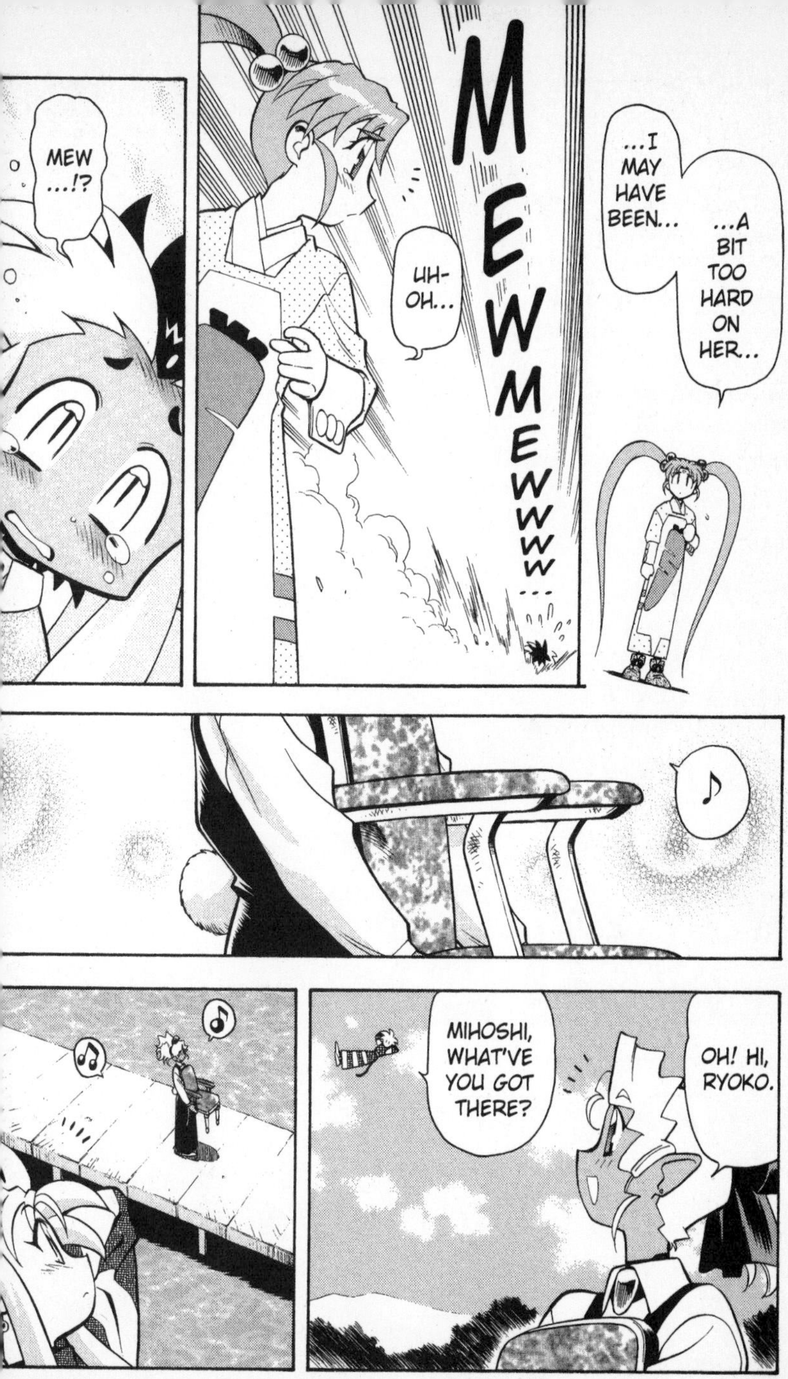
MEW ...!?
UH-OH...
MEWWMEWWWWW...
...I MAY HAVE BEEN...
...A BIT TOO HARD ON HER...
♪
♪
♪
MIHOSHI, WHAT'VE YOU GOT THERE?
OH! HI, RYOKO.

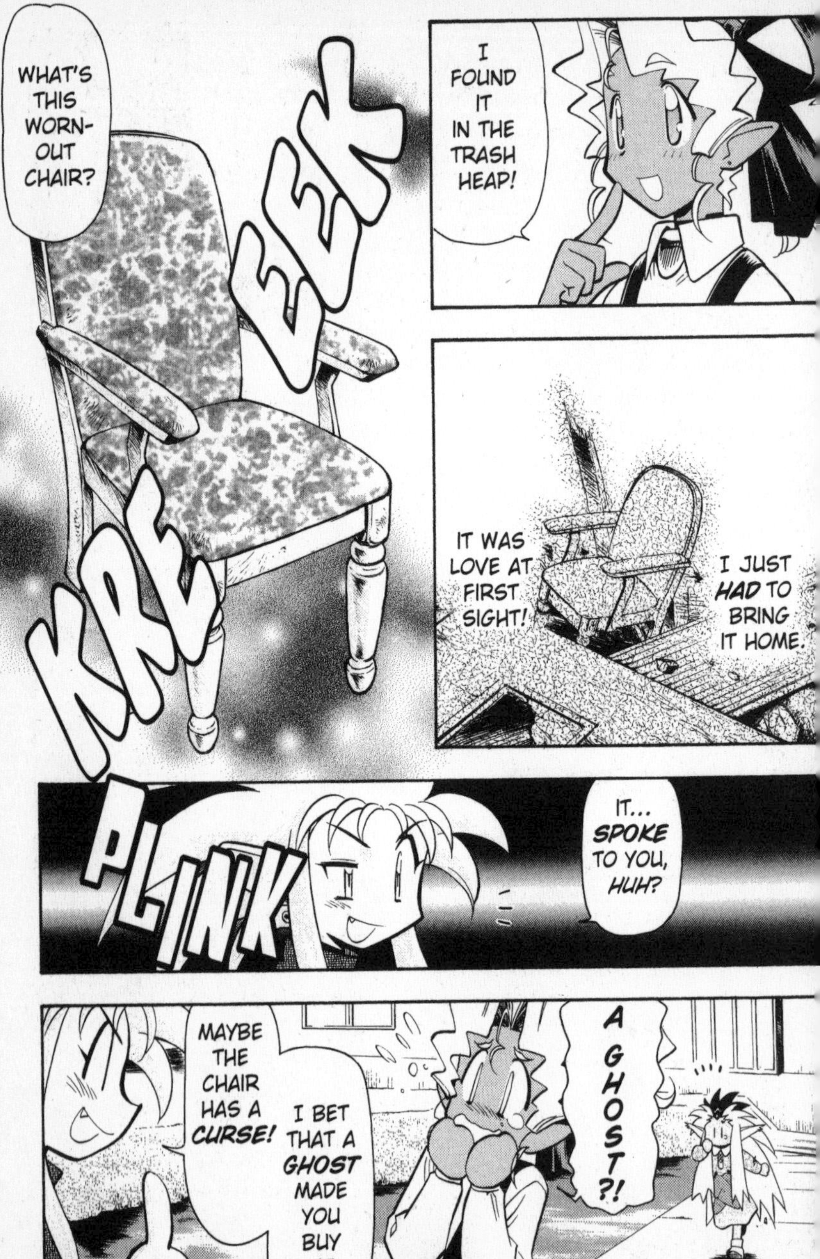
WHAT'S THIS WORN-OUT CHAIR?
KREEEK
I FOUND IT IN THE TRASH HEAP!
IT WAS LOVE AT FIRST SIGHT!
I JUST *HAD* TO BRING IT HOME.
PLINK
IT... *SPOKE* TO YOU, *HUH?*
MAYBE THE CHAIR HAS A *CURSE!*
I BET THAT A *GHOST* MADE YOU BUY IT
A GHOST?!

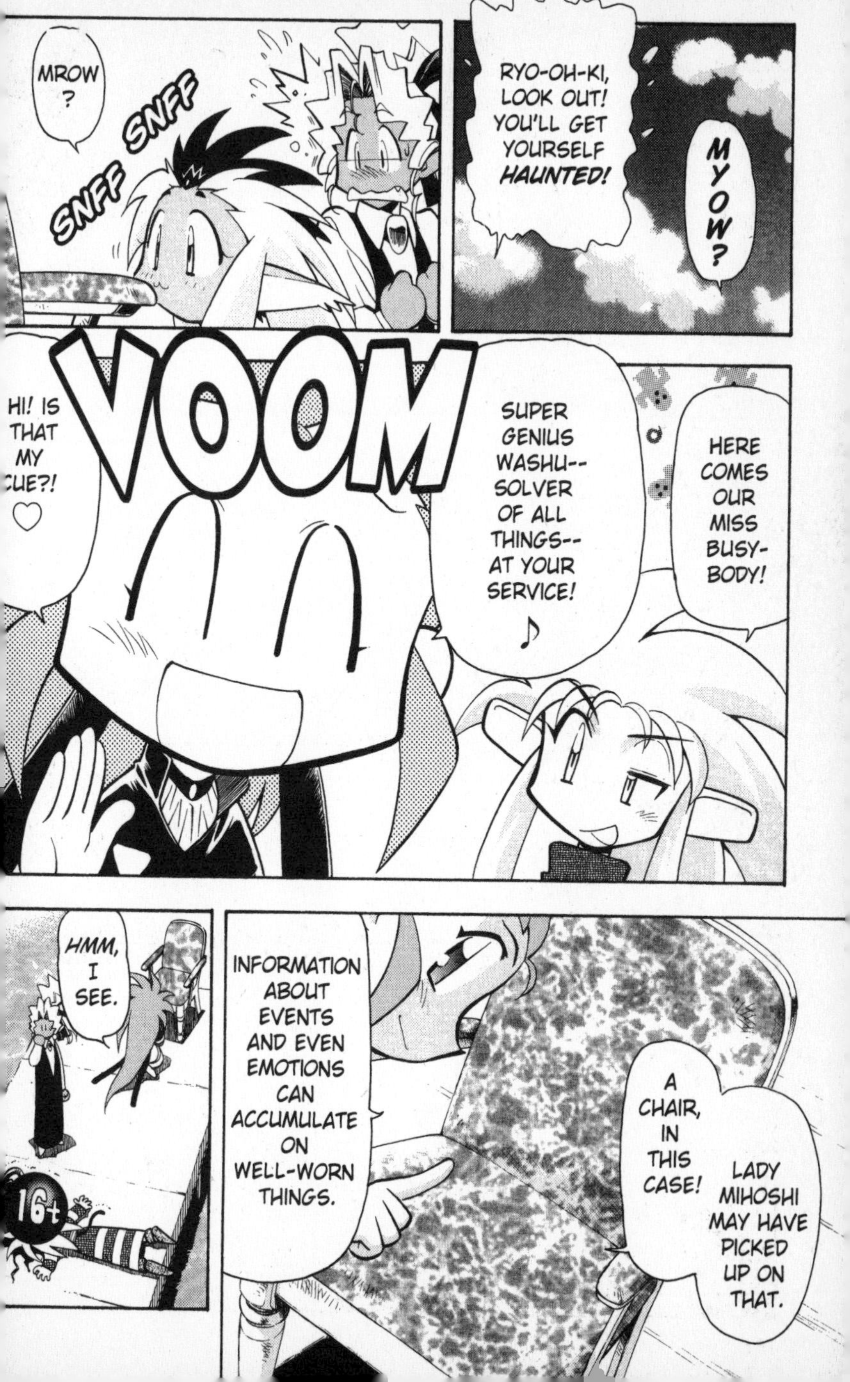

MROW ?
SNFF SNFF
RYO-OH-KI, LOOK OUT! YOU'LL GET YOURSELF *HAUNTED!*
MYOW?
VOOM
HI! IS THAT MY CUE?! ♡
SUPER GENIUS WASHU-- SOLVER OF ALL THINGS-- AT YOUR SERVICE! ♪
HERE COMES OUR MISS BUSY-BODY!
HMM, I SEE.
INFORMATION ABOUT EVENTS AND EVEN EMOTIONS CAN ACCUMULATE ON WELL-WORN THINGS.
A CHAIR, IN THIS CASE!
LADY MIHOSHI MAY HAVE PICKED UP ON THAT.
16+

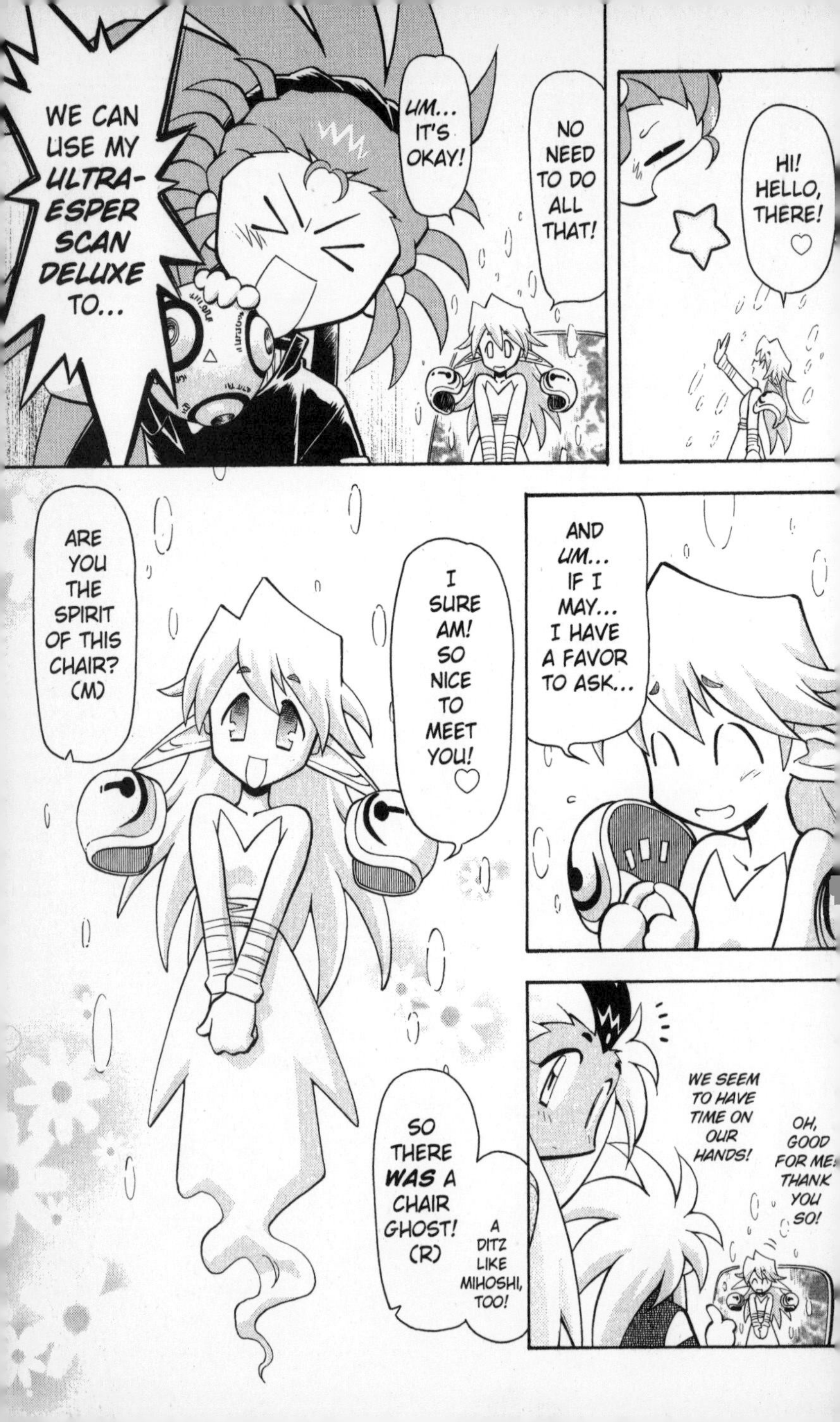

WE CAN USE MY ***ULTRA-ESPER SCAN DELUXE*** TO...
UM... IT'S OKAY!
NO NEED TO DO ALL THAT!
HI! HELLO, THERE! ♡
ARE YOU THE SPIRIT OF THIS CHAIR? (M)
I SURE ***AM!*** SO NICE TO MEET YOU! ♡
SO THERE ***WAS*** A CHAIR GHOST! (R)
A DITZ LIKE MIHOSHI, TOO!
AND *UM*... IF I MAY... I HAVE A FAVOR TO ASK...
WE SEEM TO HAVE TIME ON OUR HANDS!
OH, GOOD FOR ME! THANK YOU SO!

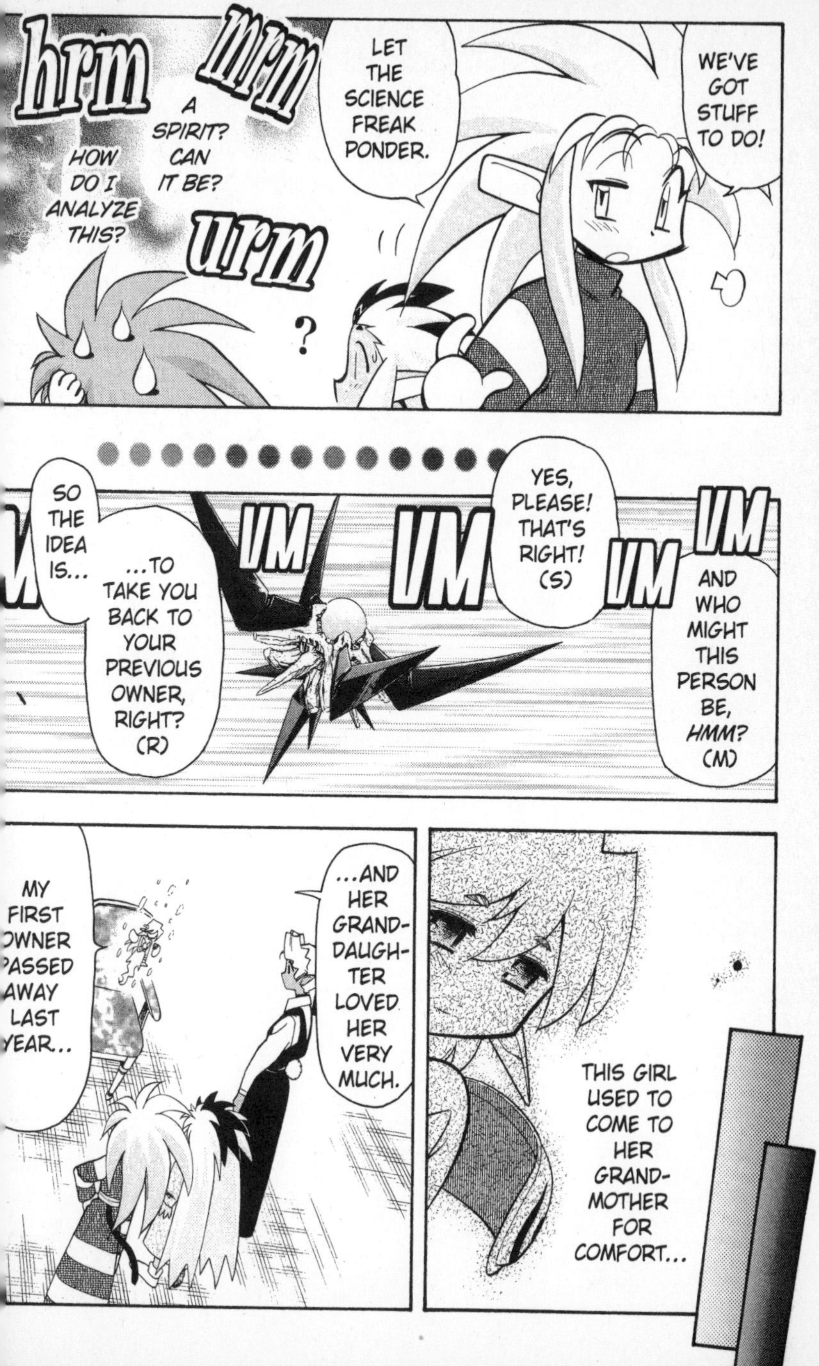
hrm
HOW DO I ANALYZE THIS?
A SPIRIT? CAN IT BE?
mrm
urm
?
LET THE SCIENCE FREAK PONDER.
WE'VE GOT STUFF TO DO!
SO THE IDEA IS...
...TO TAKE YOU BACK TO YOUR PREVIOUS OWNER, RIGHT? (R)
VM
VM
YES, PLEASE! THAT'S RIGHT! (S)
VM
VM
AND WHO MIGHT THIS PERSON BE, *HMM?* (M)
MY FIRST OWNER PASSED AWAY LAST YEAR...
...AND HER GRAND-DAUGHTER LOVED HER VERY MUCH.
THIS GIRL USED TO COME TO HER GRAND-MOTHER FOR COMFORT...

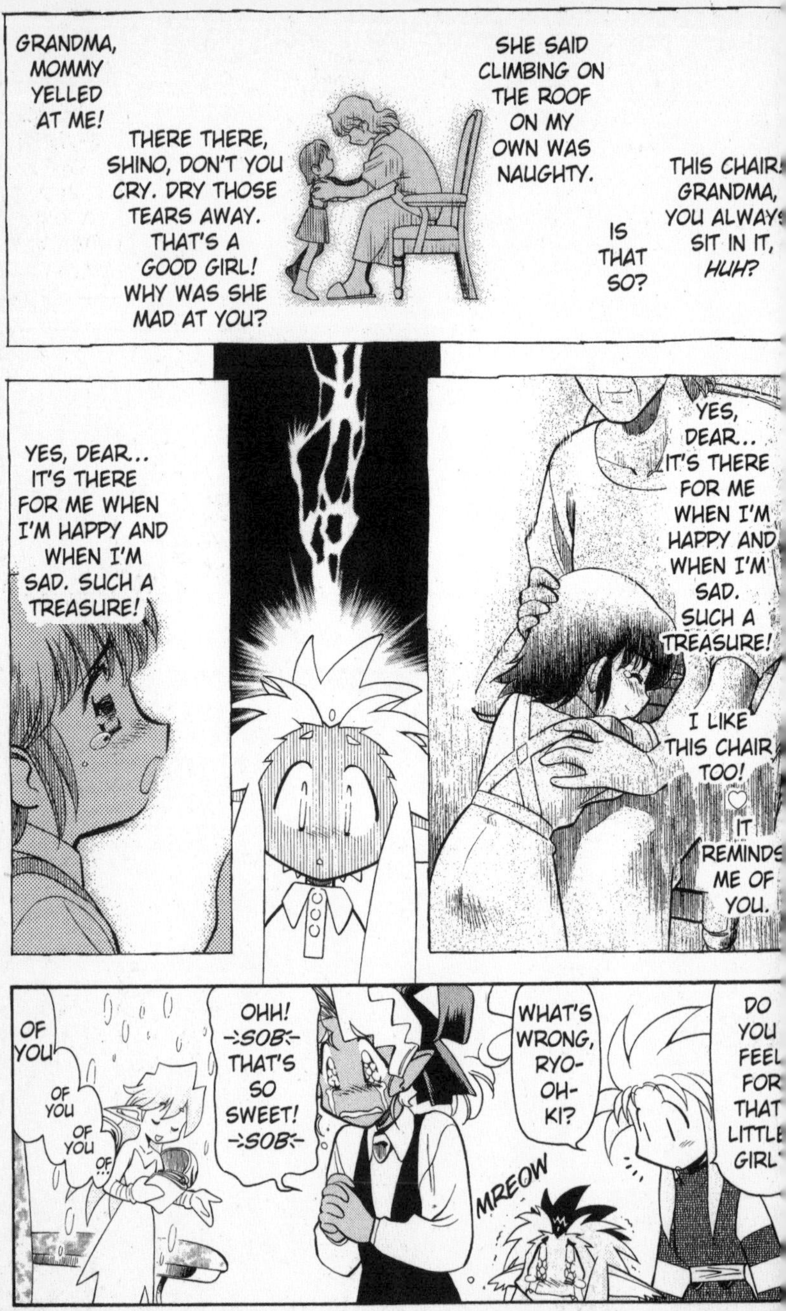

GRANDMA, MOMMY YELLED AT ME!
THERE THERE, SHINO, DON'T YOU CRY. DRY THOSE TEARS AWAY. THAT'S A GOOD GIRL! WHY WAS SHE MAD AT YOU?
SHE SAID CLIMBING ON THE ROOF ON MY OWN WAS NAUGHTY.
IS THAT SO?
THIS CHAIR, GRANDMA, YOU ALWAYS SIT IN IT, HUH?
YES, DEAR... IT'S THERE FOR ME WHEN I'M HAPPY AND WHEN I'M SAD. SUCH A TREASURE!
YES, DEAR... IT'S THERE FOR ME WHEN I'M HAPPY AND WHEN I'M SAD. SUCH A TREASURE!
I LIKE THIS CHAIR, TOO! ♡
IT REMINDS ME OF YOU.
OF YOU
OF YOU
OF YOU
OF...
OHH! -SOB- THAT'S SO SWEET! -SOB-
WHAT'S WRONG, RYO-OH-KI?
MREOW
DO YOU FEEL FOR THAT LITTLE GIRL

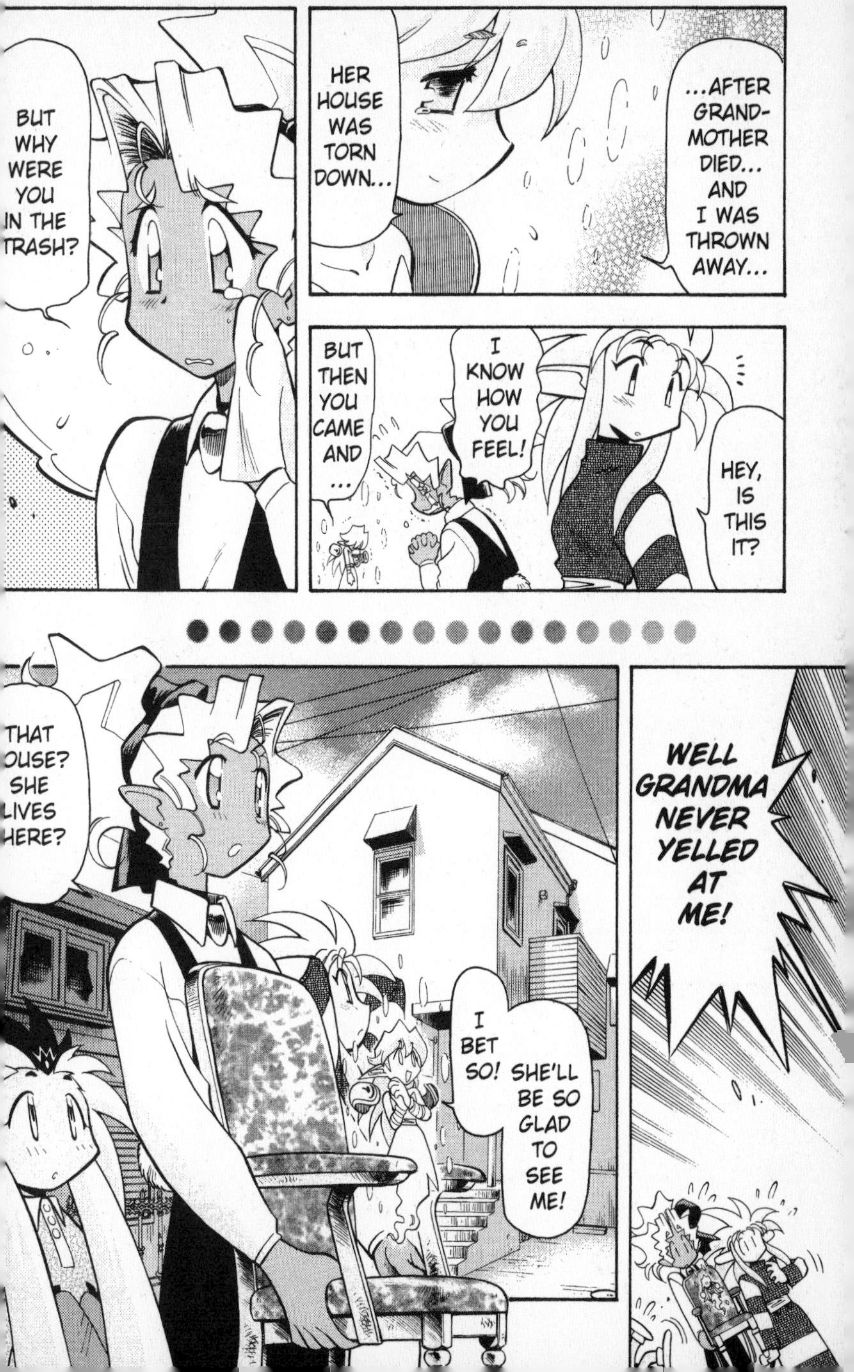
BUT WHY WERE YOU IN THE TRASH?
HER HOUSE WAS TORN DOWN...
...AFTER GRANDMOTHER DIED... AND I WAS THROWN AWAY...
BUT THEN YOU CAME AND ...
I KNOW HOW YOU FEEL!
HEY, IS THIS IT?
THAT OUSE? SHE LIVES HERE?
I BET SO!
SHE'LL BE SO GLAD TO SEE ME!
WELL GRANDMA NEVER YELLED AT ME!

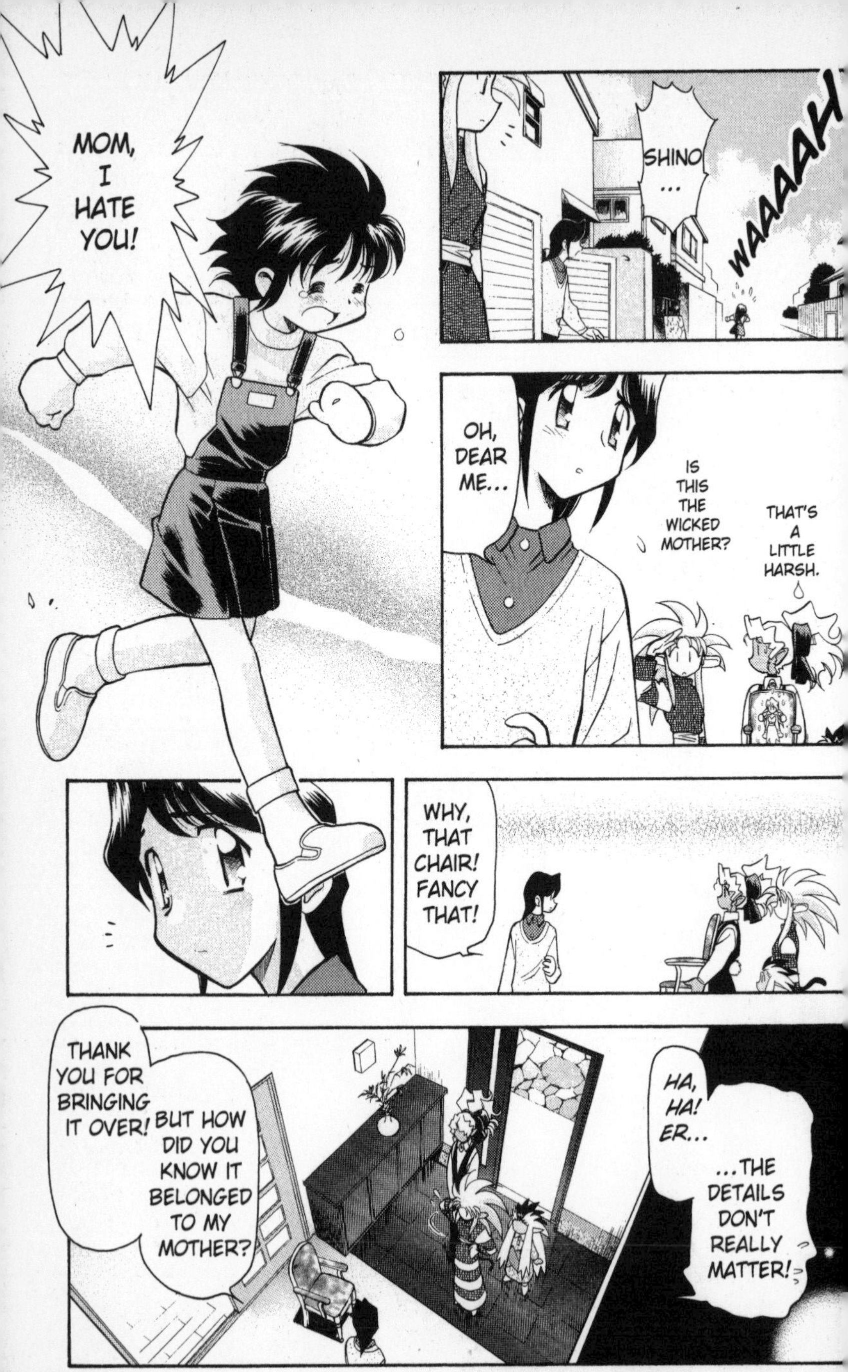
MOM, I HATE YOU!
SHINO...
WAAAAH
OH, DEAR ME...
IS THIS THE WICKED MOTHER?
THAT'S A LITTLE HARSH.
WHY, THAT CHAIR! FANCY THAT!
THANK YOU FOR BRINGING IT OVER!
BUT HOW DID YOU KNOW IT BELONGED TO MY MOTHER?
HA, HA! ER...
...THE DETAILS DON'T REALLY MATTER!

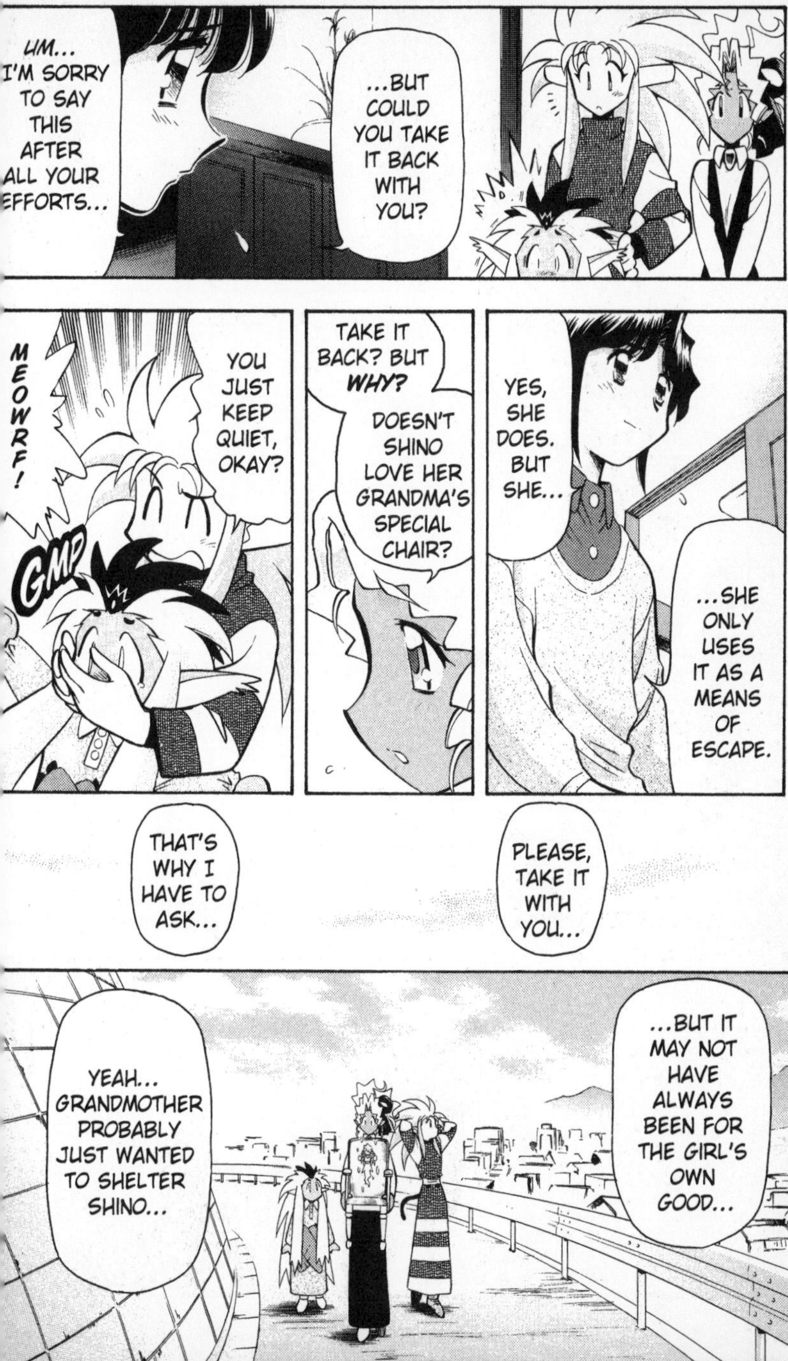

UM... I'M SORRY TO SAY THIS AFTER ALL YOUR EFFORTS...
...BUT COULD YOU TAKE IT BACK WITH YOU?
MEOWRF!
YOU JUST KEEP QUIET, OKAY?
GMP
TAKE IT BACK? BUT WHY?
DOESN'T SHINO LOVE HER GRANDMA'S SPECIAL CHAIR?
YES, SHE DOES. BUT SHE...
...SHE ONLY USES IT AS A MEANS OF ESCAPE.
THAT'S WHY I HAVE TO ASK...
PLEASE, TAKE IT WITH YOU...
YEAH... GRANDMOTHER PROBABLY JUST WANTED TO SHELTER SHINO...
...BUT IT MAY NOT HAVE ALWAYS BEEN FOR THE GIRL'S OWN GOOD...

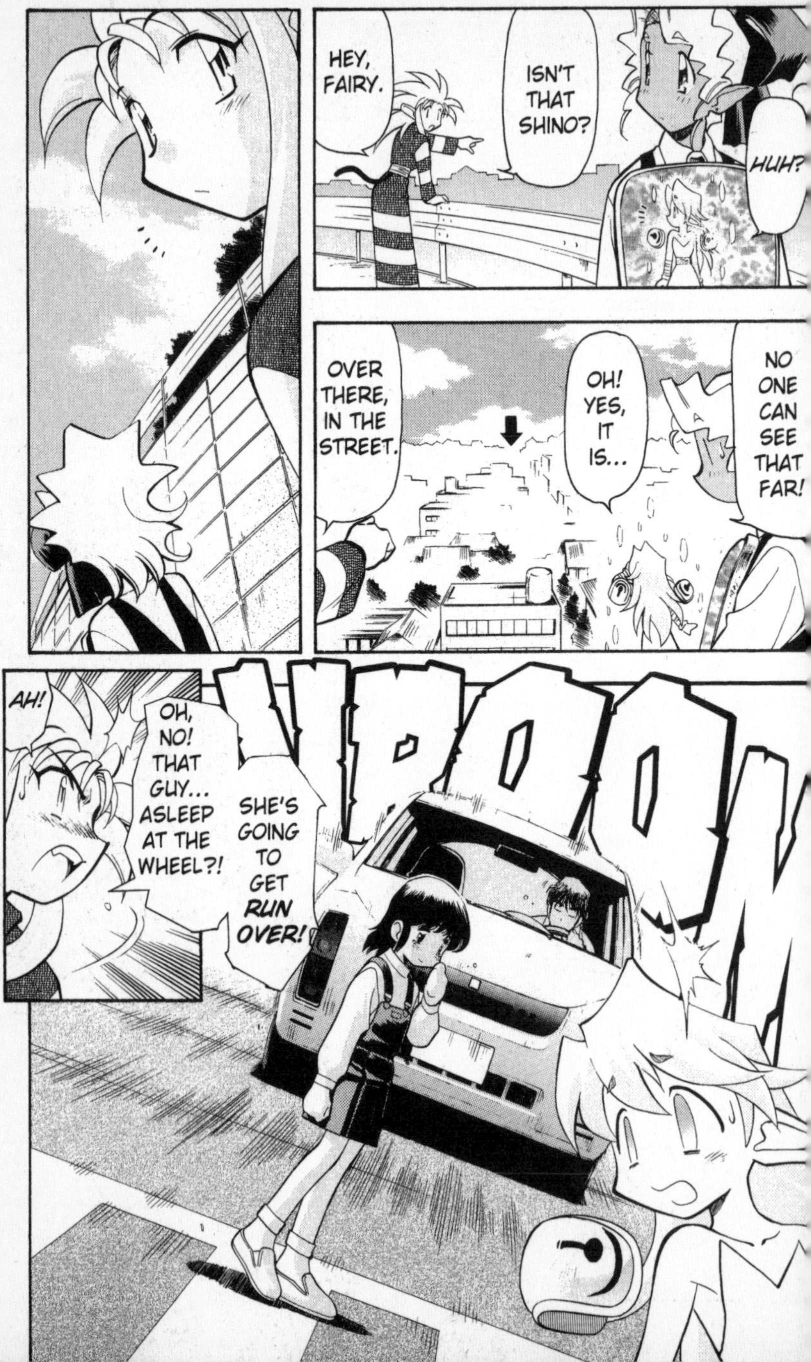

HEY, FAIRY.
ISN'T THAT SHINO?
HUH?
OVER THERE, IN THE STREET.
OH! YES, IT IS...
NO ONE CAN SEE THAT FAR!
AH!
OH, NO! THAT GUY... ASLEEP AT THE WHEEL?!
SHE'S GOING TO GET RUN OVER!
VROO

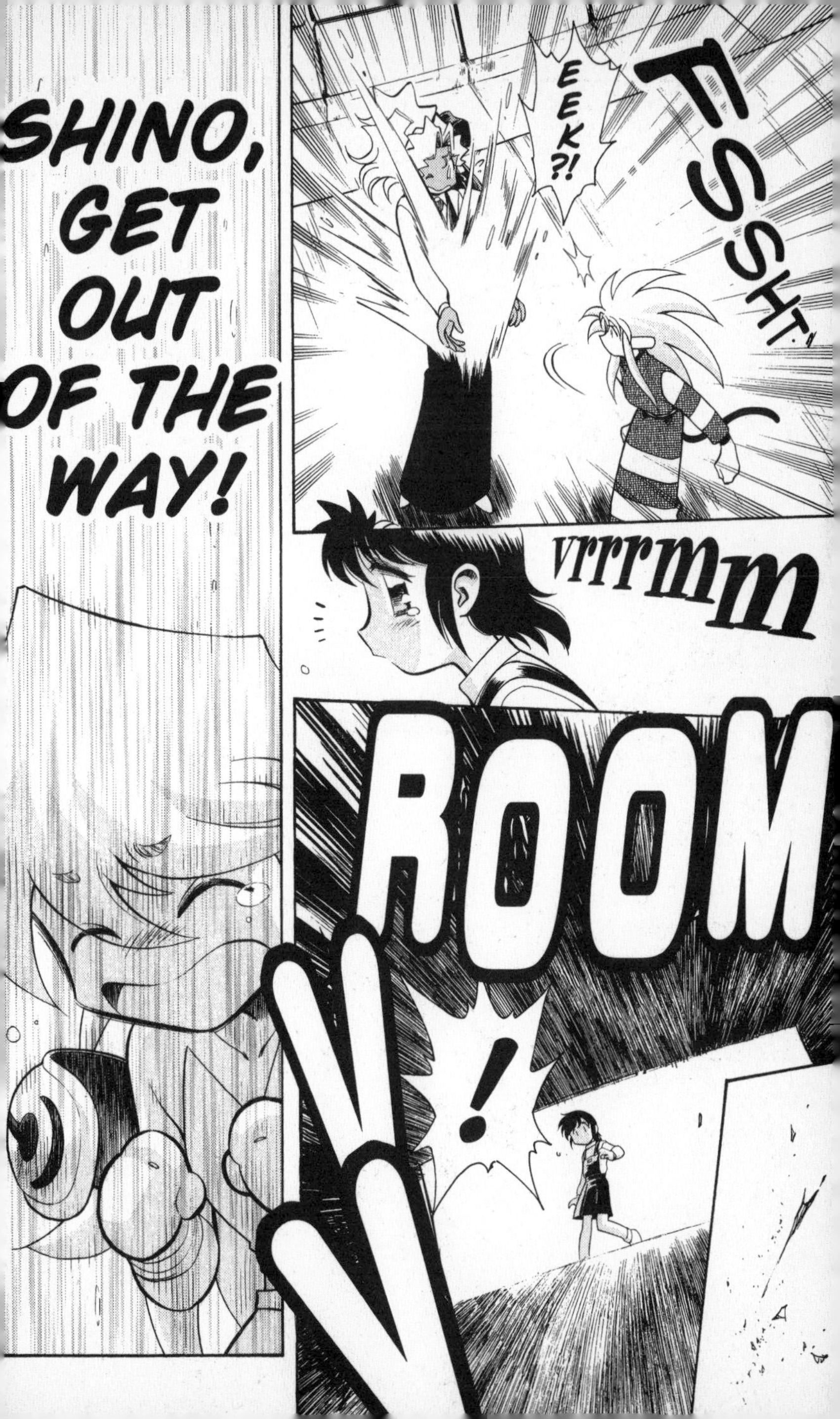
SHINO, GET OUT OF THE WAY!
EEK?!
FSSHT
VRRRMM
ROOM
V!

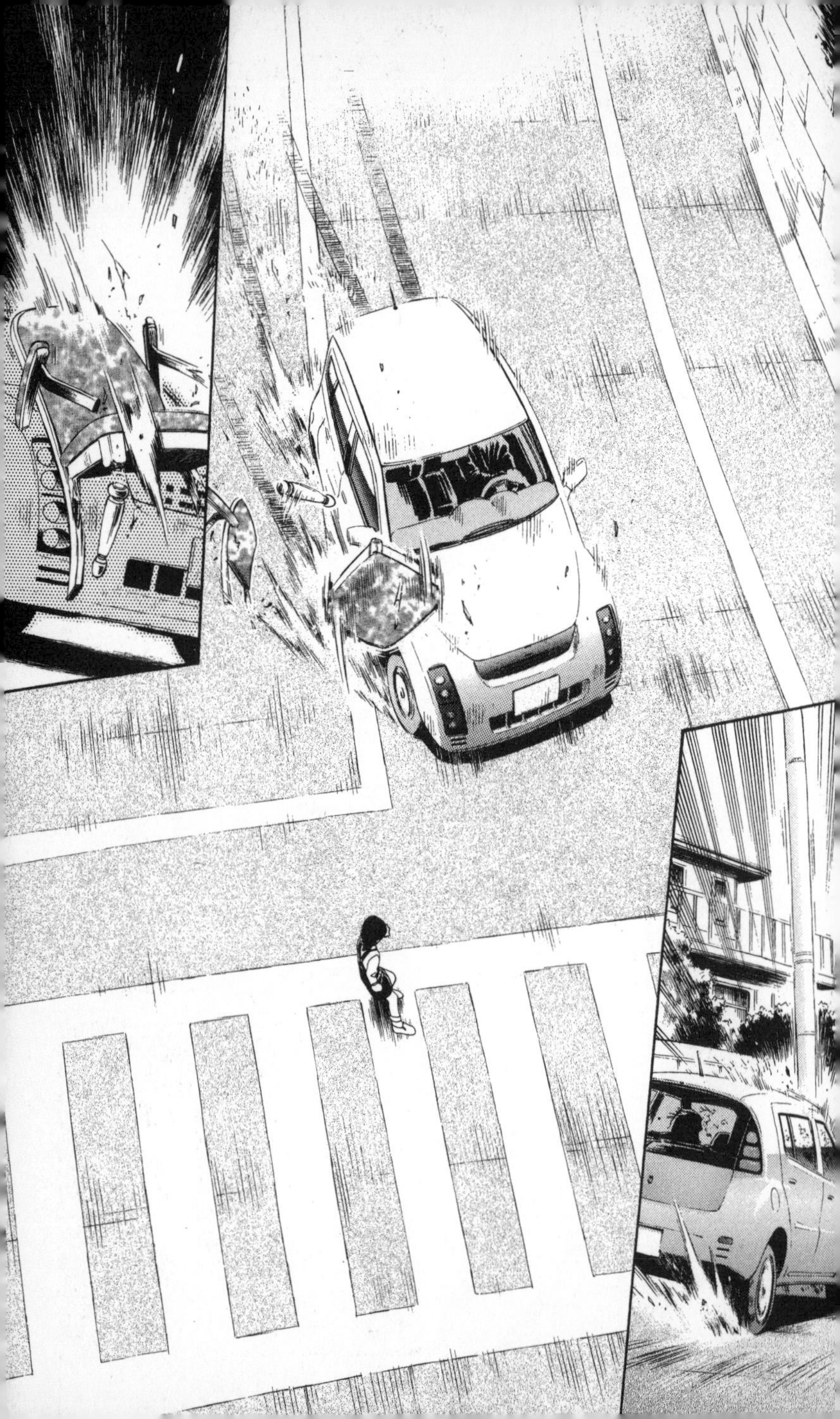

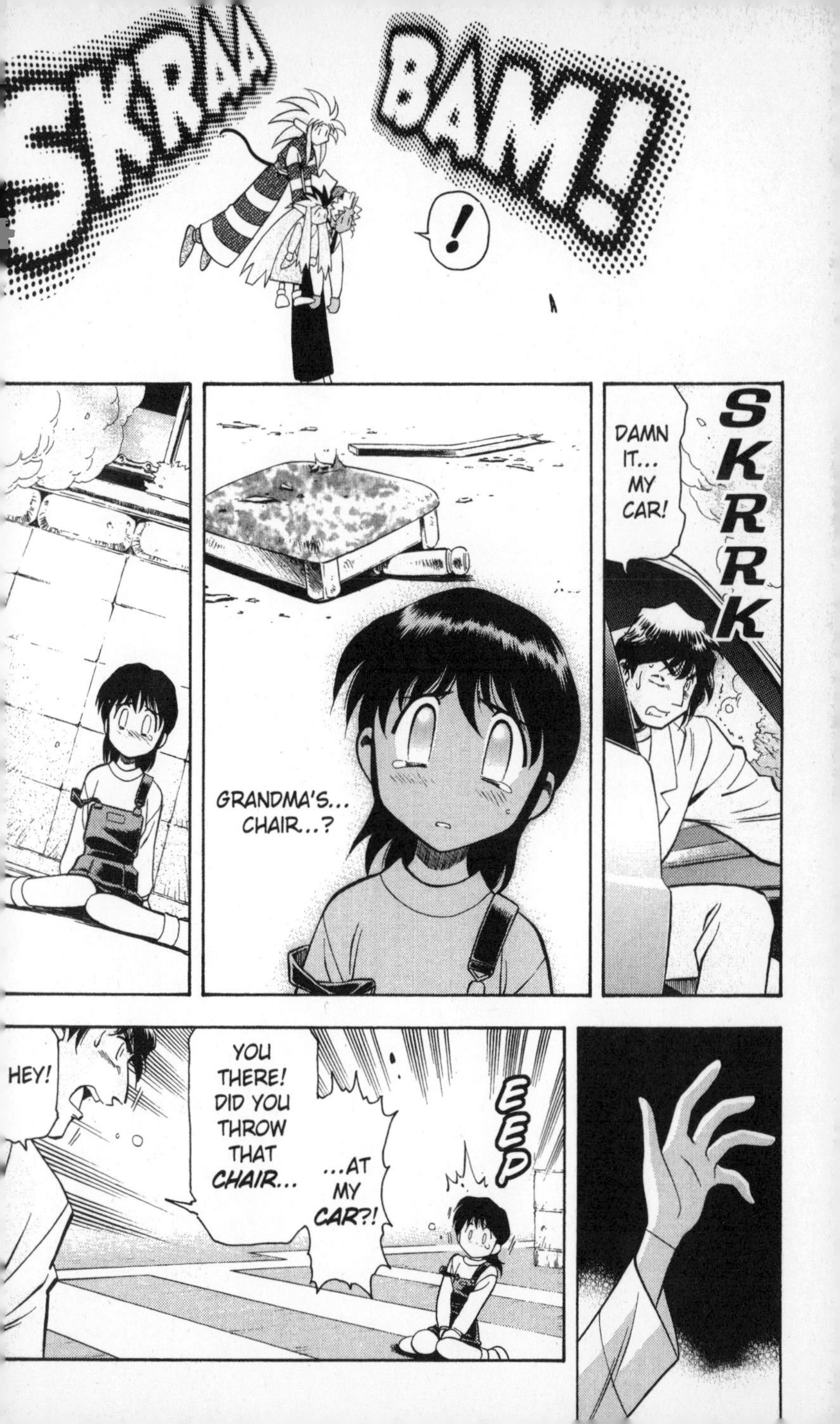
SKRAA
BAM!
!
DAMN IT... MY CAR!
SKRRK
GRANDMA'S... CHAIR...?
HEY!
YOU THERE! DID YOU THROW THAT CHAIR...
...AT MY CAR?!
EEP

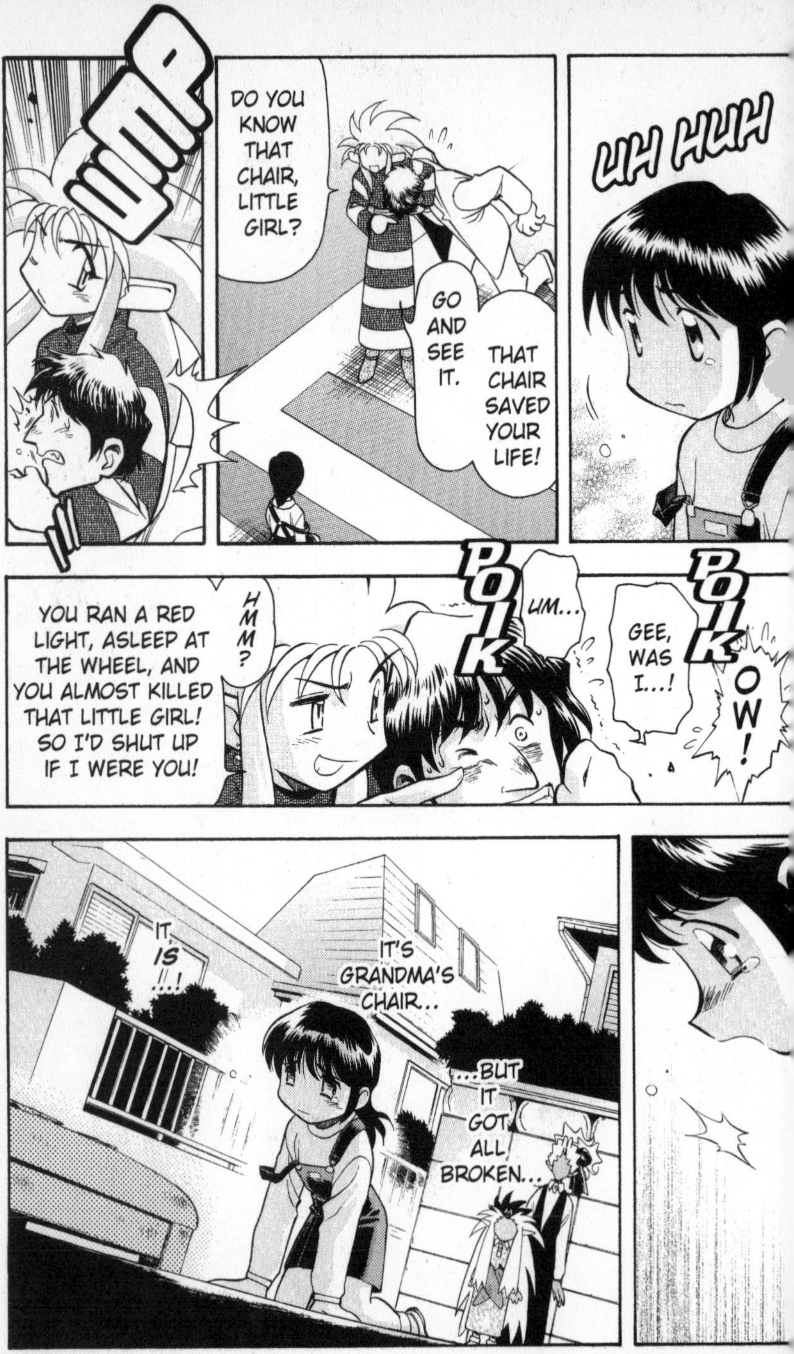
WHAP
DO YOU KNOW THAT CHAIR, LITTLE GIRL?
GO AND SEE IT.
THAT CHAIR SAVED YOUR LIFE!
UH HUH
YOU RAN A RED LIGHT, ASLEEP AT THE WHEEL, AND YOU ALMOST KILLED THAT LITTLE GIRL! SO I'D SHUT UP IF I WERE YOU!
HMM?
POIK
UM...
GEE, WAS I...!
POIK
OW!
IT IS...!
IT'S GRANDMA'S CHAIR..
...BUT IT GOT ALL BROKEN...

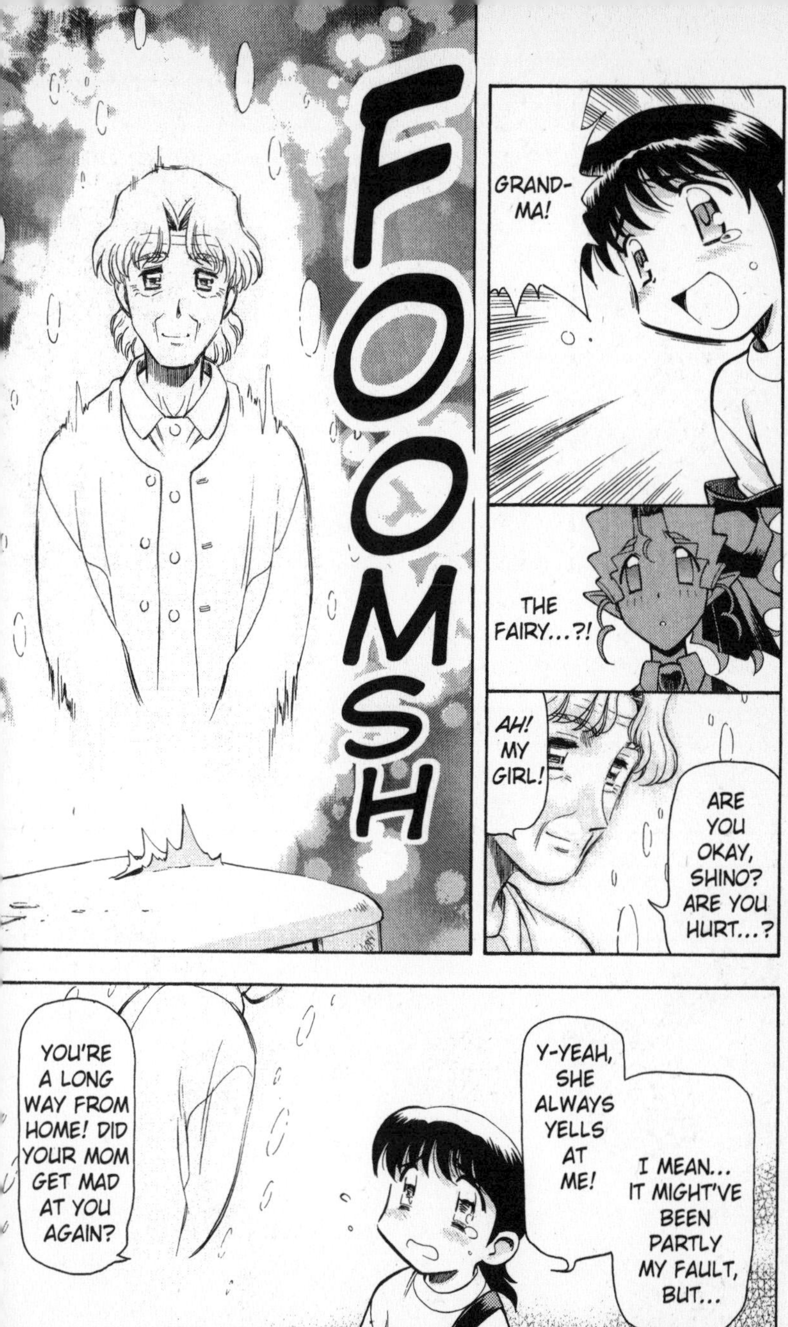
FOOMSH
GRAND-MA!
THE FAIRY...?!
AH! MY GIRL!
ARE YOU OKAY, SHINO? ARE YOU HURT...?
YOU'RE A LONG WAY FROM HOME! DID YOUR MOM GET MAD AT YOU AGAIN?
Y-YEAH, SHE ALWAYS YELLS AT ME!
I MEAN... IT MIGHT'VE BEEN PARTLY MY FAULT, BUT...

YOUR MOTHER DOESN'T *HATE* YOU, SHINO...

SHE SCOLDS YOU BECAUSE SHE *CARES*. IT HURTS HER MORE THAN IT HURTS YOU...

IT... IT DOES?

...NOT EVEN WHEN SHE'S MAD AT YOU!

YOU HAVE TO BE CAREFUL!

AND DO YOU ALWAYS TELL HER YOU'RE SORRY?

UMM...

YOU CAN'T JUST SAY THE WORDS-- YOU HAVE TO MEAN IT.

IT'S IMPORTANT TO BE ABLE TO SAY YOU'RE SORRY.

MOMMY WILL FORGIVE YOU IF YOU DO...

...AND SHE'LL BE NICE TO YOU AGAIN.

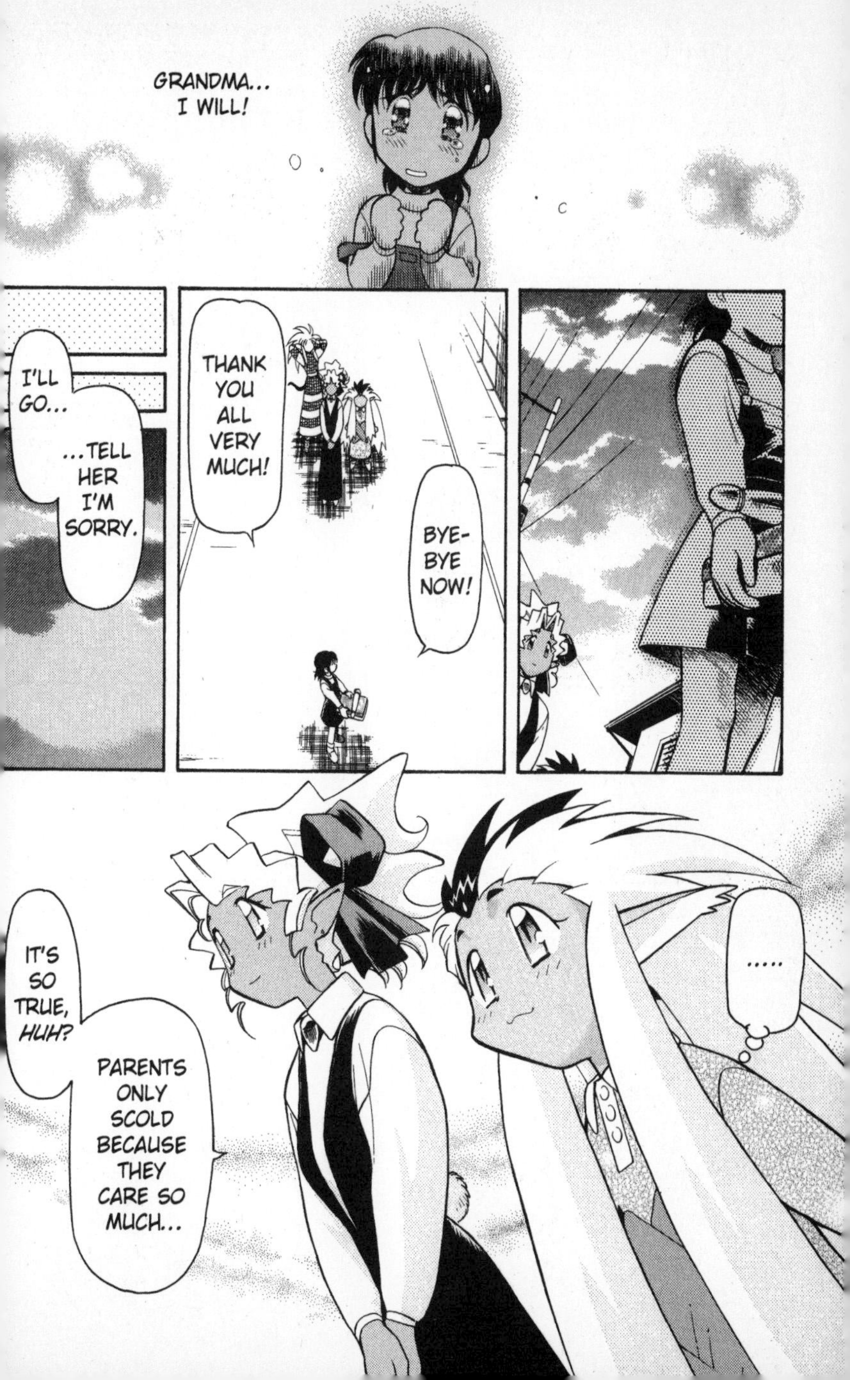
GRANDMA... I WILL!
I'LL GO...
...TELL HER I'M SORRY.
THANK YOU ALL VERY MUCH!
BYE-BYE NOW!
IT'S SO TRUE, *HUH?*
PARENTS ONLY SCOLD BECAUSE THEY CARE SO MUCH...
.....

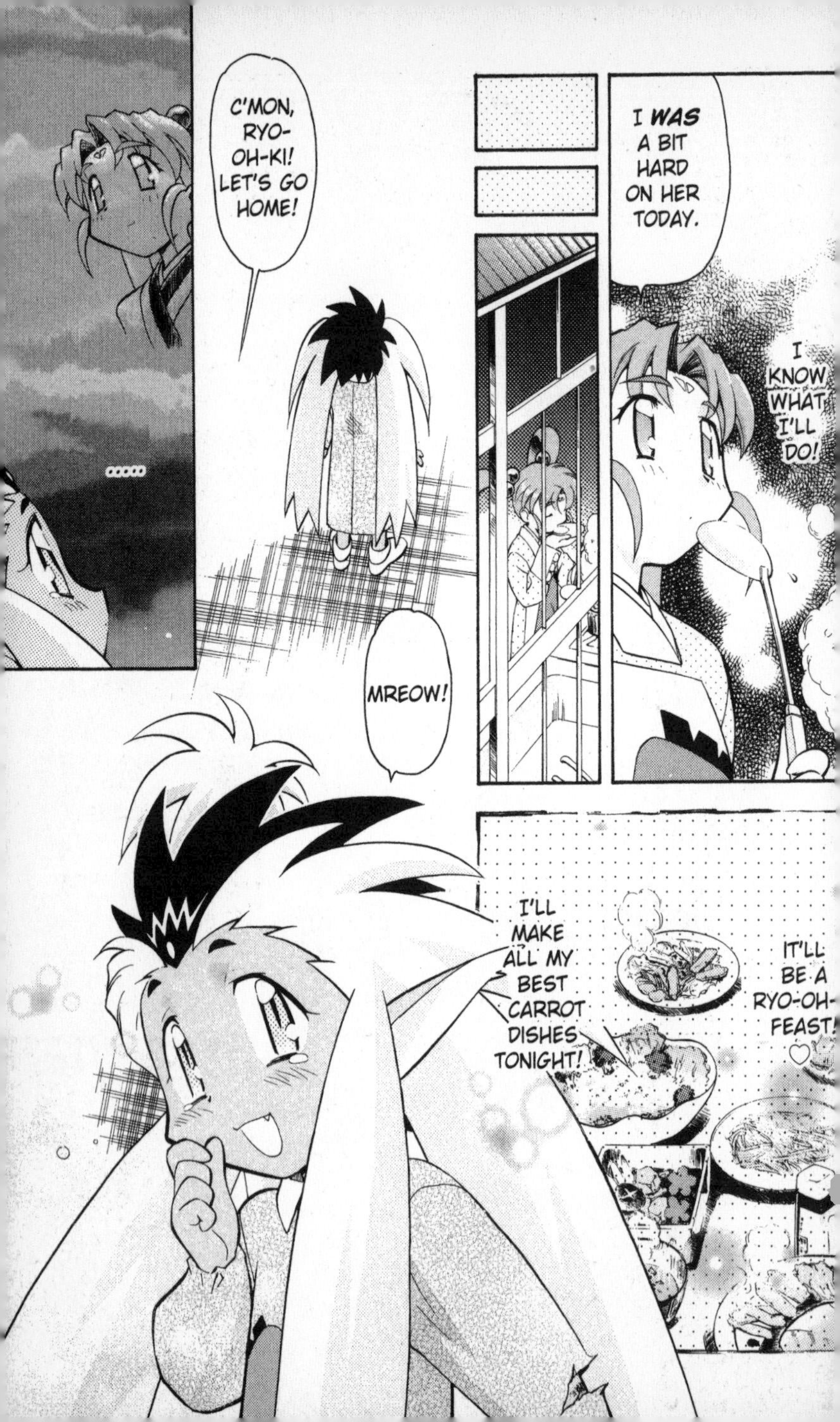
.....
C'MON, RYO-OH-KI! LET'S GO HOME!
MREOW!
I WAS A BIT HARD ON HER TODAY.
I KNOW WHAT I'LL DO!
I'LL MAKE ALL MY BEST CARROT DISHES TONIGHT!
IT'LL BE A RYO-OH-FEAST! ♡

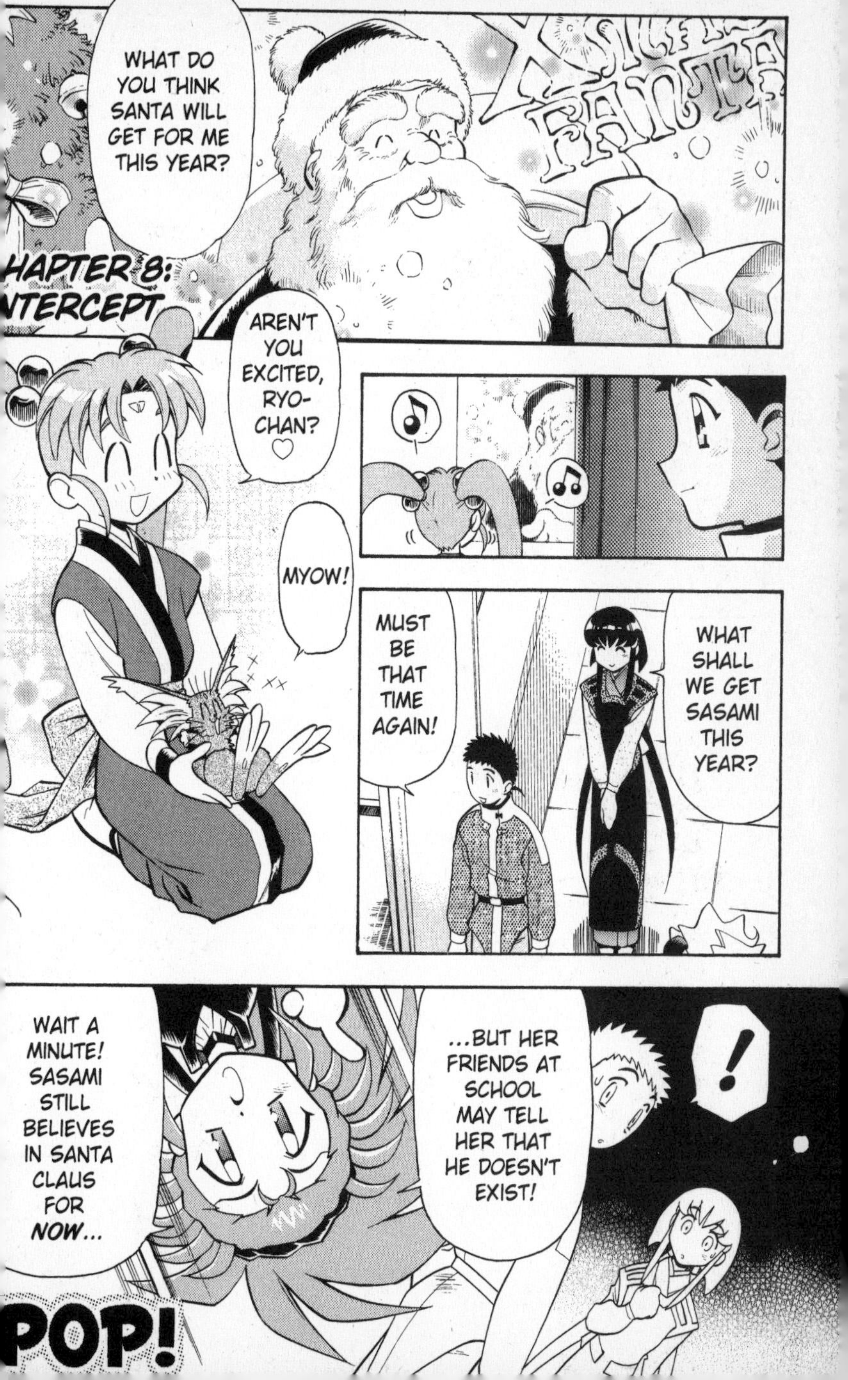
WHAT DO YOU THINK SANTA WILL GET FOR ME THIS YEAR?
HAPTER 8:
NTERCEPT
AREN'T YOU EXCITED, RYO-CHAN? ♡
MYOW!
♪
♪
MUST BE THAT TIME AGAIN!
WHAT SHALL WE GET SASAMI THIS YEAR?
WAIT A MINUTE! SASAMI STILL BELIEVES IN SANTA CLAUS FOR *NOW*...
...BUT HER FRIENDS AT SCHOOL MAY TELL HER THAT HE DOESN'T EXIST!
!
POP!

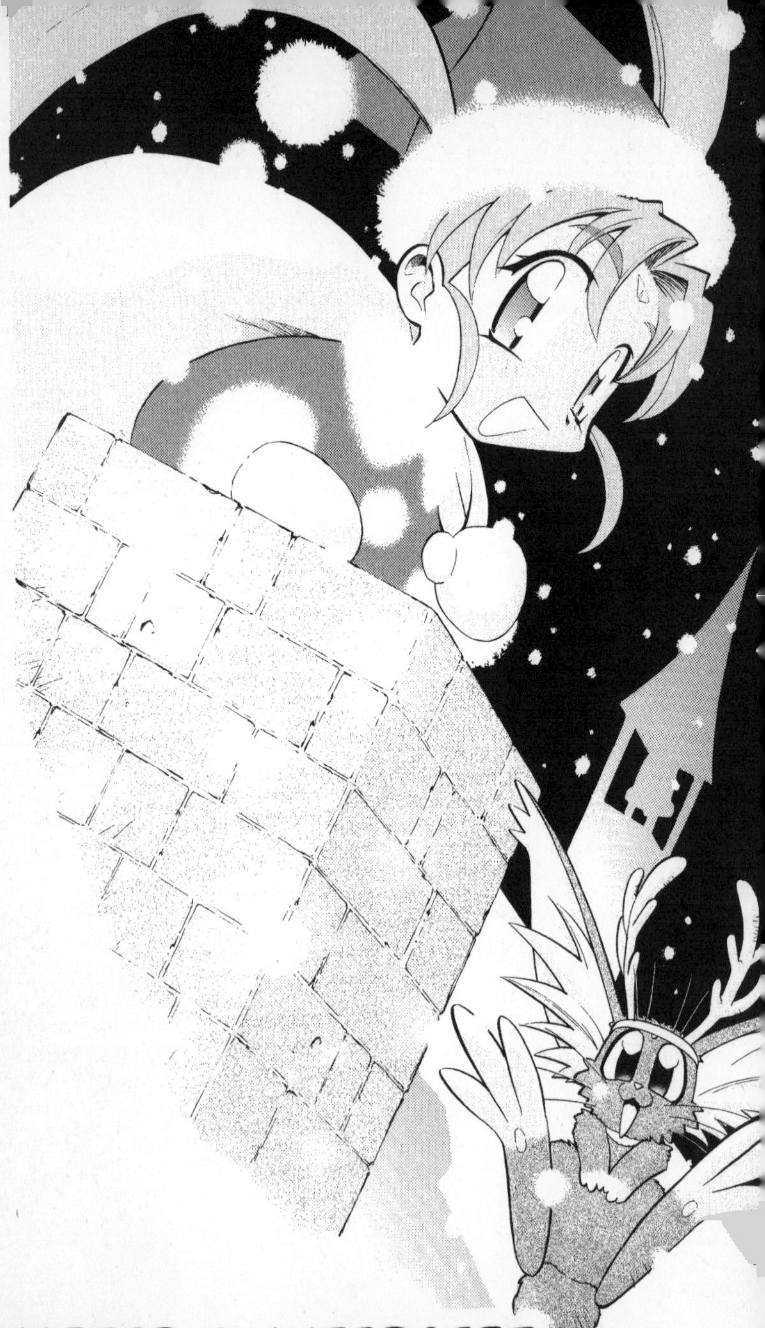

CHAPTER 8: INTERCEPT

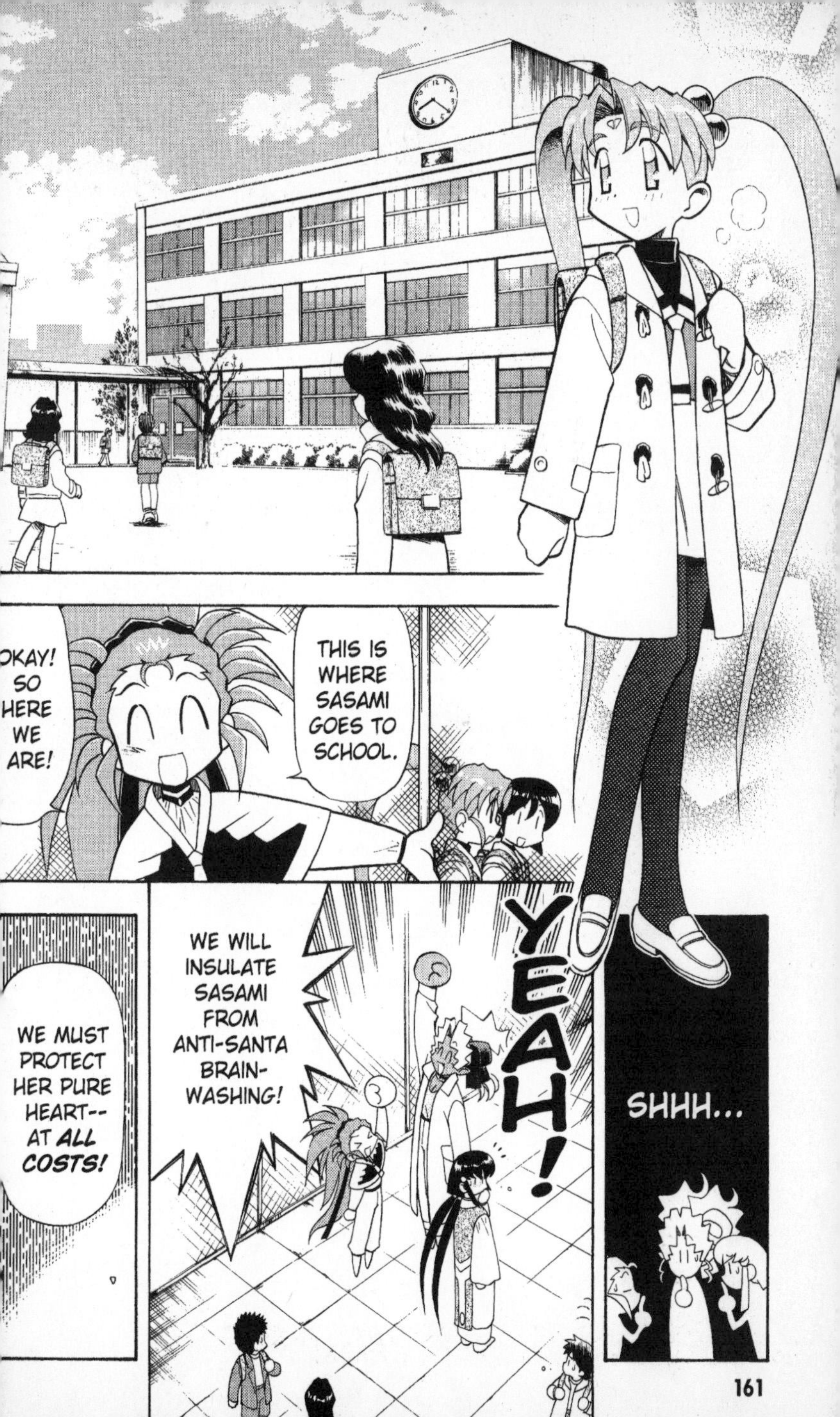

OKAY! SO HERE WE ARE!
THIS IS WHERE SASAMI GOES TO SCHOOL.
WE MUST PROTECT HER PURE HEART--AT ALL COSTS!
WE WILL INSULATE SASAMI FROM ANTI-SANTA BRAIN-WASHING!
YEAH!
SHHH...

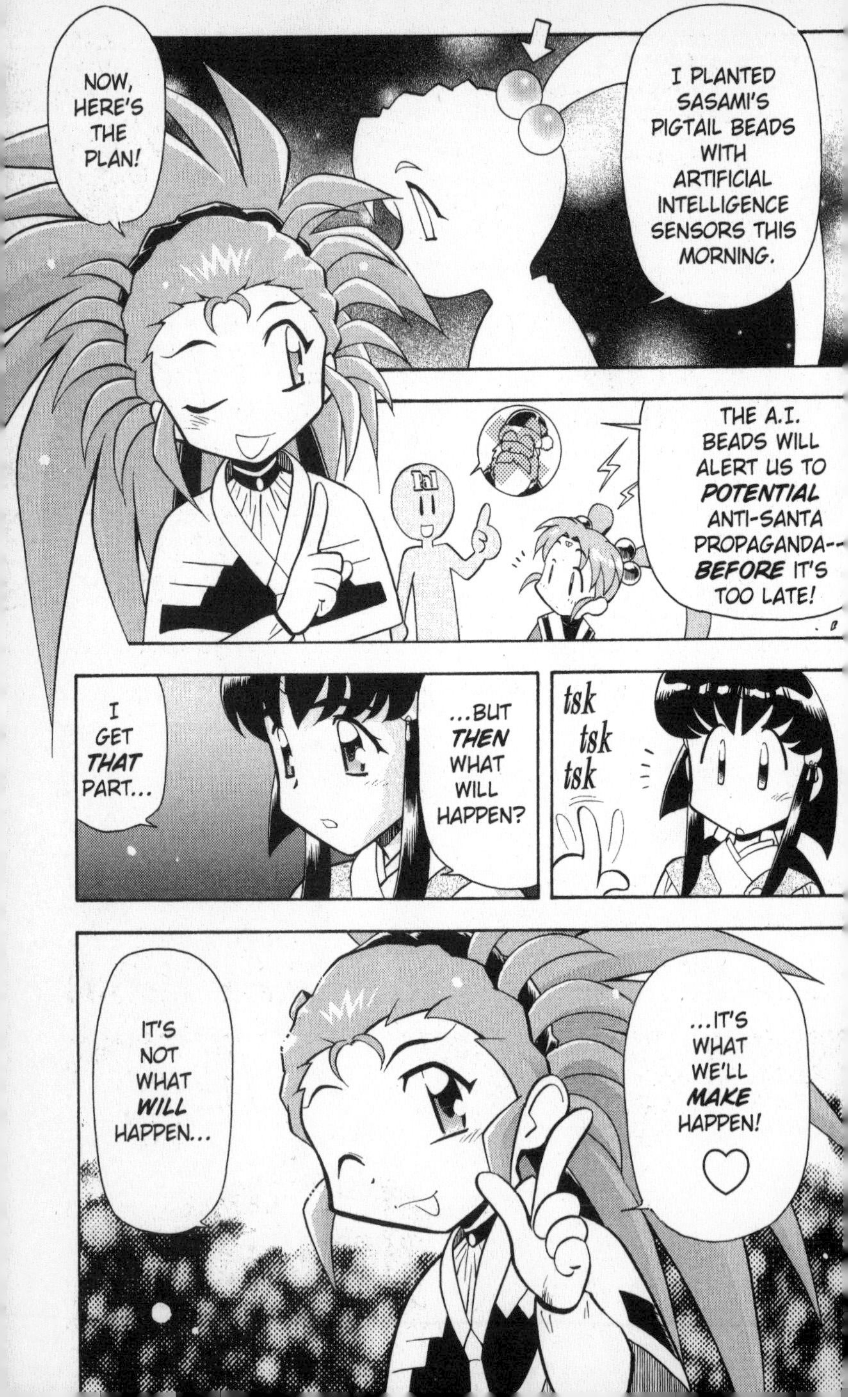
NOW, HERE'S THE PLAN!
I PLANTED SASAMI'S PIGTAIL BEADS WITH ARTIFICIAL INTELLIGENCE SENSORS THIS MORNING.
THE A.I. BEADS WILL ALERT US TO *POTENTIAL* ANTI-SANTA PROPAGANDA-- *BEFORE* IT'S TOO LATE!
I GET *THAT* PART...
...BUT *THEN* WHAT WILL HAPPEN?
tsk tsk tsk
IT'S NOT WHAT *WILL* HAPPEN...
...IT'S WHAT WE'LL *MAKE* HAPPEN! ♡

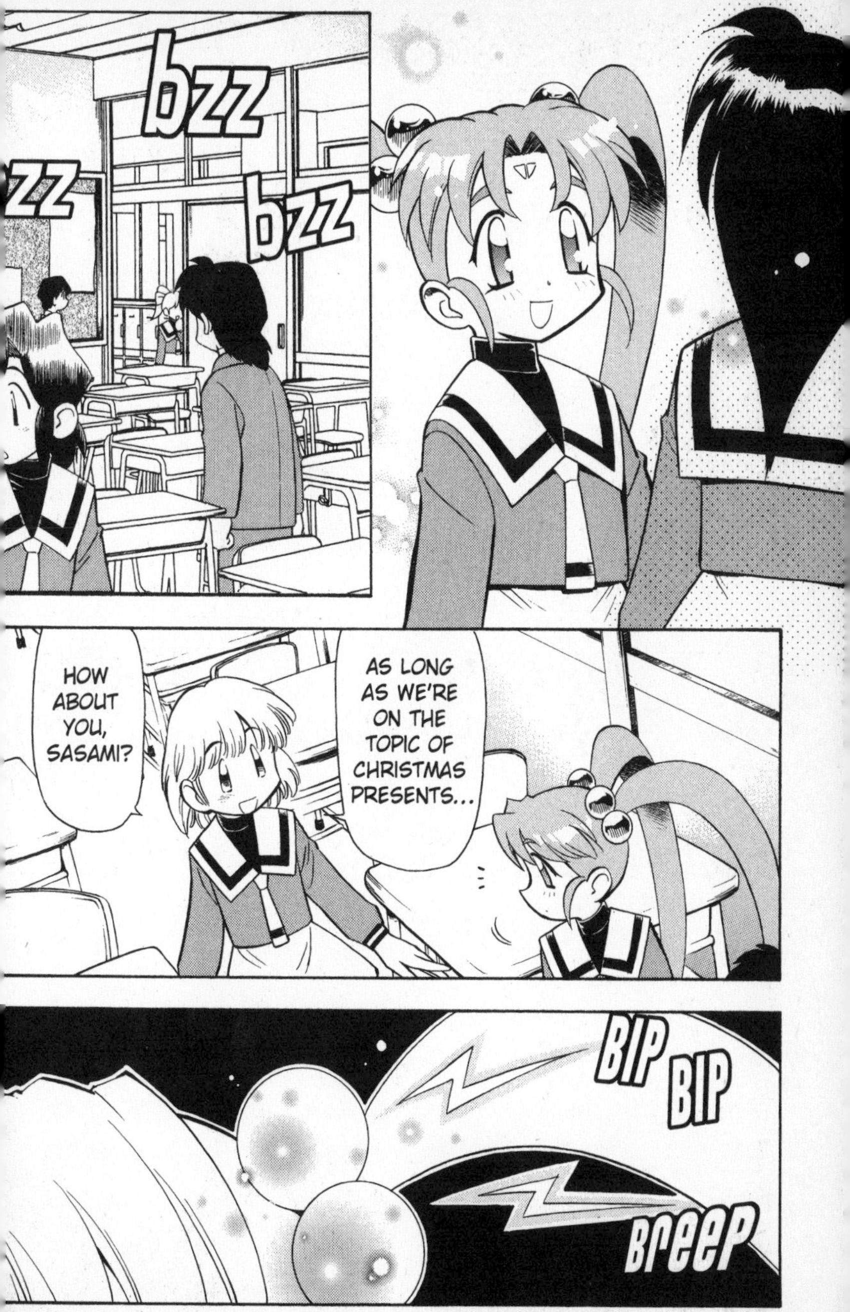

ZZ
bzz
bzz
HOW ABOUT YOU, SASAMI?
AS LONG AS WE'RE ON THE TOPIC OF CHRISTMAS PRESENTS...
BIP BIP
BREEP

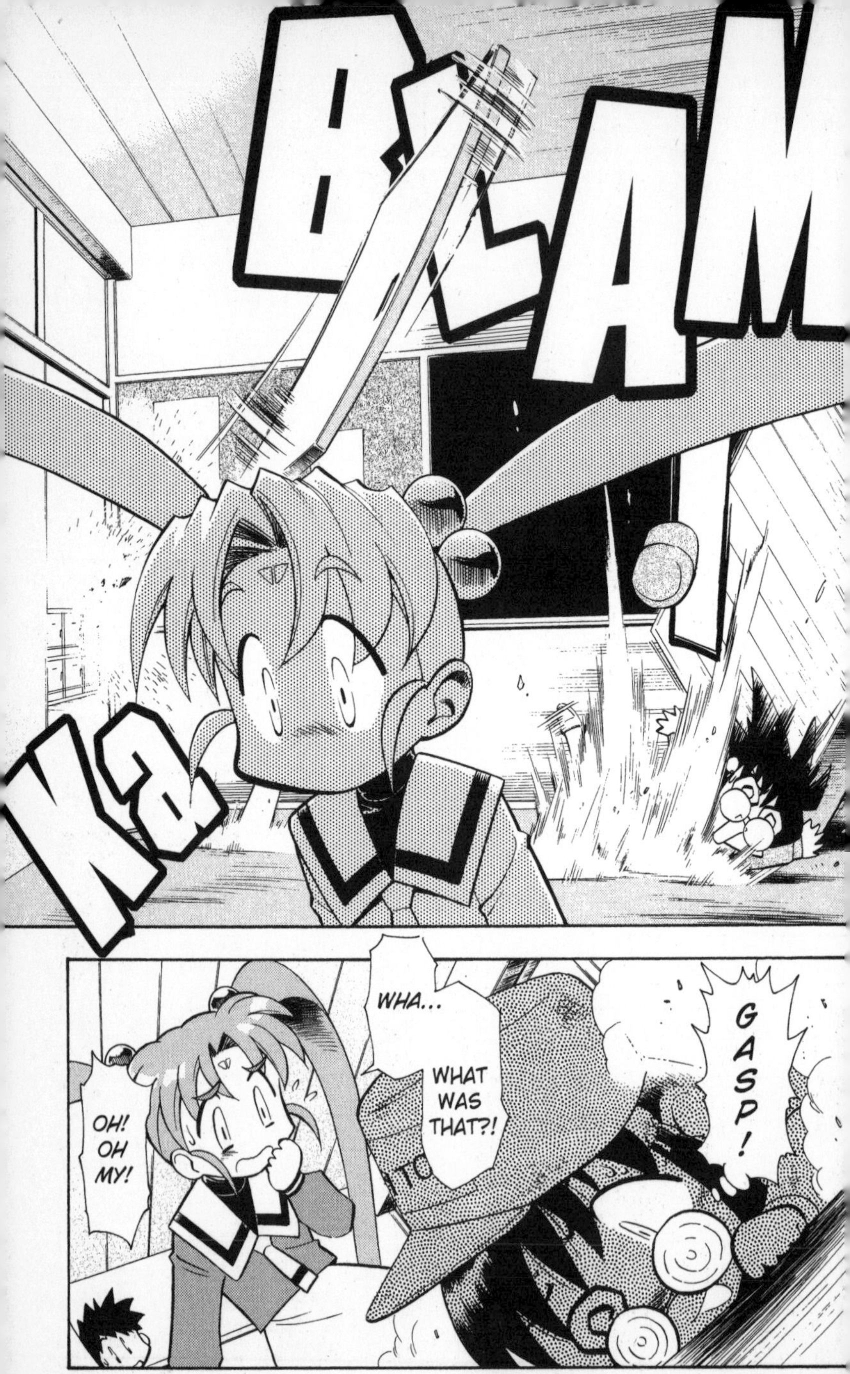
BLAM
KA
WHA...
WHAT WAS THAT?!
OH! OH MY!
GASP!

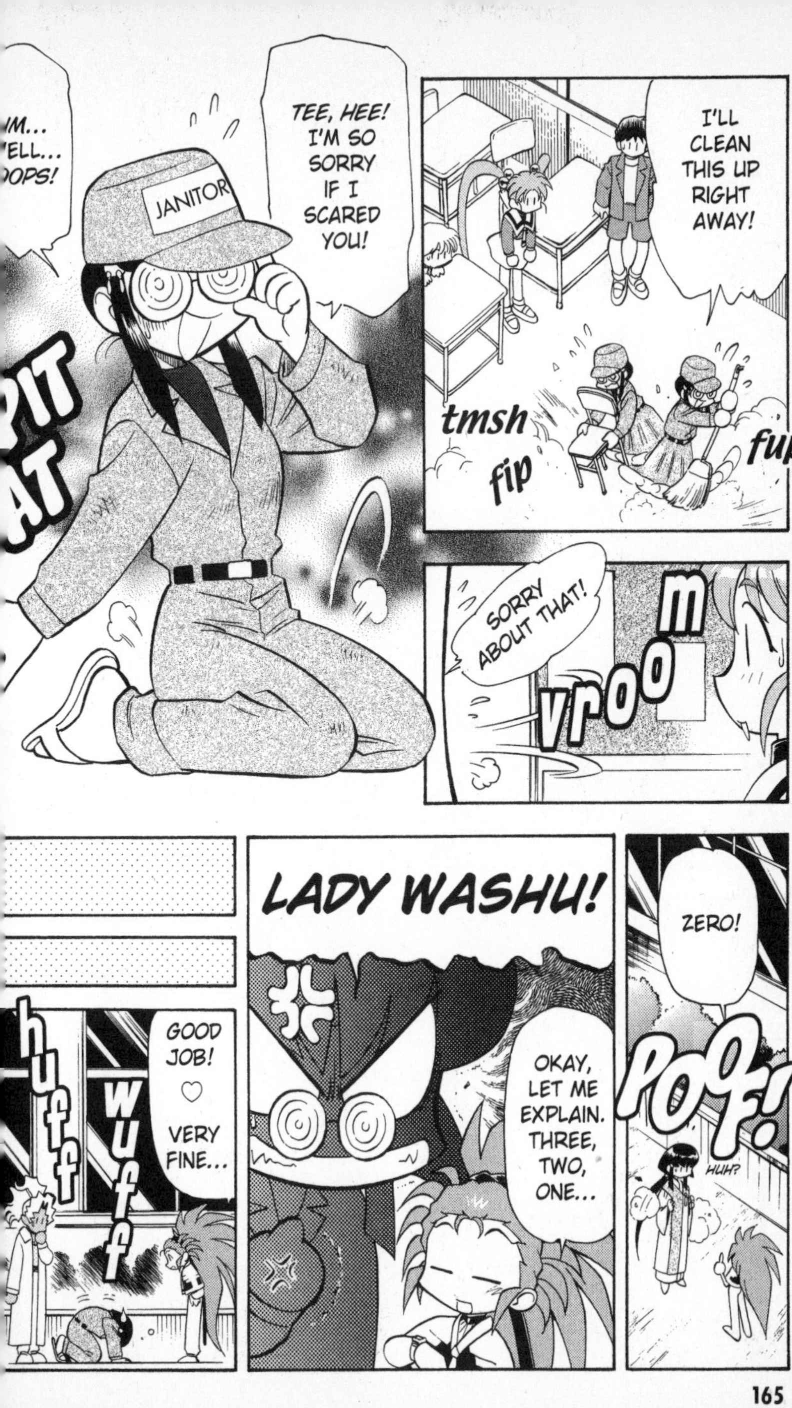
TEE, HEE! I'M SO SORRY IF I SCARED YOU!
JANITOR
I'LL CLEAN THIS UP RIGHT AWAY!
tmsh
fip
fup
SORRY ABOUT THAT!
vroooom
GOOD JOB! ♡ VERY FINE...
huff
wuff
LADY WASHU!
OKAY, LET ME EXPLAIN. THREE, TWO, ONE...
ZERO!
POOF!
HUH?

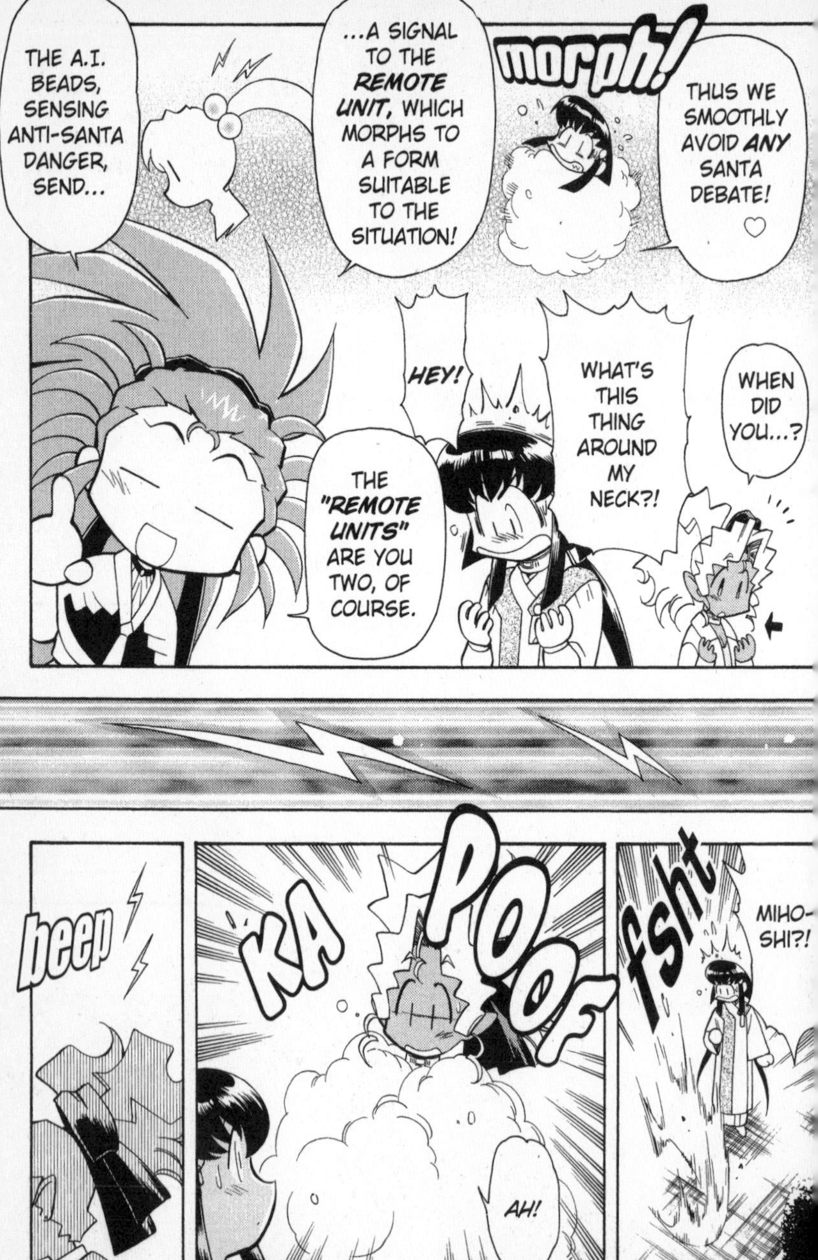
THE A.I. BEADS, SENSING ANTI-SANTA DANGER, SEND...
...A SIGNAL TO THE REMOTE UNIT, WHICH MORPHS TO A FORM SUITABLE TO THE SITUATION!
morph!
THUS WE SMOOTHLY AVOID ANY SANTA DEBATE! ♡
HEY!
WHAT'S THIS THING AROUND MY NECK?!
WHEN DID YOU...?
THE "REMOTE UNITS" ARE YOU TWO, OF COURSE.
beep
KA POOF
AH!
fsht
MIHO-SHI?!

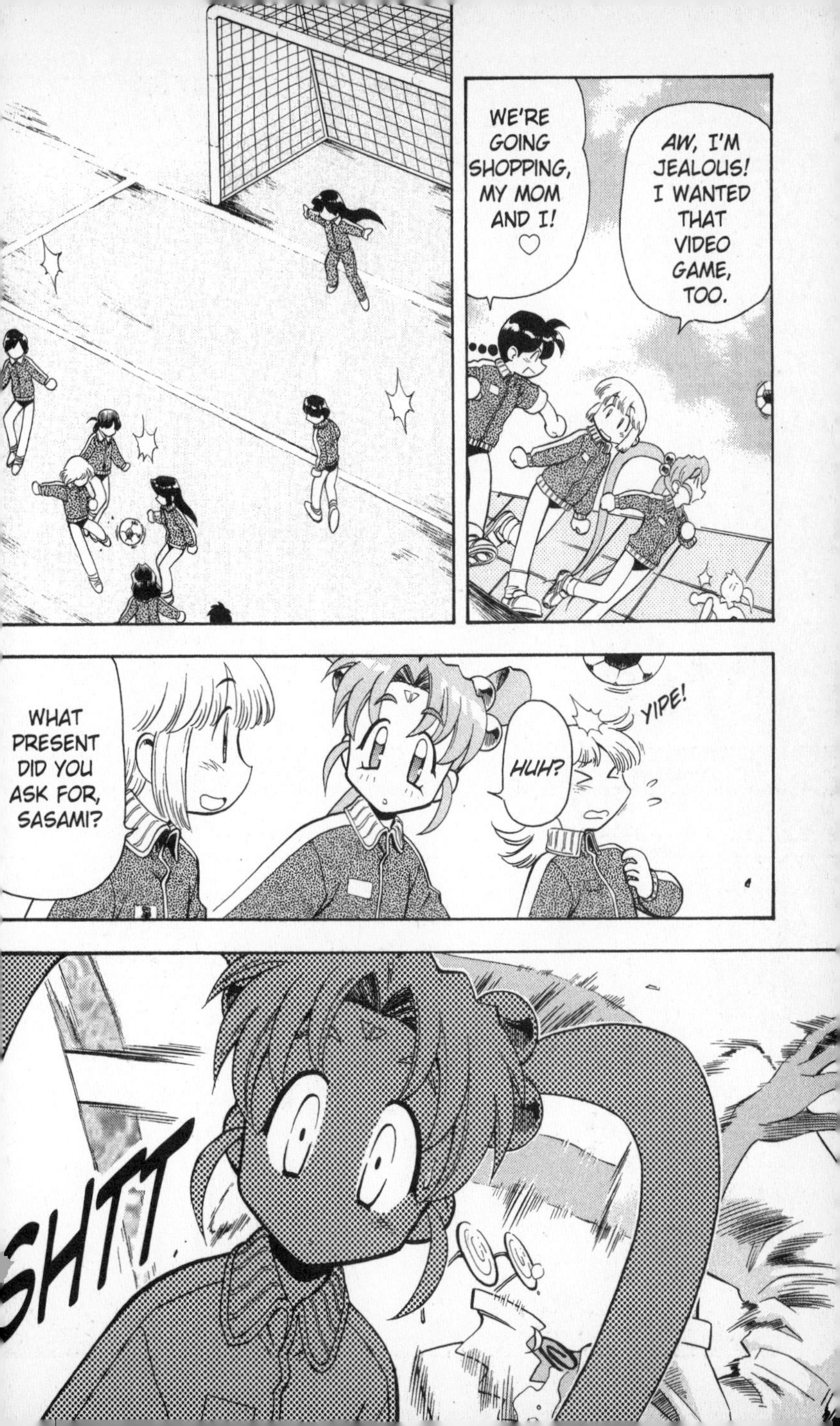
WE'RE GOING SHOPPING, MY MOM AND I! ♡
AW, I'M JEALOUS! I WANTED THAT VIDEO GAME, TOO.
WHAT PRESENT DID YOU ASK FOR, SASAMI?
HUH?
YIPE!
SHTT

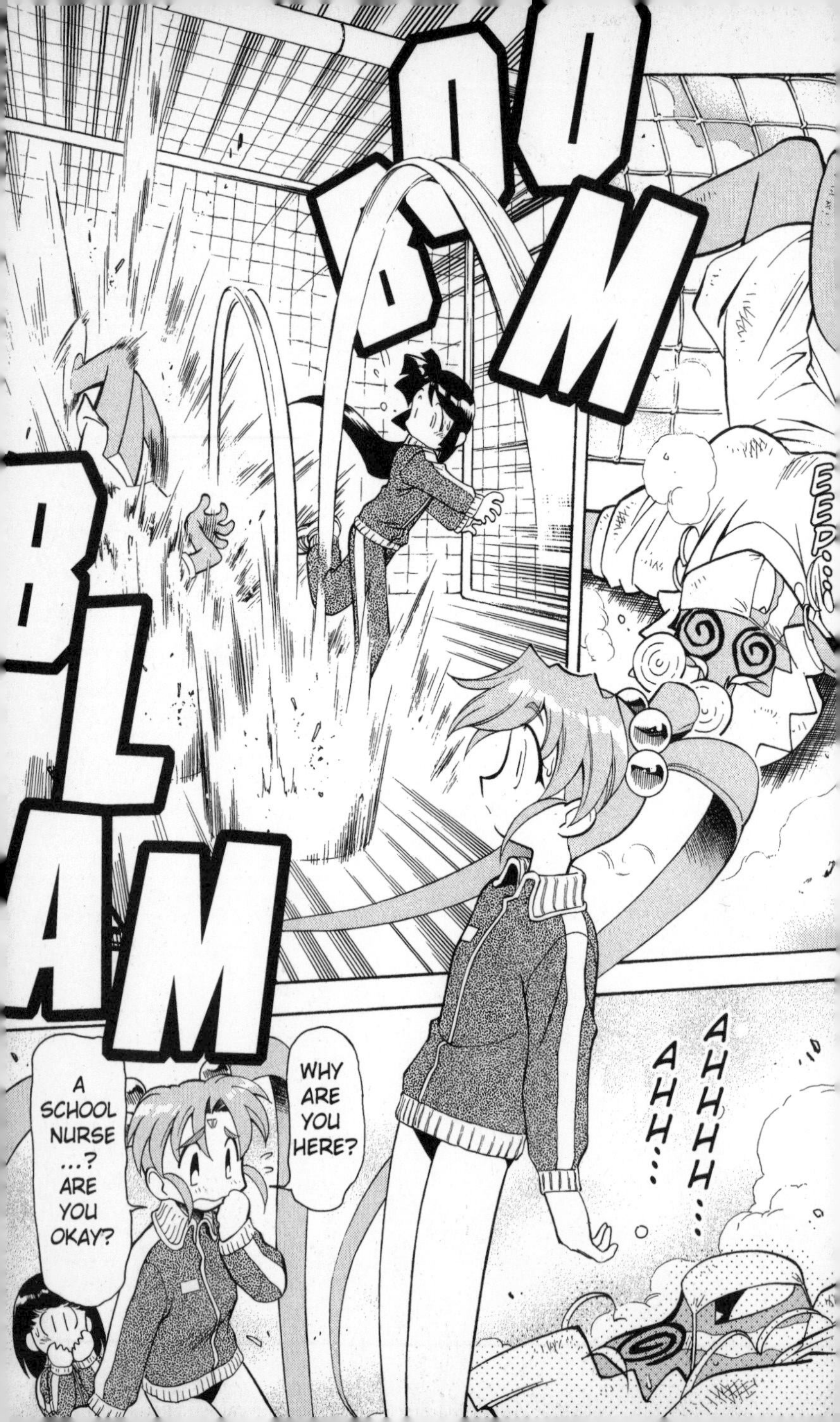
BOOM
BLAM
EEP...
A SCHOOL NURSE ...? ARE YOU OKAY?
WHY ARE YOU HERE?
AHH...
AHHHH...

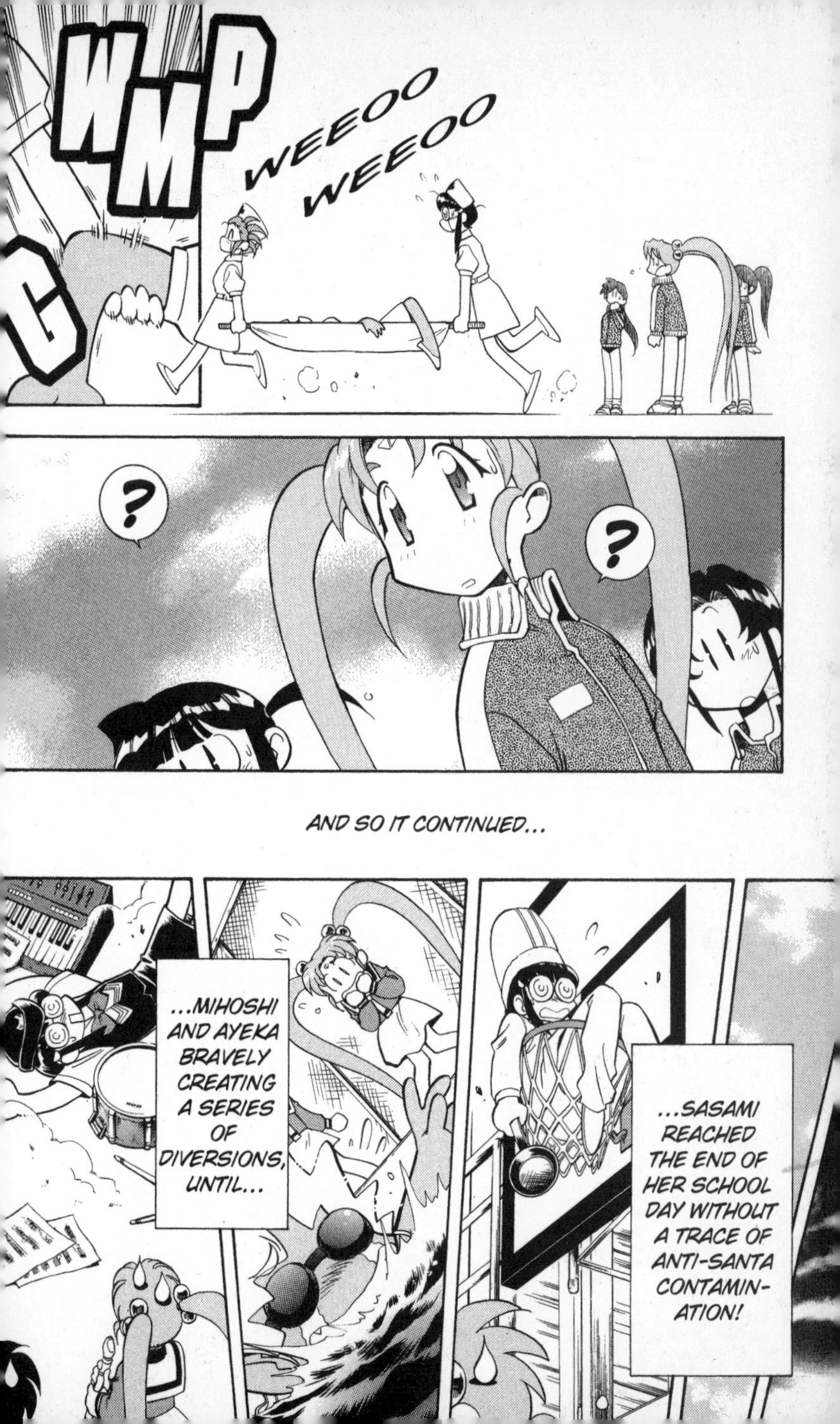
WMP
WEEOO WEEOO
?
?
AND SO IT CONTINUED...
...MIHOSHI AND AYEKA BRAVELY CREATING A SERIES OF DIVERSIONS, UNTIL...
...SASAMI REACHED THE END OF HER SCHOOL DAY WITHOUT A TRACE OF ANTI-SANTA CONTAMIN-ATION!

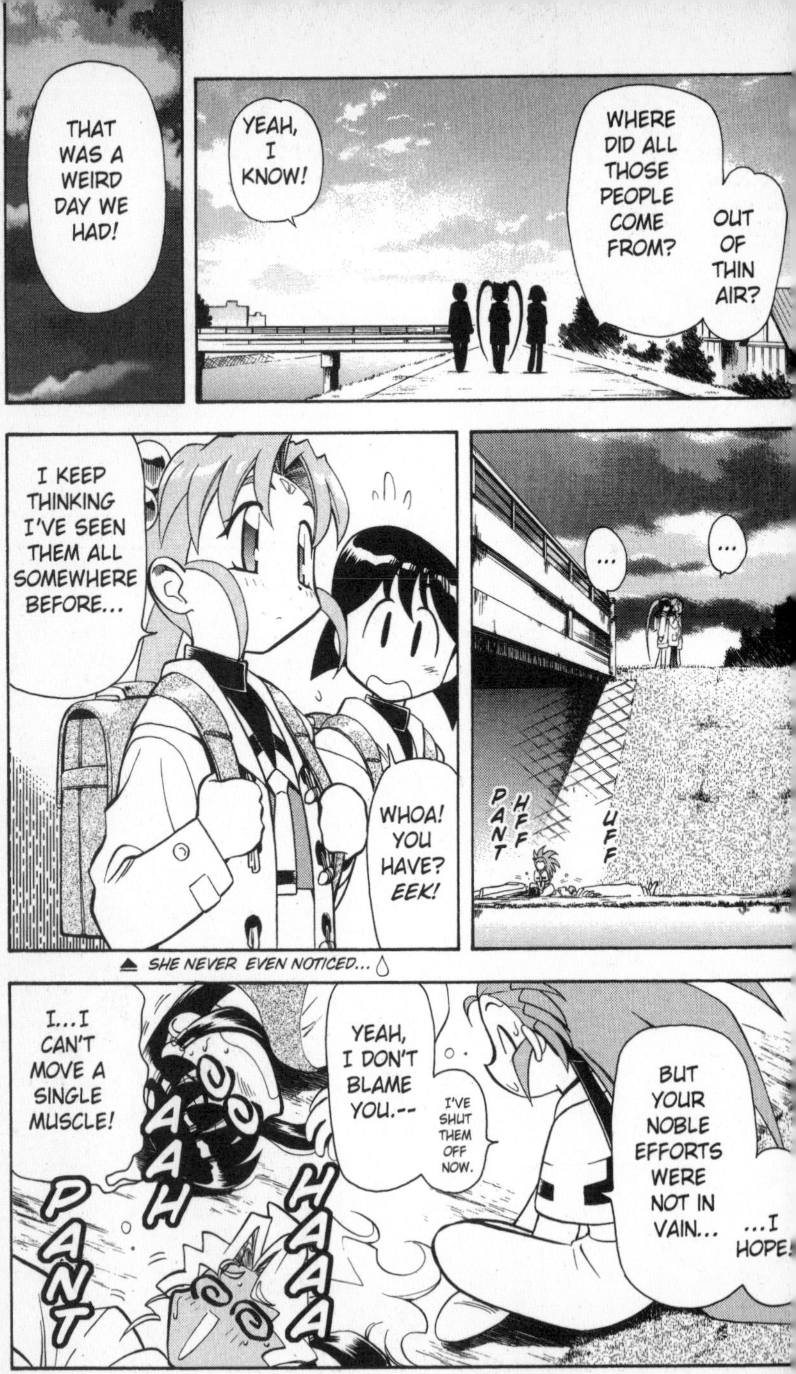
THAT WAS A WEIRD DAY WE HAD!
YEAH, I KNOW!
WHERE DID ALL THOSE PEOPLE COME FROM?
OUT OF THIN AIR?
I KEEP THINKING I'VE SEEN THEM ALL SOMEWHERE BEFORE...
WHOA! YOU HAVE? EEK!
...
...
PANT
HFF
UFF
SHE NEVER EVEN NOTICED...
I...I CAN'T MOVE A SINGLE MUSCLE!
AAH
PANT
HAAAA
YEAH, I DON'T BLAME YOU.--
I'VE SHUT THEM OFF NOW.
BUT YOUR NOBLE EFFORTS WERE NOT IN VAIN...
...I HOPE.

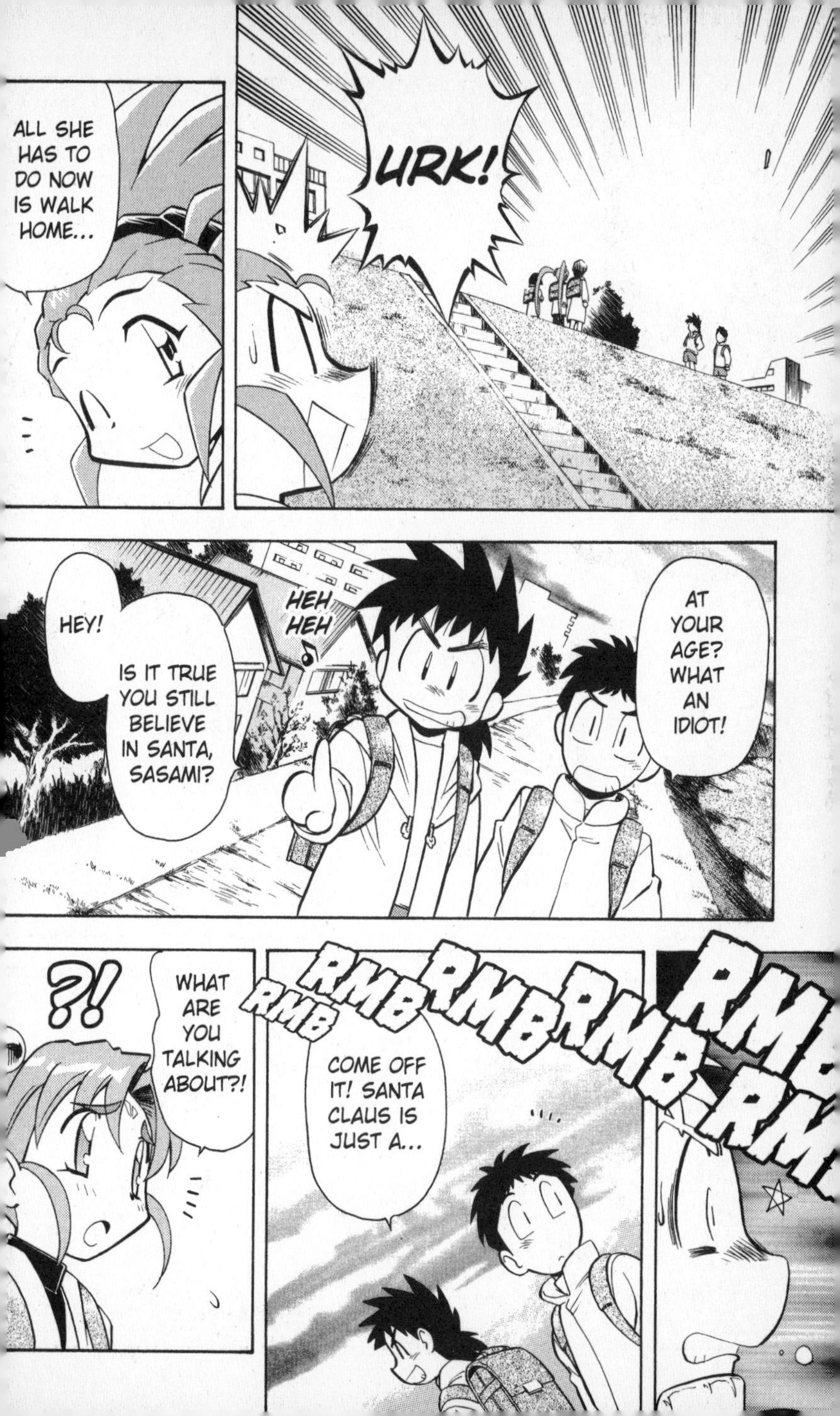
ALL SHE HAS TO DO NOW IS WALK HOME...
URK!
HEY!
IS IT TRUE YOU STILL BELIEVE IN SANTA, SASAMI?
HEH HEH
AT YOUR AGE? WHAT AN IDIOT!
?!
WHAT ARE YOU TALKING ABOUT?!
RMB RMB RMB RMB RMB
COME OFF IT! SANTA CLAUS IS JUST A...

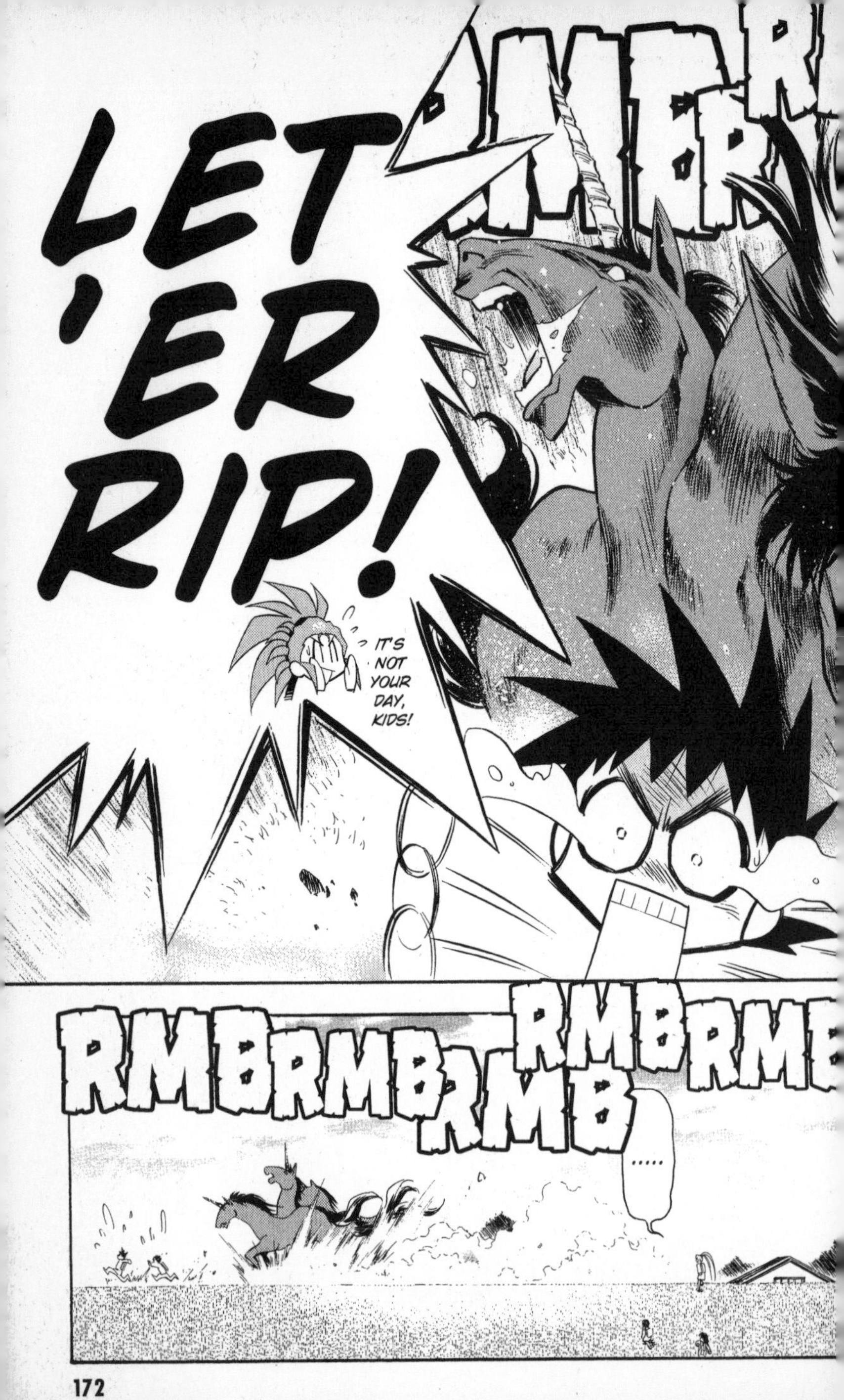
AMBR
LET 'ER RIP!
IT'S NOT YOUR DAY, KIDS!
RMBRMBRMB
RMBRMB
.....

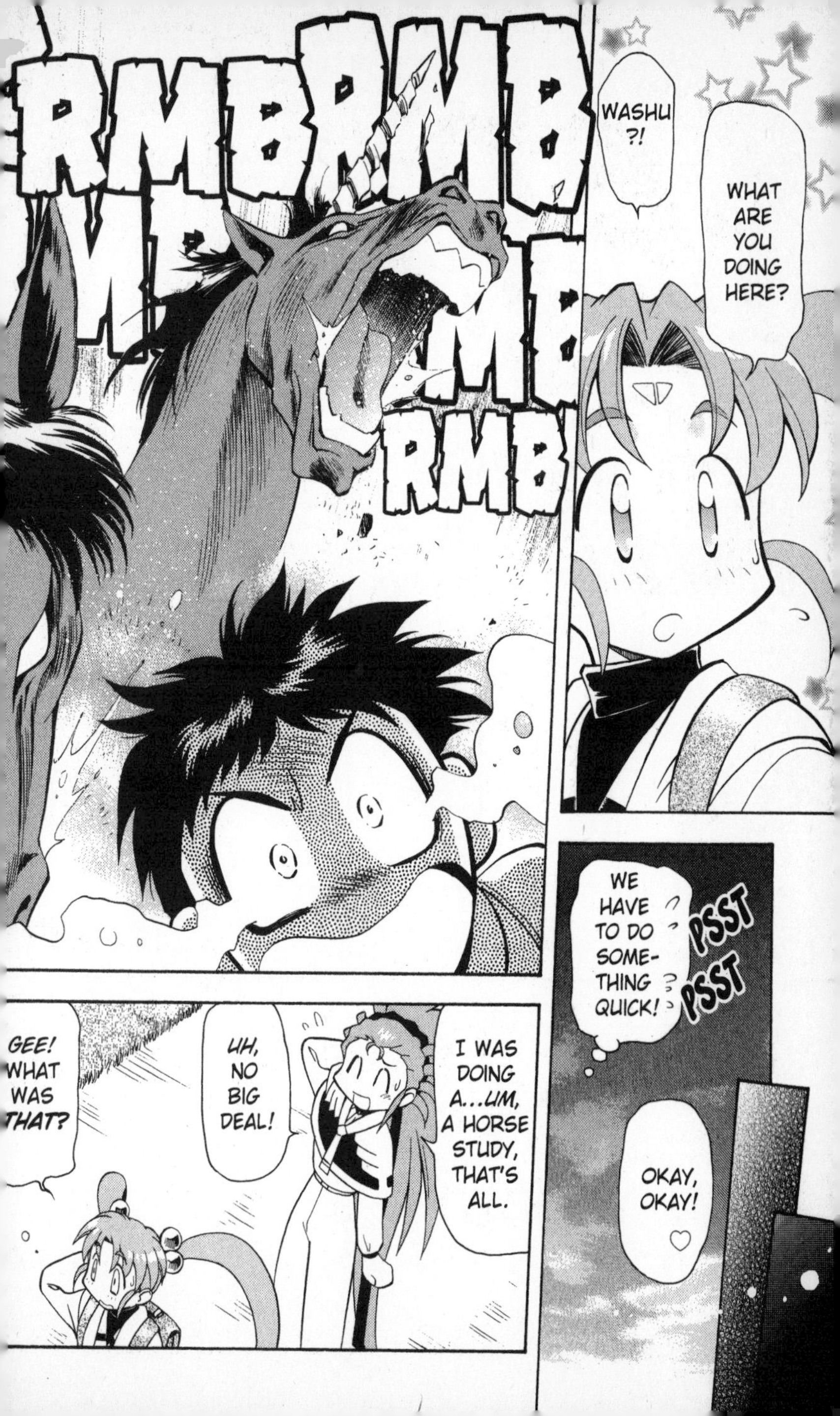
RMBRMB
RMB
RMB
WASHU ?!
WHAT ARE YOU DOING HERE?
GEE! WHAT WAS THAT?
UH, NO BIG DEAL!
I WAS DOING A...UM, A HORSE STUDY, THAT'S ALL.
WE HAVE TO DO SOME-THING QUICK!
PSST PSST
OKAY, OKAY! ♡

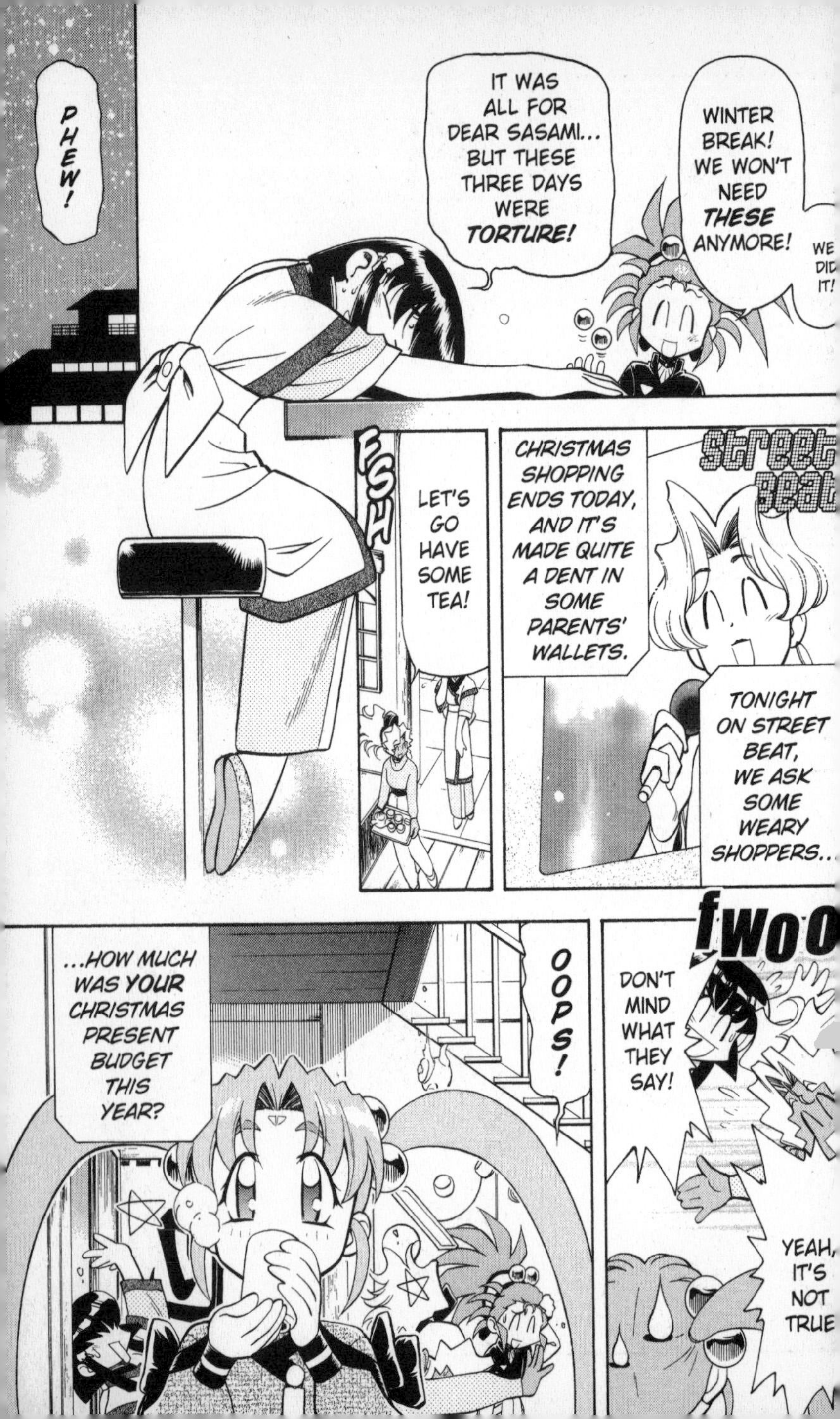
PHEW!
IT WAS ALL FOR DEAR SASAMI... BUT THESE THREE DAYS WERE TORTURE!
WINTER BREAK! WE WON'T NEED THESE ANYMORE!
WE DID IT!
FSH
LET'S GO HAVE SOME TEA!
CHRISTMAS SHOPPING ENDS TODAY, AND IT'S MADE QUITE A DENT IN SOME PARENTS' WALLETS.
Street Beat
TONIGHT ON STREET BEAT, WE ASK SOME WEARY SHOPPERS...
...HOW MUCH WAS YOUR CHRISTMAS PRESENT BUDGET THIS YEAR?
OOPS!
fwoo
DON'T MIND WHAT THEY SAY!
YEAH, IT'S NOT TRUE

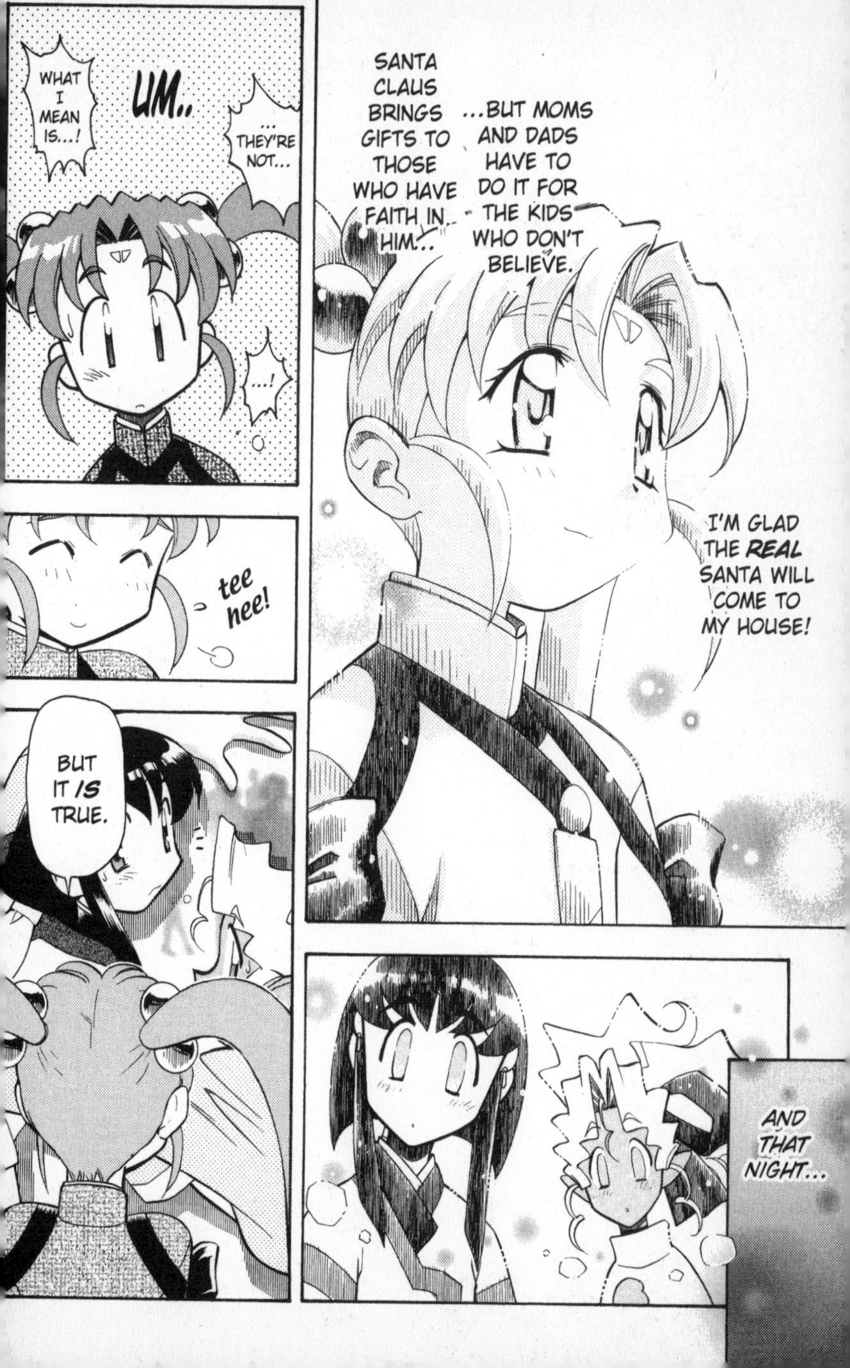
WHAT I MEAN IS...!
UM..
...THEY'RE NOT...
...!
SANTA CLAUS BRINGS GIFTS TO THOSE WHO HAVE FAITH IN HIM...
...BUT MOMS AND DADS HAVE TO DO IT FOR THE KIDS WHO DON'T BELIEVE.
I'M GLAD THE REAL SANTA WILL COME TO MY HOUSE!
tee hee!
BUT IT IS TRUE.
AND THAT NIGHT...

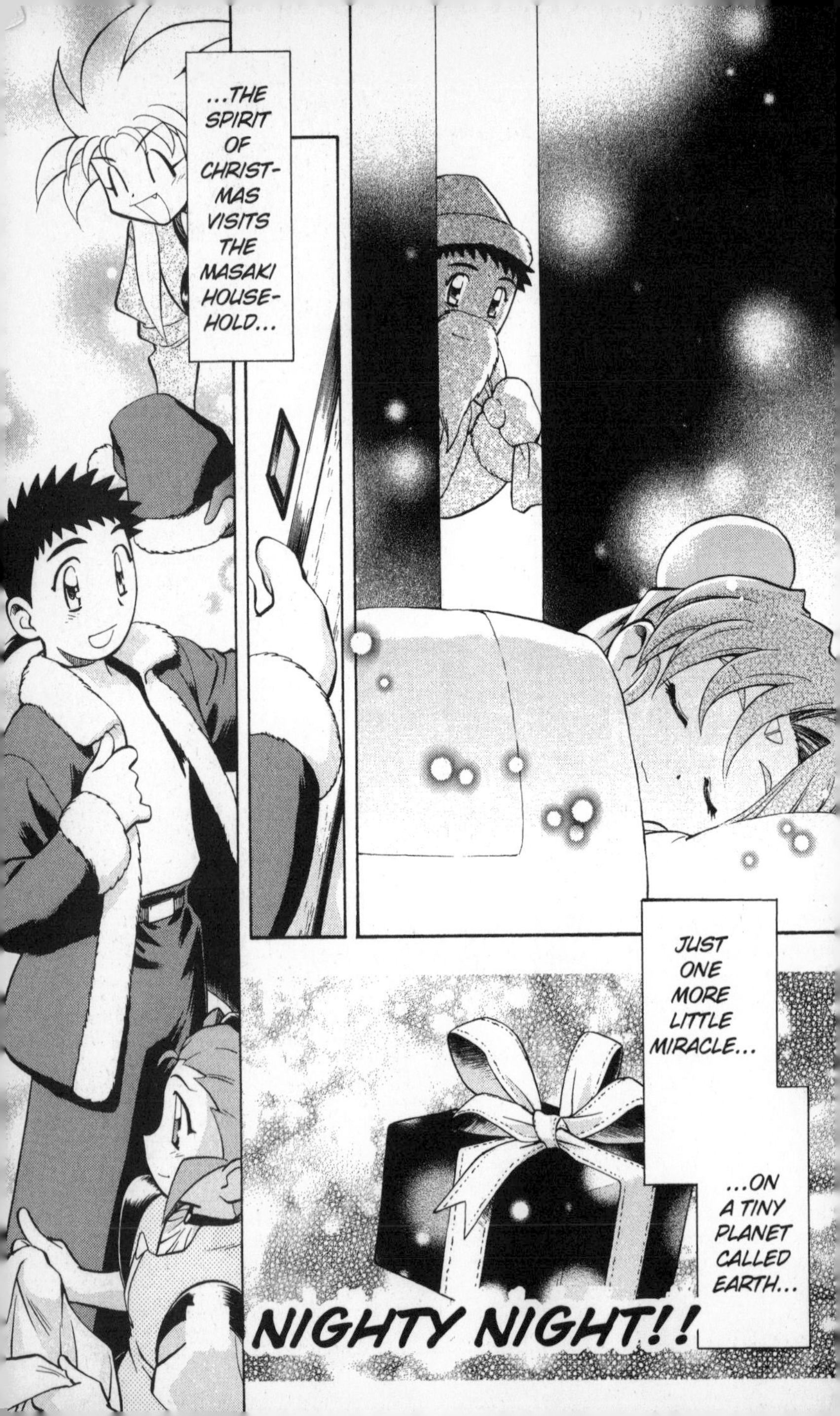
...THE SPIRIT OF CHRIST-MAS VISITS THE MASAKI HOUSE-HOLD...
JUST ONE MORE LITTLE MIRACLE...
...ON A TINY PLANET CALLED EARTH...
NIGHTY NIGHT!!

enchi Superstar!

rrently there exist three animated **Tenchi** movies. The big
reen series kicked off with **Tenchi Muyô in Love** and was
ickly followed by **The Daughter of Darkness** and **Tenchi**
rever. All three are now available on DVD and all three are
ghly recommended.

doubtedly, there will be more **Tenchi** anime in the future.
t at some point, someone in Japan or the U.S. (or maybe
en planet Jurai) will get the bright idea to make a live-
tion **Tenchi** movie. It's got to happen, right?

at's what a lot of fans are hoping for. They want to see flesh-
d-blood actors breathing life into their favorite anime char-
ters. How do I know? That's simple. I get sacks of letters from
aders who are impatiently waiting for the day Tenchi makes
s cineplex debut.

ho would (or could) play Tenchi? Or Ryoko? Or li'l Sasami?
ns are having a ball deciding which of their favorite actors
ould be picked.

ost surprising of all is the wide range of names being tossed
out. Everyone from Ozzy Osbourne to Shia LaBeouf has been
entioned as a perfect Tenchi. Never mind the age disparity.
ore than one reader wants to see Marie Osmond as Ayeka
d Chuck Norris as Yosho. And concerning Ryo-oh-ki, any
mber of celebrities (young or old) could easily don the furry
bbit suit.

rsonally, I'd prefer to see future **Tenchi** projects remain ani-
ated. A live-action film might rob the series of its magical
d sentimental properties. Do we really want to see Hilary
ff prancing around in a furry Ryo-oh-ki costume? I surely
n't.

nchi works perfectly as a cartoon. Much of what I love about
e series comes from the uniqueness of the art form. Just
nk about all the great cartoons that were ruined when they
orphed into live-action dramas.

imately, I have one bit of advice for fans who continue to
mor for a big screen **Tenchi** adventure: be careful what you
sh for. Seeing Marie Osmond flirting with Ozzy Osbourne
uld be so very, very wrong.

c Searleman
itor, **The All-New Tenchi Muyô!**

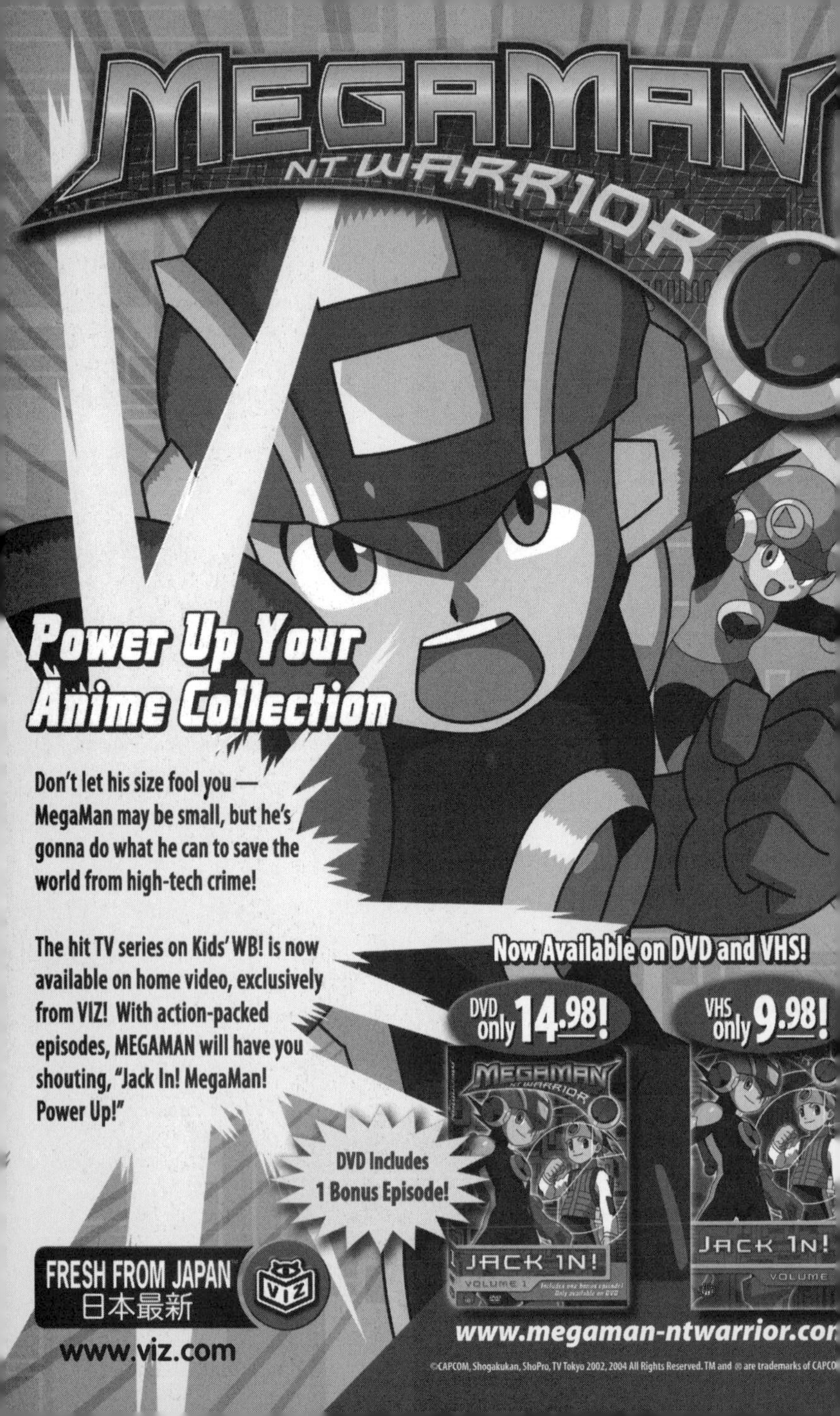
MEGAMAN
NT WARRIOR
Power Up Your Anime Collection
Don't let his size fool you — MegaMan may be small, but he's gonna do what he can to save the world from high-tech crime!
The hit TV series on Kids' WB! is now available on home video, exclusively from VIZ! With action-packed episodes, MEGAMAN will have you shouting, "Jack In! MegaMan! Power Up!"
Now Available on DVD and VHS!
DVD only 14.98!
VHS only 9.98!
MEGAMAN NT WARRIOR
JACK IN!
VOLUME 1
JACK IN!
DVD Includes 1 Bonus Episode!
FRESH FROM JAPAN
日本最新
VIZ
www.viz.com
www.megaman-ntwarrior.com
©CAPCOM, Shogakukan, ShoPro, TV Tokyo 2002, 2004 All Rights Reserved. TM and ® are trademarks of CAPCO

COMPLETE OUR SURVEY AND LET US KNOW WHAT YOU THINK!

☐ Please do NOT send me information about VIZ products, news and events, special offers, or other information.

☐ Please do NOT send me information from VIZ's trusted business partners.

Name: _____

Address: _____

City: _____ **State:** _____ **Zip:** _____

E-mail: _____

☐ Male ☐ Female **Date of Birth** (mm/dd/yyyy): ___ / ___ / ___   (Under 13? Parental consent required)

What race/ethnicity do you consider yourself? (please check one)

☐ Asian/Pacific Islander   ☐ Black/African American   ☐ Hispanic/Latino

☐ Native American/Alaskan Native ☐ White/Caucasian   ☐ Other: _____

What VIZ product did you purchase? (check all that apply and indicate title purchased)

☐ DVD/VHS _____

☐ Graphic Novel _____

☐ Magazines _____

☐ Merchandise _____

Reason for purchase: (check all that apply)

☐ Special offer   ☐ Favorite title   ☐ Gift

☐ Recommendation   ☐ Other _____

Where did you make your purchase? (please check one)

☐ Comic store   ☐ Bookstore   ☐ Mass/Grocery Store

☐ Newsstand   ☐ Video/Video Game Store ☐ Other: _____

☐ Online (site: _____)

What other VIZ properties have you purchased/own? _____

_____

How many anime and/or manga titles have you purchased in the last year? How many were VIZ titles? **(please check one from each column)**

ANIME	MANGA	VIZ
☐ None	☐ None	☐ None
☐ 1-4	☐ 1-4	☐ 1-4
☐ 5-10	☐ 5-10	☐ 5-10
☐ 11+	☐ 11+	☐ 11+

I find the pricing of VIZ products to be: **(please check one)**

☐ Cheap ☐ Reasonable ☐ Expensive

What genre of manga and anime would you like to see from VIZ? **(please check two)**

☐ Adventure ☐ Comic Strip ☐ Science Fiction ☐ Fighting

☐ Horror ☐ Romance ☐ Fantasy ☐ Sports

What do you think of VIZ's new look?

☐ Love It ☐ It's OK ☐ Hate It ☐ Didn't Notice ☐ No Opinion

Which do you prefer? **(please check one)**

☐ Reading right-to-left

☐ Reading left-to-right

Which do you prefer? **(please check one)**

☐ Sound effects in English

☐ Sound effects in Japanese with English captions

☐ Sound effects in Japanese only with a glossary at the back

THANK YOU! Please send the completed form to:

NJW Research
42 Catharine St.
Poughkeepsie, NY 12601

All information provided will be used for internal purposes only. We promise not to sell or otherwise divulge your information.